To the plethora of books written by journalists and family members about Donald Trump and his Presidency, Gregg Barak adds *Criminology on Trump*. Barak's unique take on Trump and the Trump organization evolves out of decades of studying the political economy of corporate and white-collar crime and he brings the "tools, methods and theories" of the trade to lay bare Trump's plutocracy and political corruption. It is a fascinating yet sobering tale of how money corrupts democracy and may destroy it.

— **Sally Simpson**, *Interim Chair and Distinguished University Professor, Department of Criminology and Criminal Justice, University of Maryland, USA*

Criminology on Trump offers a unique social-psychological portrait of how the two Trumps, the real Donald Trump and his alter ego *the Donald,* were shaped by, and are now shaping the institutional and cultural framework of America. Through a unique application of the tools of criminological inquiry, Dr. Gregg Barak, reveals how Trump's malign personality intersected with America's malignant capitalism to create not only a Mobster in Chief, but also Trumpism, a social movement that will likely shape America's political climate well into the future, with or without Trump. For anyone interested in the future, *Criminology on Trump* is a must read.

— **Raymond J. Michalowski**, *Arizona Regents Professor Emeritus, Northern Arizona University, USA*

Using a broad criminological perspective that draws on issues central to white-collar and elite offending, this important book provides a deep and novel analysis of Donald Trump's behaviors before, during, and after his presidency. Barak effectively exposes the fundamental shortcomings of media-driven, and relatively narrow legal interpretations of such acts, and in doing so, issues a major rationale for crucial scholarly attention toward elite criminality while setting a copious conceptual table for future research.

— **Henry N. Pontell,** *Distinguished Professor, John Jay College of Criminal Justice and Professor Emeritus, University of California, Irvine, USA*

The lifelong involvement of Donald J. Trump in a wide range of corrupt and criminal activities, continuing during his four-year presidency and in the wake of his re-election loss, is a hugely significant phenomenon in American history. Gregg Barak, in *Criminology on Trump*, has explored quite exhaustively this criminal career, and has applied some comparative and conceptual dimensions of criminology to advance a sophisticated understanding of it. Both students of criminology and of the present American political world have much of value to learn from this book. It can be regarded as a crowning achievement in Barak's long and distinguished career as a critical criminologist.

— **David O. Friedrichs**, *Author of Trusted Criminals:White Collar Crime in Contemporary Society, USA*

Scholarly, rigorous and meticulously researched, informed by criminology, political economy and psychology, this is a hard-to-put-down, forensic and ultimately terrifying analysis of Teflon Don, whose life and times Hollywood would surely not have dared to conjure up as fiction. Barak magisterially documents Trump as the source of a devastating gamut of harms, through every crime in the book spanning the five decades before, during and after his presidency, and culminating in insurrection – failed, but for which he still evades accountability. Beware then: read this book. For as Barak convinces, in a style accessible to and demanding of the widest possible readership (this is 'newsmaking criminology' at its very best), the key forces of economic and political power which have maintained Trump to date may yet combine to propel the Racketeer-in-Chief, the only POTUS twice-impeached, back into the White House.

— **Steve Tombs**, *Professor of Criminology, The Open University, England*

Award winning scholar Gregg Barak uses his critical eye to serve up a detailed and illuminating account of the decades long story of the organized deviant behaviors of Trump. In doing so he skillfully weaves together theories of personality and social structure in this fascinating and unique description of how a deviant life course emerges, and how that life course was projected as normal and even laudable in a (social) media-dominated age.

— **Michael J. Lynch**, *Professor and Director of Graduate Programs, Department of Criminology, University of South Florida, USA*

Donald Trump could be an ideal film character, like those depicted by Charlie Chaplin or Federico Fellini. But as Gregg Barak suggests, he is also the ideal subject of study for criminologists, who provide subtle evaluations of the harm caused, among others, by powerful individuals and groups. Barak takes the daunting task of analyzing the conduct of an evasive ameba and his associates, who straddle buffoonery and illegality. The book manages to position 'criminal jesters' among the forces that support and attempt to exacerbate structural inequality. This is a splendid achievement by a top critical scholar.

— **Vincenzo Ruggiero**, *Professor of Sociology, Middlesex University, England*

Gregg Barak's *Criminology on Trump* uses detailed research to demonstrate Donald Trump's modus operandi in advancing his business and political career, and how these advances were made possible by white-collar crime, abuses of power and Trump's apparent impunity. The past and present of Donald Trump are very much an American affair, and lie at the heart of American democracy. But the Trump phenomenon is of major international interest, as is this excellent book!

— **Isabel Schoultz**, *Associate Professor in Sociology of Law, Lund University, Sweden*

This work is a brilliant (and not non-controversial) analysis of the career of Donald Trump as a businessman and as a politician. However, much more than that, Gregg Barak shows also like a fine mirror the US cultural, economic, political, and institutional terrain which has enabled that career to flourish. A magistral use of criminological tools and especially of uncontested knowledge on white collar and corporate crime issues make *Criminology on Trump* a paramount example of case-study research. Since the book combines invaluable information (down to a filigree-level) together with the nimble writing-style of the author it is a clear must (a fascinating one!) for scientists and nonscientists in and outside the USA.

— **Maria Laura Bohm**, *Chair of Criminal Law and Criminology, Ludwig-Maximilians-Universität München, Germany and Associate External Professor, Faculty of Law, University of Buenos Aires, Argentina*

Barak's *Criminology on Trump* is an outstanding work aimed at challenging amnesia and denial regarding the crimes of the powerful. The book is a robust newsmaking criminology project in which Donald Trump appears as the main character. Throughout his life history, Barak didactically exposes how powerful people's lack of liability for their crimes is marked by whiteness, richness, and cis heteropatriarchy in an expanding political economy of structural inequality. Understanding the scenario in which public and private actors collude is mandatory to prevent those wrongdoings from perpetuating at the expense of nature and human rights in and beyond the US territory. Barak's book fulfills this task in a thought-provoking way.

— **Marília de Nardin Budó**, *Professor of Criminology, Federal University of Santa Catarina, Brazil*

Criminology on Trump is a must-read for those interested in a perspective on why and how Donald Trump was able to exploit our social and political systems to rise to power. What makes this work so critical is that even though Trump may be out of office, the era of Trump and Trumpism are far from over. And that's because Trump has charted a roadmap. Gregg Barak brings a well-honed lens as a social historian and criminologist to every page.

— **Abdul El-Sayed**, *Policymaker in Residence, University of Michigan Ford School of Public Policy, USA*

CRIMINOLOGY ON TRUMP

Criminology on Trump is a criminological investigation of the world's most successful outlaw, Donald J. Trump. Over the course of five decades, Donald Trump has been accused of sexual assault, tax evasion, money laundering, non-payment of employees, and the defrauding of tenants, customers, contractors, investors, bankers, and charities. Yet, he has continued to amass wealth and power. In this book, criminologist and social historian Gregg Barak asks why and how?

This book examines how the United States precariously maintains stability through conflict in which groups with competing interests and opposing visions struggle for power, negotiate rule breaking, and establish criminal justice. While primarily focused on Trump's developing character over three quarters of a century, it is also an inquiry into the changing cultural character and social structure of American society. It explores the ways in which both crime and crime control are socially constructed in relation to a changing political economy.

An accessible and compelling read, this book is essential for all those who seek a criminological understanding of Donald Trump's rise to power.

Gregg Barak is an Emeritus Professor of Criminology and Criminal Justice at Eastern Michigan University. Barak is an award-winning author and editor of books on crime, justice, media, violence, criminal law, homelessness, and human rights. He is also the co-founder and North American Editor of the *Journal of White Collar and Corporate Crime.*

Crimes of the Powerful

Gregg Barak, Eastern Michigan University, USA
Penny Green, Queen Mary University of London, UK
Tony Ward, Northumbria University, UK

Crimes of the Powerful encompasses the harmful, injurious, and victimizing behaviors perpetrated by privately or publicly operated businesses, corporations, and organizations as well as the state mediated administrative, legalistic, and political responses to these crimes.

The series draws attention to the commonalities of the theories, practices, and controls of the crimes of the powerful. It focuses on the overlapping spheres and inter-related worlds of a wide array of existing and recently developing areas of social, historical, and behavioral inquiry into the wrongdoings of multinational organizations, nation-states, stateless regimes, illegal networks, financialization, globalization, and securitization.

These examinations of the crimes of the powerful straddle a variety of related disciplines and areas of academic interest, including studies in criminology and criminal justice; law and human rights; conflict, peace, and security; economic change, environmental decay, and global sustainability.

Corrupt Capital
Alcohol, Nightlife, and Crimes of the Powerful
Kenneth Sebastian León

Domestic Violence as State Crime
A Feminist Framework for Challenge and Change
Evelyn Rose

Criminology on Trump
Gregg Barak

For a full list of the books in the series and more information, please visit: https://www.routledge.com/Crimes-of-the-Powerful/book-series/COTP

CRIMINOLOGY ON TRUMP

Gregg Barak

LONDON AND NEW YORK

Cover image: Zsudayka Terrell

First published 2022
by Routledge
4 Park Square, Milton Park, Abingdon, Oxon OX14 4RN

and by Routledge
605 Third Avenue, New York, NY 10158

Routledge is an imprint of the Taylor & Francis Group, an informa business

British Library Cataloguing-in-Publication Data
A catalogue record for this book is available from the British Library

Library of Congress Cataloging-in-Publication Data
Names: Barak, Gregg, author.
Title: Criminology on Trump / Gregg Barak.
Description: London; New York, NY: Routledge,
Taylor & Francis Group, 2022. |
Includes bibliographical references and index. |
Identifiers: LCCN 2021059446 | ISBN 9781032117928 (hardback) |
ISBN 9781032117904 (paperback) | ISBN 9781003221548 (ebook)
Subjects: LCSH: Trump, Donald, 1946—Ethics. |
Trump, Donald, 1946—Psychology. |
Presidents—United States—Biography. |
Businesspeople—United States—Biography. |
Real estate developers—United States—Biography. |
Corporations—Corrupt practices—United States. |
Criminal behavior—United States. | Political ethics—United States. |
United States—Politics and government—2017-2021.
Classification: LCC E913.3 .B37 2022 |
DDC 973.933092 [B]—dc23/eng/20220124
LC record available at https://lccn.loc.gov/2021059446

ISBN: 978-1-032-11792-8 (hbk)
ISBN: 978-1-032-11790-4 (pbk)
ISBN: 978-1-003-22154-8 (ebk)

DOI: 10.4324/9781003221548

Typeset in Bembo
by codeMantra

"I have joined the political arena so that the powerful can no longer beat up on people who cannot defend themselves"

Trump RNC Nomination Acceptance Speech,
July 2016

CONTENTS

ABOUT THE AUTHOR

Gregg Barak is an Emeritus Professor of Criminology and Criminal Justice at Eastern Michigan University, a former Visiting Distinguished Professor in the College of Justice & Safety at Eastern Kentucky University, and a 2017 Fulbright Scholar in residence at the School of Law at Pontificia Universidade Catholica do Rio Grande do Sul in Porto Alegre, Brasil. In 2003, he became the 27th Fellow of the Academy of Criminal Justice Sciences, in 2007, he received the Lifetime Achievement Award from the Critical Division of the American Society of Criminology, in 2019, the Praxis Award from the American Society of Criminology's Division on Critical Criminology and Social Justice, and in 2020, the Gilbert Geis Lifetime Achievement Award from the American Society of Criminology's Division of White-collar and Corporate Crime. Barak is the author and editor of 20 books on crime, justice, media, violence, criminal law, homelessness, and human rights. These include three award-winning books, *Gimme Shelter: A Social History of Homelessness in Contemporary America* (1991), *Theft of a Nation: Wall Street Looting and Federal Regulatory Colluding* (2012), and *Unchecked Corporate Power: Why the Crimes of Multinational Corporations are Routinized Away and What We Can Do About It* (2017). In 2020, Rutgers University published Barak's criminological memoir *Chronicles of a Radical Criminologist: Working the Margins of Law, Power, and Justice*. Barak received his bachelor's, master's, and doctorate from the Berkeley School of Criminology at the University of California.

INTRODUCTION

Criminology on Trump is about family business, habitual lawlessness, and the struggle for economic and political power. The central character Donald Trump is a con artist, a master gaslighter, and a shrewd racketeer. It is the story of how the Houdini of White-Collar Crime and the founder and CEO of the Trump Organization operated a criminal enterprise from within an incorporated organization beginning in 1980 and continuing up to and from within the bowels of the White House for four years. At the same time, it is the history of the causation of the social, psychological, and physical harms connected to the Donald and his associates before, during, and after the presidency. This book is also an account of the activities that Donald Trump pursued in order to obtain the power of Commander-in-Chief of the United States, what he then did with the power of the bully pulpit once he had achieved it, and finally the lengths to which he would go to keep from losing that power. Lastly, this is the story of what many elected and appointed politicos did or did not do to acquire or to forfeit their individual shares of Trumpian power.

This overall analysis of the underside of the rule of law begs the question: Had the Donald not become the 45th president of the United States, would he, his children, or the Trump Organization have found themselves formal defendants and legal adversaries of the people of the state of New York? My answer unequivocally would have been no way. As of January 6, 2022, the question remains open as to whether Donald Trump as the former president or any of his family members will be indicted and prosecuted

DOI: 10.4324/9781003221548-1

for criminal tax fraud and other felonies along with the Trump Organization, Inc. and its CFO Allan Weisselberg?

From the point of view of newsmaking, lawlessness, and equal justice, much of the popular discourse-surrounding Trump has to do with competing narratives. The most reverberating of these have been the dueling apocalyptic narratives traversing both old and new media platforms alike. One narrative has to do with witch-hunts, hoaxes, fake news, global elites, and the deep state engaging in a myriad of underworld or otherworld conspiracies to bring down Trump.[1] The other narrative has to do with saving the U.S. democracy from authoritarianism, recovering law and order from the damage, chaos, and trauma of Trump, and restoring American normalcy without all of the political insanity.[2] While these two narratives capture the cultural conflict, the diverse groups of people at work here, and the rival social movements of incompatible interests, desires, and visions, neither speaks to the fundamental structural conditions that generate the divisiveness between these two narratives. Without ever addressing these structural relationships, the two sides will remain at loggerheads for some time to come.

The medium as always is still the message and so far in the 21st century, social media is the medium. At the same time, the weaponizing of racism, misogyny, hate, fear, intimidation, and violence vis-a-vis social media is neither new nor unique to the United States. These sociocultural expressions of the contradictions of patriarchy, neo-colonialism, and capitalism have been around since this nation's inception. Today's Proud Boys are the contemporary versions of New England churchmen in the 1700s, the Klan riders of the 1800s, or the fervent followers of Joseph McCarthy in the 1950s. Likewise, the anti-critical race theory politicians of today that do the bidding for white minority rule and racial discrimination are very much the same as John C. Calhoun fronting for the rich plantation owners during the antebellum South.

The primary differences between the not-so-distant past of the last 75 years and the present have to do with the disbursements in the accumulation of capital. From post-WWII until around 1974, the United States experienced close to three decades of unparalleled upward social mobility as well as a rapidly expanding middle class. However, since the mid-1970s to 2022, there has been a steady increase in economic inequality, a shrinking middle class, and downward social mobility for many. Thus, the contemporary bipartisan erosion of the liberal capitalist consensus in the United States is not the primary cause of our present democratic crisis but is rather symptomatic of a much broader problem that neither the Republicans as a whole nor most of the Democrats are willing to accept. I am referring to the inability of our bourgeois democratic system to resolve the contradictions of a political economy that promises the American Dream to one and all and yet caters to the richest one percent and provides suitably for the upper ten percent. In other words, our country's present-day conflicts over identity politics, governmental failures, neoliberal policies, right-wing intransigency, and climate change not only predate Donald Trump and Trumpism, but they are all fundamentally driven by the unrelenting and expanding political economy of structural inequality.

What makes this Trump book different from the others is that it is the only one grounded in the scientific study of crime and social control. As an amalgamation of the social and behavioral sciences, criminology focuses on the pathology of harmful acts, the cultural construction of both crime and punishment, and the politics of crime control and criminal prevention. Criminology also examines the vagaries of social control and the formalities of criminal, civil, political, economic, and social justice. Contradictorily, these procedural and substantive systems of bourgeois legalities typically defend and shield the crimes of the powerful from accountability, culpability, and/or liability.

In a nutshell, criminology possesses the ideal tools, methods, and theories for sorting out and evaluating the behavior of Donald Trump and company. By scrutinizing both DJT and the United States through the lenses of social deviance, this inquiry is able to answer one basic question among others: Given the fictional biographical accounts of the "art of the deal" Trump that fly in the face of an iconic persona that reveals in great detail clashing images of whom the man exactly is, how did the Donald get away with so much destructive behavior over the course of his lifetime not to mention becoming the 45th POTUS?

In the 19th-century world of industrialized and urbanized Europe, a significant number of scholars such as Emile Durkheim, Max Weber, and Karl Marx

> sought to ground their analyses in a nuanced sense of the world as it is, and as it is becoming, not least because the phenomena of crime and disorder have so regularly been traced to the effects of social upheaval and dislocation.[3]

Early in the 21st century, the questions that have often animated my examinations of crime, regulation, and social control are those that stem from the economic, cultural, and political changes that underpin the evolving human condition. Against the interplay of moral innovation, entrepreneurship, and transgression, my analysis is fully cognizant of the continuous generation of meanings around the day-to-day routines of bureaucracy as well as during times of crises or panics. Like after the Wall Street implosion of 2008 or from the 2020 COVID-19 pandemic. These are the historical times when the old rules are often broken, amended, or replaced with new ones. These are also moments when we can learn, if we have a mind to, what we as people and our society are really made of without all the mystification.

Many social observers and investigative journalists argue that Trump deceiving others has also been about self-deception. Of those who know the Donald personally, few believe self-deception to be the correct assessment. Criminologists who study white-collar and corporate crime in relation to issues of trust, neutralization, or normalization often examine the parallel systems of deceiving others with deceiving ourselves that may or may not coexist in discrete cases of criminality. We do so as a means of trying to understand how these systems of deception operate individually and socially in order to routinize away the various forms of deviant or criminal behavior.[4] In the case of Trump, one should always appreciate his uncanny and habitual ability to cover up or suppress the facts about his "successes" and "failures" alike. He simply lies over and over and over until other persons either believe his lies or give up trying to refute them.

By means of speech or tweet, Trump had the ability as well as the power of the presidency to use the "bully pulpit" to communicate with the American people the likes of which had never been witnessed before and after social media. Trump not only drove the political narrative for at least five years, but since leaving office the former president has continued to deceive millions and millions of people into adopting disinformation, falsehoods, and fanciful lies in order to minimize, if not extricate, the Donald from any serious accountability for the damages and harms he has caused for nearly 50 years. Most recently, during his four lawless years as the Commander-in-Chief, the unleashed Trump engaged in a series of multiple defilements of the Constitutional Federal Republic of the United States. As the authors of "In-your-face Watergate: Neutralizing Government Lawbreaking and the War Against White-collar Crime" have demonstrated: "Trump exacerbated existing political differences and influenced supporters to at once ignore government crime and corruption, and accept new moral narratives that flew in the face of substantial evidence of criminality."[5]

Like virtually, all social and behavioral scientists and most other human beings, none of us are free of biases or assumptions about the world in which we live. Nor are most of us detached from our own experiences of identity formation, personal politics, social statuses, and so forth. Hence, let me be clear from the beginning of this work. While my approach to examining Trump's criminal behavior is clinical, I am also a newsmaking criminologist that tries to "make news" about crime and justice as a means of attempting to influence our public understanding of and policy responses to both individual harms and social injuries alike.[6] So while I am busy gathering my data and interpreting the mediation of crime, justice, and Trump, on the one hand, I am also engaging in the process of newsmaking criminology, on the other hand. By putting this book out there in the public domain, I am hoping that my take-a-ways or bottom lines on the criminological phenomenon of Donald Trump will become your take-a-ways or bottom lines as well.

Nine days after Trump's failed Capitol Insurrection on January 6, 2021, to prevent the electoral certification of Joe Biden as the 46th president of the United States, Sasha Abramsky writing for *The Nation* opined:

> Trump is about to metamorphose from the world's most powerful human to a financially challenged pariah, a traitor who betrayed in the starkest way possible his oath of office, a coup plotter ostracized by erstwhile political allies, business partners, lenders, and media moguls. He might retain the allegiance of a fanatical portion of the GOP base, maybe even a large portion of that base, but he will no longer command a coalition capable of winning power. Moreover, he is likely going to be chased these coming years from one criminal trial and one civil damages lawsuit to the next.[7]

I would argue that the verdict is still out as to whether the curtain has or is coming down on Trump's political career. Put another way, I contend that unless the Donald (1) is indicted and prosecuted for various crimes by the states of New York or Georgia before the upcoming 2022 midterms and/or (2) Trumpian-backed candidates take a shellacking in these midterms, Trump will be all in trying his best to recapture the White House in 2024.

Donald J. Trump's biography of deception and dishonesty has always been made possible by the willingness of others to accommodate and facilitate his crooked behavior. This type of social indulgence feeds naturally into Trump's fetish for grifting. It also satisfies Donald's narcissistic need for self-aggrandizement. Trump's immunity from wrongdoing reached a peak of sorts when kowtowing Republican officials not only denied Trump's incitement to mob violence on January 6 but also continued to promote his Big Lies about stolen elections in order to routinize across the nation their avalanche of voter suppression bills. At the same time, they all know fully well that there had been no actual widespread voter fraud and that the Donald had lost fair and square, and Biden had legitimately won the election.

Similarly, there were many Republican power brokers who continued to spread all kinds of disinformation about the January 6 assault on the Capitol, especially about the prominent roles played out by white nationalists and anti-governmental "militia" groups. For example, Rep. Andrew Clyde (R-GA) during a House Oversight Committee on the Capitol Riot in an effort to change the narrative had this to say: "If you didn't know that TV footage was a video from January the sixth, you would actually think it was a normal tourist visit."[8] One of several goals of this book is to reconsider how various theories of criminology, psychology, and political economy as well as the bodies of shared research from white-collar, corporate, and organized crime studies can assist us, criminologists and non-criminologists, to sort out the contradictory relations of the sociocultural expressions of crime and victimization, on the one hand, and of the abuses of political power and deviant behavior, on the other hand.

Donald Trump was impeached for a second time on January 13, 2021, the only president to be impeached twice. For two months prior and running up to the Republican president's failed insurrection on 1/6, Trump and his political allies had been very busy trying to stop the imaginary steal by challenging as many points as possible in the certification process of Democratic president-elect Joseph R. Biden. Post the 2020 November election, while Trump was losing more than 60 court cases and winning zero that alleged widespread and organized voter fraud, he was aided by many state-elected Republicans and other political allies so he could continue to do everything within and without his legitimate power to overturn the unfavorable electoral results in Arizona, Georgia, Michigan, and Pennsylvania. In the process, the Trumpian alliance was attempting to disenfranchise millions of democratic voters, especially blacks and other minorities from the greater metropolitan areas of Atlanta, Detroit, and Philadelphia.

Well before these efforts failed to overturn the 2020 election results, Trump had put into motion his first of two quintessential Big Lies. As far back as June of that same year, Trump was repeating Lie #1 at campaign rallies and on Twitter: The only way that he could lose the election was if the election was rigged. Wealthy allies of Trump had already spent millions on films, rallies, and other efforts to tout falsehoods about the upcoming 2020 vote. Seven months after the electoral defeat, there was the online release of *The Big Rig* in June 2021. Like the earlier media productions, this one financed by former Overstock.com CEO Patrick Byrne for $750,000 also consisted of a "loosely affiliated network of figures that have harnessed right-wing media outlets, podcasts and the social media platform Telegram to promote the falsehood that the 2020 election was rigged."[9]

Lie #2 was born less than 24 hours after voting had stopped on November 4, before tens of millions of votes had yet to be counted and when the Donald was already behind in the electoral college. This other Big Lie claimed that Trump had won the election by a landslide. Not only did both lies take hold with most Republican voters, but 47 states by the end of March 2021 had also proposed 361 bills with restrictive voting provisions. By early summer, anti-voting laws had already been passed in Republican-controlled states like Florida, Texas, and Georgia. These laws all share making it more difficult for people in general to vote. They especially interfere and infringe on the voting rights of historically discriminated groups as well as the urban poor.[10]

Although Biden received 306 electoral college votes and more than 81 million popular votes, and Trump received 232 electoral college votes and more than 74 million popular votes, by the end of 2020, some 50 million Republicans believed that president-elect Biden had stolen the election from Trump despite the experts claiming that this was the most secure presidential election in the U.S. history. Then, on certification day, January 6, 30,000 supporters invited by Trump from nearly 50 states showed up at the White House for his promised "wild" affair. After speaking for one hour and at Trump's behest, a MAGA mob of some 10,000 incited by the POTUS marched from the White House down Pennsylvania Avenue to the nation's Capitol. Once there, 800 insurrectionists proceeded to riot and occupy the lawmaking body, delaying certification for five hours, causing the injuries of hundreds of police and civilians as well as the death of five people. Meanwhile, as Donald's insurgency unfolded in real time, the former president was sitting in the White House watching it on several televisions. He was both excited and mesmerized while communicating absolutely nothing to his supporters or the nation for 187 minutes. This silence was in the face of numerous texts to Trump's Chief of Staff Mark Meadows from Don Trump, Jr. two Trumpian Fox News hosts, and several other Republican congressmen appealing to the Donald to "call off the dogs."

On February 13, 2021, the ultimate High Crimes and Misdemeanors for which the U.S. House of Representatives may indict a sitting Commander-in-Chief, the Incitement of Insurrection, fell 10 votes short of the 67 required by the Constitution for the U.S. Senate to have convicted Trump as charged. Effectively, this was the second "jury nullification" carried out by the Republican senators in 12 months. Once again, his own political party bestowed upon Trump another metaphoric mulligan or get out of jail free card. This repeated jury nullification by the opposition party allowed the president while sitting in the White House only a few blocks away from the Capitol to get away with what in other circumstances he might have been prosecuted by way of the felony murder doctrine. This is a real stretch I know. Then again had Trump been on the other side, he would have been inclined to encourage such a lawsuit against any of his political opponents, Democratic or Republican.

The Republican Party's denial of the former president's political responsibility or legal accountability for his wrongdoing proved the prescience of Trump's remarks at a 2016 campaign stop in Sioux Center, Iowa, where he boasted that his supporters would always stay loyal even if he happened to commit a capital offense: "I could stand in the middle of Fifth Avenue and shoot somebody, and I wouldn't lose any voters. OK? It's like incredible." Admittedly, this is the sad truth. An Associated Press-NORC Center for Public Affairs Research poll taken two weeks after President Biden was sworn into office found that 65 percent of Republicans believed that the election was illegitimate. And three-quarters of Republicans still maintained that Trump was a good or great president.[11]

Unpacking how and why Trump in less than 13 months escaped impeachment conviction for a second time requires interrogating how the young Donny and later the Donald escaped real accountability or liability for a lifetime of dishonesty and corrupt behavior. It also requires examining how America's corporate, political, and taxing systems have facilitated Trump's fraudulent financial schemes. I am referring specifically to the tax schemes (rackets) that he inherited from his father and has continued to perpetrate to this very day. Making sense of Trump's life of delinquency begins when Donny was two and one-half years old and was learning how to navigate his own family dynamics and privileged disadvantages.

After college and from his early twenties to his early seventies, Trump experienced limited financial losses from numerous civil lawsuits filed against him. Most importantly, Donald has so far escaped with absolute immunity from any criminal behavior. Over the course of five decades, Trump has been accused of sexual assault, tax evasion, money laundering, non-payment of employees, as well as the defrauding of tenants, customers, contractors, investors, bankers, and charities. The above list of Trump's crimes is hardly exhaustive. A typology of core, hybrid, and marginal forms of white-collar crime include corporate crime; occupational crime; avocational crime; governmental crime; state-corporate crime; crimes of globalization; financial crime; enterprise crime; contrepreneurial crime; and technocrime.[12] Trump has been credibly accused of having been involved with each of these categories of crime.

For the purposes of this investigation, the record reveals that after a couple of initial business successes followed by one investment failure after the next, Trump and company continued to amass wealth. The obvious question becomes: If his net worth and family wealth grew during these financial fiascos, then how exactly does this work? It is a lot more than a little complicated and many things are in play. For now, one person—Allen Weisselberg—and two words—"control fraud" will have to suffice.[13] In all fairness, I should underscore that the Donald and company had assistance by Uncle Sam. I am referring to the historical and operational demise of the Internal Revenue Service's capabilities of enforcing elite-level financial and tax fraud schemes. The ongoing decline in criminal enforcement has permitted corrupt autocrats, foreign oligarchs, syndicated criminals, and complicit bankers to launder trillions of dollars through Swiss, German, U.S., and other banks since the breakup of the former Soviet Union.[14] This unending failure of the United States to budget for the sufficient hiring of IRS agents specializing in the accounting frauds of the superrich has allowed DJT before and after he became the 45th POTUS to benefit from virtually little if any regulatory or law-enforcement intervention against these types of international financial crimes.[15]

During the Trump presidency, the prosecution of white-collar federal crimes in the United States predictably declined.[16] In 2020, the number of white-collar crime prosecutions was about 3,500 nationwide, its lowest level ever.[17] Meanwhile, the hundreds of civil lawsuits filed against or on behalf of Trump during one term in office broke all records involving all former presidents, including those that had served two terms in the White House. Trump's litigation tsunami as the president also echoes his pre-2017 record-setting number of some 4,000 civil lawsuits. Most of these have involved Trump as the suing plaintiff rather than as the defending respondent.[18] When the Donald loses, which is about one third of the time, he stiffs his attorneys; when he wins, the American taxpayer picks up his attorneys' fees.

No American president has been the focus of more allegations of corruption, of criminality as a basic character attribute, and of a wider range of criminal actions than Donald Trump. While other American presidencies have been closely associated with rampart corruption, including those of Ulysses S. Grant and Warring G. Harding, neither of them was directly implicated in any corruption. By comparison, claims of "personal enrichment" corruption by the U.S. presidents, while not wholly absent in the past, were never routinized into the daily operations of a U.S. president before the Donald. As for Donald's range of criminality, no president—including Richard Nixon—comes remotely close. In a parallel vein, no other American president has been accused of possessing a more pronounced disdain for and disregard of the "rule of law" than Trump.

Any discussion of the "crimes" of Trump needs to address those ultimate crimes with which he has been involved. These are not necessarily crimes in terms of specific violations of U.S. law, but rather they are crimes in the broader sense of representing massively consequential assaults, harms, or injuries against humanity. These crimes include violations of international law. Those crimes also include his administration's aggressive regulatory rollback initiatives, his promotion of white nationalism and hate crimes, his separation of immigrant children from their parents, his dealings with Iran, Yemen, and Saudi Arabia, and the responses to the COVID-19 pandemic. Regarding the latter, the former president's near-death experience with the virus and the intervention to save his life, his behavioral modeling in front of the American people, and his administration's crimes of omission, neglect, and mismanagement have been responsible according to Columbian University for the avoidable deaths of at least 250,000 lives.[19] Those estimates were before there was a vaccine for COVID-19, and the Delta and Omicron variants had not yet emerged. Similarly, the Trumpian policy prescriptions in relation to climate change have contributed to ecocide and terracide in violation of the principles of environmental justice.[20] It remains to be seen which of former president Trump's flawed and dangerous political assaults on democracy, on the pandemic, or on the environment will turn out to be his greatest legacy of depravity.

As you read the rest of this book, please keep in mind the axiom that undergirds this work: *Crime is born out of the miseries and privileges of material conditions while crime control is about who is benefitting from harming whom.* For example, one form of wage theft involves employer minimum wage violations (or paying workers below the legal limit). In the United States minimum wage violations cost workers about $15 billion in 2015 compared to about $4.5 billion lost from all the robberies, burglaries, larcenies, and motor vehicle thefts combined for that year. The percentages of dollars recovered from stolen wages or from stolen property in general averages between two and three percent annually. However, the number of state investigators who enforce minimum wage laws in the U.S. is less than 1000 while the number of law enforcement officers is more than 700,000.

Criminology on Trump is divided into three parts organized around eight chapters and followed by an Epilogue. Part I, In Advance of the Presidency, consists of Chapters 1–3. These chapters are about Trump's life before he formally enters the political arena, keeping in mind that the Donald has always been a political animal if not a politician.

Chapter 1, Family Dynamics, Privileged Disadvantages, and Coming of Age, covers time before Trump's birth and ends when he announces his candidacy for the presidency in 2015. It begins by providing a brief on the evolution of organizational crime vis-à-vis the trajectories of Benjamin Bugsy Siegel and Donald J. Trump. It also provides a protracted treatment of the sociocultural background from which the Donald would eventually reside at 1600 Pennsylvania Avenue as the White House "Mobster-in-Chief." The chapter revolves around the Trump household in the heart of Queens, New York, between 1946 and 1968 where Donald and his four siblings grew up with their father, mother, and paternal grandmother residing a few blocks away. Examined here are the central personality traits, personal values and motives, as well as the interpersonal and cultural factors shaping the character formation of DJT. His family dynamics are used to establish etiological roots of his defensive and projective mechanisms. They help to explain where Trump's episodic and transactional approaches to social, business, and ethical relations come from. They also shed light on the origins of Trump's narcissistic and sociopathic lack of empathy and human identification.[21]

Chapter 2, A Lifetime of Deviance, Deception and Dishonesty, 1970–2016, provides numerous examples of lawlessness highlighted over a span of five decades. Initially, these devious or immoral activities involve Fred Trump, Sr., son Donald, and Trump Management. Next, they involve Donald, the Trump Organization, and eventually include his three eldest children—Donald Jr., Ivanka, and Eric. These business practices reveal the family modus operandi of using lawful and unlawful behaviors to sustain and expand their wealth and power. Other pre-presidential illegalities included are the tax evasion schemes by generations of Trumps, securities frauds, and related father Fred and son Donald fraudulent violations along the way to unsuccessfully avoiding the bankruptcy of their Atlantic City casinos. In turn, the Trumps have used their ill-gotten wealth to gain legal immunity and defend themselves from future lawsuits. The story begins with the 1973 racial discrimination lawsuit involving rental apartments in

Brooklyn, Queens, and Staten Island. It previews Donald's take on lawyers, litigation, and the spinning of public narratives. The chapter then turns to the successes of the Grand Hyatt in 1978, to the building of Trump Tower in the early 1980s on a foundation of mob-sourced concrete and stolen wages, and to the litany of failed businesses and bankruptcies. This chapter ends days after Trump has won the 2016 presidential election and he has agreed to pay $25 million to settle three Trump University lawsuits, including those alleging civil fraud and racketeering.

Chapter 3, Weaponizing the Law, Litigation, and Legality, features the merging character of Donald's paternal socialization of becoming either a "winner" or a "loser" with Donald's early business and political tutelage from Roy Cohn, his legal counsel from 1973 to 1985. Throughout the time Cohn represented Trump Management, he was also a prominent fixer in New York City. Cohn was best known as the former chief counsel for Senator Joseph McCarthy. During the congressionally televised McCarthy Hearings in the spring of 1954 that lasted for 36 days with an estimated 80 million viewers tuning in to some portion thereof, Cohn's sensationalistic approach to confronting the alleged communists has been described as nothing less than demagogic, reckless, and based on unsubstantiated accusations. Based upon Donald and Roy's initial discussions of legal philosophy and legal practice as well as their consensus on the nature of lawyering, Trump first retained the services of Cohn. With Roy's assistance, Donald began fine-tuning his talents for bullying and intimidating other people. Trump also began fabricating himself as America's most famous and colorful billionaire while expanding his branding techniques from the New York tabloids and his best-selling *The Art of the Deal* to his 15-year run on NBC's *The Apprentice*.

Part II, Squandering the Presidency, consists of Chapters 4–7. They are about Trump's weaponizing of the systems of law, power, and justice for his own material and selfish interests. These chapters are also about his assault on democracy and the corrupt use of the executive branch of government for his own and allies' benefits.

Chapter 4, Campaigns and Policies of Adversity, Harmfulness, and Divisiveness, examines Trumpism and the political ideologies and electoral platforms of the Republicans in relation to those of the Democrats from Trump's earliest accounts of Birtherism and xenophobia to the draining of the swamp to deep state conspiracies to transforming the language of politics, race, and gender. The chapter underscores the roles played by Stephen K. Bannon and Stephen Miller. Bannon was the tactician behind the Trumpian ideology of nativism, combative campaigns, and the struggle to deconstruct the administrative state. Miller was one of Trump's most influential White House advisors, political speechwriters, and social architects of the immigration policies that banned Muslims from abroad and separated Latinx families at the Southern border. The chapter then turns to the rollback policies of Trump and his administration with respect to international and domestic issues. Finally, with respect to policing, prosecution, and punishment, the chapter reviews significant federal criminal justice policy intervention between 2017 and 2020.

Chapter 5, A Sinkhole of Organizational Corruption, provides a comprehensive overview of the routinization of corruption during Trump's term in office. It begins with Trump and company stocking his administration or filling the Washington swamp with free marketers, political hacks, and know-nothings. Next, the chapter explores the thoroughness of pay-to-play, the selling of public policy, and the mapping of corruption throughout Trump's authoritative state. Finally, the chapter closes with a review of the anti-democracy corruption for profit.

Chapter 6, State Organized Abuses of Power and Obstruction, explores the relationships between Donald Trump as the principal owner of the Trump Organization, Inc. and his holding the office of the presidency of the United States at one and the same time. It begins with an overview of the types of crime and criminals, white-collar and corporate, organizational and state, as well as state-corporate. The chapter then turns to a discussion of Trump's ten worst abuses of power while occupying the White House. Next, we turn to a review of Robert Mueller's investigation into the Russian interference during the 2016 presidential race, the Trump campaign collusion with the Russians, and whether Trump obstructed justice in the investigation. The chapter then pivots to the extortion of Ukrainian president Zelensky and Trump's First Impeachment trial. Finally, the chapter describes the routinization of corruption by Trump and his administration throughout the three branches of government.

Chapter 7, Pardons, Prosecutions, and the Politics of Punishment, examines Trump's unorthodox use of the pardoning power as the Outlaw-in-Chief. Donald's use of this presidential power is compared with that of former presidents as far back as William McKinley. It does so by examining the high-and-low-profile business, political, and celebrity pardons, clemencies, and commuted sentences issued early and late in his administration. The chapter then turns to a review of the ongoing civil and criminal lawsuits against the former president, as well as the pending lawsuits vs. Trump family members and the Trump Organization, Inc.

Part III, Following the Presidency, consists of the final chapter that tells the story of how Trump stoked hatred and white supremacy. How he aroused and enabled many aggrieved, angered, and cynical Americans. And how he radicalized "patriots" to take up arms and to commit violence to prevent the certification of the 46th POTUS on January 6, 2021.

Chapter 8, Insurrection, Divided Selves, and the Aftermath of a Failed Coup, begins by first focusing on the failed legal and political attempts to overturn the fairest and most secure election in the U.S. history. It highlights how the two Big Lies provided the fuel for right-wing extremist groups such as the Oath Keepers, the Proud Boys, and the Three Percenters with justifications for their violent assault on the Capitol. The lies also reinforced the ever-changing QAnon theories of conspiracy as well as a large segment of the Trumpian base. The chapter then underscores the legal and illegal actions taken by Trump and other elected and non-elected officials of the Republican Party to suppress millions of African American voters and to perpetuate the Big Lies before and after the failed election and insurrection. Next, the chapter compares a stolen election vs. election tampering and whitewashing a failed insurrection vs. investigating and covering up a failed coup. Finally, the last section of the chapter ends with a riff on Teflon Don the Racketeer-in-Chief.

After Chapter 8 is the Epilogue that talks about Trump the con and racketeer from the viewpoint of entrepreneurship, risk taking, and top dogs.

Notes

1 Paul McGuire and Tony Anderson, 2018. *Trumpocalypse: The End-Times President, a Battle Against the Globalist Elite, and the Countdown to Armageddon*. Nashville: Faith Words.
2 David Frum, 2020. *Trumpocalypse: Restoring American Democracy*. New York: HarperCollins Publishers.
3 David Garland and Richard Sparks (eds.), 2000. Criminology, Social Theory and the Challenge of Our Times. *Criminology and Social Theory*. Oxford: Oxford University Press, p. 1.
4 Joe McGrath, 2021. Self-deception as a Technique of Neutralization: An Analysis of the Subjective Account of a White-Collar Criminal. *Crime, Law and Social Change* 75: 415–432. https://doi.org/10.1007/s10611-021-09933-6.
5 Henry N. Pontell, Robert Tillman, and Adam Kavon Ghazi-Tehrani, 2021. In-Your-Face Watergate: Neutralizing Government Lawbreaking and the War against White-Collar Crime. *Crime, Law and Social Change* 75: 201–219. https://doi.org/10.1007/s10611=021-09954-1.
6 Gregg Barak, 1988. Newsmaking Criminology: Reflections on Media, Intellectuals, and Crime. *Justice Quarterly* 5 (4): 565–587. See also Gregg Barak (ed.), 1994. *Media, Process, and the Social Construction of Crime: Studies in Newsmaking*

Criminology. New York: Garland Publishing; Gregg Barak, 2020. *Chronicles of a Radical Criminologist: Working the Margins of Law, Power, and Justice*. New Brunswick, NJ: Rutgers University Press, see Chapter 4, Doing Newsmaking Criminology.

7 Sasha Abramsky, 2021. Is It Curtains for Donald Trump? *The Nation*. January 15. https://www.thenation.com/article/politics/trump-impeachment-insurrection-congress/.

8 Adam Edelman and Garrett Haake, 2021. Republican Loyal to Trump Claims Capitol Riot Looked More Like 'Normal Tourist Visit'. *NBC News*. May 12. https://www.nbcnews.com/politics/congress/republican-loyal-trump-claims-capitol-riot-looked-more-normal-tourist-n1267163.

9 Rosalind S. Heiderman, Emma Brown, Tom Hamburger and Josh Dawsey, 2021. Inside the 'Shadow Reality World" Promoting the Lie That the Presidential Election Was Stolen. *The Washington Post*. June 24. https://www.washingtonpost.com/politics/2021/06/24/inside-shadow-reality-world-promoting-lie-that-presidential-election-was-stolen/.

10 Brennan Center for Justice, 2021. State Voting Bills Tracker 2021. April 1. https://www.brennancenter.org/our-work/research-reports/state-voting-bills-tracker-2021.

11 Poll Finds 65% of Republicans Say They Don't Believe Biden's Election Was Legitimate. *MarketWatch*. Associate Press, February 5, 2021. https://www.marketwatch.com/story/poll-finds-65-of-republicans-say-they-dont-believe-bidens-election-was-legitimate-01612570478.

12 David O. Friedrichs, 2010. *Trusted Criminals: White Collar Crime in Contemporary Society*, 4th edition. Belmont, CA: Wadsworth/Cengage Learning.

13 Originally, "control frauds" referred to companies that use businesses as a means of defrauding others and making it difficult to detect and punish the frauds. See Stanton Wheeler and Mitchell Rothman, 1982. The Organization as Weapon in White Collar Crime. *Michigan Law Review* 8 (7): 1403–1426. More recently, control frauds refer not just to the organization, but also to persons, such as a CEO or a CFO, who has directed or been responsible for thefts by deception. See William Black, 2005. *The Best Way to Rob a Bank Is to Own One: How Corporate Executives and Politicians Looted the S & L Industry*. Austin: The University of Texas Press.

14 Tom Warren et al., 2020. He Was at the Heart of Two of the Biggest Dirty Money Scandals in History. *BuzzFeedNews*. September 20. https://www.buzzfeednews.com/article/tomwarren/alexander-perepilichnyy-money-laundering-scandals.

15 Casey Michel, 2021. *American Kleptocracy: How the U.S. Created the World's Greatest Money Laundering Scheme in History*. New York: St. Martin's Press.

16 Gregg Barak, 2017. Corporate Crime in the Age of Trump. *The Crime Report*. February 8. https://thecrimereport.org/2017/02/08/corporate-corruption-in-the-age-of-trump/.

17 Paul E. Pelletier, 2021. How to Actually Prosecute the Financial Crimes of the Very Rich. *The Atlantic*. May 19. https://www.theatlantic.com/ideas/archive/2021/05/prosecute-tax-fraud-financial-crimes-garland/618914/.

18 James D. Zirin, 2019. *Plaintiff in Chief: A Portrait of Donald Trump in 3,500 Lawsuits*. New York: St. Martin's Publishing Group.

19 Damian Paletta and Yasmeen Abutaleb, 2021. Inside the Extraordinary Effort to Save Trump from Covid-19. *The Washington Post*. June 24. https://www.

washingtonpost.com/politics/2021/06/24/nightmare-scenario-book-excerpt/. See also, Raymond Michalowski, 2020. The Necropolitics of Regulation. *Journal of White Collar and Corporate Crime* 1 (2): 83–85.

20 Gregg Barak, 2017. Keeping It Green: The Looming Battle with Scott Pruitt's EPA. *The Crime Report.* January 18. https://thecrimereport.org/2017/01/18/keeping-it-green-the-looming-battle-with-scott-pruitts-epa/.

21 As you read this book, keep in mind Trump's self-description of himself as "a very stable genius" and the master of messaging's Father's Day communication on June 20, 2021: "Happy Father's Day to all, including the Radical Left, RINOs, and other losers of the world. Hopefully, eventually, everyone will come together!" This "unifying" message by the former "divider-in-chief" was not aimed at the body politic as a whole but was addressed to his base of supporters, to other Trumpian Republicans, and to the Republicans in name only (RINO). The truncated message was "leaked" to the *New York Post* and shared early the next morning with the non-Trumpian world.

PART ONE

In advance of the presidency

1

FAMILY DYNAMICS, PRIVILEGED DISADVANTAGES, AND COMING OF AGE

John Joseph Gotti, Jr. (1940–2002) and Benjamin Bugsy Siegel (1906–1947) are two of the more powerful bosses in the history of American organized crime. These bosses were feared not only for their ruthlessness, but also for their willingness to exert their influence on other people's behavior. Gotti and Siegel were quite good at using other people's money to get what they wanted. They were also judicious in preventing their fraudulent conduct from giving way to liability for damages done.[1] Not only did these head honchos have close to absolute control over their extended "family" members, but their tentacles of power also spread across their interspheres of businesses, politics, and lawlessness. Yet, these 20th-century gangsters' abilities to neutralize or corrupt government officials were almost non-existent when compared to Donald Trump.

As the CEO of the Trump Organization, Inc. and even more so as the Commander-in-Chief, Boss Trump was feared for his ruthlessness and for his willingness to use anyone as well as their resources to obtain any of his desired ends. With relatively little opposition or pushback from the Republican Party, Trump and his MAGA base steamrolled the GOP and took it over in less than 18 months. Within the Department of Justice, Trump and his allies, including Attorney General Bill Barr, had the FBI investigating bogus conspiracy theories about a fraudulent or stolen election several weeks after the recounting had concluded that Biden had won. Days before and running up to the insurrection, Trump's last Acting Attorney General Jeffrey E. Rosen was resisting Donald's efforts to overturn the election and

DOI: 10.4324/9781003221548-3

was refusing to publicly cast doubt on the legitimacy of the election. Rosen was also unwilling to sign off on a letter to the Georgia state legislators asserting wrongly that they should void Mr. Biden's victory.

Throughout his lame duck administration, Trump was working harder than ever trying to overturn an election so as not to have to attempt a coup d'état as the only means left to decertify the election of Joe Biden. While he was losing 60 lawsuits alleging fraudulent elections because there was absolutely no truth to the claims, Donald was personally harassing the Department of Justice. He was doing so daily with phone calls about all kinds of allegedly fraudulent activities for them to waste their time and money investigating. Trump was also on the phone intimidating election officials in Arizona and Georgia where he was falsely claiming victory and pressurizing them to find more votes for him or to simply overturn the election because it had been rigged. In the meanwhile, his political supporters were threatening election officials in all the closely contested states, forcing several of their own Republican officials because of death threats to resign from their polling positions or not to run for re-election.

One year after the failed coup attempt and through at least the 2022 midterm elections, Trump and company will continue their big lies about a stolen election, defend the January 6th rioters as patriots evidenced at the September 18, 2021 #JusticeForJ6 rally in Union Square, and castigate the Capitol police for their overzealous brutality. Besides being the POTUS, what most differentiates the former Mobster-in-Chief from all the other nonstate mob bosses like Gotti and Siegel is that Donald's thousands of storm troopers are not per se on anybody's payroll. All but a relatively few Trumpers "pay to play" one way or the other.

At the same time, the networks around Trump's political attack dogs are paying the Donald to play. That's the kind of power that other mobsters can only dream of. In terms of personal expenditures, more than 600 of Trump's Capitol rioters will eventually have pleaded guilty to or been convicted of "obstruction of an official proceeding," "entering a restricted building with a dangerous weapon," "violent entry and disorderly conduct in the Capitol building," and lesser offenses like "trespassing." Only Stewart Rhodes of the Oath Keepers and 10 other members as of February 1, 2022 have been charged with "seditious conspiracy." Few of the financial backers or Capitol organizers, if any, will be charged with having engaged in "a rising or rebellion of citizens against their government, usually manifested by acts of violence" or with "inciting, assisting, or engaging in such conduct against the United States," including the former president who masterminded and orchestrated the January 6,

2021 insurrection. This state of affairs has reflected Trump's unchecked power by the administration of criminal law, by the U.S. Senate, by the lockstep Republican Party, and by Democratic President Biden and his Attorney General Merrick Garland.

These internal domestic power relations of constitutional and criminal laws cannot be totally separated from Trump's intertwining global tentacles of economic, political, and criminal power. Nor can these political and economic conditions be separated from the social reality that with the exceptions of the traditional elite media newspapers online and offline, Trump and his allies have dominated the dueling narratives on the social media platforms such as Twitter, Facebook, and YouTube. Trump fever has also been captured by FOX news and other alt-right media markets. In part, this has a lot to do with the psychodynamic energy or pleasure derived by millions of Americans from the fetishistic conspiracy theories juxtaposed with the cold and objective facts or the science. In part, it also has to do with a failure of the United States to have a well-funded public media system. Every other democratic country in the world does so and to varying degrees these nations have freed their mass media from corporate or state control.

Concurrently, both our mediated perceptions of Boss Trump and much of his modus operandi or transactional approach shared with other top gangsters are underappreciated. Gotti, the former boss of the Gambino crime family in New York, was also known as Black John, Crazy Horse, Johnny Boy, and Dapper Don. At the dawn of the age of "non-sticking" Teflon cookware and after being acquitted of several high-profile criminal cases in 1980, Gotti was renamed Teflon Don and that nickname stuck. When Salvatore "Sammy the Bull" Gravano, Gotti's underboss, cut a deal and agreed to turn state's evidence in 1992, Teflon Don was convicted of five murders, conspiracy to commit murder, racketeering, tax evasion, obstruction of justice, illegal gambling, extortion, and loansharking. Gotti spent the rest of his life in prison.

After his death in 2002, calling someone a Teflon Don became a derogatory term for persons that have managed to avoid responsibility for their actions. Internet searches revealed that shorty after Donald J. Trump announced his candidacy for the presidency in the late 2015, he was being referred to as Teflon Don. Beyond the shared nickname and the crimes of racketeering, tax evasion, and the obstruction of justice, Trump like Gotti has also been accused of committing numerous other crimes, including one of Donald's most lucrative specializations, money laundering. The Houdini of White Collar Crime has yet to be criminally prosecuted for any of his lifelong and habitual patterns of injurious and harmful behavior.

Trump's politics of "law-and-order" before, during, and after the presidency are at loggerheads to say the least with his life course of lawlessness that only escalated during his four-year occupation of the White House. Over the arc of Donald's business and political verve, he has always sought out and worked with a variety of unsavory criminal offenders. These lawbreakers comprise violent felons, con artists, swindlers, as well as Mafia and Russian mobsters. Joseph Weichselbaum and Felix Henry Sater are two high-profile criminals that over several decades have had very close relationships with Trump. The international cocaine trafficker and three-time felon, Weichselbaum, was Trump's personal helicopter pilot in the 1980s and more recently was a lessee of a luxury Manhattan apartment owned by Trump.[2] Soviet-born Sater, a Russian Jewish émigré, is a real estate developer and mobster-businessman with five known aliases.

Felix is also a former managing director of Bayrock Group LLC, a real estate conglomerate based in New York City. In 1998, he copped a deal, pleaded guilty, and cooperated with the government's case involving a $40 million stock fraud scheme orchestrated by the Russian mafia.[3] Having been convicted of first-degree assault in 1993 for stabbing a man and serving one year in the county jail, and since avoiding prison for high stakes financial fraud five years later, Sater has led an unusual double life. He has worked as an informant for FBI investigations of organized crime, especially ones involving international money laundering.[4] At the same time, in 2006 when the collaboration between the Trump Organization, Bayrock Group, and Tamir Sapir known as the Trump SoHo project began, Felix was a senior advisor to Donald and the Trump Organization. During the construction of the $450 million, 46-story, and 391-unit hotel condominium, he also played a major role in labor relations. In the middle of Trump's 2016 campaign for the president, Sater was also busy working with Michael Cohen in pursuit of the elusive Trump Tower Moscow.[5]

Bugsy Siegel and Teflon Don Trump

Benjamin "Bugsy" Siegel and "Teflon" Donald Trump came from contrasting neighborhoods and socioeconomic backgrounds, lived in very different times, and yet they both became organizationally very powerful crooks. Using power in very similar ways, one controlled several vices and unions for less than two decades. The other has controlled numerous illegal business practices for more than 40 years and corrupt party politics since 2017. Benjamin Siegel was the son of poor Jewish immigrants raised in the crime-ridden tenement-lined streets of Brooklyn. Born into abject poverty at the turn of the 20th century, Benny was without capital of any kind. His sources of acquiring money and power were self-made. On the other side of the tracks, little Donny inherited social capital and he became the beneficiary of several trust funds very early in life. His paternal grandmother and father set up the trusts when he was three years old. By the age of eight, without lifting a proverbial finger, master Donny had become a millionaire.

During outlaw rises to the pinnacles of power, Siegel and Trump utilized mostly disparate forms and methods of racketeering. Even with their often differing though not mutually exclusive modus operandi and their dissimilar class backgrounds, these major fraudsters share many individual characteristics and attributes in common. Both men attained celebrity status and became social memes that captured the cultural imagination.[6] Siegel had several nicknames, including the one he gave himself Bugsy for his volatile temper. Many nicknames have been bestowed on Donald Trump,[7] including the one that he is most known for—*the Donald*. In the early 1980s, several years after Ivana Marie Trump, a Czech-American businesswoman relocated from Canada to become Trump's first wife in 1977, her referencing of "the Donald" in conversation with other people caught on and stuck.

Like the real estate operator from New York City, the earlier underworld figure referred to himself as an investment broker. Bugsy made a sizeable contribution toward transforming the dusty little Nevadan town at the beck and call of cowboys, miners, and cross-country travelers looking for a handful of saloons, poker tables, and brothels into the Gambling Mecca of the World, the American Gomorrah known as Las Vegas. So, Siegel is, indeed, worthy of the investment broker moniker.[8] Like Trump, Siegel had multiple public personas. Because of his affable manner, matinee-idol looks, and expensive haberdashery, Siegel was also regarded as an actor manqué, a sportsman, a playboy, and a womanizer. The ever-charismatic mobster also became one of the early front-page "big shot" gangsters. Both before and after nightly television, Bugsy Siegel like the Donald made for very good copy in newspapers, magazines, and books. After being dead for three quarters of a century, he still does as evidenced by several recent biographies, including the 2021 publication of *Bugsy Siegel: The Dark Side of the American Dream* written by best-selling journalist and contributing *Vanity Fair* editor Michael Shnayerson.

While their social histories and curriculum vitae are dissimilar, there are many extracurricular activities that these two men share. Bugsy reflects "old" school gangsters of physical intimidation and vice in transition to becoming syndicated or organizational criminals. Donald Trump has been "newer" school or reflective of the next generation of criminal enterprises with their legal and political fixers, Ivy League MBAs, familiar boards of directors, and non-disclosure agreements.[9] There are similarities and many overlapping dimensions of organized traditional crime and corporate organizational crime, especially with respect to their expansive activities and abilities to avoid and escape criminalization. Legally, the main difference is that the former crimes are viewed as part and parcel of a criminal enterprise, while the latter types of crimes are viewed as auxiliaries of legitimate occupations,[10] making them much less likely to be pursued.

Bugsy's swan song or his final creative endeavor was developing the Flamingo Hotel and Casino in Las Vegas, Nevada. In spring of 1947, it reopened to rave reviews after the first opening one year before had been a complete flop. The Flamingo soon became an overwhelming success, launching an era of gambling, desert glamour, and the next generation of legitimized organized criminals with their degrees from the best universities. Long before he established his presence in Las Vegas, Siegel had built a widely successful criminal empire by way of assassinations, bootlegging, and gambling.

Born February 28, 1906, into a poor Jewish family in the Williamsburg section of Brooklyn where Irish and Italian gangs ruled, Bugsy was already extorting money from pushcart peddlers on NYC's Lower East Side as a pre-teenager. In 1918, he met fellow hooligan Meyer Lansky. Not long after they established the Bugs-Meyer Gang—a band of Jewish mobsters that ran a group of contract killers under the name of Murder, Inc.[11] Siegel was also a boyhood friend to Al Capone. Once upon a time at his aunt's home, the young Bugsy hid the "Fonz" short for Alphonse from a police warrant for a murder rap. During his youth, he first smoked opium and by his late teens was involved in the drug trade. By his mid-thirties, he had become a diet and health freak working out daily.

By contrast, Trump has never been a drinker of alcohol or a user of drugs, though he has always lived on junk food and diet drinks. For the record, as an adolescent on his way to graduating in 1964 from the New York Military Academy, Donny was a decent high school athlete. As an "adult child," Trump's primary form of physical exercise comes from driving golf carts and golf balls over rolling green hills. When he is not moving his ball for a better shot or taking 12-foot gimme putts, and even with his strange and unorthodox swing, he is not considered a bad player. Nowadays, his golfing usually occurs either at Mar-A-Lago Club in Palm Beach, Florida, where he and his family now live or at one of his 14 other golf clubs. Full disclosure: The Trump golf courses have lost more than $315 million over the last two decades.[12]

In the 1920s, after Mafia kingpin Charles "Lucky" Luciano and several other Italian gangsters had organized themselves into a national syndicate, Siegel became a key player in "doing away" with many of New York's veteran gangsters. In 1931, he was hired as one of four hit men to execute Sicilian mobster Joe "the Boss" Masseria. During this period, Siegel was known for his muscle, violence, and prowess with guns. After the 21st Amendment was passed repealing Prohibition in 1933, Bugsy left the field of bootlegging and turned to gambling. Siegel relocated to the West Coast in 1937, settling in Beverly Hills where he set up a slew of gambling dens and several offshore gambling ships. At the same time, he was busy consolidating the existing prostitution, narcotics, and bookmaking rackets in Southern California. In nearby Hollywood, he worked with his syndicate associates to establish motion picture related rackets.

Quite often, Siegel borrowed money from celebrities not intending to pay them back knowing that they would never ask him for the money. During his first year in Hollywood, he is alleged to have accumulated more than $400,000 in loans from movie stars such as George Raft, Clark Gable, Gary Cooper, and Cary Grant.[13] Bugsy, always the entrepreneur, initially devised a plan for extorting and thereafter forming alliances with Warner Brothers, 20th Century Fox, and MGM studios. First, he would take over a trade union like the Los Angeles Teamsters or the Screen Extras Guild. Next, he would stage strikes in order to force the studios to pay him off so the unions could start working again. In no time, Siegel had become the most powerful person in Hollywood without a studio.

By 1939, his wife and two young daughters moved into the palatial Beverly Hills estate where Bugsy regularly hosted parties and rubbed elbows with Hollywood moguls and starlets.[14] In 1941, Siegel was tried for the murder of fellow mobster Harry Greenberg and he was acquitted in 1942. During this West Coast period, he maintained relationships with politicians, businessmen, attorneys, accountants, and lobbyists who all fronted for him. In 1945, Siegel and his long-time girlfriend Virginia Hill—publicly known for being the glamorous Hollywood couple with violent altercations—moved to Las Vegas to oversee the construction of the Flamingo. One year later in 1946, Bugsy and his childhood sweetheart Esta Krakower who had married in 1929 divorced. Esta and the teenage girls left Beverly Hills and moved back to New York.

Bugsy in old-school gambling parlance became a victim of a "casino cooler" gone afoul. Traditionally, a casino employee usually a cocktail waitress or a gambler working for the house—the cooler—appears at a roulette wheel, a blackjack or craps table, where the casino has been "taking a beating" in order to infuse streaks of distraction or bad luck for the legitimate players. And in the process to reap more winnings for the house. However, things worked out differently when the "deep pockets" funding the Las Vegas Flamingo venture, the Eastern crime syndicate, and their senior accountant Meyer Lansky learned that the construction cost overruns originally budgeted for $1.5 million, which had by the end of the project soared to more than $6 million, were due to a combination of Bugsy's mismanagement and his skimming.

Just two months after Bugsy's dream of launching a gambling mecca in the middle of the desert had indeed materialized, he was brutally killed by a fusillade of bullets crashing through his girlfriend's living room window in Beverly Hills while he was reading *The Los Angeles Times*. Lansky was so enraged by the betrayal of his old friend that he had Bugsy eliminated old style. Moments after the killing, three of Meyer Lansky's cohorts would enter the Las Vegas Flamingo and declare it taken over. Of course, Lansky denied any knowledge of the crime. No one was ever charged with the killing of 41-year-old Bugsy Siegel and to this day the case remains open. Several decades later during the launching of the Jersey shore casino hotels into the big-time world of gaming and entertainment, Trump would also be cashing in until he was not.

House of Trump

Back in the 1940s when Fred Trump, Sr. bought the land and built the redbrick Georgian colonial with 20-foot columns, the borough of Queens was 95 percent Caucasian or white-skinned. As for the upper-middle-class neighborhood of Jamaica Estates where their home would be located, it was even whiter. When Donald was born in 1946, the plans for constructing the 4,000-plus square feet home were being completed. Located on a half-acre plat only a few blocks away from where the Trumps were living in a smaller home, the family would move into their new home about a year later. In the 1950s, according to Mary L. Trump, when the first Italian American family moved into the neighborhood, her grandfather had been offended.

As the Trump family referred to it, The House was the most impressive residence on the block, situated on a hill overlooking the Midland Parkway, a wide tree-lined thoroughfare. The House was far less grand than many of the surrounding hillside mansions in the northern area of Queens. In fact, the six-bedroom house was only 2,000 square feet. This material reality would contribute to Donald's psychological feelings of inadequacy, insecurity, not measuring up, and a lack of intimacy. Together, these relative material and psychological deprivations served to motivate the young Donald to venture to Manhattan and Atlantic City. These landscapes were the "big leagues" of real estate development where his father Fred had never ventured. Donald reasoned that he could get out from under his dependence on dad and his father's dominating control at the same time. A different geographical scene and type of building structures would also mean that Donald would be able to establish his own identity apart from his dad's. It also meant to a lesser degree that the two developers would not have to work together on projects. Not least of all, the big leagues would provide Donald with an opportunity to best his father at his own game of real estate development. After spending some 20 years on this pathway to development, Donald had achieved little of the anticipated material and psychological rewards he was seeking.

Frederick Trump (1869–1918)

Donald's paternal grandfather emigrated from the former Kingdom of Bavaria at age 16. The former Friedrich anglicized his name to Frederick when he became a U.S. citizen in 1892. During the Klondike Gold Rush in Northwestern Canada, between 1896 and 1899, he amassed a fortune by opening a restaurant-hotel-brothel in Bennett, British Columbia, and a restaurant and hotel in Whitehouse, the capital city of the Yukon. When Frederick returned to his native home in 1901, now Kallstadt, Germany, he deposited 80,000 marks in the village treasury. Failing to regain German citizenship, he returned to New York with the equivalent purchasing power of about a half a million euros in 2014. Frederick died during the first wave of the Spanish flu pandemic. After his death, his fortune was passed on to his wife and son. Eventually, that money would end up funding the Trump family's first residential real estate ventures in the New York area.[15]

Elizabeth Christ Trump (1880–1966)

Donald's paternal grandmother married Frederick in 1902 while he was trying to secure his citizenship in Germany. Elizabeth was also a native of Kallstadt, born as the daughter of Phillip and Marie Christ who each had prominent lineages dating back to the early 17th and 18th centuries, respectively. After the death of her husband Frederick, she used the inheritance to go into business with her underage son.

Fred Trump, Sr. (1905–1999)

Donald's father at the age of 18, in partnership with his paternal grandmother, began a career in home construction and sales. In 1923, he and his mother founded E. Trump & Son, which eventually morphed into the Trump Organization run by DJT since 1971 until he supposedly handed off the leadership to his sons Donald Trump, Jr. and Eric Trump while he was the president. In 1927, Fred, Sr. was arrested at a Ku Klux Klan rally for failing to disperse. In the 1960s not long before his death, Woody Guthrie wrote about his contempt for his racist landlord Fred Trump and put these words to verse:

> I suppose
> Old Man Trump Know
> Just how much
> Racial Hate
> he stirred up
> In the blood pot of human hearts
> When he drawed
> That color line
> Here at his
> Eighteen hundred family project.[16]

In 1973, the Civil Rights Division of the U.S. Department of Justice filed suit against Fred and Donald for racist practices.

During and after WWII, not wanting to offend his Jewish tenants, Fred denied his German ancestry and pretended to be Swedish. Like his father, Donald also pretended to be Swedish until the early 1980s. Fred was forever a frugal man who despite his wealth never moved out of their upper-middle-class home in Queens. As a creature of habit, he employed the same secretary for 59 years. Over the course of his real estate development career, he built 27,000 apartments in New York City. Before turning to apartments, he first built single-family homes in Queens, New York and then federally subsidized barracks for servicemen and their families in several cities during WWII. Over the years, according to *The New York Times*, Fred gave Donald at least $410 million helping him to stay afloat while avoiding or in between bankruptcies. Two years before his death in 1999, Fred's fortune was estimated to exceed one billion dollars.[17]

Mary Anne MacLeod Trump (1912–2000)

Known as Donald's mother, Miss MacLeod was one of ten Scottish children born into a family of poverty who spent most of her adult life as a Scottish-American philanthropist married to Fred Trump. At 18, she was one of tens of thousands of young Scotts that immigrated to Canada or the

United States. After arriving in New York, Mary lived with one of her sisters on Long Island and worked as a domestic servant for at least four years before meeting Fred Trump at a party and marrying him at the Madison Avenue Presbyterian Church on January 11, 1936. Not long thereafter, Mary has a Scottish domestic of her own. Within a dozen years, she was the mother to five children, three boys and two girls, including Donald John Trump that she gave birth to on June 14, 1946, at New York City's Jamaica Hospital in the borough of Queens. Involved with charities and social clubs, Mary could also be seen chauffeured around Queens in her rose-colored Rolls Royce with the vanity plates "MMT" collecting the money from their chain of commercial laundries.

Maryanne Trump Barry (1937–)

Donald's eldest sister was an American attorney and a retired U.S. federal judge. In 1974, Maryanne became an Assistant U.S. Attorney. President Ronald Reagan appointed her to the United States District Court for the District of New Jersey in 1983. In 1985, she recused herself from a drug-trafficking case because of Donald's relationship with the accused trafficker.[18] However, the "good jurist" did not remove herself from conspiring with her siblings over the years to defraud the Internal Revenue Service and the American taxpayers out of hundreds of millions of dollars. In 1999, President Bill Clinton appointed Judge Barry to the United States Court of Appeals for the Third Circuit. Shortly after the Donald was sworn into office, Barry took a leave of absence and would retire in 2019 without having returned to the bench. In 2018, *The New York Times* published an investigative story that Barry, her father and siblings, engaged in fraudulent and illegal activities in order to limit the estate and gift taxes stemming from Fred's real estate holdings.[19]

Fred Trump Jr. (1938–1981)

Donald's older brother Freddy and the first son of Fred and Mary, and the father of Fred III and Mary L. Trump, though he achieved spent much of his short adult life as the object of his father and younger brother's constant devaluing and degrading. He had graduated with a B.A. in business from Lehigh University in 1960, served as the president of Sigma Alpha Mu, completed ROTC, and entered the Air National Guard as a second lieutenant. He worked on and off for his father, and in 1966, he was identified in local newspapers as the vice president for E. Trump & Son, but their personalities were very different. So, he left the business to pursue his dream of becoming a pilot and did so briefly for TWA before his repeated inebriation ended his flying career. After several domestic incidents, his wife Linda Clapp asked him to leave in 1970. Fred maintained a relationship with his children and ex till close to the end of his life in 1981. During those intervening years, he worked periodically doing maintenance for Trump Properties. He lived on his own, exhausted his trust, and eventually moved into the unfinished attic in the House of Trump. He died of a heart attack caused by alcoholism at age 42.

Elizabeth Trump Grau (1942–)

The middle child Elizabeth worked for Chase Manhattan Bank. Before entering the world of banking, she graduated from Kew-Forest School and Southern Seminary College. She married James Grau in 1989, a producer of documentaries and sports movies. Reportedly, she has a home near Donald's Mar-a-Lago resort in Palm Beach and a condo in NYC's Trump Palace.

Robert S. Trump (1948–2020)

Donald's younger brother by two years, Robert, worked on Wall Street before becoming a senior executive in the Trump Organization. He graduated from Boston University with an economics major in 1970, played soccer, and was the MVP and team captain in 1969. During his employment, he managed the real estate holdings outside of Manhattan. He was also the president of Trump Management, a business owned by the Trump siblings. Robert served on other business boards; most notably, he was an investor and served on the board of directors for the very successful ZeniMax Media, parent company to Bethesda Softworks, a position he occupied from 1999 to his death in 2020.

A very stable genius

When journalist Michael Wolff raised questions concerning the mental stability of the 45th president in *Fire and Fury: Inside the Trump White House* (2018), the Donald responded with what became a series of tweets, establishing himself as what else, *a very stable genius*: "Actually, throughout my life, my two greatest assets have been mental stability and being, like, really smart." In fact, Trump argues that his life's achievements have qualified him not only as smart, but also as "a very stable genius at that." Nevertheless, the talkative Trump would have trouble sitting still for one 50-minute session of introspection, let alone years of weekly psychoanalysis or other on the couch therapies. For that matter, Trump does not do either retrospection or prospection very well.

This is a product of many things, including Donald's impulsiveness and restlessness as well as his suspected form of dyslexia, a subtle neuropsychological condition or "language-processing disorder" that has affected his "emotional, cognitive, and social development."[20] Mostly though, it has been the product of two other emotional dynamics at work. On the one hand, Donald has viewed therapy as a form of weakness. In a 2004 *Playboy* interview, he dismissed the couch as a "crutch." On the other hand, in a 2014 conversation with biographer Michael D'Antonio, he spoke in a bit more detail about his aversion to the therapeutic: "I don't like to analyze myself because I might not like what I see. I don't like to think too much about the past."[21]

Besides our own observations of Donald's public performances, we may rely on dozens of secondary assessments by many well-known members of the psychological community[22] as well as on one primary account from Donald's psychologist niece Mary Trump.[23] None of these mental health professionals except for Trump's niece has sat with the Donald and his family even once, let alone countless times as a member of the extended family. So, let's continue with these armchair diagnoses of the Donald by highlighting the "findings" of these secondary accounts as they will help us to better understand the complexity of his emotional temperament and confounding behavior.

First, there are 27 contributors to the edited volume, *The Dangerous Case of Donald Trump* (2017), who all agreed that because Donald's behavior was negatively affecting the mental health of the American people like no other president before him, the need for diverse kinds of therapy seemed like a good idea. These experts also underscored what everybody paying attention to the political affairs of the United States knows about Trump. The Donald has always made bizarre and outlandish claims that totally contradict the factual reality of the evidence. Nevertheless, Trump publicly lives out the fantasy as real and only in privacy does he rarely acknowledge that these talking points are "total bullshit." The actual truths or falsehoods of his statements are irrelevant to Trump so long as they are reinforcing what he perceives as being in his interests, namely strengthening and expanding his base of anti-Democrat and anti-democratic followers. Such as his foolish rhetoric about why the death penalty should have been applied to the innocent Central Park Five, why the imaginary birthplace of President Barack Hussein Obama should have disqualified him from holding office, or why the Donald himself won the rigged 2020 Presidential election and should be reinstated as the Commander-in-Chief.

At the last day of the Conservative Political Action Conference on February 28, 2021, the former president spoke publicly in Orlando, Florida for the first time since leaving office on January 20. The Donald continued to propagate his false claims of Democratic fraud and voter rigging. Throughout his 90-minute speech, Trump creatively and repeatedly reiterated how the 2020 election was stolen from him. While his adoring crowd was lapping up the lies and the attacks on his Democratic and Republican enemies alike, Trump was also tantalizing them with the possibility that he would run again in 2024. And, naturally how he would win again for a third time. Donald was not and is not deluded about the election outcome; he knows perfectly well that he lost fair and square. The PAC performance was the same old intense act of a self-absorbed and aggrieved Trump lying about his 2020 election defeat. The show was full of the usual unhinged hyperbole and wrath, from his attacks on foes to the hatred of immigrants to the unconstrained nativism and white supremacy. Donald's reruns from earlier staged productions also included the charges that Biden and the left were leading the country toward radicalism and socialism.[24]

When it comes to speaking untruths or telling lies, "Trump made 30, 573 false or misleading claims as president. Nearly half came in his final year,"[25] which suggests that the very stable genius might have been what constitutes for him "loosing it." Once again from Donald's point of view, telling the truth has no inherent value and honesty often is at odds with how Trump sees his vested interests, ergo all the lies. As the documentary filmmaker Errol Morris of such classics as "The Thin Blue Line" and "The Fog of War," and his recent release, "My Psychedelic Love Story" has philosophically waxed about lying, self-deception, and truth-telling in his review of *Amoralman* (2021):

> Lying is ubiquitous. Why should it be otherwise? There are far more reasons to lie than to tell the truth. Isn't lying *beneficial*? Often, it is. And the importance of truth telling--is it a fiction we tell ourselves? A fairy tale? A form of self-deception? Our *original lie*? (Emphases in the original).[26]

Finishing his thought, Morris adds: "we have this absurd belief that we are truth-tellers, or at least that we're capable of occasionally telling the truth."[27]

One of the more provocative theses for explaining the behavior of DJT comes from *The Strange Case of Donald J. Trump: A Psychological Reckoning* written by Dan P. McAdams. McAdams argues that Trump is a person that lacks an inner life story. That Trump is an "episodic man" who "compulsively lives in the moment, without an internal story to integrate his life in time."[28] As the episodic man, Donald moves through life "from one battle to the next, striving, in turn to win each battle he fights." However, "the successive battles do not really build to form a readily defined war," they do not include "clearly defined foes, stable alliances" or "clear issues of contention that drive the antagonists apart." Finally, "if life is continual warfare, if war never ends, then all there is to convey is the daily fighting, which at most, produces an ephemeral victory here and there (and short-term defeat as well), but no ultimate" resolution.[29]

As already noted, Trump is not introspective, retrospective, or prospective: "there is no depth; there is no past; there is no future."[30] While D'Antonio's biography discusses the Donald as a master "spinner of tales" that invokes many powerful narratives which project images of a successful businessman or a larger-than-life celebrity or reality TV star, McAdams maintains that Donald Trump has no psychologically compelling tale to spin about himself because he does not see himself as an ordinary person. Rather Donald sees himself as a superhero appearing episodically. Similarly, Tony Schwartz, the ghostwriter for Trump's best-selling *The Art of the Deal* (1987), which helped to erect the public's perception and the mega myth of the Donald as a great dealmaker, has often referred to Trump as an empty vessel. Schwartz has recalled on television and elsewhere that he found it highly unusual while working with Donald that the man remembered next to nothing about his childhood. Having also failed to reveal the real Trump behind the mask in *Trump and Me* (2016), author Mark Singer claimed that Trump had achieved "an existence unmolested by the rumblings of a soul."[31] As the fired former director of the F.B.I., James Comey told the editor David Remnick for a live taping of *The New Yorker Radio Hour* about his one-on-one private dinner with the president in the White House: "I think he has an emptiness inside of him" as well as "a hunger for affirmation, that I have never seen in an adult."[32]

In discussing introspection, the world of private consciousness, and what do humans usually see when they peak inside of themselves, McAdams brings up the 19th-century best seller, *The Strange Case of Dr. Jekyll and Mr. Hyde*. He reminds us of Freud's conception of the human psyche and the private world of impulse and desire. Dr. Jekyll's keen insight of course was that the private Mr. Hyde inside of him was as real as the public

Jekyll, perhaps more so. As Dr. Jekyll also observed of Mr. Hyde, human beings are split in two, or maybe more.[33] Originally referred to by The Diagnostic and Statistical Manual of Mental Disorders as "multiple personalities," this condition is presently referred to as "dissociative identity disorder." It was made famous in the 1957-film drama based on the book by the same name, *The Three Faces of Eve*, written by psychiatrists Corbett H. Thigpen and Hervey M. Cleckley. The award-winning movie starred Joanne Woodward as the fictitious Eve White, Eve Black, and Jane. The actual case study was based on the life of Chris Costner Sizemore, a timid and self-effacing wife and mother who still fearing and trying to avoid a terrible childhood experience had established 16 different personas as her psychological defenses.

McAdams' point is that Donald Trump has turned the strange case of Jekyll and Hyde on its head as he refuses "to acknowledge the kind of duality (or multiplicity) that Dr. Jekyll, and most modern men and women apprehend."[34] Conversely, McAdams contends that Trump is like Mr. Hyde *without* Dr. Jekyll. The Donald is not many things, but one primal thing that lives mainly in the moment of a vibrantly emotional world: Making him so "authentic" to many people and so "strange" to many others. This is also what gives Donald "the primal charisma that continues to enthrall millions of Americans, even as it repulses millions more."[35]

All the mental professionals who have investigated Trump's psyche from far seem to know that Donny never had a close or intimate relationship with either his mother Mary or his father Fred. In and of itself, this is not particularly unusual. A lot of people go through life without close or intimate relations with at least one if not both parents. Moreover, this does not preclude by any stretch of the imagination or deny the fact that Donald and his four siblings as well as their parents and paternal grandmother, were a typically "bonded" family in that they shared emotions, interests, and experiences together. Before we turn to the specifics of where Trump's lack of intimacy with his parents comes from and how that has affected his cognitive and social transactions throughout his life, we need to ground ourselves in the theoretical implications of securing (or not) the confidence of love, the power of the parental gaze, and the integration of the mirror stage during childhood development.

From as early as six months, humans need to be confident that they are loved so that they can risk hating the very persons who love them. This emotional security makes one feel safe enough to express their full range of feelings. However, if one feels emotionally insecure, then one retreats not only from nuance and complexity, but even from feelings of ambivalence.

At the same time, inconsistent or irregular bonding especially between a mother and an infant can lead to a "mature" adult's inability to internalize parental love enough to build genuine self-esteem. As we will see, Trump's deficit of healthy self-esteem has rendered him dependent on others, especially the media whose attention Donald craves in place of his mother's lacking childhood gaze.

For example, Trump's addiction to Twitter and to stadiums full of MAGA sycophantic crowds have been beyond his control and ability to break free from—not that he wishes to—though his opportunities to speak in front of large crowds has diminished since he exited the Oval Office on January 20, 2021. In the case of the press core and other talking heads, Trump has struggled to accept or acknowledge that his need is so great for their admiration, affirmation, and reassuring gazes that he "bridles against his dependency on the media, denying the legitimacy or the importance of the press."[36] In different words, when the media presents an unadmiring reflection, Donald experiences their criticism as asserting a level of autonomy that he knows that he does not possess. These exchanges trigger his blurred memories of disharmonic experiences with his mother. His reactions are more often the same consisting of resentment, dismissal, and threats. In fact, Donald has become "so dependent on the press that he must reassure himself that the opposite is true," and so he "fights back against anything that challenges his denial."[37] Similarly, losing to "sleepy" Joe Biden was so humiliating to Donald's sense of worth and so threatening to his ego that his heightened defense mechanisms of denial and projection automatically kicked into motion.

During little Donny's formative interactions with his mother Mary Trump, she was periodically absent because of physical illnesses and emotional needs of her own. This lack of developmental nurturing plays out in both Donald's lifelong attitudes toward women and in his limited abilities to embrace empathy, ambivalence, and complexity. Psychoanalytically, "at some point after the infant has begun to internalize the affirming power of his mother's gaze, he comes face-to-face with the power of the gaze of another—himself."[38] According to French psychoanalyst Jacques Lacan, the "mirror stage" first occurs some six months after birth when the infant encounters his own reflection and needs his mother's reassuring loving gaze. What happens when the infant sees himself in a mirror or in a selfie is that the image appears "to possess more integration and self-control than he knows or physically experiences in his chaotic existence as an infant."[39] In turn, the reflected image establishes "an ideal version of the self that the individual will typically spend a lifetime pursuing—always inevitably reminding himself of the frustrating distance between the real and ideal selves whenever he repeatedly and inevitably falls short."[40] Infants without the empowering benefit of regularly receiving and returning their mother's loving gazes will have a more difficult time confronting the gaps between their real and ideal selves. In the case of little Donny, the experience of the reassuring gaze was also exaggerated by his restless, hyperactive tendencies.

The formation of Donald's personality and character structure is important for understanding what makes Trump tick, what motivates him, what frightens him, and how he engages with the psychological tensions between these. Justin A. Frank, the Washington, DC psychiatrist-psychoanalyst who has also written books about presidents Obama and Bush on the couch before writing one on Trump believes that Donald is motivated by and has always identified with his parents' most threatening qualities to his well-being: The "maternal remoteness" of Mom and the "paternal tyrannical demands" of Dad.[41] Accordingly, Frank shares one anecdote from Donald that helps us to understand how Donny could never provide his mother with what she wanted from him, without at the same time displeasing his father. He was referring to his mother's identification with the pomp and circumstance of the royal British family as getting more of her attention than her own family did. And how Donald has always struggled to recreate that which had captured his mother's gaze or attention. In the eyes of his father, Donald's preoccupation is with his own lack of authenticity and deep-seated ambivalence about being a fake, a con, a fraudster, and so on. Making these matters more complicated for Donald was his father's owned mixed condemning and condoning of the con artist that his son had become. When, for example, the Donald compared his Trump Tower home to Versailles and his father spoke "the unspeakable truth of the con behind the illusion."[42]

Takeaways from Donald's niece[43]

Though volumes have been written on Trump perhaps more than on any other human dead or alive, very few authors have sought to understand why little Donny grew up to become the Toddler-in-Chief. In psychologist Mary Trump's prologue of her first book, *Too Much and Never Enough* that sold a whopping 1.3 million books in its first week of publication, she foreshadows one of the culturally puzzling observations about Donald Trump. How was it that Donald's character flaws and aberrant behavior that were so well known publicly in the United States had been subjected to so little scrutiny by the mainstream media or by the political vetting processes of the Republican Party?

What I find particularly fascinating especially considering McAdams' discussion of Dr. Jekyll and Mr. Hyde is Mary Trump's discussion of the 1994 film based on Mary Shelley's novel, *Frankenstein*. She quotes Frankenstein's monster when he says, "I do know that for the sympathy of one living being, I would make peace with all." The monster goes on to say, "I have love in me the likes of which you can scarcely imagine and rage the likes of which you would not believe. If I cannot satisfy the one, I will indulge the other." MLT then references a quote from an *Esquire* essay by Charles P. Pierce: The Donald "doesn't plague himself with doubt about what he's creating around him. He is proud of his monster." In fact, the Donald exults the monster, "glories in its anger and its destruction and, while he cannot imagine its love, he believes with all his heart in its rage. He is Frankenstein without conscience."[44]

Then, Mary Trump says pointedly in her analysis with one crucial difference that the description of the monster is more appropriate for Donald's father:

> Fred's monster—the only child of his who mattered to him—would ultimately be rendered unlovable by the very nature of Fred's preference for him. In the end, there would be no love for Donald at all, just his agonizing thirsting for it. The rage, left to grow, would come to overshadow everything else.[45]

Mary continues, "the atmosphere of division that my grandfather created in the Trump family is the water in which Donald has always swum, and division continues to benefit him at the expense of everybody else."

More holistically, the histories and complexities of the political, social, and economic beliefs that Donald has espoused before, during, and after the presidency have been superficially grasped by him mostly because he would not bother to learn what is necessary because it has always been for him both boring and difficult to accomplish. Nonetheless, Donald is very astute and can be laser-focused amidst his own sown confusion and uncertainty. He generally understands the bigger picture and almost always understands "bottom lines" even though he does not seem to be familiar with the routine workings of macroeconomics or even of the basic concept of Net Present Value taught at all business schools and used today as the most common tool for evaluating whether investments are likely to be profitable. When asked about these and other economic principles, Trump simply talks diversionary nonsense. Over and over, Trump revealed his ignorance and how abundantly clueless he is about the workings of economics. No matter though because in the larger scheme of things these facts have been ignored, even after his first Secretary of State Rex Tillerson, former CEO of ExxonMobil, called Trump a "fucking idiot."

The Donald has always been challenged in everyday speech by syntax unless he has the benefit of a scripted speech to read. In the arenas of mass and social media, however, Trump has certainly succeeded as one of the great communicators of our time. Most significantly, Donald has always been able to navigate—to fake his way—through the chaos or damage that he causes, seemingly extricating himself from suffering from any of the negative or social costs he creates. As much as Donald is "out of control" he is also driven by the fears of not measuring up, and worse, of becoming another "loser" son like his older brother Freddy. Rather than becoming his father's image of a genuine "winner" or "killer" to assuage or massage his mental well-being, Donald became a grifter, a faker, and a teller of tall tales. Instead of the art of the deal that was more hype than real, a more appropriate moniker for the Donald would be the "art of the con."

For all the talking that Trump does, most of it is very general, nonspecific, vague, and superficial. When it comes to talking about his parents, he is guarded both consciously and unconsciously, and usually only speaks in empty platitudes. In other words, Donald has not revealed much about his interactions with either of his parents growing up, especially his mother except to say how "great" they both were. One of his more revealing slips of the tongue comes from a Q&A at the end of Donald's self-help book co-authored with Bill Zanker, *Think Big: Make It Happen in Business and Life* (2007), when he responds to a question about the best advice his parents ever gave him:

> "My mother was a wife who was really a great homemaker. She always said, 'Be happy!' She wanted me to be happy. My father understood me more and he said, 'I want you to be successful.' He was a very driven kind of guy. That's why *I'm so screwed up*, because I had a father that pushed me pretty hard. My father was a tough man, but he was a good man. He was a kind man, and he would tell me to always do something you love. Now I am happy, so I ended up doing what both of my parents wanted me to do" (emphasis added)[46]

When it came to the challenged parenting from Mary Anne, MLT speculates about her grandmother's neediness as stemming from growing up in an inhospitable environment that Mary Anne rarely spoke about. The "family" therapist was more familiar with her grandmother's post-surgical needs. As Donald was over two years and Robert was less than a year, Maryanne found their mother in the early morning hours near the girls' bathroom hemorrhaging and passed out. By the afternoon, she had already had an emergency hysterectomy. Mary Anne underwent two more surgeries the following week and after several months had pretty much recuperated but not without physical and emotional scarring. MLT presents a family scenario where the five children were "essentially motherless" growing up. Fred, Sr., cold and physically distant, was no motherly substitute of warmth and comfort to his enfant boys nor was his own mother Elizabeth who lived nearby and came regularly with prepared meals in their mother's physical absence during her stays in the hospital and while at home recovering. However, Elizabeth was no more physically affectionate than her son was. As for the live-in housekeeper, she had her hands full doing the housework. And there was no nanny live-in or otherwise, so at 12 Maryanne becomes the surrogate mother filling the void as best she can. For example, she sees that Donny and Robbie were bathed in the evenings and readied for bed.

Whatever the exact reasons for Mary's lack of full presence for her children's emotional development, "she was the kind of mother who used her children to comfort her rather than comforting them. Her attention and caregiving were more about when it was convenient for her rather than when the children needed her. With respect to her three sons, she basically tossed her hands up in the air as though there was nothing that she could do for them. "Often unstable and needy, prone to self-pity and flights of martyrdom, she frequently put herself first."[47] As for Fred's absence from parenting, apart from Donald—for better or worse—he was pretty much indifferent to his children. Raising the children and maintaining the home were after all "women's work." Though Mary ran the household and Fred was always away from home working hard and philandering as well, he always ruled the House of Trump.

MLT describes Trump, Sr. as stoic and as someone who did not seem to have any emotional needs. She also describes him as a "high-functioning" sociopath or a person suffering with antisocial personality disorder, an affliction that affects about three percent of the population or 1 in 100 adults with males constituting about 75 percent of those diagnosed. As Mary writes about children with a sociopathic parent, "especially if there is no one else to mitigate the effects, all but guarantees severe disruption in how children understand themselves, regulate their emotions, and engage with the world." She also points out how her grandmother was "ill-equipped" to deal with her own marital problems because of Fred's "callousness, indifference, and controlling behaviors." Finally, Fred's "lack of real human feeling, his rigidity as a parent and a husband, and his sexist belief in a woman's innate inferiority likely left her feeling unsupported."[48]

In the scheme of human development and social interaction, much of all behavior by infants and toddlers revolves around attachment or bonding—the search for comforting or positive reinforcement—a smile to elicit a smile or tears to prompt a hug—from the caretaker. Donny and Robbie missed their mother's reassurance and were distressed by her absence. Fred was no substitute caretaker. He did not believe that children were his job; that was women's work. Even under normal circumstances, Fred considered the needs or demands of his children on him to be an annoyance. And the greater the distress shown by the little boys, the more Fred rebuffed them, as the children's neediness set up a dangerous tension in the Trump household. Rather than little Donny or his younger brother's biologically designed attachment behaviors triggering soothing and comforting responses from their father in the absence of their mother, these needs provoked anger or indifference from Fred. The boys quickly learned that "needing" something was akin to despair and hopelessness, and equivalent to humiliation.

Thus, when Mary became ill and Donny lost his main source of what had been inconsistent human comfort, connection, and love from his mother, he then found himself dependent on a father who barely met any of those needs. As MLT tells it, Fred's self-interest skewed his priorities:

> His care of his children, such as it was, reflected his own needs, not theirs. Love meant nothing to him, and he could not empathize with their plight, one of the defining characteristics of a sociopath; he expected obedience that was all. Children don't make such distinctions, and his kids believed that their father loved them or that they could somehow earn his love. But they also knew, if only on an unconscious level, that their father's "love," as they experienced it, was entirely conditional.[49]

Niece Mary argues further that Donald and the rest of his siblings were "isolated not just from the rest of the world but from one another," and that they were without the ability to find solidarity with each other, and this was one of the reasons that Freddy's "brothers and sisters ultimately failed him; standing up for him, even helping him, would have risked their father's wrath."[50]

As for Donald's coping mechanism, early on he developed powerful yet primitive defenses, "marked by increasing hostility to others and a seeming indifference to his mother's absence and father's neglect. The latter became a kind of learned helplessness over time because...it insulated him from the worst effects of his pain," it also made it extremely difficult" for him to have "any of his emotional needs met at all because he became too adept at acting as though he didn't have any." As Donald's resentment and anger grew in relation to his suppressed needs, his victimization sensibility and grievance mentality grew into a bullying, disrespect, and aggressiveness toward others.[51] In the moment, these styles of behavioral interactions often serve to mostly diffuse anger. However, even in the moment whether they accomplish their objective or not, they are most often pyrrhic victories. Overtime, these types of behavioral interactions are increasingly destructive and harmful.

Ironically, these behaviors became hardened into Donald's personality because "once Fred started paying attention to his loud and difficult second son, he came to value" these types of social interaction. Put another way, Fred Trump "came to validate, encourage, and champion the things about Donald that rendered him essentially unlovable and that were in part the direct result of Fred's abuse."[52] However, Mary McLeod Trump was not an adoring fan. According to *Vanity Fair* at 78, she once asked Ivana Trump, her soon-to-be-ex-daughter-in-law, a pointed question: "What kind of son have I created?" That was in 1990 when Donald and Ivana were publicly divorcing, and he was running around with model Marla Maples, his second wife to be (1993–1999). In his early forties at the time, Trump was floundering in hundreds of millions of dollars in debt, facing financial ruin, and experiencing high-profile humiliation.[53]

A calculating and compulsive liar

In my view, the public diagnoses of Trump by the various talking heads have over hyped his conditions of egocentricity and narcissism. In an age of selfies, self-promotion, and branding, to varying degrees millions of people are consumed with themselves as part of the normative "culture of narcissism."[54] As MLT underscores, the media obsession on the evolution of Trump's development should be less about whether or not the Donald's symptoms and behaviors meet the DSM-5th edition's criteria for "malignant narcissism" or "narcissistic personality disorder" and perhaps more about whether or not he meets the criteria for "antisocial personality disorder" or "dependent personality disorder" or in the most extreme "sociopathy" as each of these conditions may be more significant when it comes to discussing Trump's chronic criminality, arrogance, and disregard for the rights of others.[55] Of course, the dilemma for professional or amateur shrinks is to figure out first whether the Donald is simply lying and manipulating reality, and second whether he and millions of other Americans are actually living in these illusions of reality, conspiracy, and misinformation.

Personally, I think the case can be made that Trump is a calculating and compulsive liar, often a symptom of both antisocial personality disorder and paranoia. At the same time, Trump is a meglomaniac with delusions of greatness as well as a "manic-depressive" personality with an emphasis on the "m" over the "d" rather than someone suffering from "bipolar disorder" with its long episodic attacks of depression and suicidal tendencies. However, I do not believe that Donald is self-deluded or that he believes the fabrications that he deceptively cons and assists others into believing and living their lives by. It has been suggested that self-deceivers may hold contradictory realities at the same time, storing truths in their unconscious minds and fictions in their conscious minds. It has also been argued that the practice of repeating lies and rehearsing fictions in the conscious memory, can overtime replace the facts as they originally were.[56] I still contend that the Donald is not self-deluded, nor has he replaced either the facts or the science in his mind with his desired fictions and quackery. As for the perpetual lying or the constant spilling of lies these are simply the means to Trump's desired ends. It is mostly scripted performance stuff. In a feedback loop of sorts, Trump, the MAGA base, and the Fox News propaganda machine are delivering and playing back to each other exactly what they all cannot get enough of.[57]

Indeed, Donald may be crazy both as a fox and in the pejorative meaning. Trump has certainly suffered from "mental illness" throughout his whole life. To put it simply, Donald is not the most stable person emotionally. On the contrary, he is usually hypermanic and often frantic, always suppressing anger and rejection, and intermittently experiencing relatively short bouts of depression. Trump is never calm or at peace with himself. Donald often feels trapped by circumstances he cannot shake, control, or escape from. With respect to Donald's psychic integration or state of mind, it is one of constant anguish, pain, and frustration as well as the seeds of his mental instability. A condition of concern by those advisers and others surrounding the former president from the beginning to the ending of his administration. For example, as evidenced by DOJ discussions about invoking the 25th Amendment and removing Trump from office after firing FBI Director James Comey,[58] or by the phone calls made by General Mark Milley to his Chinese counterpart just before the 2020 election and immediately after the Capitol riots.[59]

Not unrelated to self-delusion is rationalization or what criminologists refer to as neutralization theory. This social-psychological theory posits that wrongdoers will rationalize their wrongdoing in ways that allow them to justify or to excuse their actions. In their original formulation, Gresham Sykes and David Matza posited five "techniques of neutralization." These included three "denials" of responsibility, harm, and victimization as well as two "projections," condemning the condemners and appealing to higher loyalties.[60] While Trump employs all five techniques of neutralization on a regular basis, most often Donald prefers using projections rather than denials. The latter techniques are psychologically comforting and more compatible with Donald's Hobbesian worldview or meta-narrative of "every man for himself" or "dog-eat-dog" or "the law of the jungle" or "survival of the fittest."

Trump employs these techniques of neutralization primarily as instruments to further perpetuate both his legitimate and his illegitimate behaviors. In the case of perpetual wrongdoing, these rationalizations are enabling. On the one hand, they allow Trump to avoid rather than confront those realities that are not self-validating or are in opposition to Donald's personal agenda and self-interests. On the other hand, they also facilitate Trump in dodging or eluding the consequences of his past and present bad behavior or wrongdoings. However, Donald's adversarial or Hobbesian justifications for his wrongful behavior, whether preceding or following the actions under inspection, have little to say about Trump's lack of empathy, mutualism, and love as part of the motivation or causation behind Trump's frenzied and destructive behavior. At the end of the day, many and perhaps most but certainly not close to all violators of the law, especially white-collar offenders want to view themselves as moral and law-abiding people to assuage their guilty consciences or to satisfy their remorseful superegos. Because Donald's powers of empathy are underdeveloped and his superego is undersized characteristic of a sociopathic state of mind, they have neutralized his identification with the harmfulness he causes and with the immorality that he endorses.

As for all of those Trumpians who have drunk the Kool-Aid, their attractiveness to collective self-delusion has to do with the magical content, to the endurance of the white Anglo-Saxon Western mythic resistance to the rise of certainty or to foregone conclusions that accompany empirical knowledge and scientific reasoning, and to the machinery of the popular imagination.[61] In other words, what Donald and his two key advisors, Stephen Bannon and Stephen Miller, understood to a tee was that the gaps or disconnects between fact and fiction or between what people want to believe and what they actually know in the United States and elsewhere, are the objects of those historical conditions that have always been useful for exploiting irrationality, superstition, and conspiracy. Meanwhile, everyone else in America who have found the Kool-Aid toxic, or the anti-Trumpians, have been trying their best to escape from the former Chief-of-Darkness' nightmare of chaos, cruelty, and destruction.

Additionally, I think that a case can be made that most elected Republicans and power brokers, unlike Representative Elizabeth Lynne Cheney from Wyoming, for example, are unconcerned about whether Trump is guilty of treason or is an insurrectionist. In fact, the Trumpian Republican Party has the former president's back. Nor are Republican leaders concerned about whether Donald is pathological, delusional, or harmful to the body politic or to democracy, so long as they can leverage Trump's criminal power and exploit his political base for their own naked power. With respect to the Trumpian takeover of the Republican Party and the removal of Cheney from her House GOP leadership position in May 2021 for opposing the Big Lies, a CBS News poll found that 80 percent of Republicans agreed with her ousting because she's not on message with the party (69 percent), she's wrong about the 2020 election not being stolen (57 percent), she did not support Trump (52 percent), and lastly, disloyalty should be punished (34 percent).[62]

After four decades of observing the very public Donald J. Trump, investigating him as an etiological person of interest over some five years, and based on my integrated approach to the social-psychological evolution of the man, he seems to be representative of those personality formations that were common for nuclear families of white upper middle classes post-WWII where the socialization and parenting practices were grounded in gendered, racist, and patriarchal relationships. Plenty of other males growing up in similarly privileged conditions then and now also feel entitled and share these personality imbalances.[63] This stated, the Donald appears to reveal a slew of normative and complex maladies a bit more intense than that of his male peers.

These social relations are also indicative of an array of nuclear family dependent disorders characteristic of the white upper and upper middle classes. For example, a University of Michigan study of American College students found that "narcissistic exhibitionism scores among affluent boys at elite private schools were almost twice the average scores of a more diverse sample."[64] At least on the surface, while Trump conforms to such pathologically negative labels as "narcissistic" or "sociopathic" or "megalomaniac," I prefer to think of him instead as a disturbed, frustrated, and angry neurotic white guy suffering from legacies of cognitive and nurturing deficits rather than from some serious or deep-seeded psychoses emanating from early parental abuse or neglect.[65]

In Marxian terminology, Donald is "alienated" from himself and others. In Durkheimian terminology, Donald came of age during a period of "anomie" and social upheaval. In Mertonian terminology, Donald is an "innovator" experiencing emotional and psychological distress. All these circumstances are a function of the structural contradictions "between the political and economic arrangements, on the one hand, and the culturally defined aspirations and goals, on the other hand."[66] All of these structural *and* agency determined models apply to Trump. In these models of criminality, perpetrators are either trying to conform culturally to acquired wealth by violating the law or they are violating the law as nonconforming perpetrators simply trying to survive. As we will see in some detail in the next chapter, the Donald is obviously a case of the former. At the same time, Trump's habitual lawlessness has always been about economic accumulation and/or subsequently political survival.

The Marxian-Freudian framework used by me to explain the outlaw behavior of Trump and his enablers/supporters/corrupters was first posited and examined by Hans H. Gerth and C. Wright Mills in their classic textbook, *Character and Social Structure: The Psychology of Social Institutions* (1953).[67] One other social-psychological dynamic of importance to underscore is Donald's relatively lifelong cloistered and delimited social interaction. I am referring specifically to those institutional settings or restricted territorial spaces that have amplified Trump's psychological Goffman-like dependency on other people.[68] Hidden away and sheltered within his own-bubbled psychological existence, and living within a bubbled social existence more generally, each of these functions to fuel Trump's underlying feelings of inadequacy or insecurity. Because Trump has not actually ever lived fully independent from his father in the free world or without his organization and protective apparatus in place to support him, Donald continues to doubt his abilities and feels both weak and vulnerable.[69] This has always been the case whether Donald was living in the House of Trump as a young boy, at the New York Military Academy as a troubled adolescent, or as an egocentric adult at Trump Tower, the White House, and Mar-a-Lago.

When Donald joins up and goes to work for his father in the late 1960s, he becomes a part of the third generation of Trumps that have acquired their wealth through the housing and hospitality industries. Discounting the revenue accrued from his grandfather's brothels in Canada, Donny and his siblings were all born into their father and grandmother's "crime family."[70] In the United States, their wealth has always been accumulated both legally and illegally. These revenues have always been transferred mostly illegally to the next generation as a way of avoiding the taxes that should be normally due. Initially, the five siblings all benefitted from the fraudulent schemes of their father. After Freddy died and then Fred, Sr. passed, the four remaining siblings conspired to deprive their niece Mary Trump and nephew Fred Trump III of some 20 million dollars that they divided up among themselves.[71] When the fourth generation of Trumps came of age, Donald Jr., Ivanka, and Eric—in one capacity or the other—they all became active participants in the family businesses of organizational crime.

As we turn to Chapter 2, let me point out that the Trump Organization owns hotels, golf clubs, and other properties as well as a global brand that has encompassed book deals, TV shows, and Trump-emblazoned skyscrapers. The organization is a family holding business that consists of some 500 or so limited liability companies,[72] which according to tax records for 2018 employed a total of 3,500 persons with only 122 earning an annual income of $100,000 or more.[73] Historically, these businesses have engaged in legitimate activities as well as illegitimate activities characteristic of "criminal enterprises." Michael Cohen, Trump's personal attorney and long-time fixer before flipping on the Boss, and Stephen Bannon, the former president's political tactician, have described the Trump Organization as a criminal enterprise. They are hardly alone.

Back in 2019, Bannon, also the architect of Trump's "deconstruction of the administrative state," predicted that Donald's "finances would in all likelihood bring about his political demise, especially when the people finally realize that he is not the billionaire he claims to be, but just another scumbag."[74] After the Southern District of New York indicted the Trump Organization and its CFO Allen Weisselberg on several counts of criminal fraud, July 1, 2021, Bannon's predictions about Donald's finances bringing him down are starting to look prescience. One year earlier in August 2020, Bannon was arrested and charged with defrauding donors from a private fundraising effort, called We Build the Wall, to help bolster the president's initiative along the Mexico border.[75] No problem, however, because Steve knew that he had one of Trump's get out of jail free cards. As one of the former presidents' collaborators in most things dirty, Bannon received his pardon from Trump a few days before Christmas. At the time, both men were busy doing everything in their power to overturn the results of the 2020 election, including the instigation of the storming of the Capitol on January 6, 2021.

Notes

1 Joseph D. Pistone, 2005. *The Way of the Wiseguy: The FBI's Most Famous Undercover Agent Cracks the Mob Mind.* Philadelphia: Running Press. George A. Manning, 2005. *Financial Investigation and Forensic Accounting.* Boca Raton, FL: CRC Press.

2 David Cay Johnston, 2016. *The Making of Donald Trump.* New York: Melville House Publishing.

3 Rosalind S. Helderman and Tom Hamburger, 2016. Former Mafia-Linked Figure Describes Association with Trump. *The Washington Post.* May 17. https://www.washingtonpost.com/politics/former-mafia-linked-figure-describes-association-with-trump/2016/05/17/cec6c2c6-16d3-11e6-aa55-670ca-bef46e0_story.html. See also, Tom Burgis, 2017. Russia-Born Dealmaker Linked to Trump Assists Laundering Probe. *Financial Times.* July 6.

4 Andrew Rice, 2017. Felix Sater: The Original Russian Connection. *Intelligencer.* An adapted version from an August 7th issue of *New York Magazine.* https://nymag.com/intelligencer/2017/08/felix-sater-donald-trump-russia-investigation.html.

5 Matt Apuzzo and Maggie Haberman, 2017. Trump Associate Boasted That Moscow Business Deal 'Will Get Donald Elected'. *The New York Times.* August 28. https://www.nytimes.com/2017/08/28/us/politics/trump-tower-putin-felix-sater.html.

6 Morris "Moe" Greene is a fictional character based on the character and personality of Bugsy Siegel that appeared in Mario Puzo's 1969 novel *The Godfather* and the 1972 film of the same name directed by Francis Ford Coppola.

7 Since at least 2015, friends, enemies, and comedians alike have adorned Donald J. Trump with numerous nicknames and memes, including one of my favorites from the list of the 15 most popular, Screaming Carrot Demon, which never stuck. See Katherine Webb, 2019. 15 Hilarious Nicknames Donald Trump Has Been Called, August 27. https://www.cheatsheet.com/entertainment/15-hilarious-nicknames-donald-trump-has-been-called.html/. Not to be outdone, the Donald has also made an art form out of nicknaming his political opponents from Little Marco to Crooked Hillary to Sleepy Joe.

8 As Stephen Birmingham wrote in his *The Rest of Us: The Rise of America's Eastern European Jews.* New York: Little, Brown & Company, 1984: "He is to Las Vegas what Benjamin Franklin is to Philadelphia. Las Vegas was Benny Siegel's vision, his grand design. Had it not been for his dream, there might be nothing there at all." See also Larry D. Gragg, 2015. *Benjamin "Bugsy" Siegel: The Gangster, the Flamingo, and the Making of Modern Las Vegas.* Santa Barbara, CA: Praeger.

9 Donny never obtained any degree beyond his liberal arts undergraduate bachelors in business without honors from the University of Pennsylvania in 1968. This was two years after Trump had transferred from Fordham University where he completed his freshman and sophomore years.

10 Neal Shover and Andy Hochstetler, 2002. Cultural Explanation and Organizational Crime. *Crime, Law and Social Change* 37 (1): 1–18. https://doi.org/10.1023/A:1013399001934.

11 Biography. https://www.biography.com/crime-figure/bugsy-siegel.

12 Eliza Relman, 2020. Trump Has Lost More Than $315 Million on His Golf Courses Over the Last 20 Years, Bombshell Report Finds. *Insider.* September 28. https://www.businessinsider.com/trump-lost-millions-on-golf-courses-tax-returns-report-2020-9.

13 Michael Shnayerson, 2021. *Bugsy Siegel: The Dark Side of the American Dream*. New Haven, CT and London: Yale University Press.
14 Although I have no way of knowing whether Siegel came off as a rube or not to the Beautiful People that he hobnobbed with because Bugsy may not have known which fork to use, I do know that Trump, a lifelong Democrat and political contributor to the likes of President Bill Clinton and to Senator Hillary Rodman Clinton, was never received by the economic or social elite, was often mocked and made fun of, and for the most part was known for his tastelessly showy hotels.
15 Natalie Obiko Pearson, 2016. Donald Trump's Grandfather Friedrich Trump Ran a Restaurant, Bar, and Brothel in British Columbia. *Bloomberg*. October 26. https://www.bloomberg.com/features/2016-trump-family-fortune/.
16 FirstDraft, 2016, Woody Guthrie Wrote of His Contempt for His Landlord, Donald Trump's Father. *The New York Times*. January 25. https://www.nytimes.com/politics/first-draft/2016/01/25/woody-guthrie-sang-of-his-contempt-for-his-landlord-donald-trumps-father/.
17 Kaitlin Menza, 2020. 16 Things You Didn't Know about Donald Trump's Father, Fred. *Town&Country*. August 25. https://www.townandcountrymag.com/society/money-and-power/g9229257/fred-trump-facts/.
18 David Cay Johnston, 2018. The Donald and His Sister, Federal Judge Maryanne Trump Barry, Both Took Helicopter Flights with a Guy Who Had a Lot of Ways to Get People High. *Protect*. December 16. https://www.thedailybeast.com/the-drug-trafficker-donald-trump-risked-his-casino-empire-to-protect.
19 David Barstow, Susanne Craig and Russ Buettner, 2018. Trump Engaged in Suspect Tax Schemes as He Reaped Riches From His Father. *The New York Times*. October 2. https://www.nytimes.com/interactive/2018/10/02/us/politics/donald-trump-tax-schemes-fred-trump.html.
20 Justin A. Frank, 2018. *Trump on the Couch: Inside the Mind of the President*. New York: Avery, p. 213.
21 Dara Lind, 2016. Trump in 2014: "I Don't Like To Analyse Myself Because I Might Not Like What I See." *Vox*.
22 Bandy X. Lee, (ed.), 2017 *The Dangerous Case of Donald Trump: 27 Psychiatrists and Mental Health Experts Assess a President*. New York: Thomas Dunne Books. See also, Dan P. McAdams, 2020. *The Strange Case of Donald J. Trump: A Psychological Reckoning*. New York: Oxford University Press.
23 Mary R. Trump, 2020. *Too Much and Never Enough: How My Family Created the World's Most Dangerous Man*. New York: Simon & Schuster.
24 E.J. Dionne, 2021. The GOP Is Trapped in Trump's Rendezvous with Yesterday. *The Washington Post*. February 28. https://www.washingtonpost.com/opinions/the-gop-is-trapped-in-trumps-rendezvous-with-yesterday/2021/02/28/976e1f70-7a12-11eb-85cd9b7fa90c8873_story.html?utm_medium=email&utm_source=newsletter&wpisrc=nl_opinions&utm_campaign=wp_opinions.
25 Glenn Kessler, 2021. Trump Made 30, 573 False or Misleading Claims as President. Nearly Half Came in His Final Year. *The Washington Post*. January 23. https://www.washingtonpost.com/politics/how-fact-checker-tracked-trump-claims/2021/01/23/ad04b69a-5c1d-11eb-a976-bad6431e03e2_story.html.
26 Errol Morris's Book Review in *The New York Times* (March 21, 2021, p. 12) of *Amoralman: A True Story and Other Lies* by Derek DelGaudio, 2021. New York: Alfred A. Knopf.

27 Ibid.
28 Quoted from the inside cover jacket of McAdams, 2020.
29 McAdams, 2020: 20.
30 Ibid: 3.
31 Quoted in Ibid: 3.
32 The New Yorker, 2018. James Comey on His Infamous Dinner with Trump. *The New Yorker Interview.* April 23. https://www.newyorker.com/news/the-new-yorker-interview/james-comey-on-his-infamous-dinner-with-trump.
33 Ibid: 3.
34 Ibid: 3.
35 Ibid: 5.
36 Frank, 2018: 214.
37 Ibid: 24.
38 Ibid.
39 Ibid.
40 Ibid.
41 Ibid: 16.
42 Ibid: 17.
43 Mary L. Trump has written an interesting and informative book about Trump and family from the perspective of being Donald's niece and a psychologist. Aside from the fact that Donald and his lawyers tried unsuccessfully to stop her book from being published, his defenders would say that Mary is biased and others with no skin in the game, would say that she is less than objective. Because less than two months after her book was published, she filed a civil suit in the State Supreme Court in Manhattan, accusing Donald, his sister and retired judge Maryanne Trump Barry, and their brother Robert Trump, who died in August 2020, of fraud and civil conspiracy that began in 1981 when her father, Fred Trump Jr., unexpectedly died, leaving her at age 16 with a small stake in the family empire worth tens of millions of dollars, and ends nearly 40 years later when Mary learns that the Donald and his siblings, quoting from the lawsuit, "used their position of power to con her into signing her interests away."
44 Ibid: 14.
45 Ibid.
46 Quoted in Frank, 2018: 20–21.
47 Mary Trump, 2020: 23.
48 Ibid: 24.
49 Ibid: 26.
50 Ibid: 25.
51 Ibid: 26–27.
52 Ibid: 27.
53 Michael Kruse, 2017. The Mystery of Mary Trump. *Politico.* November 5. https://www.politico.eu/article/donald-trump-the-mystery-of-mary-trump/.
54 Christopher Lasch, 1979. *The Culture of Narcissism: American Life in an Age of Diminishing Expectations.* New York: W.W. Norton.
55 Symptoms of "sociopaths" include a lack of empathy, a facility for lying, abusive behavior, an indifference to the rights of others, and to right and wrong in general.
56 Joe McGrath, 2021. Self-deception as a Technique of Neutralization: An Analysis of the Subjective Account of a White-Collar Criminal. *Crime, Law and Social Change* 75: 415–432. https://doi.org/10.1007/s10611-021-09933-6.

57 Adam Serwer, 2021. *The Cruelty Is the Point: The Past, Present, and Future of Trump's America.* New York: Penguin Random House.

58 Dan Mangan, 2019. Justice Department Officials Discussed If Trump Could Be Removed as President via 25th Amendment after Firing FBI Director James Comey: Andrew McCabe. *CNBC.* February 24. https://www.cnbc.com/2019/02/14/andrew-mccabe-doj-officials-discussed-using-25th-amendment-to-remove-trump.html.

59 Bob Woodward and Robert Costa, 2021. *Peril.* New York: Simon & Schuster.

60 Gresham M. Sykes and David Matza, 1957. Techniques of Neutralization: A Theory of Delinquency. *America Sociological Review* 22 (6): 664–670.

61 Phillip Ball, 2021. *The Modern Myths: Adventures in the Machinery of the Popular Imagination.* Chicago, IL: University of Chicago Press.

62 Anthony Salvanto, Fred Backus and Jennifer De Pinto, 2021. CBS News Poll: Republicans Weight in on Liz Cheney and Direction of GOP. *CBS News.* May 16, 2021. https://www.cbsnews.com/live/video/20210517101124-a-new-poll-by-cbs-news-shows-a-majority-of-republican-voters-approving-of-the-decision-to-remove-rep-liz-cheney-from-her-leadership-pos/.

63 James W. Messerschmidt, 1997. *Crime as Structured Action: Gender, Race, Class, and Crime in the Making.* Thousand Oaks, CA: Sage. See also, James W. Messerschmidt, 2004. *Flesh and Blood: Adolescent Gender Diversity and Violence.* Lanham, MD: Rowman & Littlefield.

64 Quoted in Shimi Kang, 2015. How the Wealthy Are Disadvantaged: How Upper and Upper Middle Class Kids are at Risk. *Psychology Today.* December 1. https://www.psychologytoday.com/us/blog/the-dolphin-way/201512/how-the-wealthy.

65 Gregg Barak, 2003. *Violence and Nonviolence: Pathways to Understanding.* Thousand Oaks, CA: Sage Publications.

66 Gregg Barak, 2009. *Criminology: An Integrated Approach.* Lanham, MD: Rowman & Littlefield, p. 255.

67 "The basic variables of their 'working model' include the central concept of social role, defined as 'recurrent interactions' which form 'patterns of mutually oriented conduct.' The concept plays a triple function entering into the *description* of both the person *and* the social structure and is also the conceptual linkage between the two." Cultural Apparatus. https://culturalapparatus.wordpress.com/intellectual-craftsmanship/character-and-social-structure/. Retrieved March 5, 2021.

68 Erving Goffman, 1961. *Asylums: Essays on the Social Situation of Mental Patients and Other Inmates.* New York: Anchor Books.

69 As we will see later, there is also a structural legal apparatus that protects powerful law violators keeping them mostly beyond incrimination. See Donald Black's *The Behavior of Law* first published in 1976 and the reissued, *The Behavior of Law: Special Edition*, published in 2010 by Emerald Group Publishing, UK.

70 Fox Butterfield, 2018. *In My Father's House: A New View of How Crime Runs in the Family.* New York: Vintage Books. See also, Andrea Bernstein, 2020. *American Oligarchs: The Kushners, the Trumps, and the Marriage of Money and Power.* New York: W.W. Norton & Company; Vicky Ward, 2019. *Kushner, Inc.: Greed. Ambition. Corruption: The Extraordinary Story of Jared Kushner and Ivanka Trump.* New York: St. Martin's Press.

71 Alan Feuer, 2020. Mary Trump Sues President and Family, Claiming Fraud of Millions. *The New York Times*. September 24. https://www.nytimes.com/2020/09/24/nyregion/mary-trump-suing-trump-family.html.

72 Limited liability companies also known as shell companies exist for the most part without active business operations or assets. While these types of corporations are not necessarily illegal, they are often used illegitimately, to disguise business ownership from law enforcement or the public. Business entities may use them legitimately to raise money for startups, to conduct hostile takeovers, or when they are about to go public. They may also be used legitimately and illegitimately to avoid paying taxes. Donald has used LLCs mostly as vehicles for passing business revenue to his own individual tax returns, which is typically as a lower tax rate. Donald has also used them to protect his individual assets for when his companies go out of business or file for bankruptcy, in order to prevent his investors or partners when they become suing plaintiffs from coming after his personal money beyond what they themselves had invested.

73 Mike McIntire and Russ Buettner, 2021. In Case against Trump's Company, Echoes of His Father's Tactics on Taxes. *The New York Times*. July 4: Front page.

74 Edward Helmore, 2019. Bannon Described Trump Organization as 'Criminal Enterprise,' Michael Wolff Book Claims. *The Guardian*. May 29. https://www.theguardian.com/us-news/2019/may/28/bannon-trump-organization-criminal-enterprise-comments-michael-wolff-book.

75 Phillip Rucker and Robert Costa, 2017. Bannon Vows a Daily Fight for 'Deconstruction of the Administrative State'. *The Washington Post*. February 23. https://www.washingtonpost.com/politics/top-wh-strategist-vows-a-daily-fight-for-deconstruction-of-the-administrative-state/2017/02/23/03f6b8da-f9ea-11e6-bf01-d47f8cf9b643_story.html.

2

A LIFETIME OF DEVIANCE, DECEPTION, AND DISHONESTY, 1970–2016

From the commercial success of the Western genre first realized by Zane Grey, author of more than 80 titles, including his best-selling *Riders of the Purple Sage* (1912) made into five films to Francis Ford Coppola's *The Godfather* trilogy produced in 1970, 1972, and 1990 to the Home Box Office television series, *The Sopranos* (1999–2007), outlaws and mobsters have enthralled American audiences. Part of Trump's appealing deviancy has been about his macho persona and how he represents the best alternative to politically correct and woke culture. And yet at gala events and political rallies, his tough guy act and his image of authenticity are pure fabrications. As the saying goes, Trump "is as phony as a three-dollar bill." Much of Trump's attraction though has to do with his chauvinistic attitudes of white supremacy, racism, and misogyny. Donald's disdain for people of color and his objectification of women are well documented in biographies dating back to the 1970s.[1]

In terms of being an *outlaw*, Trump is the real deal. Meaning that Donald is habitually breaking laws of all kinds, while he remains free at large to take care of his businesses as usual. Donald is also an outlaw within a community of outlaws because he has no moral compass, and he has no loyalty to anyone beside himself. In a few words, Trump has no honor among thieves, and he has no honor among the law-abiding. The Donald is not an outlaw out of negligence or unfamiliarity with the illegalities of the marketplace, the Constitution, or civil laws. On the contrary, Trump knows the subtle differences between lawfully right and unlawfully wrong.

DOI: 10.4324/9781003221548-4

Moreover, Donald appreciates that the legal system and the laws distinguishing between right and wrong, justifiable and not justifiable, legal and illegal are fluid in theory and practice, and they are subject to valuation and interpretation. Trump also understands that the administration of justice can often be malleable. Based on Trump's unmatched number of lawsuits as both plaintiff and defendant, Donald generally knows the rules of the legal games as well as anyone with the exceptions of those who litigate the law for a living. Should Donald not know where the lines are drawn between lawlessness and lawfulness, it then becomes the business of his arsenal of attorneys to find out where those lines are supposed to be as they seek to evade or move them.[2] Unlike most powerful people who may go up to the lines of wrongdoing and have some reluctance of stepping over, Donald has no such inhibitions especially when it comes to bending, if not breaking, those legalities standing in the way of his pursuing the objects of his needs or desires.

In terms of being a mobster, Boss Trump has always intermingled his legitimate affairs of business with those illegitimate affairs of organized crime.[3] Like his father, the Donald has not only been well connected to politicians of all stripes and ideologies but also to all kinds of mobsters and criminals. Throughout his professional life, the Donald has conducted everyday business with a variety of syndicated criminals. These have included individual members belonging to the Bonanno, Colombo, Gambino, Genovese, Lucchese, and Scarfo crime families.[4] Back in the day when the young Donald was just starting out, if one wanted to successfully compete in the biggest New York and New Jersey real estate markets or in the emerging casino industries, then assistance in one form or the other from organized crime could help to grease the wheels of a project or to seal the deal.

As Trump told a panel at the Museum of Television and Radio in Los Angeles in 2004 shortly after he had signed his first contract to do "The Apprentice" that he had been tentative about signing on with the reality TV show because of all the mobsters that frequent his place of work. "I [didn't] want [TV] cameras all over my office, dealing with contractors, politicians, mobsters and everyone else I have to deal with in my business."[5] More than a decade later, during one of his moments of public candidness, Donald stated what he would be more inclined to say privately or only to a group of his biggest donors: "winners team up with mobsters, losers don't." The point is that DJT has been running a family based criminal enterprise for close to 50 years. For four of those years as the president of the United States, Trump not only managed but he also expanded his looting and corruption from the Oval Office. As Trump told *The New York Times* shortly after winning the 2016 presidential election: "In theory I could run my business perfectly and then run the country perfectly."[6] In everyday practice, however, Trump ran the affairs of state as much as he runs his business affairs. Flying by the seat of his pants or by helter-skelter.

Trump advises his readers in *Think Big and Kick Ass: In Business and Life* (2007) that people need to be paranoid and should trust no one because people are "all out to steel you blind." This was what father Fred thought and the way he behaved. Fred, Sr. was also a tightwad with his and other people's money. Donald is a "chip off the old block" only a more extreme version. Both men spent much of their adult lives stealing from the U.S. taxpayers, hording their ill-gotten profits, and cynically telling themselves that everyone else was doing the exact same thing. Donald's take on mistrust has to do not only with his view of people, but also with his deeper insecurities and lack of self-trust. Combine Donald's all-encompassing lack of trust with his intimate knowledge of his own deception and dishonesty, and we find an "alter ego" pretending in the late 1980s and early 1990s to be an imaginary pitchman, John Berry or John Barron, allegedly working for the Trump Organization. On the one hand, Trump was too cheap to hire a real public relations person. On the other hand, Trump understood that nobody else could ever capture his poppycock narratives as well as he could. Accordingly, Trump found himself using these pseudonyms while contacting the media talking mostly in third person. Yet slipping unconsciously back in forth and speaking in the first person.[7]

We learn from the same book about the sanctity of Trump's grievance and revenge mentality:

> I love getting even when I get screwed by someone—yes, it is true… Always get even. When you are in business you need to get even with people who screw you. You need to screw them back fifteen times harder…go for the jugular, attack them in spades![8]

We also learn about the pleasure that Donald derives from hurting others or inflicting pain. One story shared is about a former employee that Trump had hired and assisted with her early career development. By the early 1990s, years after the woman had left Trump Management and had become successful running her own business, Trump who was then financially hemorrhaging approached her to collect on "one favor in return." She declined his invitation because she found it to be ethically inappropriate. Subsequently, she fell on hard times herself. According to Trump, the woman lost her business, her home, and her "gold digging" husband. These changed circumstances made Trump very happy. Donald also reveals that whenever people would call him up for job recommendations about the woman, he would always go out of his way "to make her life miserable."

Additionally, Trump shares some of the personality traits or social characteristics of other powerful gangsters. I am referring to Donald's street smarts, to his depravity, destructiveness, and megalomania. Like other mobsters, Trump has his own entourage of enablers and trails of ingratiating "yes" people. But the reasons behind Trump's success beyond his savvy marketing are complicated. As Michael Cohen, Trump's personal attorney and fixer[9] for more than a decade has written. The Boss cannot be reduced to merely that of "a cheat, a liar, a fraud, a bully, a racist, a predator, and a con man."[10] Among his other qualities, Trump is authoritarian, charismatic, corrupting, intelligent, kleptocratic, and persuasive. When it comes to greed and venality, Trump is an expert par excellence; he also knows how and whom to exploit in bringing out the worst in people. As for those persons that are repulsed by Trump or have become objects of disloyalty or disobedience to Donald for whatever real or imagined reasons, then payback, getting even, and seeking revenge become the orders of the day. As for confronting his former loyalists, political allies, business associates, consensual lovers, or anyone else that Trump believes has betrayed him by failing to go along with one or more of his unethical schemes, no one is ever safe, including his own family members. No matter how unseemly the desired collusion—laundering money, obstructing justice, inciting an insurrection—anyone who challenges or resists Trump in the world of business or in the world of politics is someone to be fired, put down, and crushed.

Back in 2005, while Trump and Felix Sater were in Denver working on two business deals, the Donald made his way by limousine some 60 miles north to Loveland, Colorado to make some "talking cash" by giving an inspirational presentation on how to succeed in life and business to a small group of Republicans. Of course, whenever Trump gives a non-scripted speech, the probabilities are pretty good that something outrageous will flow from his lips. On this occasion, Trump was pontificating on one of his favorite topics—losers—telling the audience: "I love losers because they make me feel so good about myself."[11] As we all know, the Projector-in-Chief used to spend an enormous amount of time on Twitter and other social media until he was kicked off, always harping about "winners" and "losers." Recall too that Trump prefers not to look back into his past because of what he does not like to see, namely those things he dislikes about himself as well as the truth about his less than stellar business performances. Rather than revisiting episodes from his past and reflecting on them honestly, Trump prefers to consciously reside in one of his favorite default positions of either denial or alternative reality.

Businesswise, for example, Donald is hypersensitive about all his investment fiascoes that as a politician he has tried so hard to conceal from the world. Whether we are talking about financial bankruptcies or failed enterprises, the Donald has one of the greatest losing records of all time. Among those former companies of his that no longer exist: Trump Steaks, Go Trump, Trump Airlines, Trump Vodka, Trump Mortgage, Trump: The Game, Trump Magazine, Trump University, Trump Ice, The New Jersey Generals, Tour de Trump, Trump Network, and Trumped! As for the Trump gaming and hospitality corporations that have sought bankruptcy protection these include: Trump Taj Mahal, Trump's Castle, Trump Plaza Casinos, Trump Plaza Hotel, Trump Hotels and Casino Resorts, and Trump Entertainment Resorts.[12] Even before his father died, is it any wonder that conventional banking or lending institutions had stopped doing business with the Donald, and that Trump had become dependent on the underground economy, money laundering, and syndicated criminals for raising venture capital?

During Trump's presidency when he had spoken or tweeted something for its desired and predictable negative reactions from the political opposition and/or fake media and it was considered "over the top," his advisors and other public defenders would often chime in trying to downplay his offensive remarks. Their lame refrains were always the same: "Oh the president wasn't serious; he was only joking." Sometimes, Trump would let the "dead dog lie," mostly though he would double down and push back against his own protectors. Whether Trump was joking or not was usually not the point. Besides Donald does not have much of a sense of humor in the first place. This deficit is not unrelated to the former president's emotional inability to really connect or empathize with other human beings. Because virtually all his social or public interactions are transactional in nature. They are almost always devoid of human reciprocity beyond his empty superficiality.

These missing emotional qualities, including his lack of humor except at the expense of others, are deeply psychological. They are also reflective of the fact that Trump has spent his whole life trying to be taken seriously by others who thought of him mostly as amusing or worse. Hence, except for when the Donald is making fun of other people, he rarely jokes about anything at all. When he does crack a serious joke, he usually does so among his confidants in private. Even then, these jokes are rarely if ever self-effacing. In short, comedy is not one of Donald's fortes.

Whether as a celebrity or as a politician, Trump has always been the butt of publicly shared jokes. As the pre-president, president, and post-president, Donald has experienced unmatched and unrelenting comedic mockery from late night television hosts like Stephen Colbert, Jimmy Fallon, or Trevor Noah to the Doonesbury comic strips by Gary Trudeau to the remarks of Seth Meyers at the 2011 annual White House Correspondents Association Dinner in Washington, DC. Even President Obama roasted Trump that evening for a full five minutes, delighting in several zingers aimed at the man who questioned whether he was a legitimate president. Among some of Barack's best lines were,

> No one is happier, no one is prouder to put this birth certificate matter to rest than the Donald. That's because he can finally get back to focusing on the issues that matter, like: Did we fake the moon landing? What really happened at Roswell? And where are Biggie and Tupac?[13]

In fact, by the middle of his presidency, Trump was so disturbed by the constant ridiculing that he wanted the DOJ to stop *Saturday Night Live* and other late night comedians from teasing him.[14]

Always keep in mind that what Donald needs from people more than money and love is to be liked and respected rather than feared or dreaded. For example, Trump does not actually gather much emotional satisfaction from his MAGA political base. Because the Donald like Hillary Clinton views these groups of supporters as belonging in that "basket of deplorables." What Donald really, really wants is to be accepted by those he allegedly detests and rails the most against. I am referring to the mainstream media, the Hollywood elites, and the financially powerful people. However, Donald's self-doubts, insecurities, and hyper defense mechanisms always get in the proverbial way of his satisfying his basic human needs. Trump's continuing denigration and disparagement of those adversaries that he desires approval from is a classic illustration of sour grapes or reaction formation. His negative attitude or anger toward the "fake" news, the Hollywood elites, and so on is a product of the fact that he has never been able to achieve their approval, let alone their adulation. After all, most of these people think not only that he is a dangerous joke, but also that he is to put it delicately not a very likeable person.

Grifting the myth of the self-made billionaire

To reiterate, Donald is a person driven primarily by insecurity, gluttony, and selfishness without much or any of the empathy and humanity stuff. With the notable exception of Donald's ever-present bullying or intimidation of others, the lack of empathy and identification with the other people was not always the case. In the late 1970s and early 1980s when the Donald was first "going out on his own" before the success of the Trump Tower and his image as the flamboyant developer took off, the Trump Organization, consisting of Donald and three other executives, retained the best and brightest personnel. They also used high-quality subcontractors whenever possible. Back then, Trump listened to his hired professional help more than he wanted to. Donald pretty much allowed them as much power as they required for them to successfully carry out their tasks for him. With respect to the organizational conduct for a relatively small number of people, it meant a couple of things.

First, these individuals often had to ignore Trump because either he did not know what he was talking about or the Donald was trying to violate a contractual agreement with his suppliers, workers, subcontractors, and so on. Second, these skilled builders had to be willing to accept the blame for the mistakes that Trump made. For example, when Trump would demand that they use cheaper materials than what was called for resulting in their having to redo the job and spending more money. Back in those earlier days, Trump was still very much aware of his limitations. Unlike his father who knew a great deal about construction, Donald knew next to nothing about low-rise or high-rise construction, retrofitting buildings, or anything about the trades. So, at the beginning, Trump's only real successful business ventures were dependent on others doing his bidding as well as the heavy lifting.[15] As a consequence, before the fleeting early success came to Donald, there was a time when he displayed decency and even on occasion empathized with his associates or employees.

These humanistic sentiments began to fade during the construction of the casinos in Atlantic City.[16] Which is somewhat strange as Donald once again "knew next to nothing about the casino industry, including the rules of the games."[17] It was not that even as his investment ventures were going from bad to worse, as many talking heads opine, that Trump came to believe his own hype. Trump only wants people to think he believes his own hype. Rather, the actual story has more to do with the big con and the mythmaking of the self-made billionaire. It all began with Donald's first major profile that appeared in *The New York Times* on November 1, 1976:

> He is tall, lean and blond, with dazzling white teeth, and he looks ever so much like Robert Redford. He rides around town in a chauffeured silver Cadillac with his initials, DJT, on the plates. He dates slinky fashion models, belongs to the most elegant clubs and, at only 30 years of age, estimates that he is worth "more than $200 million."[18]

Yet years later, Donald acknowledged to casino regulators that his 1976 taxable income was only $24,594. The truth of the matter, the bottom line, or letting the con out of the bag, Donald over the course of his life has probably made less than a billion dollars on his own. Most of his wealth has come from the aid of his father and subsequently his siblings too. DJT and the familia simply appropriated Fred's empire with Donald taking the lion's share. If that was not enough, years later he tried to alter his father's will—much to his father's anger—so that he could employ his old man's fortune to further mediate against his failing business concerns.

For the profile story, the newsmaking and clever Donald took the female reporter on a chauffeured driven tour of what he referred to as his job. Actually, these were daddy's not Donny's projects. Trump also talked about the Manhattan hotel that he planned to convert into the Grand Hyatt without mentioning the construction loan was guaranteed by his father. The tour continues to the Hudson River railroad yards where he planned to develop without referencing that the rights to do so were purchased by his father's company. Donald then took the reporter to

> 'our philanthropic endeavor,' the high-rise for the elderly in East Orange (bankrolled by his father), and to the apartment complex on Staten Island (owned by his father), and their 'flagship,' Trump Village, in Brooklyn (owned by his father), and finally Beach Haven Apartments (owned by his father).[19]

Over the years, Fred also leased the Cadillac and paid for the chauffeur. Shortly after *The Times*' article ran, Fred set up additional trusts for his children, seeding each of them the equivalent of $4.3 million in 2018 dollars. By the early 1980s, when Trump "was already proclaiming himself one of America's richest men," he still "remained on his father's payroll," drawing an annual salary, once again in 2018 dollars, of $260,000.[20]

The story of Trump is also about how he is an excellent marketer without any ethics. As he spoke to the New York reporter: "So far, I 've never made a bad deal." True enough. Then again, at that time in his life, Donald had not really made any deals of his own. Over the next two decades despite a terrible track record of losing in business, the Barker-in-Chief was able to successfully promote the winning Trump Brand. This was part and parcel of or predicated on the myth that Donald had started out with a small million-dollar loan from his father that he had to pay back with interest. Nothing could have been further from the truth as his farther was always fronting him money that he never paid back with or without interest. Success wise, according to tax records, Trump was able to make a small fortune of $197 million directly from The Apprentice over 16 years. It is also estimated that $230 million in value has flowed from the fame associated with the television show.[21]

Not like a slight majority of Americans today who seem to care about the social realities of life, Trump could care less about these realities or about truth, fairness, and justice. Donald only believes in those realities (or fantasies) that he thinks are in his personal best or vested interests. The same can also be deduced from his sycophantic Trumpian followers and 72–78 percent of Republicans who believe that Biden is not the legitimate president. These political enablers of the Donald have both knowingly and unknowingly consumed and spread the Big Lies about a stolen election and who won. At the same time, by ignoring, excusing, or relishing in the habitually abusive, abominable, and destructive behavior of Trump, these political supporters have only helped to sustain Trump's deceptive and dishonest conduct.

Even after the president's insurrectionists were calling for the execution of the VP and Twitter accounts were trending "Hang Mike Pence," former Vice President Pence was *all in* with the Trumpian Big Lies as he still has pipedreams of returning to the White House as the president in 2024. From yesteryears Monty Python's Flying Circus and wearing my own Pythonesque cork hat so to speak, I can envision the allegedly affable Mike busily and happily building his own gallows as he simultaneously runs around shouting to the onlookers, "Hang Mike Pence, Please, Hang Mike Pence." The point being that these strengths of loyalty to Trumpian power are even more miraculous given Trump's one-way street of loyalty where he is so quick to have his own people discarded or thrown under the proverbial buses whenever it serves his needs to do so. It has been stated by more than a few insiders that when "push ever comes to shove," that Trump's children Donald, Jr., Ivanka, and Eric know perfectly well that they are not safe or immune from their father's wrath of selfishness. They are very aware that Donald helped his father screw over his older brother's children and their offspring's rightful monetary inheritance after Fred, Jr. passed in 1981. They are very aware that one decade later their father had tried to alter their grandfather's will by making him the soul executor of the state to the disadvantage of his siblings.

In the case of not being who he really is or in terms of the "art of the fake," Donald can usually do whatever it takes to accomplish the "con," the "grift," or the "graft." For example, political pundits, social commentators, and just about everyone for that matter were all surprised to discover in 2015 that the lifelong amoral, pro-abortion, pro-homosexual, and Democratic contributor had become the beloved favorite of the evangelical voters. Besides putting a lot of energy into getting their backing, as well as promising to appoint conservative judges to low and high courts alike, to work against abortion, gender, and human rights for all, Donald was also able to play to both the desires and vanities of some of the most famous evangelicals in the United States, including Jerry Falwell Jr., Pastor Darrell Scott, and Reverend Robert Jeffress. He did so by tapping into the long dead Protestant preacher Norman Vincent Peale from New York City and the author of *The Power of Positive Thinking* for the entire materialistic gospel that Peale was worth.

Meanwhile, the Donald was also successfully conning them into believing that he had experienced a moment of conversion. As Johnnie Moore, the unofficial leader of Trump's evangelical advisory board has been quoted, "I absolutely believe he's a born-again Christian." Similarly, the Rev. Franklin Graham, faith adviser to Trump's White House and son of the late Billy Graham, "I think there's no question he believes."[22] Point of information: After Trump's 2015 meeting with the evangelical leaders on the 25th floor of Trump Tower and the ritualistic laying of their hands on his germophobic body, Donald had a brief exchange privately with Michael Cohen when he stated: "Can you believe people believe that bullshit?"[23] His fixer had organized the meeting, thanks to an IOU that Michael had called in from Jerry and Becki Falwell.[24]

Throughout his life, Trump has been very capable of manufacturing fraudulent images portraying himself as anyone but the person he is. This was especially the case when he was living part-time in the White House as the president and Gaslighter-in-Chief. As Cohen testified before the U.S. Congress on February 24, 2019, about the contradictions of human nature:

> Mr. Trump is an enigma…He is complicated, as am I. He does both good and bad, as do we all. But the bad far outweighs the good, and since taking office, he has become the worst version of himself. He

> is capable of behaving kindly, but he is not kind. He is capable of committing acts of generosity, but he is not generous. He is capable of being loyal, but he is fundamentally disloyal.[25]

Michael also informs us that before his betrayal of the former president, he was not only part of the Trump Organization, but that in some ways he knew Donald "better than his own family did, because I bore witness to the real man, in strip clubs, shady business meetings, and in the unguarded moments when he revealed who he really was."[26]

For the record, despite Trump and Cohen's intimate relationship, Michael always addressed Donald as Boss in private and as Mr. Trump in public. While the Donald may not actually be an old school mobster, part of his modus operandi is the same, especially when it comes to pushing other people around or circumventing law and order. As I have been arguing, most of Trump's behavior has been a product of his father's socialization to the world of business and to the political culture of high stakes real estate development in New York City and elsewhere. In order to understand Donald's cruelty and his sadistic orientation to the world, and to appreciate the types of emotional connections that these forge with his political base's feelings of alienation and powerlessness, for example, it is necessary to drill down further into Fred Trump's real estate empire worth about a billion dollars two years before his death in 1999. After this review, we can then turn to the joint criminality of father and son as well as to those illicit activities involving the Donald and his siblings.

In an October 3, 2018 article for *The Atlantic* entitled, The Cruelty Is the Point, Adam Serwer underscores that "President Trump and his supporters find community by rejoicing in the suffering of those they hate and fear."[27] From a different angle, Obama has voiced: "Trump is for a lot of white people what O.J.'s acquittal was to a lot of Black folks – you know it's wrong, but it feels good."[28] If the primal charisma of Donald and his cruelty are both attractive to millions of people and repulsive to millions of people—at the same time—depending on the objectification of the other, then part of the success of this dynamic has to do with the Donald having tapped into and exploited the evolution of America's "putdown" or "smackdown" culture.

From the covert forms of racist elephant jokes popular in the United States as well as the UK during the late 1950s and early 1960s to the overt forms of playing the Dozens in African American communities even to this day. Back in the day, these elephant jokes had to do more generally with repudiating established wisdom, rejecting authority, and dismissing conventional questions and answers.[29] As for the Dozens, these have often involved two contestants increasingly insulting each other in front of others until one of them gives up.[30] Not to be ignored of course, there have always been the patriarchal degradations and negative labeling associated with gender, sexism, and misogyny.[31]

Among the most well-known genre of public putdown television shows were *The Dean Martin Celebrity Roast* that aired from 1974 to 1984 and the *Comedy Central Roast* that premiered in 2003 and by the end of 2019 had aired 17 specials. Who could ever forget the funniest and queasiest of them all, the over-the-top *Celebrity Deathmatch*? The stop-motion clay animated series created by Eric Fogel for MTV ran from May 1998 to June 2002. It aired 75 episodes of celebrities engaging in highly stylized wrestling matches known for gory violence, physical injuries, missing body parts, spraying blood, and eventually death. Over the past decade, we have witnessed in similar fashion the weaponizing of irony and satire to advance political agendas of all persuasions.

For example, in sync with the ideological left are late night TV hosts such as Stephen Colbert or Jimmy Fallon who use piercing humor, irony, satire, and parody to communicate anti-racist, sexist, or homophobic remarks to denigrate the right. In turn, the alt-right media in sync with the Donald have adopted ersatz or false seriousness to engage in coordinated online harassment and trolling campaigns against not only these left leaning comedians, but also aimed at other liberal institutions, including mainstream media talking heads and university faculties who are viewed as engaging in political correctness or censor culture and the production of geek culture. While these individuals and institutionalized entities weaponized against may be confronted with hatred and threats of violence, they are not the primary targets of these putdowns. Rather their targets are the "normie" audiences that as a result of the controversy created by the alt-right might hopefully be turned off and better yet "redpilled." Whereby, for example, they conclude that white, straight, and Christian men are in fact "under siege and that mainstream institutions are complicit in attacking them."[32] In sum, using similar strategies as the progressive comedians of the left the alt-right mediations in reverse are trying to advance their white supremacist, anti-Semitic, misogynist, and quite often deadly, serious agendas.

In response to Serwer, niece Mary has written about how cruelty was what father Fred was all about and how it played out with respect to Donald's lifelong struggle for legitimacy:

> One of the few pleasures my grandfather had, aside from making money, was humiliating others. Convinced of his rightness in all situations, buoyed by his stunning success and a belief in his superiority,

> he had to punish any challenge to his authority swiftly, and decisively and put the challenger in his place. That was effectively what happened when Fred promoted Donald over Freddy to be president of Trump Management.
>
> Unlike my grandfather, Donald has always struggled for legitimacy—as an adequate replacement for Freddy, as a Manhattan real estate developer or casino tycoon, and now as the occupant of the Oval Office who can never escape the taint of being utterly without qualification or the sense that his "win" was illegitimate. Over Donald's lifetime, as his failures mounted despite my grandfather's repeated—and extravagant—interventions, his struggle for legitimacy, which could never be won, turned into a scheme to make sure nobody found out that he's never been legitimate at all.[33]

Barbara A. Res is an attorney, an electrical engineer, and a former executive vice president in charge of construction at the Trump Organization from the late 1970s to the middle 1990s. As the author of *Tower of Lies: What My 18 Years of Working with Donald Trump Reveals About Him* (2020), Res has shared a sympathetic and critical portrayal:

> In the beginning Donald was glamorous and brash, even handsome. Sure, he was a showman, but he also had charm and moments of humanity, especially with some of us who worked closely with him. I saw him bully people below him and make idle threats, but what New York boss didn't—especially in the construction world? You had to be tough or you wouldn't survive one second on those sites or in those meetings. Trump thought of himself as a 'killer.' That is what you had to be to succeed, and he only wanted "killers" to work for him. Trump thought that I fit that mold. The man I knew so well and worked with for almost twenty years, who gave me a break in construction at a time when women were not given such breaks, my once narcissistic but ultimately human boss is now just a hate-filled and amoral person.[34]

As Res encapsulates at the beginning of her book. "It's not hard to look at the trajectory of his entire life and spot an unmistakable pattern: The bigger he got as a name, the smaller he got as a person."[35]

At the beginning of the 2016 campaign, Donald was taking credit for breaking the glass ceiling for women by hiring women like Barbara Res way back when. However, in a characteristic style, Donald had failed to mention any of them by name. Later in the campaign when Trump was attacking the woman who had successfully developed Trump Tower on his behalf, he never failed to mention Res by name. Back when Donald first hired Barbara to head up construction for the Trump Organization in 1980, he had told her: "So I want you to be me...Make the decisions I would make. [Think of yourself as] Donna Trump. You know, direct the work—the day-to-day things. I'm just gonna be too busy."[36] This had nothing to do with Trump being too busy. Rather, it was because the Donald who had a fair amount of knowledge about the operations of father Fred's real estate empire knew absolutely nothing about hotel construction not to mention the reconstruction of hotels. Nor did Donald ever learn any of the nitty-gritty about such ventures.

Res also points out that Donald liked to surround himself with strong women. Beside herself as the head of the Trump Tower development project, other assertive women included the leasing agent, the condo sales manager, and the head of advertising. The Donald was comfortable with these killers because no matter how insecure he was and how lacking in genuine self-confidence he possessed, Trump was always "confident that no matter how accomplished or intelligent they were, they could never be a threat. He was superior just because he was a man."[37] Res has also acknowledged that it did take her a while to see beyond the public persona illusion that Donald had worked so hard to create and "into the racism, sexism, and xenophobia that he carefully hid. Ironically, these things are now part of his brand."[38]

What Res leaves out of her account when detailing Trump's usage of concrete over the use of steel girders in his high rising buildings was his relationship with and dependence on a legion of concrete racketeers. These included Mafia chieftains Anthony "Fat Tony" Salerno and Paul Castellano. The two of them secretly owned the firm S & A Concrete. They controlled not only the price of concrete, but also whether the unions would cooperate when needed. Cementing their relationship was the fact that Salerno and Castellano were also old clients of Donald's personal attorney and fixer Roy Cohn.

In the tradition of father Fred and grandfather Friedrich

While Fred, Sr. thought of Donald's failures as a bad reflection on himself, he continued to throw "good money after bad money" or to "cover all his bets" as a means of trying to sustain his own empire. Some 80 years earlier when Fred was 12, his father had died from the Spanish flu and the young master became the "man" of the house. Despite a sizable inheritance, his mother Elizabeth Trump was having tough times making ends meet. So as a high school student, Fred began taking odd jobs to help with the family finances. He also began to seriously study the building trade, learning everything there was about the business, as it had always been his dream to become a builder. Only a sophomore in high school and with his mother's backing, he began building and selling garages. A short time thereafter, Fred was on to single-family houses. In 1927, Elizabeth and Fred incorporated their home construction and sales business becoming E. Trump & Son. By 1936, Trump had some 400 workers digging foundations for houses that were selling from $3,000 to $6,250. In 1938, the *Brooklyn Daily Eagle* referred to Fred Trump as the Henry Ford of the home-building industry.

After WWII, Fred began to diversify from building and managing single middle-class family houses in Queens and Brooklyn as he had done during the 1930s to taking on other types of building projects. These ventures were funded by the Federal Housing Administration (FHA) and spread across low-income neighborhoods from Coney Island, Bensonhurst, and Sheepshead Bay to Flatbush and Brighton Beach in Brooklyn to Flushing and Jamaica Estates in Queens. In 1947–1949, the FHA underwrote his largest project to date, Shore Haven, located in Bensonhurst, Brooklyn. It comprised 32, 6-story buildings and a shopping center spread over 30 acres. Nine million dollars was paid directly to Fred for the construction. Having described the rental tenants that would occupy his 2,201 apartment units as "unwholesome," Fred took the money as he realized immediately the fortune that he was about to make. In 1950, he built the Beach Haven Apartments near Coney Island, a slightly larger project procuring a whopping $16 million from the FHA.

During this period, Fred developed close ties with the leaders of the Brooklyn Democratic Party, the New York State political machine, and the federal government. Many of these politicos were also major players in the real estate industry. Fred became a member of an exclusive beach club on the south shore of Long Island and later the North Hills Country Club. These were excellent places to entertain, impress, and rub elbows with the men best positioned to funnel governmental funds into his pockets. If getting funding or tax breaks meant sucking up and kowtowing to more powerful and better-connected men, then Fred an iron-fisted autocrat at home and in his office was all in. The taxpayers were not the only source of raising capital for Fred's construction projects. Shortly after WWII ended, Fred partnered with Willie Tomasello, an associate of the Genovese and Gambino Mafia families in New York. When cash was short, Tomasello was always able to provide operating capital on short notice. He also ran interference with the unionized bricklayers, carpenters, and teamsters. As David Johnston points out, "just as Friedrich Trump had engaged in illicit businesses to build his fortune in the late nineteenth century, his son Fred Trump turned to an organized crime associate as his longtime partner to build his own."[39] Several decades later, Donald would do business with the heads of the very same families.

As the sayings go, the acorn or the apple doesn't fall far from the tree, or "like father, like son," Fred was never shy about not telling the truth when it served his purposes. Whether he was pretending to be Swedish when he was German or lying about his actual age in order to seem more precocious than he was. Fred was neither modest nor humble. He was living *The Power of Positive Thinking* before Peale wrote the best-selling book in 1952. Unlike Donald, it appears that Fred had no self-doubts or was not lacking in self-confidence. Like his son, Fred also had a propensity for self-promotion, showmanship, and often trafficked in hyperbole.

In 1963–1964, Fred built Trump Village in Coney Island for $70 million subsidized with funding from the State of New York. By the early 1970s, Fred's rental apartments were generating about $50 million a year. That would turn out to be his biggest and last major project. Subsidies from the government or organized crime were not the only ways that Fred acquired capital. He routinely skimmed money from his building contractors and shortchanged the IRS in commonly rigged rituals by those in the building industry of New York and elsewhere. As Johnston learned from talking with building contractors who had sat "across from Fred's plain desk, proposing to do plumbing, window, and electrical work." They would present "a plain envelope" and "Fred would take a second to test its weight in his hand before putting it into a drawer. Then he would listen to the pitch about contract terms for work" to be done.[40] As Johnston further explains:

> The cost of these secretive extras was built into the contract cost when it could be passed on to Uncle Sam or tenants. Otherwise it reduced the profit the contractor made. This was, and remains today, a widespread but illegal practice unless the cash payments are reported on income tax returns—which of course would defeat the purpose of the inducements. It's a low-risk crime: Unless the party handing over the envelope is a government agent and the bills are marked, who's to know? The practice also meant there was little need to withdraw cash from bank accounts, thereby leaving no records for tax authorities to discover during an audit.[41]

During this period, Fred was still very much involved with New York politics and with Donald's first major venture—the acquisition and redevelopment of the Commodore Hotel in downtown Manhattan next to Grand Central Terminal. This was 1975 and Fred who had given money lavishly to NYC Mayor Abe Beame (D), 1974–1977, was able to call in his chits for his son's project. Donald received for what became the Grand Hyatt Hotel an unprecedented 40-year tax break that ended in April 2020. According to the city's Department of Taxation and Finance that financing of the redevelopment has cost New York City $410,068,399.55 in forgone revenue.[42] With Fred as with Donald, everything was always "great," "couldn't be better," "fantastic" and so on. Then again, from time-to-time things went afoul for Fred. On three significant occasions Fred Trump found himself subject to government investigations into various forms of corruption and fraud.

In 1954, as part of a probing inquiry of the FHA operations by the U.S. Senate Hearings Before the Committee on Banking and Currency, he was one of the contractors investigated for profiteering. During the questioning, Fred was called out for "outright misrepresentation" referring to "his practice of valuing his properties at top dollar for government mortgages while using much lower assessments for tax purposes."[43] This has been a habitual practice engaged in by father and son throughout their real estate careers.

In 1966, the New York State Investigations Commission examined him about overcharging the government. At the public hearings held in January of that year, Fred suffered the worst public humiliation of his career. After testifying for several hours about an array of abuses in Trump Village, the commission chairman, Jacob Grumet, asked the state housing officials whether there was any way to prevent Fred Trump from obtaining any future contracts with the state? The answer at least with respect to NYC and Mayor Beame was no. One decade later as already noted, Fred was able to pass the city government's largesse off to Donald for his first real estate venture. When threatened legally by the state, Fred returned $1.2 million to New York that he had claimed that he had kept for estimated billing overcharges.[44]

In October 1973, the Justice Department filed a civil rights suit accusing the Trump firm, its chairman Fred Trump, and its 27-year-old president Donald Trump of violating the Fair Housing Act of 1968. Approximately one-half of Fred's empire of 27,000 apartments or 14,000 rental units of his were front and center of another real estate scandal. Not for profiteering or overcharging, but for racial discrimination. See the United States vs. Fred

C. Trump, Donald Trump and Trump Management, Inc., filed in the U.S. District Court for the Eastern District of New York. The complaint for injunction reads, the

> defendants, through the actions of their agents and employees, have discriminated against persons because of race in the operation of their apartment buildings, among other ways, by: Refusing to rent dwellings and negotiate for the rental of dwellings with persons because of race and color, in violation of Section 804 (a)...

Recall that a decade earlier, Woody Guthrie had put pen to verse about his contempt for his racist landlord. In fact, before the Fair Housing Act of 1968 and before Donald two years later went to work for his father full time, on at least seven occasions, people seeking apartments had filed complaints about alleging "discriminating practices" with the New York City Commission on Human Rights. Those earlier complaints had always been individually resolved by offering apartments to each minority, which rather than alleviating discriminatory housing served to perpetuate segregated housing within the apartment complexes owned by Fred Trump. Only this time was different. The federal investigators gathered evidence from undercover black and white would-be renters or "testers" of discriminatory patterns that played out across Queens and Brooklyn. The investigators discovered that Trump employees were secretly coding applications for whites and minorities. Then directing "blacks and Puerto Ricans away from buildings with mostly white tenants, and [steering] them "toward properties that had many minorities."[45]

In the wake of the Fair Housing Act, this was one of the highest profile racial discrimination cases of the many filed in federal courthouses across the United States. After all redlining and racial discrimination in housing was not unique to New York City, it was common in virtually every city and state in the union. The other big NYC landlords involved in the civil lawsuit "settled quickly to avoid nasty publicity, agreeing to keep track of the racial mix of tenants, to advertise to non-whites, and to take other steps to comply."[46] Not the Trumps.

The Trumps retained Roy Cohn to represent them. This was the first time that Donald found himself in the spotlight and he would make the most of the 20-month legal battle. While becoming a regular presence on newspaper front pages, the Donald demonstrated his brash and combative style. After working out their defense strategy, Donald held a press conference on December 12, 1973, at the New York Hilton announcing a $100 million counterclaim. They were maintaining that the government had knowingly made false and misleading statements about their racial discrimination. And the government was trying to force them to lease apartments to people on welfare, which had absolutely nothing to do with the legal case against the Trumps. It was just Roy and Donald spinning their practices of racial profiling and trying to confuse the issue and to deflect away from what they were guilty of. Trump had stated to the media that if we are compelled to rent to welfare recipients, then "there would be a massive fleeing from the city of not only our tenants, but communities as a whole."[47]

In his affidavit, Donald rejected the view that their business practices were based on race: "I have never, nor has anyone in our organization ever, to the best of my knowledge, discriminated or shown bias in renting our apartments."[48] Counselor Cohn filed his own affidavit in the case claiming: "No matter what the outcome of this case," the "damage is never going to be completely undone because you are never going to catch up with" the negative "initial headlines" in the newspapers. In January 1974, at a hearing in federal district court in Brooklyn, the Trumps sat waiting to see whether the suit and countersuit would continue. The government provided plenty of evidence of the techniques used by the Trump Organization to deny blacks, Puerto Ricans, and other minorities' equal treatment. Cohn's response was to accuse another lawyer, not the one arguing the case against the Trumps, of "soliciting false testimony and conducting a 'Gestapo-like' interrogation of Trump employees."[49] Federal Judge Edward R. Neaher allowed the government to proceed with its original suit. The federal judge dismissed Cohn's claims of official misconduct as "utterly without foundation" as he also dismissed the Trumps' counterclaims.

Although the litigation philosophy or strategy of Cohn and Trump is that one should always fight rather than fold because once you cave in, you get a reputation as someone who settles. Without the facts or the law on their side, the Trumps folded and settled this case as they have many other cases. The government proclaimed in their press release that the legal case had been "one of the most far reaching" of its kind to end racial discrimination in housing. Meanwhile, the Donald following in the footsteps of his father spun the stinging loss by offering a simple and quotable narrative: "In the end the government couldn't prove its case, and we ended up making a minor settlement without admitting any guilt."[50] What most people back then or now are not aware of is that the government routinely lets corporate offenders settle cases without acknowledging their wrongdoing so long as they promise to stop unlawfully doing what they were doing.

In this instance, there was not even so much as a fine. The settlement only required that they stop their discriminatory practices and run some advertisements aimed at nonwhite tenants.

It's not what you know, it's who you know

The more popular catchphrase, "It is not what you know, but whom you know," refers to people getting ahead in business based on connections through family and friends rather than based on their own skills or knowledge. In the world of illegitimate business affairs, relationships or connections—networking in contemporary parlance—are even more important than competence because these are often tied to the nefarious worlds of power. Of course, it is always better to be knowledgeable, competent, and well connected. As in the cases of Maryanne Trump Barry and Jared Corey Kushner; she was and he is, both talented and connected.

After a successful career working in the U.S. Attorney's Office for the District of New Jersey from 1974 to 1983, Maryanne was nominated to the U.S. District Court for the District of New Jersey by President Ronald Reagan on September 14, 1983, confirmed by the U.S. Senate on September 30, and filled the vacated seat on October 6. Sixteen years later, President Bill Clinton nominated Barry to the U.S Court of Appeals for the 3rd Circuit on June 17, 1999. Upon her elevation to the Third District Court of Appeals in 1999, Barry resigned from the district court of New Jersey. The backstory of Barry's first appointment to the bench was that she had asked Donald for his assistance. Donald contacted Roy Cohn, Roy contacted Reagan, and it was done.[51]

Jared Kushner, the husband of Ivanka Trump and father of her three children, served as a senior advisor to his father-in-law and as the Director of the Office of American Innovation throughout Donald's four years of the presidency. Jared's father was a friend of both Clintons providing them with endorsements and money for their political campaigns. Jared's paternal grandparents were Holocaust survivors and Jared was raised in a modern Orthodox Jewish family in Livingston, New Jersey. Jared is one of the few persons in the world that Donald trusts. In 2019, he was said to have a net worth of $800 million.

JCK has been called the Acting President, the Decision-maker, the Main Artery to Trump's clogged heart, and The Prince of Everything because as Jared likes to explain: "Everything runs through me." Jared has also been referred to as Donald Trump's Junior Partner in Crime. Then again, he has been called Donald Trump's A$$-Kissing Son-in-Law as well as The Outlaw Son-in-Law. His most popular nicknames have included: The Clown Prince, Javanka, Vanilla ISIS, and The Good Boy. Word is that Jared can play the Donald like a violin but that he does not do so. Instead, he prefers instead allowing Trump to pretty much be himself. Probably nobody in the Trump Administration had as much influence over Donald as Jared did except for Stephen Miller.

Despite Jared's other monikers like Trump's Aide de Kampf, Little Prince Daisycakes, and the COVID Kid, Donald relied on Jared for almost everything. Donald after all was far too busy watching cable news and tweeting. During the 2016 presidential campaign, Jared helped to develop and run Trump's digital media strategy. Kushner was a key player in the First Step Act signed into law in 2018. This criminal justice reform bill was a lot "more bark than bite" as it only applied to federal prisoners. He also authored the Trump peace plan for dismissing the Israeli-Palestinian conflict. Jared was involved as well in the talks regarding the Middle East Peace Process, which in 2020 led to the signing of the Abraham Accords as well as to other normalization agreements between Israel and various Arab states. Perhaps the worst of Kushner was the influential role he had in Trump's playing down the COVID-19 response.

There is a very interesting backstory of Jared Kushner. Before becoming a White House advisor in 2017 at the age of 36, his impressive curriculum vita includes among other things: American investor, heir, real estate developer, and newspaper publisher. Kushner is the son of the former real estate developer Charles Kushner. From 2004 to 2006 Charles was incarcerated after pleading guilty to 18 counts of assisting in the filing of false tax returns, one count of retaliating against a federal witness, and one count of lying to the Federal Election Commission. The *Insider* headline read on December 23, 2020: "Trump pardoned Jared Kushner's dad Charles, who was convicted of tax crimes, witness tampering, and illegal campaign contributions."[52]

While at Columbia Law School and before that as an undergrad at Harvard,[53] he worked part-time in his dad's real estate empire the same as Donald had done during his undergraduate years at the University of Pennsylvania. When his father went to prison and Jared took over the management of Kushner Companies at age 23, his career took off like gangbusters. Over the next ten years, with both borrowed and suspected Russian laundered money,[54] Jared purchased close to $7 billion in property, mostly in New York City, including the office building at 666 Fifth Avenue for a then-record price of $1.8 billion. He acquired other types of properties as well buying the Observer Media, publisher of the New

York Observer. In 2014, with his brother Joshua and Ryan Williams, he co-founded the former Cadre, subsequently RealCadre LLC, an online real estate investment platform whose business partners included Goldman Sachs and billionaire George Soros.

Jared was not able to obtain Top Secret Security clearance until May 2018 when President Trump had to intervene on his son-in-law's behalf. There were issues having to do with lacking full disclosures of all his business investments, some of his omitted business dealings all together, conflicts of interests, and even profiting from policies that he was advocating for within the administration. When the billionaire families merged in 2009, it may not have been a marriage made exactly in heaven, but it was certainly the merging of two families composed of plenty of greed, ambition, corruption, and power to go around.[55] In many, but not in all ways, Jared was the ideal son-in-law for Donald's beloved daughter, Ivanka. Jared was also savvy enough to understand as he told Bob Woodward in an interview for *Rage* (2020), the president "basically did a full hostile takeover of the Republican Party." And, that Donald's takeover had nothing whatsoever to do with policy and everything to do with attitude.

Thinking about Bugsy, the Donald, and the Prince of Everything, by their middle thirties, these venture capitalists were all very well connected and at the top of their games, for better or worse as it were. An obvious difference between Bugsy, Donald, and Jared, only one of these men was self-made. The other two were born with golden spoons in their mouths. Not only do Jared and Donald share the tendencies to be less than truthful, but they are also fortunate enough to have their derrieres protected by their fathers and other powerful people. In the case of Jared's Top Secret Security Clearance that the State Department denied him, he had his father-in-law. In the case of Trump, for example, the acquisition of the very lucrative casino and gaming licenses for Atlantic City should have been denied by the several omissions and lies that were discovered and ignored during the speeded-up application process which Donald had manipulated.

Securing those gambling licenses from the State of New Jersey in 1981 was one of Trump's better get overs. Though Donald was caught being dishonest and should have been disqualified from obtaining the licenses for the obvious red flag reasons, he received them in a record-breaking short period of time. This story is well worth telling because it demonstrates the audacity as well as the ingenuity of Trump, not to mention those politicos that were running interference and doing Donald's bidding with the gaming commission. As the Donald bragged in *The Art of the Deal* (1987), he had succeeded in limiting the New Jersey attorney general's background investigation when he had applied for his first casino owner's license. At the time, the state of New Jersey's vetting process was detailed and comprehensive as it did not want Atlantic City becoming a mob-run Las Vegas East. The state even sent detectives overseas to interview people and verify documents. Applicants had "to fill out about fifty pages of details, including every address where they had lived in the past decade, any insurance claims, and any government investigations, civil or criminal."[56]

When Trump learned that the licensing process and inquiry would take 18 months, he immediately set about to rearrange the process in order to prevent more rather than less scrutiny into his past. With the assistance of Nick Ribis, a New Jersey attorney, Trump cut a deal of sorts with the New Jersey Attorney General John Degnan who was about to make a bid for the governorship and with G. Michael Brown the head of the New Jersey Division of Gaming Enforcement (DGE). Donald convinced and threatened them into abbreviating the investigation and ultimately overlooking things that should have denied the Donald's casino owner's license. First, Trump played the young and innocent card, he was "clean as a whistle" and at 35 years of age, how much wrongdoing could he have been involved with. Next, in order to expedite the approval process, Trump threatened not to build in Atlantic City where he had already purchased a prime property at the center of the Boardwalk. He also pointed out that his Grand Hyatt Hotel, next to Grand Central Terminal in midtown Manhattan, could accommodate a casino should the Empire state legalize casino gaming. As Donald pointed out, that wouldn't be very good for Atlantic City business or for Degnan's political future. And should Degnan oblige Trump with the licensing, Donald would become a vocal opponent of casino gambling outside of the state of New Jersey. This is pretty much Trump's playbook—smoke, mirrors, threats, and promises—when it comes to making deals to this day.

Degnan agreed to Trump's terms because he did not need a lawsuit or the adverse publicity during what turned out to be his failed bid for New Jersey governor. He did not guarantee that the application would be approved per se. However, if Donald cooperated and did not make waves, then the investigation could be reduced from 18 to six months. Of course, Donald did not fully cooperate. In response to some questions, he had to lie or leave them blank. For example, when asked whether he had been investigated for any reason by an agency of the government, the final official report filed by the DGE made no mention of two cases involving Trump and dealt with two others in a footnote indicating that these were not included when he submitted his original application. The first case was the

Justice Department's 1973 lawsuit for racial discrimination that we have already discussed. When asked in his casino application about whether he had ever been accused of any civil misconduct, which would have included racial discrimination, Donald checked the "no" box.

The second of these cases was a 1979 grand jury investigation into how Trump had acquired an option to buy the Penn Central railroad yards on the West Side of Manhattan. Trump was interviewed twice by the FBI and told that he was a target of the grand jury. Fortunately for the Donald, the five-year statute of limitations ran out before the investigation was complete. Trump was never charged. In 1980, the U.S. Attorney in Manhattan briefly investigated Trump for a third time about his acquisition of the Commodore Hotel for the purpose of remaking it into the Grand Hyatt. The old Commodore also owned by the Penn Central Transportation Company was related to the same bankruptcy residue and whether the debtors in the case were cheated. No charges were ever filed. A fourth omission had to do with the FBI subpoenaing and questioning Donald in 1980 about his dealings with mobster and convicted felon, John A. Cody. A close associate of the Gambino crime family and head of the local teamsters' unions, Cody also controlled the flow of ready-mix concrete in New York City, something Trump depended on for the building of Trump Tower, 1979 to 1983. Once again, no charges were ever filed.

In capital letters, the cover page of the application reads: FAILURE TO ANSWER ANY QUESTION COMPLETELY AND TRUTHFULLY WILL RESULT IN DENIAL OF YOUR LICENSE APPLICATION. As it turned out, Donald's omission on his application was of no negative consequence. When the DGE report was finished in record time and turned over to the Casino Control Commission, there was no mention that Trump had been involved in multiple federal investigations. There was not even any reference to two of the cases that made the newspapers, or to one of the reporters that had been interviewed about the cases by the DGE, as Johnston writes:

> The DGE gave Trump a pass on his failure to disclose. In a footnote to its 199-page report, the DGE said that just before completing its work, Trump had "volunteered" the information that he had failed to disclose. It was an early sign of what two Casino Control commissioners would later say was a pattern of DGE favoritism to Trump.[57]

Years later, Trump's relationship with the mob would be exposed when law enforcement witnesses observed Trump meeting at Cohn's town house with Salerno. Turns out that John Cody never received an apartment from Trump as suspected of union cooperation. However, Trump did help a woman friend of Cody's get a $3 million mortgage to pay for three apartments without any loan application. She modified one of them with an indoor pool for herself. Cody also had invested $100,000 of his own money in her apartments, and he often stayed there overnight. After Cody had been convicted in 1982 of racketeering, imprisoned, and was no longer in control of the union, Trump sued the woman for alteration work to the tune of $250,000. She countersued Trump for $20 million. Never settle Trump did so for $500,000 when her court papers accused Trump of taking kickbacks from his contractors, and such evidence could become the basis of a criminal proceeding against Trump. Soon after, federal prosecutors brought a major case against eight mobsters. Charges included inflating the price of concrete for Trump's East 61st Street apartment building.

Donald on his own, well not exactly

The Donald is fond of saying, "I built what I built myself." In virtually every era of Mr. Trump's life, his "finances were deeply intertwined with, and dependent on, his father's wealth." By the time Donny was 17, dad had given his favorite son "part ownership of a 52-unit apartment building." Soon after graduating from the University of Pennsylvania, Donald "was receiving the equivalent of $1 million a year from his father." That figure had risen to $5 million annually by the Donald's 40s and 50s. When Fred Trump hired Donald full time, he made him like no other ordinary salaried employee. Donald became Fred's property manager, his landlord, his banker, and his consultant. Donald was given loan after loan; many were never repaid. That's not all. Fred provided money for Donald's employees:

> money to buy stocks, money for his first Manhattan offices and money to renovate those offices. He gave him three trust funds. He gave him shares in multiple partnerships. He gave him $10,000 Christmas checks. He gave him laundry revenue from his buildings.[58]

Much of Fred's "giving" was structured looting from him to reduce annually his own bottom-line taxability, to sidestep gift taxes, to avoid inheritance taxes, and to ensure the future of the family empire. *The New York Times*' investigation had documented 295 streams of revenue that Fred, Sr. had created to enrich all his children and their offspring. However, shortly after Fred, Jr. died in 1981, his wife and children were cut off from the revenue streams, and these were divided up among the four remaining siblings. The records also reveal that as the Donald "careened from one financial disaster to the next, his father found ways to give him substantially more money" than his three siblings received. By 1975 when Donald was only 29 and before he had sold his first Manhattan apartment, he had collected $9 million in 2018 dollars from his father.

In the mid-1980s, at the time when the Donald was first making his entrée into Atlantic City, Fred hatched a brilliant plan to start depleting his holdings and wealth, sharply increasing the flow of his money to his children, in effect, establishing a mini empire within his larger empire. The plan involved not only transferring eight of his buildings to his children, but also creating several revenue streams in the process. Fred converted seven of these buildings into cooperatives and helped the kids' covert the eighth. "That meant inviting tenants to buy their apartments, generating a three-way windfall for Donald Trump and his siblings, from selling units, from renting unsold units and from collecting mortgage payments."[59] According to The Times article, there was

> no evidence to be found that the Trump children had to come up with money of their own to buy their father's mortgages. Most were purchased from Fred Trump's banks by trusts and partnerships that he set up and seeded with money.[60]

The icing on this "financial cake" was that Fred Trump made his four living offspring his bankers, unleashing a big new source of revenue for the Donald and his siblings. Talk about a real "sugar daddy" with all types of benefits.

It was only a short matter of time before Fred and his companies were extending large loans and lines of credit to DJT. The flow of cash was so constant at times it was as if Donald had his own Money Store or Daddy, Inc. Some of these loans were never paid back, others became gifts, and most were interest-free without any repayment schedules. For example, after the 1987 stock market crashed and the economy was still reeling, the Donald was doubling down, thanks to father Fred's ever-expanding line of credit. "He bought the Plaza Hotel in 1988 for $407.5 million. He bought the Eastern Airlines shuttle fleet in 1989 for $365 million" and renamed it the Trump Shuttle.[61] By 1990, the ultimate silent partner had already transferred the 2018-dollar equivalent of more than $46 million to Donald.

This was at the time when the Trump Taj Mahal casino was opening in Atlantic City. It would shortly be hemorrhaging and in need of at least a

$1 million a day infusion just to cover its debt. Similarly, this was the same year that Fred Trump's bookkeeper, Howard Snyder, would be dispatched to Trump's Castle casino with a check to purchase $3.35 million worth of casino chips without placing a bet in order to help raise the necessary funds to make an $18.4 million bond payment due at the end of the year. This was the very same year that the Donald went around his father's back, had one of his own lawyers drawing up an amended estate will, and tried unsuccessfully to get his old man's John Hancock on the document. The 85-year-old Fred already suffering from dementia was still astute enough to "smell a rat." He quickly turned to sibling federal judge and daughter Maryanne Trump Berry. After she read the "codicil" to the will, she too smelled the Donald. Among other things, the amended will would have protected Donald's portion of the inheritance from his creditors, his first wife, Ivana Trump, and gave him sole control over his father's estate. Judge Maryanne and Fred found new estate lawyers to represent them with the charge: "Protect assets from DJT, Donald's creditors." They did so.[62]

Sibling fraud and transferring daddy's empire

Though Fred's business empire was built on the back of government financing, he loathed paying taxes and he would do anything to avoid them. Mostly, he was busy steering money away from the Internal Revenue Service and siphoning it off to his five children. In much the same way, the Donald and his siblings with the blessing of their father and his closest advisors in the early 1990s devised and implemented an "inheritance plan" to convert Fred and Mary Anne's apartment buildings worth many hundreds of millions of dollars into their shared wealth to avoid huge inheritance taxes rates of 55 percent when Fred died in 1999.[63] This family business practice of thieving and defrauding the government by moving money around represents a classic win-win scheme of cheating. First, the offending heirs to the estate do not have to shell out for their fair share of inheritance taxes. Second, the siphoning parties as well can reduce the amounts of actual profits and taxes they owed.

Executed over the next decade, this plan blended traditional and unorthodox strategies and techniques. Rewriting Fred's will to legally maximize his tax avoidance was an example of the former. Devising a fraudulent scheme in which they, the offspring siblings gained ownership of their father's buildings without having to spend a penny of their own, was an example of the latter. The mountain of cash was ipso facto turned into a molehill of cash, and hundreds of millions of dollars that otherwise would have gone to the U.S. Treasury went instead to the children of Fred Trump. As part of an ingenious conspiracy to funnel money to his children, the Trump siblings incorporated a company named All Country Building Supply & Maintenance to overcharge Fred Trump for repairs and improvements on his properties. All County had no corporate offices and its only other purpose was to make large cash gifts to his children and to disguise them as legitimate business transactions to avoid the 55 percent inheritance taxes.[64]

All County systematically overcharged Fred Trump for thousands of individual items, while Fred and his staff continued to negotiate with the vendors as they always had. In turn, the Trumps used the padded All County invoices to justify higher rent increases from their tenants. "State records show that after All County's creation, the Trumps got approval to raise rents on thousands of apartments by claiming more than $30 million in major capital improvements. Tenants repeatedly protested the increases, almost always to no avail."[65] The simultaneous self-dealing at the heart of this fraudulent arrangement is illustrated by Robert Trump whose father paid him a $500,000 annual salary. Robert also approved the payments made by Fred to All County generating invoices that fell to Fred's favorite nephew John Walter. Walter was also the person that computerized the payroll for Fred Trump. Not only was Walters on the payroll for his services but so too was an assistant paid to work on Walter's side businesses. Many years later, when interviewed for *The Times* article in 2018 and long after the statute of limitations had lapsed, Adam S. Kaufmann, a former chief of investigations for the Manhattan district attorney's office, was quoted as saying, "All of this smells like a crime." Mr. Kaufmann also believed that the Trumps' use of All County Building Supply and Maintenance would certainly have warranted investigation for "defrauding tenants, tax fraud and filing false documents." Just another business-as-usual day in the world of the Trump Organization.

Trump's most public and recent settlement occurred just days after he became the president-elect in November 2016. As an ABC News story reported, attendees of Trump University will be getting paid back as victims of Donald Trump's fraudulent university. Judge Gonzalo Curiel, a federal judge in the Southern District of California, finalized the $25 million settlement to be paid from the now-defunct real estate seminar called Trump University in the spring of 2018. The final actual amount of relief to the Trump victims exceeded the number that the class-action lawsuit initially negotiated. The federal judge remarked that the "settlement marked a stunning reversal by President Trump, who for years refused to compensate the victims of his sham university." Judge Curiel's statement added further, "My office won't hesitate to hold those who commit fraud accountable, no matter how rich or powerful they may be." The Trump Organization spokesperson had a very different spin. He claimed that when the lawsuit was originally filed back in 2013, Mr. Trump had "no doubt" that Trump University would prevail should the case go to trial. However, once the Donald was elected the president, the "resolution of these matters" became a priority, so Trump could focus on running the country or something to that effect.[66]

Notes

1 With respect to racial animus, one has only to look to the 1973 housing and racial discrimination lawsuit filed by the DOJ against Fred Trump and Donald Trump, which will be discussed later in this chapter, or to Donald's full-page advertisements to give the Central Park Five the death penalty for the violent raping and near death of the Central Park Jogger in 1989 that they were falsely convicted of and later exonerated by a confession of the guilty party, for which Trump would still not apologize for 30 years later. As for the physical objectification of women, since the 1980s at least 26 women have publicly accused Trump of sexual assault of one kind or another.

2 James D. Zirin, 2019. *Plaintiff in Chief: A Portrait of Donald Trump in 3500 Lawsuits*. New York: St. Martins Publishing Group.

3 As Robert J. Sampson and John H. Laub argue in *Crime in the Making: Pathways and Turning Points through Life*. Boston, MA: Harvard University Press, 1993, criminality is neither constant nor inconsistent with noncriminal behavior and is affected by changing social forces over a life-course.

4 David Cay Johnston, 2016. *The Making of Trump*. Brooklyn, NY: Melville House.

5 Quoted in Amanda Luz Henning Santiago, 2019. Trump's Mob Connections. *City & State New York*. September 27. https://www.cityandstateny.com/politics/2019/09/trumps-mob-connections/176871/.

6 Eliza Collins, 2016. Trump: I Could Run Both My Business and Be President 'Perfectly'. *USA Today*, November 22. https://www.usatoday.com/story/news/politics/onpolitics/2016/11/22/trump-organization-white-house/94292010/.

7 Michael D'Antonio, 2016. Donald Trump's Long, Strange History of Using Fake Names. *Fortune*. May 18. https://fortune.com/2016/05/18/donald-trump-fake-names/.

8 Quoted in Johnston, 2016: 24.

9 A "fixer" is a person who makes illicit or devious arrangements for other people.

10 Michael Cohen, 2020. *Disloyal, a Memoir: The True Story of the Former Personal Attorney to the President of the United States*. New York: Skyline Publishing, p. 17.

11 Ibid: 22.

12 SahidFawaz,2016.HereAreAllofTrump'sBankruptciesandFailedBusinesses.Labor 411. September 8. https://labor411.org/411-blog/here-are-all-of-trump-s-bankruptcies-and-failed-businesses/.

13 Amy B. Wang, 2017. Did the 2011 White House Correspondents' Dinner Spur Trump to Run for President? *Chicago Tribune*. February 26. https://www.chicagotribune.com/nation-world/ct-white-house-correspondents-dinner-trump-20170226-story.html.

14 After watching an episode of *Saturday Night Live* in March 2019, an incensed Trump tweeted:

> It's truly incredible that shows like Saturday Night Live, not funny/no talent, can spend all of their time knocking the same person (me), over and over, without so much of a mention of 'the other side.' Like an advertisement without consequences. Same with Late Night Shows. Should Federal Election Commission and/or FCC look into this?

Quoted in Asawin Suebsaeng and Adam Rawnsley, 2021. Trump Wanted His Justice Department to Stop 'SNL' From Teasing Him. *Daily Beast*. June 22. https://www.thedailybeast.com/trump-wanted-his-justice-department-to-stop-snl-from-teasing-him.

15 Barbara A. Res, 2020. *Tower of Lies: What My 18 Years of Working with Donald Trump Reveals About Him*. Los Angeles, CA: Graymalkin Media.

16 Ibid.

17 Johnston, 2016: x.

18 David Barstow, Susanne Craig and Russ Buettner. 2018. Trump Engaged in Suspect Tax Schemes as He Reaped Riches From His Father. *The New York Times*, October 2. https://www.nytimes.com/interactive/2018/10/02/us/politics/donald-trump-tax-schemes-fred-trump.html.

19 Ibid.

20 Ibid.

21 Mike McIntire, Russ Buettner and Susanne Craig, 2020. How Reality-TV Fame Handed Trump a $427 Million Lifeline. *The New York Times*, September 28. https://www.nytimes.com/interactive/2020/09/28/us/donald-trump-taxes-apprentice.html.

22 Quoted in Sarah Pulliam Bailey, Julie Zauzmer and Josh Dawsey, 2020. Trump Mocks the Faith of Others. His Own Religious Practices Remain Opaque. *The Washington Post*. February 14. https://www.washingtonpost.com/religion/2020/02/14/trump-mocks-faith-others-his-own-religious-practices-remain-opaque/. See also, Cohen, 2020: 125–133.

23 Quoted in Cohen, 2020: 133.

24 Nick Anderson, 2021. Liberty University Sues Ex-president Jerry Falwell Jr., Seeks More Than $10 million, Alleging Breach of Contract and Cover-up of Scandal. *The Washington Post*, April 16. https://www.washingtonpost.com/education/2021/04/16/liberty-university-jerry-falwell-jr-lawsuit/.

25 Ibid: 19.

26 Ibid: 17.

27 Adam Serwer, 2018. The Cruelty Is the Point. *The Atlantic*. October 3. https://www.theatlantic.com/ideas/archive/2018/10/the-cruelty-is-the-point/572104/.

28 Quoted in Ben Rhodes, 2021. *After the Fall: Being American in the World We've Made*. New York: Random House.

29 Elliott Oring, 2003. *Engaging Human*. Champlain: University of Illinois Press.

30 Harry Lefever, 1981. Playing the Dozens: A Mechanism for Social Control. *Phylon* 42 (1): 73–85.

31 Edwin Schur, 1984. *Labelling Women Deviant: Gender, Stigma, and Social Control.* New York: Random House.
32 Viveca S. Greene, 2019. "Deplorable" Satire: Alt-Right Memes, White Genocide Tweets, and Redpilling Normies. *Studies in American Humor* 5 (1): 67. https://www.jstor.org/stable/10.5325/studamerhumor.5.10031.
33 Mary R. Trump, 2020. *Too Much and Never Enough: How My Family Created the World's Most Dangerous Man.* New York: Simon & Schuster, pp. 200–201.
34 Res, 2020: 3.
35 Ibid: 6–7.
36 Quoted in Ibid: 31.
37 Ibid: 31.
38 Ibid: 2.
39 Johnston, 2016: 14–15.
40 Ibid: 15–16.
41 Ibid: 16.
42 Andrea Bernstein, 2020. Trump Pushed for a Sweetheart Tax Deal on His First Hotel. *ProPublica.* January 22. https://www.propublica.org/article/trump-pushed-for-a-sweetheart-tax-deal-on-his-first-hotel-its-cost-new-york-city-410-068-399-and-counting.
43 Ibid.
44 Wayne Barrett, 1992. *Trump: The Deals and the Downfall.* New York: HarperCollins.
45 Michael Kranish and Robert O'Harrow, Jr., 2016. Inside the Government's Racial Bias Case Again Donald Trump's Company, and How He Fought It. *The Washington Post,* January 23. https://www.washingtonpost.com/politics/inside-the-governments-racial-bias-case-against-donald-trumps-company-and-how-he-fought-it/2016/01/23/fb90163e-bfbe-11e5-bcda-62a36b394160_story.html.
46 Johnston, 2016: 36.
47 Quoted in Ibid.
48 Ibid.
49 Johnston, 2016: 38.
50 Ibid.
51 Trump, 2020.
52 Azmi Haroun, 2020. Trump Pardoned Jared Kushner's Dad Charles, Who Was Convicted of Tax Crimes, Witness Tampering, and Illegal Campaign Contributions. *Insider.* December 23. https://www.businessinsider.com/trump-pardoned-charles-kushner-jared-father-crimes-2020-12.
53 Jared's admission to Harvard was aided by his father's $2.5 million endowment gift to the university.
54 David Enrich, 2019. Deutsche Bank Staff Saw Suspicious Activity in Trump and Kushner Accounts. *The New York Times.* May 19. https://www.nytimes.com/2019/05/19/business/deutsche-bank-trump-kushner.html. See also, Grace Panetta and Sonam Sheth, 2019. The FBI Is Reportedly Investigating Deutsche Bank over Money-laundering Regulation Compliance, Including Transactions Connected to Jared Kushner. *Insider.* June 19. https://www.businessinsider.com/fbi-investigating-deutsche-bank-for-money-laundering-kushner-transactions-2019-6.
55 Vicky Ward, 2019. *Kushner, Inc.: Greed. Ambition. Corruption. The Extraordinary Story of Jared Kushner and Ivanka Trump.* New York: St. Martin's Press. See also, Andrea Bernstein, 2020. *American Oligarchs: The Kushners, the Trumps, and the Marriage of Money and Power.* New York: W.W. Norton & Company.

56 Johnston, 2018: 41.
57 Ibid: 45.
58 Barstow, Craig and Buettner, 2018.
59 Ibid.
60 Ibid.
61 Ibid.
62 Ibid.
63 Ibid.
64 Ibid.
65 Ibid.
66 Aaron Katersky and M.I. Nestel, 2018. Judge Finalizes $25 Million Settlement for 'Victims of Donald Trump's Fraudulent University'. *ABC News*. April 9. https://abcnews.go.com/US/judge-finalizes-25-million-settlement-victims-donald-trumps/story?id=54347237.

3

WEAPONIZING THE LAW, LITIGATION, AND LEGALITY

Lawsuits especially in litigious and celeb-oriented societies like the United States garner much attention. Not unlike professional sports, litigation involving big business, entertainment, politics, or individual grievances has long been considered one of America's favorite pastimes. Similarly, lawsuits are considered by many people to be highly emotional and dramatic affairs. Apart from high-profile litigation or criminal adjudication, however, most lawsuits are terribly boring, barely sufferable, and usually inconsequential to all but a handful of people. As the saying goes, the only winners in lawsuits are the lawyers, presuming that they get paid for their services.[1] Otherwise, for those caught up in lengthy legal battles whatever side of the conflict, most litigants find the experience to be costly to their pocketbooks, reputations, and mental wellness. As someone who has been involved in more than 4,000 legal battles since 1973, the Donald is clearly an exception to this legal rule. He loves his litigation as much as his cans of diet coke and boxes of fast food. As a real estate tycoon, entrepreneur, entertainer, and politician, Trump boasts: "I've taken advantage of the laws. And frankly, so has everybody else in my position."[2] Regarding the "Projector-in-Chief," virtually everything that DJT accuses everyone of doing to him is usually a case of "the pot calling the kettle black."

Estimates have varied as to the number of unnecessary deaths caused by the Trump administration's response to the coronavirus pandemic, from the misleading public statements and the lack of federal assistance to states, to the testing delays and industry influence.[3] In fairness to Trump, it did

DOI: 10.4324/9781003221548-5

not help that the United States has no national or integrated health care system or that the Center for Disease Control (CDC) did not have its act together. With respect to 545,000 deaths by the airing of CNN's documentary, "COVID WAR: The Pandemic Doctors Speak Out" on March 28, 2021, Dr. Deborah Birx, the White House coronavirus response coordinator under the former president, stated that had the cities and states been able to aggressively fight COVID-19 after the first surge, as many as 400,000 lives would have been mitigated against. Former CDC Director Dr. Robert Redfield spoke about how the former Health and Human Secretary Alex Azar on more than one occasion wanted him to revise the CDC's Morbidity and Mortality Weekly Report on the deaths and the disease as well as on various recommendations to the public.

At the same time, critics of Redfield, a Trump appointment to head the CDC with an illustrious yet controversial career dealing with HIV/AIDS and opioids, argue that the White House failing to protect the credibility of the massive agency outmaneuvered Redfield. Specifically, they refer to the executive branch "meddling into science-based CDC guidance involving school closings and religious gatherings."[4] While there was a constant COVID-19 war going on in the Trump White House between the science and the politics, only Dr. Anthony Fauci, the director of the National Institute of Allergy and Infectious Diseases who could not be fired by Trump, would on occasion push back publicly against the former president's spurious virus claims, especially about how well the United States was doing. None of the other scientists or members of Trump's U.S. Coronavirus Task Force, including its head Vice President Mike Pence, ever spoke out on behalf of science over politics.

If the lawsuits come charging Trump with criminal negligence typically defined as gross or reckless disregard for human life, resulting in serious injury or death, Trump and his lawyers will be well prepared for his defense. There were Trump's incriminating comments made to Bob Woodward—acknowledging that "This is deadly stuff" and that he always tried to "play down" the virus so as not to panic the people or the stock market—recorded during interviews in February 2020. There were also his repeated statements about the coronavirus throughout the spring and summer of 2020 that were in direct conflict with information that Trump knew was untrue. Moreover, his personal behavior in the White House, during official ceremonies, and at campaign rallies not only spread the COVID-19 wherever he was or went, but his manifest disdain for safety involving the wearing of masks and social distancing served as a model for and was mimicked by millions of other science deniers.[5] Trump's influence in the

United States certainly contributed to the anti-vaccine and anti-mask mania that had persisted throughout the second year of the pandemic.

Within 24 hours after the CNN documentary aired, Trump attacked Fauci and Birx referring to them as "self-promoters," something that the Donald has specialized in his whole life. The Donald also doubled down on the fact that he intentionally ignored their science because they "had bad policy decisions" that would have put "millions of lives at risk" and kept "our economy from reopening," which "would have led us directly into a COVID caused depression." In essence, Trump has once again convicted himself of criminal negligence as he continues, "I only kept Dr. Fauci and Dr. Birx on because they worked for the U.S. government for so long – they are like a bad habit!" Talk about a bad habit, the master of lies finished his statement by telling us "Time has proven me correct."[6] Actually, on this subject and others, the Donald has been proven correct only in the world of conspiracy theories and alternative time and space dimensions.

Persons can easily argue that Trump was not only knowingly careless or mistaken, but that he also acted with clear and deadly consequences for others in ways that no reasonable person would have. In short, Trump knew the risks of COVID-19 and chose not only to ignore the science, but also to undermine it. Trump preferred to spread the contagion and disinformation everywhere he went offline and online, negatively affecting his most loyal political allies. Nevertheless, any litigation both politically and legally would have an uphill battle trying to prove that Trump directly caused the deaths of specific people, let alone that he was liable for the collective suffering of hundreds of thousands of people.

Hence, the prosecution's burden in the United States vs. Donald J. Trump would be to establish murder beyond a reasonable doubt and that will never find its way into a criminal court. A plaintiff's class action civil suit with the burden to prove guilt by a preponderance of the evidence is not out of the question, but it too is very unlikely. Either way, Trump knows that whatever he has tweeted and stated publicly so long as he says it obliquely for why he did or did not do something is of little legal consequence. Should the government or a class action civil lawsuit be filed against Trump, he will most likely file a counter lawsuit for greater damages than the ones he is being sued for.

Since Donald hired Roy Cohn in 1973 to defend his father and himself from the racial discrimination suit filed against them by the U.S. Department of Justice, this has been a fundamental part of his litigious modus operandi. The courts for having no legal foundation whatsoever dismiss the vast majority of Trump's countersuits. Exceptions do occur when the opposing litigants with their lacking resources and staying power decide to fold altogether or settle the case to Donald's liking. As for the likelihood of COVID-19 lawsuits involving Trump, most likely they will never occur. At the same time, perhaps the Donald's most pernicious and deadly legacy will be the needless numbers of Republican deaths that have occurred in primarily Trumpian red states from the Delta Variant post the availability of the vaccines. Many if not most of these can be directly connected to Trump's politicalization of the pandemic, his spreading of misinformation, dismissal of the science, and modeling of inappropriate behavior.[7]

Over the course of his lifetime, especially during his first real campaign for the presidency, while POTUS and as the former president, Trump weaponized the law, litigation, and legality. He also transformed everyday speech with his norm-shattering brashness and word choices full of hate speech and blasphemy. In the process, his demagoguery weaponized language in contemporary politics and forged a new kind of presidential power never seen before. Trump accomplished his linguistic slight of tongue by tapping into the political differences of the left and right. He also tapped into the local and global currents of right-wing populism, xenophobic fear mongering, white victimhood, and a resurging patriarchy. Not only would his Trumpian sycophants and alt-right media adopt a similar discourse, but so too would much of the liberal-based media as well as his anti-Trumpists' detractors.[8]

Where's my Roy Cohn?

Roy Cohn (1927–1986) was a lawyer, a rabid anti-communist, a closeted homosexual, a homophobe, a Jewish anti-Semite, a misogynist, a legal warrior on behalf of the House Un-American Activities Committee, and a registered Democrat who almost exclusively supported Republicans.[9] Cohn was also Trump's mentor, friend, and advisor-in-chief. He escorted Mary Anne Trump to the opening of Trump Tower in 1983. During the ribbon-cutting ceremony, Roy posed for photos with Donald, his mother, and New York Mayor Ed Koch. When Cohn was dying of AIDS in March 1986, Trump gave him a farewell dinner party in Florida, a $200,000-a-place setting tribute to the ruthless real-life villain of the law. Two months later at Cohn's disbarment hearings "for reprehensible conduct," Trump testified as a character witness swearing that Roy was "loyal" and "possesses the highest degree of integrity."

Cohn was disbarred. He died two weeks later. Michael Cohen, another personal attorney and Trump "fixer" for more than a decade, was disbarred in 2018 from the State of New York. This occurred at the same time as he was sentenced to three years in federal prison and fined $50,000 following his guilty plea to tax evasion and campaign finance violations on behalf of Donald. Rounding out Trump's "trifecta" of personal attorneys and fixers was his most recently retained Rudy Giuliani, former Mayor of NYC, who a New York court suspended on June 24, 2021, from practicing law in the state, citing his work on behalf of the former president. Not to mention that Rudy has been under investigation since 2019 for matters related to Ukraine and his business dealings with two indicted Soviet-born associates. Coincidentally, these U.S. prosecutors are from the same Manhattan office of the Southern District of New York that once upon a time Giuliani oversaw.

Cohn taught Trump the art of the linguistic lie or how to lie unabashedly as a fundamental way of moving through life. As Cohn's apprentice, Donald would eventually take the art of his teacher's lie to an even lower level of transparency. For example, Trump became perfectly comfortable denying former lies of his that everybody else knew he had uttered or tweeted. Donald's primer on the law included Cohn's three rules of litigation where neither the facts nor the law matter: Never settle, never surrender; Counterattack, counter-sue immediately; and No matter the outcome, always claim victory. Over the course of his litigious life, Trump was better at adhering to rule numbers two and three than rule number one because the social reality of legal facts may dictate this outcome. Cohn also taught Trump other related lessons, including but not limited to focusing on short-term victories, employing any unscrupulous means necessary to achieve them, doing end-runs around the judicial systems, fixing disputed outcomes, and the value of always defending yourself by going on the offensive. These "defensive offensive" moves often require attacking and bashing your opponents with lies and falsehoods about them. Nonetheless, they are often apt to lower an opponent's credibility.

When it comes to learning (1) how one becomes a criminal, (2) why something becomes a crime providing the opportunity of labeling someone as criminal, and (3) whether or not that label will be applied or not and to whom, I would be delinquent not to give a shout out to the individual and collective body of works of the three Edwins of 20th-century criminology: Lemert,[10] Schur,[11] and Sutherland.[12] With respect to the "father" of white-collar crime and his learning theory of criminality, "differential association," Sutherland posited that crime is learned primarily through intimate actions of communication with other individuals but also by way of secondary or mass groupings of people where persons learn the values, attitudes, techniques, and motivation conducive to criminal behavior. According to Sutherland, the modeling of criminality increases or decreases depending on the "frequency, duration, priority, and intensity" of a person's engagement with the competing patterns of criminal and anticriminal interactions. With respect to Donald's early socialization and subsequent coming of age, there were his two father figures. Both Fred Sr. and Roy were fully engaged in illicit activities much of their lives as were the other persons that Donald saw crossing the criminal pathways of these men. Ergo, Donald's imprinted claims that everybody else is cheating and dishonest too. So why pick on him? It's not just unfair; it's a witch-hunt.

Two years after graduating college, Trump was making his move from Queens to Manhattan, living in a crummy little apartment at Third Avenue and 75th street on the East Side with a view of a water tank. Almost every night, Donald was out trying to hook up with beautiful women and powerful men associated with Le Club and Studio 54. After joining Le Club, not unlike an upper-middle-class anthropologist Trump found himself hobnobbing with and learning the ways of the rich from mostly old white men adorned by striking young women from New York and abroad. As he was studying the wealthy one evening, Donald met the infamous Roy Cohn whose reputation had already preceded him. Trump knew that Cohn could be vicious and was quite willing to brutalize other people on behalf of his clients.

In other words, Donald knew that Roy was not exactly a Boy Scout. Moreover, when he discovered that Cohn had spent more than two thirds of his life under indictment for one charge or the other, Donald became more fascinated by the outlandish attorney. Before Cohn was retained to represent the Trumps in their Title VIII lawsuit with the Justice Department, the young Donald and Roy had to come to terms about litigious relationships. Trump's story is that he had told Cohn that he did not like lawyers because they delay deals from happening, tell you no and why you cannot do something, and that they are always looking to settle rather than fight cases. Cohn agreed, which surprised Trump. Most importantly, the young 27-year-old whose father put him in charge of dealing with their legal problems had found an attorney whose loyalty to his client would always trump his integrity for the law. The rest is history: Roy became not only Donald's legal counsel but also his business mentor and "like a second father" as the pre-politician Trump used to say.

Cohn left Donald with his "take no enemies" approach to conflict resolution whether personal, political, or legal. There were other indelible imprints of behavior that Cohn bestowed on Trump. For example, the never married gay misogynist as well as a bonafide propertyless multimillionaire who never owned any property in his legal name taught Donald the value of getting the most out of his three prenup agreements with wives Ivana, Marla, and Melania. Similarly, Cohn taught Trump the value of media "catch-and-kill" contracts to silence other women that he had had long time affairs with such as Karen McDougal, a *Playboy* centerfold model. The Donald also learned the value of one of his most used means for suppressing the truth from coming out—the nondisclosure agreements (NDAs). Trump's well-known NDAs have been used to silence former employees, associates, and so on, not to mention his former sexual liaisons with the pornography actress and director Stormy Daniels.

One might have thought that NDAs were safer than hush money payments, especially ones made during the final days of the 2016 presidential campaign. Think again. While Trump's attorney Michael Cohen went to prison for paying off Ms. Daniels on behalf of the Donald with the latter's signatures on some of the hush money checks, the Federal Election Commission, thanks to two Republican commissioners, dismissed the case against Trump. These commissioners lamely claimed that the matter was "not the best use of agency resources" because the "public record is complete."[13] What about Trump's admission of guilt or his criminal conviction and his orange jumpsuit?

Plaintiff or defendant doesn't really matter to the Donald

Before Trump became the president in 2017 and over the course of four decades, he was arguably the greatest litigant of all time. According to *USA Today* and to the American Bar Association, from 1986 to 2016, Trump had been involved on the order of 3,500 to 4,000 lawsuits, proceedings, and investigations. A Google search for "Trump lawsuits" yielded in less than one second roughly 21 million hits.[14] In about 60 percent of the legal cases, he was the plaintiff. In some 500 cases, judges dismissed plaintiffs' claims against Trump; hundreds of other cases ended with the available public record unclear about the resolution. Trump has sued and been sued for both business and personal reasons. His legal targets have included personal assistants, celebrities, mental patients, prisoners, unions, rival businesspeople, and his own family members. Trump's win-loss record is an impressive one, winning 451 times and losing only 38 times. By the way, when Trump loses a law case, he usually stiffs his lawyers for malfeasance, incompetence, or whatever. In some of those instances, Donald has then found himself in litigation with his former attorneys trying to collect their money for services rendered.

Trump has ironically sued others for fraud, for breach of trust, for breach of contract, for violation of the Racketeer Influenced and Corrupt Organizations Act, for government favoritism, for libel, and for misappropriation or adulteration of the brand name TRUMP. Except for the last offense, Trump has repeatedly violated all the other crimes that he has sued other people for. Concurrently, Trump has been sued for race and sex discrimination, sexual harassment, fraud, and breaches of trust, money laundering, defamation, stiffing his creditors, and defaulting on loans. Whether as plaintiff or defendant what is important to underscore is that neither the facts nor the laws are of importance to the Donald because:

> Whether he was entitled to the benefit of the law, or whether he could support his positions with evidence, or whether his claims stated a cause or action, or whether he was really damaged was irrelevant to Donald Trump. What was important was to use the lawsuit to attract attention, to exert economic pressure, and to prove he was the kid on the block not to be messed with. And his adversaries largely gave way during his rise to celebrity and power.[15]

Throughout Trump's professional career, he has always been at war with legal standards and normative rules that he regards as made to be broken, or avoided at all costs to all parties, including himself. His lifetime of adjudication is found in a lengthy background of litigation accompanied by a pathological pattern of lying in which Donald's particular style of intimidating evolved and morphed into one courtroom episodic drama after another like a reality TV show. As James Zirin, former assistant U.S. attorney for the Southern District of New York, writes in *Plaintiff in Chief: A Portrait of Donald Trump in 3500 Lawsuits*, it should have surprised nobody familiar with Trump's legal history that when he became the president that "he would seek to weaponize the justice system, use his power to bend the law, attack his enemies and critics, and claim victory when there was none."[16]

Most importantly, the former president used his time in the White House to stave off the prosecution by Manhattan district Attorney Cyrus R. Vance Jr. (D) and New York Attorney General Letitia James (D) of the Trump Organization and his associates, until July 1, 2021 when the organization and its CFO Allen Weisselberg were arraigned on multiple criminal charges alleging a 15-year tax scheme that was still going on as of June 30, 2021.[17] Straight out of the Cohn-Trump playbook, the Trump Organization released one of their classic assaults on the prosecutors rather than an affirmative defense of the indicted CFO or Donald's organization:

> Allen Weisselberg is a loving and devoted husband, father and grandfather who has worked for the Trump Organization for 48 years. He is now being used by the Manhattan District Attorney as a pawn in a scorched earth attempt to harm the former President. The District Attorney is bringing a case involving employee benefits that neither the IRS nor any other District Attorney would ever think of bringing. This is not justice; this is politics.[18]

Donald's remarks on the indictment were a bit less polished than his organization. He attacked the prosecutors as being part of the "radical left" and also for being "rude, nasty, and totally biased." The Donald with his usual refrain tells us how he is being persecuted and how this is the ultimate witch-hunt, "the crime of the century." Fearing that one of his loyal employees may eventually flip on him, Trump true to form tells us further how the prosecutors are "in search of a crime" and that they "will do anything to frighten people into making up the stories or lies that they want."[19]

Of course, this is simply part of Trump's preparation for litigation should it come to that. After all, he and his legal team know that neither the law nor the facts are on their side. And they are hoping that neither will matter as much as the political hullabaloo that they intend on raising for the benefit of at least one member of the jury, should the judge allow the trial to turn into a political circus. As David Frum, author of *Trumpocalypse: Restoring American Democracy* (2020), has correctly put it: "Trump worked all of his life on the theory that law can be subordinated to political favors and political pressures. That theory has carried him this far—and it's pretty far, all things considered."[20]

Unlike the thousands of other lawsuits up to now, none have raised the possibility that at the end of the day, the Trump Organization may become an organization of the past and that the Donald may, indeed, be in that orange jumpsuit.[21] Regardless of the outcome, as Zirin argues, Trump's lifetime of litigation especially as plaintiff but also as a defendant has always been about Trump's psychological need to be a winner rather than a loser:

> Trump wakes up every morning with an irrepressible desire to win, to win big, and to win soon. Trump is a day trader. The finish line for him is always only hours away. Over the years of his professional history, he became more than litigious: he acquired a litigation mentality. He was possessed of an ugly combativeness coupled with the natural mendacity of a born salesman and promoter.[22]

However, the lawsuits themselves were means rather than ends, usually ending without winners or losers, and mostly settlements closed to public disclosure, where the Donald could always claim that he was victorious. Hence, Trump sued at the drop of a hat or as often as he played 36 holes of golf in one day. "He sued for sport; he sued to achieve a sense of control; and he sued to make a point. He sued as a means of destroying or silencing those who crossed him." Trump uses the law whether he is the plaintiff or the defendant as a means of bullying and punishing his adversaries regardless of who they are. As the Plaintiff-in-Chief, his "pattern was more 'float like a butterfly' than 'sting like a bee'." As was often the case, "he would sue and, shortly thereafter, drop the case. He sued to make headlines, for the entertainment value, and to reinforce his power over others."[23] When Trump is the defendant in a lawsuit, he plays offense or weaponizes the law as much as he can, but most of his legal energies in these cases are expended on hurdling over or sidestepping the law. Whether as a plaintiff or as a defendant, Trump's barks are usually worse than his bites.

Zirin has categorized plaintiff Trump's litigation in a very interesting way:

- If you partner with Donald Trump, chances are you will wind up litigating with him.
- If you question his professed net worth as overstated, he will sue you for defamation.
- If you enroll in his university or buy one of his condominium apartments, chances are that you will want your money back.
- If you purchase a membership in one of his golf clubs, you may find that there were misrepresentations, or that you paid more to join than did some of your fellow members, and you will want a refund.
- If you make a deal with him, you better get it in writing.
- If you are a lawyer, an architect, a subcontractor, or even a dentist, you better get paid up front.
- If you render honest service to him, he will stiff you for your fee and threaten to charge you with malpractice if you dare sue.
- If you are a critic, you better write a rave review...If you venture an opinion that publicly criticizes him, you may be sued for libel.
- If you use the Trump name in a business he had never had anything to do with, he will sue you even if the Trump name is on your birth certificate.
- If you are a rapper, find someone else to dis or you will wind up in court.

- If you are pretty woman and you get too close to him, you may need to watch your ass, your breasts, or anything else he finds attractive… Then, if you try to sue him [for sexual assault], he will defame you or deny it ever happened.
- If he lives or does business in a locality, he is likely to sue the local government or the state for tax abatement, or even the nation-state as he did Scotland.
- If you are an Indian tribe entitled to operate a gambling casino under the law, you are in his crosshairs—he will question your lineage and claim that you don't look like an Indian.
- If you buy his bonds, the debt will be compromised when he files for bankruptcy.
- If you marry him, get an independent lawyer to draw up an airtight prenup giving you lots of money the moment he is dissatisfied with your companionship or is unfaithful and says, "You're fired."
- If you divorce him, he will not let go but will sue you years after the final decree.
- If he takes you for a roll in the hay, he will attempt to buy your silence with six-figure hush money sums paid by wire transfer out of an off-shore account owned by a shell LLC.
- If you sue him, a counterclaim for damages in excess of your net worth is almost inevitable.[24]

As the Plaintiff-in-Chief, "Trump's Greatest Lawsuits: The Greatest Hits" have included[25]:

1973, Trump vs. United States Justice Department
1983, Trump vs. Central Park South Tenants
1986, Trump vs. the NFL
1990, Trump vs. Marvin Roffman
1992, Trump vs. Palm Beach County
1995, Trump vs. George Houraney
1995, Trump vs. Palm Beach County
1997, Trump vs. Jill Harth
1997, Trump vs. Palm Beach County
2006, Trump vs. Warner Books
2008, Trump vs. Deutsche Bank
2010, Trump vs. Tarla Makaeff and Art Cohen
2013, Trump vs. New York Attorney General
2017, Trump vs. Washington, Minnesota, and Hawaii

2018, Trump vs. Stormy Daniels
2019, Trump vs. Deutsche Bank and Capital One

I would add to Trump's greatest hits, his class action lawsuits filed against Facebook, Google, YouTube, and Twitter as well as their CEOs on July 7, 2021, in the Southern District of Florida for suspending his accounts five months earlier because of his incitement to violence at the Capitol on January 6, 2021.

Among other claims, unspecified punitive damages, and remedies called for such as ending the blacklisting and censorship, these lawsuits allege that the private companies are violating Trump's First Amendment rights. Without going into details, it is not likely that the case will even get to discovery because First Amendment "free speech" does not apply to private companies, but only to the state and governmental agencies.[26] No matter, the Insurrectionist-in-Chief is really using this lawsuit as another form of harassment and as a grift for generating one more revenue stream from his small time donors. More importantly, for 70 percent of the Republicans who believe in conspiracies of the Deep State and/or that Biden and company had stolen the 2020 election, Trump's legal case being tossed out of court will simply become more evidence of these false claims.

Trump vs. the National Football League

Trump vs. the NFL was the United States Football League vs. the National Football League in 1986. Make no mistake about the lawsuit, however, Donald J. Trump led the charge and retained the attorneys for the case. Had Donald not purchased the New Jersey Generals for as much as $9 million or as little as $5 million in the early 1980s and convinced the 11 other league owners as well as David Dixon the USFL founder, to move their schedule from the spring to the fall and to sue the NFL under the Sherman Antitrust Act, the upstart league might have become only the second professional football league besides the American Football League (AFL) to successfully compete with and eventually merge with the NFL as full partners or equal franchises.

Between 1983 and 1986, the USFL captured the attention of millions of Americans. Initially conceived as a spring/summer sport, games were played in such notable venues as Soldier Field in Chicago, the New Orleans Superdome, and Giants Stadium in New Jersey. The league also introduced innovations that the fans liked such as instant replay, the option after scoring a touchdown of going for two points rather than one, and a style of offense that opened the aerial game. In its first two years, the USFL was able "to produce TV ratings and game attendance that nearly rivaled" those of the NFL. Superstar quarterbacks Jim Kelly and Steve Young, running back Herschel Walker, defensive end Reggie White and others, spurred the early success of the league on with well over budgeted salaries. Consequently, the predicted financial losses were bigger by $1.3 million per team than the league had anticipated with a loss of almost $40 million in its first year of operation, or an average of $3.3 million per team.

> Prior to the 1985 season, the league was offered nearly $250 million in cable and network TV contracts. Despite the apparent early success, within 6 months the league would be in financial ruin and most of its players and owners would soon be forgotten.[27]

Also forgotten about the tragedy of the USFL and its legal battle with the National Football League that brought about the league's demise was the role played by the Donald.

Serial sports entrepreneur Dixon and other USFL founders "had started the league as a way for people not rich enough to buy an NFL team (like Trump) to invest in commercial sports."[28] Dixon's strategy:

> was low-risk and low-cost. It called for patience and careful execution to grow the business until it could go head-to-head with the NFL. A crucial part of the strategy was to play in the spring rather than compete with the NFL's wealth, seven decades of fans, and monopoly in the fall season.[29]

Trump had little interest in or patience for Dixon's strategies. Instead, like a high stakes gambler he endowed the USFL with the showmanship of P.D Barnum. Tryouts to become New Jersey General's cheerleaders or "Brig-A-Dears" occurred in the basement of Trump Tower just before Christmas. To promote the team Trump then sent the scantily clad young Brig-A-Dears to bars without security where they were mistaken for hookers. More significantly, to build the Generals audience, Trump signed top college players, including Heisman Trophy-winning quarterback Doug Flutie for well over the maximum USFL salary, as he paid top dollar to lure several pros away from the NFL.

After only one season, Trump convinced the other USFL owners in a meeting in New York on May 9, 1984, to move to a fall schedule beginning in 1986. Later in the year, he convinced the owners of the USFL to sue the NFL under the Sherman Antitrust Act that makes it a felony to monopolize or try to monopolize any business. Roy Cohn signed the lawsuit. As Trump announced the lawsuit on October 18, 1984, Roy introduced their lies and stated that he had a secret list of NFL owners that had come together as a committee "created exclusively for the purpose of combatting the USFL." When Cohn was asked for the names or proof, he simply stated that "We have reliable reason to believe we know whom they are and what they are doing."[30] In response to an ABC television reporter's question about moving its schedule to the fall, Trump had a wonderful one liner: "If God wanted football in the spring, he wouldn't have created baseball."

The federal court trial lasted 48 days and the USFL on Donald's advice retained Harvey D. Myerson, a colorful attorney with no expertise in antitrust litigation. Most of the trial was filled with mind-numbing testimony about law and economics. Trump also testified bringing not necessarily his "A game" of lying to the fore. While Donald claimed that NFL commissioner Pete Rozelle had tried to buy him off by offering him an NFL franchise in exchange for blocking the USFL's proposed move to the fall and for preventing the filing of the lawsuit, the judge was unimpressed and the jury did not buy it. Naturally Rozelle denied ever making any such offer to Trump. In the end, this "he said he said" was irrelevant. After five days of deliberation, the jury found for the USFL that the NFL had violated the Sherman Antitrust Act and awarded the plaintiffs $1.00 which could have been tripled to $3.00 under antitrust law. Keep in mind that the USFL sought damages of $567 million, which could have been tripled to $1.7 billion.

It's complicated law and in my humble opinion contradictory as for all practical purposes the NFL has been exempted from the Sherman Antitrust Act. It is fascinating legalese especially the back-and-forth testimony of the parties. Nevertheless, it is not worth getting into the weeds over—since antitrust monopoly law is seldom invoked let alone enforced.[31] The USFL appealed the damages award to the U.S. appellate court that agreed with the lower federal court. The U.S. Supreme Court refused to hear the case on appeal. The USFL became an interesting side note in the history of the NFL. A useful bottom line: "the smart business strategy of David Dixon had been fumbled by a disastrous Trumpian legal gamble."[32]

A quarter of a century later, Trump was still meddling in the affairs of the NFL. In 2008 he offered campaign cash to the U.S. Senator Arlen Spector in exchange for his dropping a probe into the illegal spying of the New England Patriots. Shortly after the NFL had concluded its own investigation of the New England Patriots' videotaping of its rival teams, the

Pennsylvania senator had called for an "independent investigator to determine how many games the Patriots had illegally videotaped, how deeply the videotaping of opposing coaches' signals affected the integrity of their games, and why the NFL had destroyed all evidence" following its investigation.[33] At the time, Trump was a friend of both Patriots owner Robert Kraft and the late senator who he had politically supported for years with maximum donations. As a headline from an ESPN news report revealed on May 26, 2021: "Son, ghostwriter of late senator says Trump intervened to stop probe of Patriots' Spygate scandal."

While taking part in the making of an unrelated ESPN documentary, *Small Potatoes: Who Killed the USFL?* that aired in 2009, Trump grew angry when questioned about whether suing the NFL and not remaining with the spring schedule was a smart strategy. As he pulls off his microphone and exits the interview, Trump retorts that such a league would have been only "small potatoes." The documentary by Mike Tollin has the Donald summarizing his thoughts about the USFL after some 25 years: "It was a nice experience. It was fun. We had a great lawsuit." Before the documentary was televised Tollin had sent a rough cut of the film as a courtesy to Trump. Trump was not pleased with the product and how he came off as the one who had killed the USFL. So, the Donald responded in typical Trump fashion. He took a thick, felt-tip pen to Tollin's letter before mailing it back and wrote: "A third rate documentary and extremely dishonest—as you know. Best wishes," signed in his distinctive style with a "P.S.—You are a <u>loser</u>" (underlined in the original).[34]

Deutsche Bank vs. Donald Trump vs. Deutsche Bank

One of the more provocative counterclaim lawsuits filed by Donald Trump over the years would have to be the one he filed against Deutsche Bank in 2008 who had sued him after he had defaulted on a personally guaranteed $40 million loan repayment. The Trump countersuit sued the bank for $3 billion. It relied on the *force majeure* clause in their lending agreement that included the critical catchall phrase, "any other event or circumstance not within the reasonable control of the borrower."[35] Black's Law Dictionary has defined "force majeure" as an event or effect that can be neither anticipated nor controlled for. Legally like an Act of God. In this instance, these events could include something that would interfere with the completion of a building project such as riots, floods, or strikes. Before filling in some of the more important known and unknown speculative facts about the ongoing relationship between Deutsche Bank and Donald Trump, allow me to cut to the chase—the court dismissed Trump's counterclaim. But that's only part of a rather complicated legal story where both parties may be guilty of related crimes, including conspiracies to defraud.

Over the course of three decades, Deutsche Bank has lent Trump somewhere between $2 and $3.5 billion as estimates vary. The business relationship between Trump and the bank began in 1990 and lasted precariously through the Trump administration. The U.S. House of Representatives subpoenaed Deutsche's banking financial records of the 45th president. On July 9, 2020, in the case of Trump vs. Deutsche Bank AG, the U.S. Supreme Court ruled 7-2 to vacate and remand or to overturn a lower court's ruling. The majority opinion argued that the lower court's decision to turn over the documents failed to adequately account for the "separation of powers" concerns.[36] Six months later, January 11, 2021, following the Capitol Insurrection, Deutsche bank announced that it would no longer do any business with Donald Trump. When the former president left office ten days later, the Trump Organization still owed the bank about $340 million in outstanding loans.[37]

Trump's relationship with Deutsche Bank first emerged following the failures of his Atlantic City casinos and after the Trump Shuttle had defaulted on its loans and went out of business. Consequently, Trump was well known as a cash-strapped New York City businessman with shaky credit. As *New York Times* finance editor David Enrich recalls:

> His record of defaulting on loans and stiffing his business partners was very long and very well-documented. Any mainstream financial institution that had competent risk management systems in place – there is no way they were going to do business with Donald Trump.[38]

Enrich describes the bank as a "second-tier player" in the world of banking at the time that Deutsche became involved with Trump. The bank was:

> …so hungry for profits, for short-term profits, and so hungry to make a name for itself in the United States that it was really eager to just disregard any red flags that presented themselves with clients. Trump would default on a bond offering. He would sue the bank. And yet, time after time, Deutsche Bank executives kept going back to him for more business.[39]

Despite financial and legal conflicts with each other, why did the Trump Organization and Deutsche Bank remain business allies all those years? Could it be that these two financial entities had mutually overlapping criminal activities? For example, when Trump's now-defunct foundation "set off alerts in a computer system designed to detect illicit activity," why did the executive financial officers at Deutsche Bank reject their anti-money-laundering specialists' advice in 2016 and again in 2017 to report "multiple transactions involving legal entities controlled by Donald J. Trump and his son-in-law, Jared Kushner," to "a federal financial-crimes watchdog"?[40]

In the early 1990s, Deutsche Bank went from that of a nonentity on Paternoster Square as well as on Wall Street to becoming one of the leading players in these financial capitols. At the time, Edson Mitchell headed up Deutsche's London office and led the bank's charge into the mega financial league. Mitchell has been described as an impulsive, charismatic, and energetic salesman. "Largely through the force of his personality and through the power of persuasion of having a few billion dollars at his disposal to spend on hiring people," Mitchell employed thousands of people that he lured away first from Merrill Lynch and then from the rest of Wall Street. In no time, Deutsche Bank had become "one of the most aggressive places to work on Wall Street."[41]

Under CEO Josef Ackerman that began in 2002, the "reckless taskmaster" established an outlandish goal of increasing the bank's profitability in two years by 600 percent. Ackerman could get "extremely angry" and he could blame his subordinates for their failures not only privately but also publicly. So, his underlings were sufficiently bullied to be scared of him. To survive and succeed, his minions set out to make Ackermann's mandate their own personal missions. Not unlike Trump subordinates, these folks were afraid of doing anything that might incur Ackerman's wrath. The entire incentive structure within the bank quickly changed as did the decisions as to whether to make loans or enter other transactions. "If it wasn't going to be enormously profitable in the immediate term, they just wouldn't do the business anymore."[42]

Not surprisingly, the bank was engaged in things that were more about the interests of the bank than the interests of their customers. As an international bank headquartered in Germany with a presence all over the world and a large operation in the United States, Deutsche was supposed to adhere to the U.S. law that imposed very strict sanctions on the nations of Iran, Syria, Myanmar, and Libya. However, the German bank chose to ignore those restrictions and found a very lucrative market with little competition for servicing those sanctioned countries. To conceal their activities, they engaged in the practice known as "stripping" where they would remove any references to the sanctioned nations so as not to alert the U.S. regulators or their American computer systems.

> And over a period of several years, they engaged in billions of dollars of business with entities that, in Iran's case in particular, were very closely tied to the Iranian military and were later blamed for really helping finance a lot of terrorism that was going on in Iraq after the Iraq War.[43]

During the same period, most "Western banks were very wary of doing business with Russians" because a lot of their "money came through corruption or kleptocracy."[44] This was not the case with Deutsche Bank. With its long history as one of the few Western banks doing business with Russian customers, Deutsche was well positioned and its money laundering business became a very lucrative enterprise. By the early 2000s, in addition to the oligarchs, there were a lot of other Russians vis-à-vis suspicious means getting very rich in rubles very quickly. However, to get this wealth out of Russia, it became necessary to convert rubles into euros, dollars, or pounds. Using shell companies and other fraudulent means, Deutsche "arranged for a number of workarounds for Russians where they could move their money to a country like Latvia, and then have it wired into the U.S."[45] With and without the help of Deutsche Bank, much of that laundered money found its way to purchasing Trump condos. In fact, records "show that more than 1,300 Trump condominiums were bought not by people but by shell companies, and that the purchases were made without a mortgage, avoiding inquires from lenders."[46]

As recently as January 2021, Deutsche Bank entered a "deferred prosecution agreement" with the U.S. prosecutors to avoid criminal charges under the U.S. Foreign Corrupt Practices Act that forbids companies operating in the United States from paying bribes abroad. Inclusive of the bank's executive leadership, the scheme "knowingly and willfully conspired" to hide and falsify payments made to phony financial consultants. The bank paid a fine of $130 million for its bribes in Saudi Arabia, Abu Dhabi, Italy, and China. The agreement put to rest the allegations that the German bank had devised a "scheme to conceal corrupt payments and bribes" to encourage business around the world. In recent years, Deutsche Bank has also "paid hundreds of millions of dollars in penalties for anti-money laundering lapses."[47]

Returning to Trump's 2004 loan application to Deutsche Bank and to Deutsche Bank's 2005 loan to Trump that resulted in DB vs. DJT vs. DB in 2008. Based on the application, DB concluded that Trump was worth $788 million, and its real estate department loaned him $640 million to finance about 75 percent of the construction of Trump International Hotel and Tower in Chicago. After the global financial implosion in late 2008, Trump defaulted on his personally guaranteed payment of $40 million in order to pay down the loan as he had agreed to. In response to Deutsche suing Trump for the overdue money, he not only denied liability alleging that the financial crisis was a force majeure that prevented him from fulfilling his contract, but also that DB had aided and abetted this financial event. So, the Donald argued that he was owed a lot of money and countersued the bank for $3 billion alleging lender liability for undermining the project, predatory practices, and damages to his brand and reputation.

Putting aside the fact that the construction project was completed on time, was unimpeded by the financial crisis, and that Trump had the money to make the payment, he was simply trying to creatively take advantage of the global financial crisis and the fact that banks like Deutsche were in trouble. Once again in classic Trump fashion, he was turning a claim against him back on the plaintiff whether it had any basis. As Donald has uttered about this counterclaim: "I figured it was the bank's problem, not mine." Of course, Deutsche argued otherwise and the New York court agreed dismissing Trump's countersuit. However, Trump may have known better because two years later in 2010, the parties settled and extended the loan term for another five years. And until the January 6th Insurrection in 2021, the private wealth department of the bank continued to do business with Trump.

Cruelty lawsuits, enhanced branding, and threatening to sue

Make no mistake, many of Trump's lawsuits have nothing to do with winning or losing a claim or counterclaim. They are about payback, punishment, or threatening to inflict some type of pain. These lawsuits are a means that allow Trump to act maliciously toward others. They might be referred to as "cruelty lawsuits." In these cases, one might also say that Trump gets off by tormenting his enemies. Other lawsuits are about enhancing the Trump brand and/or defending his name and reputation. In some of these instances, including his bankrupted New Jersey gambling ventures, he sued to have his name removed from the casinos he founded and no longer controlled before they were eventually demolished. Finally, there are the threatened and/or related lawsuits that have absolutely no chance that the action will stand up in a court of law. What really holds most of these actual or threatened lawsuits together are the psychological damages to Trump's fragile ego that may have somehow been assaulted.

The noteworthy examples of cruelty or spiteful lawsuits might include Trump suing an ex-wife or a political comedian as he has done. In 1992, Trump sued his first former wife Ivana for $25 million dollars (about the same as she received from the divorce in cash and property). Trump accused her of fraud after she publicly discussed Donald's financial and business affairs. Ivanka Trump had violated the "gag order" from their divorce settlement agreement not to discuss any of the details of their relationship whether business or marital. The Donald sued Ivana the woman whose nickname for him has stuck all these years for the "willful, deliberate and surreptitious disclosure." He also sued his former wife in the New York State Supreme Court for cohabiting since their divorce with the Italian industrialist, Ricardo Mazzucchclli, thereby relieving him of his annual alimony payments of $400,000. The final outcomes of these two settled lawsuits remain sealed.

On a contradictory lighter note, the third case involves one of Trump's serious gaslighting endeavors about his predecessor President Barack Obama's birthplace that lasted for several years before being put to rest. In 2013 after the Donald stated that he would donate $5 million to charity if Obama would release to the public his personal documents, Bill Maher appeared on NBC's *The Tonight Show.* Maher making fun of Trump joked about how he would pay the Donald $5 million if he could prove that his father was not an orangutan. Losing no time, Trump sent Maher a copy of his birth certificate. Trump then sued Maher for a sum of $5 million when the latter failed to deliver him the $5 million. The Donald dropped the case as he surely knew that his case would have been laughed out of court because joke contracts are not legally binding or enforceable.

With respect to Trump's penchant for threatening or suing former business associates or family members or journalists who have penned books to prevent their publications because they would expose the "real" Donald and, therefore, harm his reputation such as when his former "fixer" Michael Cohen or niece Mary Trump were about to publish their tell-all books. Typically, Trump sends these authors and their deep pocket publishers, cease-and-desist libel letters. These suits, however, usually never materialize because of something called the First Amendment that Donald is quite familiar with. A couple of notable exceptions have included Trump suing in 1984 the *Chicago Tribune* and the newspaper's Pulitzer Prize winning architecture critic, Paul Gapp, and his suing *The New York Times* and its reporter Timothy L. O'Brien in 2008.

In the former libel case, Trump filed it in the U.S. District Court in the Southern District of New York claiming that he suffered $500 million in damages. Gapp had written a piece in the *Sunday Tribune Magazine's* "design" column ridiculing Trump's proposal and final construction of the world's tallest skyscraper at the time. The Tribune and Gapp filed a Rule 12(b)(6) motion to dismiss on the grounds that Gapp's statements and his artist's renderings were protected opinions. District Judge Edward Weinfeld agreed and the case was dismissed.[48] In the latter libel case, the publication in 2005 of *TrumpNation: The Art of Being the Donald* by *New York Times* reporter Timothy L. O' Brien, cited three unnamed sources close to Trump that claimed the real estate mogul and reality TV star was not a billionaire. The sources stated that he had a net worth of between $150 and $250 million rather than some several billion dollars the Donald has maintained on many occasions. So, Trump sued O'Brien in 2008 seeking $5 billion, claiming that the book had hurt his reputation and branding. One year later, the court ruled in O'Brien's favor and dismissed Trump's case.

Cliff Sims, a former White House communications aide and special assistant to the president, filed one interesting and recent lawsuit. Sims first crafted Trump's messaging for the 2016 campaign and then from inside the West Wing. Shortly after leaving the Trump administration, Sims authored the best-selling *Team of Vipers: My Extraordinary 500 Days in the Trump White House* and sued Trump alleging that his campaign organization's arbitration claims against him for violating an NDA that he may have signed in 2016 were selectively denying him from invoking his First Amendment rights based on whether the Donald viewed the tell-all as flattering. Judge Collen Kollar-Kotelly, citing a "separations-of-powers" issue and echoing a D.C. Circuit Court of Appeals that had denied an initial ruling that Democratic lawmakers were entitled to sue the president over violation of the Emoluments Clause of the U.S. Constitution: "In reviewing the parties' arguments concerning subject matter jurisdiction, the Court is most concerned about its ability to grant declaratory or injunctive relief against the President of the United States."[49]

No matter though. Trump reasoned that *Team of Vipers* had not actually attacked or denigrated him as he first thought. Upon further reflection, the Donald realized that the vipers referred to his subordinates. According to Trumpian logic, those subordinates are also not a reflection of Trump. More importantly, Trump needed Sims' messaging skills. Hence, Trump rehired him in June 2020 to take care of the messaging operation for Trump's re-election campaign. These lawsuits are almost always for ways for Trump to communicate, release tension, and occasionally negotiate a settlement. It is certainly not about right or wrong or even about winning and losing. It is primarily about flexing his legal power in business, political, and social relationships. It is lastly almost always a transactional and vacuous endeavor.

Notes

1 Steve Reilly, 2016. USA Today Exclusive: Hundreds Allege Donald Trump Doesn't Pay His Bills. *USA Today*. June 9. https://www.usatoday.com/story/news/politics/elections/2016/06/09/donald-trump-unpaid-bills-republican-president-laswuits/85297274/. For example, at

> least 60 lawsuits, along with hundreds of liens, judgments, and other government filings reviewed by the USA TODAY NETWORK, document people who have accused Trump and his businesses of failing to pay them for their work. Among them: a dishwasher in Florida, a glass company in New Jersey. A carpet company. A plumber. Painters. Forty-eight waiters. Dozens of bartenders and other hourly workers at his resorts and clubs, coast to coast. Real estate brokers who sold his properties. And, ironically, several law firms that once represented him in these suits and others.

For the record, Trump and his companies have prevailed in more of these legal disputes than they have lost for "failing to pay small businesses and individuals" because they usually resort to

> tying them up in court and other negotiations for years. In some cases, the Trump teams financially overpower and outlast much smaller opponents, draining their resources. Some just give up the fight, or settle for less; some have ended up in bankruptcy or out of business altogether.

As the circumstances laid out in these claims and other lawsuits reveal, Trump and his companies either "have a poor track record hiring workers and assessing contractors, or that Trump businesses renege on contracts, refuse to pay, or consistently attempt to change payment terms after work is complete."

2 AZ Quotes.

3 American Oversight, 2021. The Trump Administration's Response to Coronavirus. January 20. https://www.americanoversight.org/investigation/the-trumpadministrations-response-to-coronavirus.

4 Sanjay Gupta, M.D., 2021. Autopsy of a Pandemic: 6 Doctors at the Center of the US Covid-19 Response. CNN. March 26. https://www.cnn.com/2021/03/26/health/covid-war-doctors-sanjay-gupta/index.html.

5 Francis T. Cullen, Amanda Graham, et al., 2021. The Denier in Chief: Faith in Trump and Techniques of Neutralization in a Pandemic. *Deviant Behavior*. doi: 10.1080/01639625.2021.1918035

6 Benjamin Din, 2021. Trump Lashes Out at Fauci and Birx after CNN Documentary. POLITICO 03/29. https://www.politico.com/news/2021/03/29/trump-fauci-birx-cnn-documentary-478422. Within two months, Trump and his allies were lionizing the former president for his "heroic foresight" during the pandemic, villainizing Anthony S. Fauci, and calling for a Congressional investigation. See Matt Viser and Yasmeen Abutaleb, 2021. Trump

and His Allies Try to Rewrite, Distort History of Pandemic While Casting Fauci as Public Enemy No. 1. *The Washington Post.* June 5.

7 A Washington Post-ABC News Poll conducted in early July 2021 found that 86 percent of Democrats had received at least one COVID-19 vaccine shot, and only 45 percent of Republicans had. Moreover, only six percent of Democrats stated that they would probably decline the vaccine, while 47 percent of Republicans stated that they would probably not be inoculated.

8 See Janet McIntosh's (2020). Introduction: The Trump Era as a Linguistic Emergency. In McIntosh, Janet and Mendoza-Denton, Norma (eds.), *Language in the Trump Era: Scandals and Emergencies.* Cambridge: Cambridge University Press, pp. 1–44.

9 Roy Cohn, RationalWiki. https://rationalwiki.org/wiki/Roy_Cohn.

10 See, for example: Edwin Lemert, 1951. *Social Pathology.* New York: McGraw-Hill; Charles C. Lemert and Michael F. Winter (Eds.), 2000. *Crime and Deviance: Essays and Innovations of Edwin M. Lemert.* Lanham, MD: Rowman & Littlefield.

11 Edwin M. Schur was prolific having written at least twelve books. See his fourth, fifth, ninth, and tenth titles respectively: *Law and Society: A Sociological View* (1968), New York: Random House; *Our Criminal Society: The Social and Legal Sources of Crime in America* (1969), New York: Prentice-Hall; *The Politics of Deviance: Stigma Contests and the Uses of Power* (1980), New York: Prentice Hall; and *Labeling Women Deviant: Gender, Stigma, and Social Control* (1984), New York: Random House.

12 See, for example, Edwin H. Sutherland, 2004. *White Collar Crime: The Uncut Version*2004 with an Introduction by Gilbert Geis and Colin Goff. New Haven, CT: Yale University Press; *Principles of Criminology*, revised edition (1934), Philadelphia, PA: J.B. Lippincott Company; and *The Professional Thief* by a Professional Thief, annotated and interpreted by Edwin Sutherland, Chicago, IL: The University of Chicago Press.

13 Namita Singh, 2021. Review of Trump's Hush Money Payment to Stormy Daniels Dropped by US Election Commission. *Independent.* May 7. https://www.independent.co.uk/news/world/americas/us-politics/donald-trump-stormy-daniels-scandal-b1843546.html.

14 James D. Zirin, 2019. *Plaintiff in Chief: A Portrait of Donald Trump in 3500 Lawsuits.* New York: St. Martins Publishing Group, p. xii.

15 Ibid: xvi.

16 Ibid: x.

17 Shayna Jacobs, David A. Fahrenthold, Josh Dawsey and Jonathan O'Connell. Trump Organization and CFO Allen Weisselberg Arraigned on Multiple Criminal Charges as Prosecutor Alleged a 15-year Tax Fraud Scheme. *The Washington Post.* July 1. https://www.washingtonpost.com/politics/trump-business-weisselber/.

18 David Frum, 2021. Trump Is Preparing for the Worst. *The Atlantic.* July 1. https://www.theatlantic.com/ideas/archive/2021/07/trump-organization-allen-weisselberg-indictment-new-york/619340/.

19 Quoted in Ibid.

20 Ibid.

21 As of July 1, 2021, I personally think that the Trump Organization will become history. I also suspect at the end of the day that if Donald is indicted, that sooner or later he will cut a deal to avoid prison, and then claim a personal victory.

22 Ibid: x–xi.
23 Ibid: xi.
24 Ibid: xiv.
25 Valerie Keene, 2021. Donald Trump Settlement & Lawsuits—History of Legal Affairs. *Crush the LSAT.* February 21. https://crushthelsatexam.com/deep-dive-donald-trumps-long-history-of-lawsuits/.
26 Frank LoMonte, 2021. Trump Can't Beat Facebook, Twitter and YouTube in Court – But the Fight Might Be Worth More Than a Win. *Naked Capitalism.* July 9. https://www.nakedcapitalism.com/2021/07/trump-cant-beat-facebook-twitter-and-youtube-in-court-but-the-fight-might-be-worth-more-than-a-win.html?utm_source=feedburner&utm_medium=email&utm_campaign=-Feed%3A+nakedcapitalism+%28naked+capitalism%29.
27 Boris Kogan, ND. USFL v. NFL: The Challenge beyond the Courtroom. 1–21. https://www.law.berkeley.edu/sugarman/Sports_Stories_USFL_v_NFL__-_Boris_Kogan.pdf.
28 David Cay Johnston, 2016. *The Making of Donald Trump.* Brooklyn, NY: Melville House, pp. 51–52.
29 Ibid: 52.
30 Quoted in Ibid: 54.
31 If you are interested, then read Kogan, ND for an insightful review and analysis of the arguments and counter-arguments.
32 Johnston, 2016: 56.
33 Andrew Callahan, 2021. ESPN Report Alleged Donald Trump Offered Late Senator 'Money' to Stop 'Spygate' Investigation. *Boston Herald.* May 26. https://www.bostonherald.com/2021/05/26/espn-report-alleges-donald-trump-offered-late-senator-money-to-stop-spygate-investigation/.
34 Ibid: 57.
35 Quoted in Floyd Norris, 2008. Trump Sees Act of God in Recession. *The New York Times.* December 4. https://dealbook.nytimes.com/2008/12/05/trump-sees-act-of-god-in-recession/.
36 Trump v. Deutsche Bank AG, 2020. SCOTUSblog: Independent News & Analysis on the U.S. Supreme Court. July 9. https://www.scotusblog.com/case-files/cases/trump-v-deutsche-bank-ag/.
37 Reuters, 2021. Deutsche Bank Won't Do Future Business with Trump: Report. *Business Today.* January 12. https://www.businesstoday.in/current/world/deutsche-bank-wont-do-future-business-with-trump-report/story/427713.html.
38 David Enrich quoted in an interview with Terry Gross, 2020 about his book, 'Dark Towers' Exposes Chaos and Corruption at the Bank That Holds Trump's Secrets." Heard on Fresh Air, *National Public Radio.* February 19. https://www.npr.org/2020/02/19/807191309/dark-towers-exposes-chaos-and-corruption-at-the-bank-that-holds-trump-s-secrets.
39 Ibid.
40 David Enrich, 2019. Deutsche Bank Staff Saw Suspicious Activity in Trump and Kushner Accounts. *The New York Times.* May 19. http://www.nytimes.com/2019/05/19/business/deutsche-bank-trump-kushner.html.
41 Dave Davies, 2020. From the Written Highlights That Accompany the Terry Gross' *Fresh Air* interview with Enrich about his book, 'Dark Towers' Exposes Chaos and Corruption at the Bank That Holds Trump's Secrets." February 19. https://www.npr.org/2020/02/19/807191309/dark-towers-exposes-chaos-and-corruption-at-the-bank-that-holds-trump-s-secrets.

42 Ibid.
43 Ibid.
44 David Enrich quoted in Gross' Fresh Air, 2020.
45 Davies, 2020.
46 Thomas Frank, 2018. Secret Money: How Trump Made Millions Selling Condos To Unknown Buyers. *BuzzFeed News*. January 12. https://www.buzzfeednews.com/article/thomasfrank/secret-money-how-trump-made-millions-selling-condos-to.
47 Spencer Woodman, 2021. Deutsche Bank Agrees to Pay $130 Million in Latest Major US Penalty. International Consortium of Investigative Journalists. January 12. https://www.icij.org/investigations/fincen-files/deutsche-bank-agrees-to-pay-130-million-in-latest-major-us-penalty/.
48 Susan E. Seager, N.D. Donald J. Trump Is A Libel Bully But Also A Libel Loser. Media Law Resource Center. https://www.medialaw.org/component/k2/item/3470-donald-j-trump-is-a-libel-bully-but-also-a-libel-loser#startOfPageId3470.
49 Eriq Gardner, 2019. Judge Is Hesitant About Ordering Trump to Back Off Nondisclosure Agreements. *Hollywood Reporter*. August 1. https://www.hollywoodreporter.com/business/business-news/judge-is-hesitant-ordering-trump-back-nondisclosure-agreements-1228516/.

PART TWO

Squandering the presidency

4

CAMPAIGNS AND POLICIES OF ADVERSITY, HARMFULNESS, AND DIVISIVENESS

In 2020, the United States experienced its highest voter participation rate since 1900 and a record turnout of more than 156 million voters. Trump, the incumbent Republican President while receiving more popular votes than any Republican candidate before him, including Ronald Reagan, still lost the popular vote by more than seven million votes to his Democratic challenger Joe Biden. The Donald also lost the Electoral College by 74 votes receiving 232 compared to Biden's 306. Four years earlier, Republican candidate Trump lost the popular vote to Democratic candidate Hillary Clinton by almost three million votes. The Donald still won the Electoral College vote tally by 77 receiving 304 votes compared to 227 for Hillary. In the context of American exceptionalism, these and other presidential elections have always raised questions about the unfair practices in which the people of the United States elect their president every four years.

In those cases, certifying presidents where the real losers—those with less votes—become the legitimate winners raise two related questions about the contradictory nature of the outcomes of our past two presidential elections: First, what kind of electoral system does the United States have when the 2016 candidate with three million votes less than the losing candidate receives essentially the same number of Electoral College votes as the 2020 winning candidate with seven million votes more than the losing candidate? Second, what kind of "democratic" electoral system does the United States have when its 2016 winner with three million fewer votes than its loser receives a marginal victory of 77 Electoral College votes

DOI: 10.4324/9781003221548-7

compared to the marginal victory of 74 received by its 2020 winner with seven million more votes than the loser? Answers to both questions are the same. From its birthing, the United States has always had a constitutionally corrupt electoral system that should have been abolished along with the institutions of slavery of which it was an integral part of.

Trump became the fourth presidential candidate in the U.S. history to lose the popular vote and to legally steal the presidency at the same time. Without the Framers of the Constitution having created the undemocratic Electoral College system as part of the infamous *three-fifths compromise* to form a union between the North and the South, presidential elections to this day would not still be skewing elections in favor of rural over urban voters and white voters over black voters. Like the three previous real losers, Trump was sworn in as the president in 2017 because the Electoral College system was set up to override the popular vote and to deny outcomes based on one person-one vote.[1] Moreover, had Trump only lost the past election by some six million votes, he probably would have legally stolen this election too.

Aside from the politically obsolete and unfair Electoral College system, other social forces contributed to the success of Trump's two presidential campaigns. These included and were not limited to judicialism, nativism, populism, racism, sexism, evangelicalism, authoritarianism, white supremacy, and conspiracy theory. During the 2016 political contest, there were also the powerful "never Hillary Clinton" or the "Lock Her Up" chants led by the former Army General Flynn, not to mention HRC's less than stellar campaign performance. Two weeks before the election, there was the FBI Director James Comey's breaking with tradition and exonerating, yet making disparaging remarks about Hillary's emails and private server. This bit of news critically deflected media attention away from the nine women who had publicly come forward to claim that the Donald had sexually assaulted them after the Trump Access Hollywood video revealed Trump enthusiastically bragging and objectifying women with television personality Billy Bush.[2] As usual, Trump's best defense was to categorically deny any and all charges while counterattacking and going on the offensive against those women and HRC for their horrible lying and dishonesty.

Following Trump's trouncing by Hillary at the first presidential debate in late September, for example, the Donald turned to harder ball than usual even for him during the second debate calling out the Secretary of State for her corruption involving affairs of state and the Clinton Foundation. At the final debate in Las Vegas on October 19, 2016, moderated by Fox News' Chris Wallace, Trump double-downed on his narratives of criminal Hillary and even went so far as to label the Clinton Foundation a criminal enterprise.[3] Then on October 29th at an Arizona rally as the race was coming to an end, Trump ratcheted up his law-and-order critique of Hillary. The Projector-in-Chief went for Clinton's political jugular. A one-two, knockout punch as it were: "A vote for Hillary is a vote to surrender our government to public corruption, graft, and cronyism that threatens the survival of our constitutional system itself." And then, the aspiring authoritarian with a lifetime of lawlessness ended with this zinger: "What makes us exceptional is that we are a nation of laws and that we are all equal under those laws. Hillary's corruption shreds the principle on which our nation was founded."[4]

While channeling his long-time deceased mentor Roy Cohn, Trump in the moment was successfully appropriating Comey's critical remarks by merging them with the anti-Hillary conspiracy theories. These had been picking up momentum with the 2015 publication of *Clinton Cash: The Untold Story of How and Why Foreign Governments and Businesses Helped Make Bill and Hillary Rich.*[5] By July 2016, the book had sold more than 200,000 copies. The former president William J. Clinton and first lady Hillary Rodham Clinton together had weathered several scandals from Arkansas to the District of Columbia, including Bill's impeachment trial as well as the uncertain suicide of their close friend and former Deputy White House counsel Vince Foster. This money scandal story was different, however. The politically retired Bill and now Hillary, the former U.S. Senator from New York and former U.S. Secretary of State, were never able to shake this book and other Steve Bannon choreographed productions of how the Clintons in less than one decade had gone from living with legal debts of two million dollars to being worth $130 million dollars.[6]

Long before the primary race ended for the 2016 Republican nomination, there was literally nothing that Trump could say or do no matter how absurd or dangerous that phased his base of supporters. This was certainly not the case with the pre-Trumpian Republican power brokers who were all quick to do an about face and get on board the Trump train. Perhaps Senator Lindsey Graham from South Carolina was the biggest hypocrite of all but of course where Trump is concerned there is plenty of competition. Lindsey as most people already know went from "anybody but Trump" in 2016 during the Republican primary race to flying side-by-side with the president on Air Force One. By 2018, he had also become one of the former president's few regular golf-playing buddies. The pompous blowhard told Wolf Blitzer of CNN in March 2016:

> This is not about whom we nominate anymore as Republicans as much as it's who we are. This is a fight for the heart and soul of the

> Republican Party. What is conservatism? If it's Donald Trump carrying the conservative banner I think not only do we lose the election, but we'll be unable in the future to grow the conservative cause. The more you know about Donald Trump, the less likely you are to vote for him. The more you know about his business enterprises, the less successful he looks. The more you know about his political giving, the less Republican he looks.[7]

Apparently, that is not necessarily the case because after the 2016 election, all Graham needed to know more about was the political power that Trump possessed. In quick fashion, Lindsey performed a 180-degree pirouette and became one of the former presidents' most loyal suck ups. Fast-forward to the 2020 election and Graham was singing a much different tune as one of Donald's staunchest defenders. In response to a reported two-dozen GOP lawmakers, including rank-and-file as well as party leaders who had refused to announce publicly whether or not they would back Trump for a second term in office something quite unusual for a sitting president, Graham told CNN's Manu Raju: "As to the 2020 presidential race, the Trump movement is real" and the Donald "will be our nominee, I'm confident of that, and I will support him."[8]

As for his Trumpist followers, they were all in regardless of whether the former president was for or against an issue, had no position on an issue, or knew nothing about an issue. They were also all in no matter how absurd, crazy, or foul the Donald could be. For example, in August 2019 on the two-year anniversary of the white nationalist weekend of rallies in Charlottesville, SC, where a car driven by a hatemonger deliberately plowed into a peaceful group of counter demonstrators and killed a woman and injured more than a dozen others, the reflections from Trump on this melancholy occasion were par for the course. The Trumpian leader's take on the situation was to draw moral equivalents between those engaging in public displays of aggressive hate and those demonstrating earnestly against hate when he claimed among other things, "you also had people that were very fine people, on both sides." By the end of four years of Trump's corruption, incompetence, and misbehavior politics, the nation's Capitol was more chaotic, divided, and irrational than ever before. It all culminated with the Capitol riots on January 6. Of course, Trump and his Trumpian followers were not making moral equivalents about the 5,000 Capitol insurrectionists and the more than 20 million peaceful Black Lives Matter protestors. On the contrary, in classic doublespeak, the Donald was speaking about the violent insurrectionists as patriots, and he was speaking about the BLM peaceful demonstrators as thugs. Trump also referred to NYC Mayor Bill de Blasio's BLM plan of action as a "symbol of hate."

Meanwhile, the anti-democratic precursors to the partisan stalemate had been developing since the 1994-midterm elections and the anointment of the Republican Speaker Newt Gingrich to the House of Representatives. It picked up momentum during Presidential Obama's two terms in office. First, there was the emergence of the Tea Party Republicans in 2009. And then when Republican Mitch McConnell became a majority leader of the U.S. Senate in 2014. Several nicknames have been conferred on the Republican majority leader each with its own story. These include Moscow Mitch, Midnight Mitch, and Massacre Mitch. In preference to my own nickname, The Turtle, I believe that Mitch's own self-described moniker, the Grim Reaper, is the best of all these derogatory names.

Senate Majority Leader McConnell was the first U.S. senator from either party to publicly state not once but several times that he would "just say no" to virtually anything that the opposition might want to propose or is even obligated to do no matter how beneficial or overwhelmingly popular it might be with the American people. Besides having the power to do so, the Grim Reaper does so for no other reasons than (1) the Democratic legislators have proposed the bill or (2) a Democratic president had nominated someone that requires senate confirmation. McConnell gives a whole new meaning to the word, chutzpah. As the most powerful Republican senator since 2009, Mitch has made "just say no" or obstructing any business from across the aisle the only real agenda of the Republican Party besides earmarking money for mega corporations and the superrich. Meanwhile, Mitch and the Republicans have brought forth no alternative policies or an affirmative agenda of any kind. I mean—bupkes, diddlysquat, and nada—whether we are talking about health care, infrastructure, climate change, law enforcement, poverty, inequality, or whatever.

For example, for nine months, the McConnell prevented the U.S. Supreme Court from having nine justices after the death of Associate Justice Antonin Scalia in early 2016. Mitch simply denied the U.S. Senate from holding hearings, let alone voting up or down, for President Obama's nomination of the U.S. Court of Appeals for the District of Columbia Circuit Judge Merrick Garland to the U.S. Supreme Court. Mitch's rationale was that selecting the replacement for Scalia was too close to the next presidential election and that the court should wait until afterward. Two years later after Associate Justice Rugh Bader Ginsberg died on September 18, 2020, Sabotage Mitch turns around with less than two months to go before the November 2020 election and rushes through

President Trump's nomination to the court in a matter of four weeks' time. Either way one looks at this political hypocrisy, McConnell picked up two Republican nominated justices that were denied the Democrats. The result being that the Supreme Court instead of having five Republican and four Democrat justices sitting on the court, it now has six Republicans and three Democrats constituting the most conservative court in modern history. Ironically, Trump's three conservative nominations to the highest court in the land as well as hundreds of other judicial appointments will be among the most concrete legacies of the most lawless president in U.S. history.

This antagonistic and growing stockpile of anti-democratic do-nothingism by Republican lawmakers has been accumulating for more than two decades before the lifelong Democrat Donald threw his hat into the political arena as a Republican candidate for the president. When Trump ascended to the White House, along with his chronic abuse of power came the accelerated erosion of the Republican Party as it morphed overnight into the anti-democratic Trumpian party. The takeover was aided by Robert Mueller's circumscribed or botched investigation into the relationship between Trump campaign higher-ups and the Russian intervention into the 2016 election as well as the obvious obstruction of justice by the former president during the special investigation. Attorney General Bill Barr made a significant contribution as well to the takeover by specifically misrepresenting and suppressing Mueller's findings regarding Russian collusion leading up to the election as well as the former president's active obstruction of justice. Not that the U.S. intelligence agencies' subsequent conclusions that Russia had indeed interceded on behalf of Trump in both the 2016 and 2020 elections would have made any difference to the vast majority of his MAGA supporters or to all but a few handfuls of Republican officials elected locally, statewide, or nationally.[9] On the contrary, the "Russian hoax" that was anything but a hoax, the non-existent attempts by a conspiratorial "Deep State" to unfairly pursue Trump, and the Republicans' first impeachment trial to acquit Trump all helped to advance the former president's very impressive vote tallies in his failed bid for a second term.

As important as each of these factors was in the accumulation of Trump voters, it was Donald's media savviness and his ability to influence much of the political reporting that was more important. With respect to the first election, Trump received almost free wall-to-wall coverage running up to the election. As Michael Cohen has explained:

> If interest in Trump was waning, even just a little bit, he'd yank the chain of the media with an insult or racist slur or reactionary

> outrage—and there would be CNN and *The New York Times* and Fox News dutifully eating out of his hands.[10]

Right, left, moderate, tabloid, radio, television, Internet, Facebook, and so on were all covering the Trumpian false narratives that only served to strengthen his power overtime.

Even when the talking heads and other mainstream media finally caught on that the Donald was playing them like fiddles, they would still reappear on network news and cable television shows talking about the need to reduce their coverage of his disgraceful remarks and actions. For various personal and professional reasons, they could not turn away from Trump's manufactured chaos and drama. Like Donald, the astute or ignorant media could not help themselves, nor could they or Donald ever really get enough of each other. They needed the Donald as much as the Donald needed them because the different kinds of ratings of each were interdependent on the words of the other. Their exchanges were often both symbiotic and symbolic. Donald used the media and the media used Donald. At the end of most days, Trump displayed more genius at exploiting them to his advantage than certainly vice versa. Also, there were often the Plaintiff-in-Chief's "threats of litigation to deter news organizations from looking behind the curtains of the seemingly all-wise and all-powerful man."[11] After becoming the president, this lifelong strategy of Trump's would finally lose most of its punch especially after the Donald had become a security risk to the well-being of the United States.

Looking back, the Donald had been toying around with the idea of running for president since the 1980s. Mostly for the purposes of promoting himself, the Trump brand, and even as a means of commodifying politics and negotiating his last contract with NBC's *Celebrity Apprentice*. Before 2016, Trump had dipped his feet momentarily into more than one political race for the presidency. Those undertakings had turned out to be "cash cows" for the former president. As one can argue, Trump's fictitious narratives about himself that he has arduously constructed for more than four decades had combined with his adroit expertise in newsmaking and media manipulation. They paid off far better than the Donald had ever imagined they would. Neither Trump nor his campaign ever thought that he would win the election and become the 45th president of the United States.

When surprisingly he won the election, his branding value took a downturn with his affluent clientele who wanted his name removed from the skyscraping condominiums where they resided, for example. However, winning the first election and losing the second election reaped sizable material gains for the Donald, the latter by a long shot even more than the former. During his occupancy of the White House, the former president routinized profitable emoluments vis-à-vis the Trump International Hotel Washington only a few blocks from the White House and at his Mar-a-Lago Golf Club in Florida as well as at Trump National Golf Club Bedminster, New Jersey. Following his electoral and popular defeat for a second term in 2020, there were the political war chests worth hundreds of millions of dollars that he accumulated for his political and personal use as part of his Big Lies and Stop the Steal campaigns.

Trump first tested the political waters when he publicly proposed himself as the running mate for the first President George Bush in 1988. The job went to the former Republican Vice President Dan Quayle who decades later would advise Vice President Pence not to overturn the election on January 6. Back in July of 1988, the Donald had arrived in Atlantic City on his yacht, the *Trump Princess*, where cheering crowds had greeted him without his having to pay any out-of-work actors to show up as he did when he announced his actual candidacy for the presidency in 2015. Johnston reports that a "phalanx of teenage girls jumping up and down, squealed with delight as if they had just seen their favorite rock star." As Trump and first wife Ivana took an escalator upward this time into Trump's Castle Casino, the crowd continued to cheer them on. Donald loved it especially when "one man shouted loudly, 'Be our president, Donald'."[12] Trump was no doubt catching a political fever that he would nurture and eventually turn into several moneymaking schemes.

In 2000, he had a short-lived bid for the presidency on the ticket of the Reform Party, a fringe political group that counted its members in the tens of thousands rather than in the tens of millions. Trump understood that a third party run stood no chance of winning the presidency. However, he had figured out that there was money to be made from running for political office. The Donald claims in this "run" that he had arranged a million-dollar deal involving his giving ten motivational speaking events hosted by Tony Robbins. Accordingly, the short-lived presidential candidate "coordinated his campaign appearances around the speeches so the campaign would pay for the use of his Boeing 727 jet."[13]

Once again in 2012, Trump declared his candidacy. While most talking heads were taking him seriously, Lawrence O'Donnell, host of MSMBC's The Last Word, was speculating that Trump had an alternative motive than 1600 Pennsylvania Avenue. He opined that the Donald was simply hustling a better contract with the NBC television network for his *Celebrity Apprentice* show. When he dropped out of the race because his television audience needed him more than the White House did, journalists concluded that this short-lived campaign had been a ruse of some kind. Therefore, when the Donald once again announced in 2015 that he was running for the Republican Party's nomination, Trump was met with a great deal of disbelief. However, this time things were different:

> Trump's ratings were in decline. His show was at risk of being cancelled. To Trump, a man who reads the New York tabloids religiously, I knew that just about the worst fate he could imagine for himself short of death, would be waking up to these *Daily News* and *Post* covers: "NBC to Trump: You're Fired."[14]

Now think about the campaign launching in 2015 when Donald and Melania descended the Trump Tower escalator to the hotel lobby. Waiting below were the sensitivities of most New Yorkers and guests hanging around the hotel lobby that day. Like most politicos—left, center, and even right—they were all a gashed at the foul, racist, and xenophobic garbage spilling from Trump's oratory lips that late afternoon in June. To suppress that reaction in that upscale setting as much as they could, the fixer Cohen had been at work arranging things for the Boss by planting in the gathered crowd out-of-work New York actors as 50 dollars a pop. On cue, they all heartily applauded and cheered wildly for Trump. The talking heads and politicos were all immediately dismissive of Trump's campaign before it had even begun.

In 2016, the alleged multibillionaire talked a good game of self-financing his own campaign. He never did so of course, not one thin dime of his own money. Instead, as usual, Trump was making out like a bandit with a large share of his campaign money raised "spent paying himself for the use of his Boeing 757, his smaller jet, his helicopter, his Trump Tower office space, and other services supplied by Trump businesses."[15] You might be asking yourself, "Is this even legal?" Yes, it is. According to the anticorruption campaign law, Trump is obligated to pay charter rates for his aircraft and market prices for services from his other businesses in order "to prevent vendors from underpricing services to win political favors—a legacy of a time when no one imagined that a man of Trump's presumed immense wealth would buy campaign services from himself."[16] In short, the prevailing law still ensures that Trump would make a profit from his 2016 campaign, win or lose, just like he did in 2020. Nevertheless, the Attorney General for the District of Columbia sued the president-elect's 2017 inaugural committee, the Trump Organization, and his children in January

2020 for, among other things, the improper expenditures of $300,000 for a private party that enriched the family business.[17]

Before diving into the rest of this chapter, the time has come to share Donald's take on business elites and corporate power vs. political elites and governmental power. Trump does not hold our political leaders in the same high esteem as he does our economic leaders. In part, this is because real economic superstars intimidate the Donald very much. He shows no similar deference to political superstars. In part, this is because Trump views powerful CEOs as the smartest guys in the room. In his mind, they are the real winners and killers in all societies, democratic or authoritarian. These power brokers know how to take out the competition, eat them alive, and spit them out. Afterward, these "killers" reabsorb and make them over as underlings. In realpolitik terms, Donald knows who is filling his or any other politico's campaign war chests. Thereby greasing or making possible their play in the game of political rackets should they "choose" to play. Thanks to Citizens vs. United, Trump also appreciates the fact that it is the financially rich and corporate wealthy who are the ones buying politicians and not vice versa.

As for politicians themselves, Donald disses both Republicans and Democrats alike, even the most powerful ones as he views most of them as not very strong or cutthroat enough in their dealings for his personal taste. They either do not know how or they are not inclined to do whatever is necessary to take care of business. Unless push comes to shove most of them would rather not break the rules or lie, slander, and libel their opponents or cruelly attack and harm others or negatively label their adversaries at the drop of a proverbial hat. Lately, however, this has radically changed especially with the Trumpian wantabes who have become outrageous too. Think of the tag team of GOP Matt Gaetz-Marjorie Taylor Greene who receive celebrity treatment from the Trump base at MAGA rallies but lack any real power on the Hill. More importantly, to the Donald, politics is just another racket for generating wealth.

The other power-hungry politicians have all learned that it was Donald's gift for the verbal assault and his lubricated potty mouth that allowed him with no actual political experience or knowledge about the workings of government to walk all over the field of 21 competing primary Republican candidates. In less than 30 days, he took the lead for the nomination and rarely ever looked back. Less than a year later, Trump had secured the Republican Party's nomination. And one year after that the politically powerful Republican naysayers of Donald Trump had either been silenced or converted into public kowtowing brown noses. Although I can only speculate here, it appears that Boss Trump took over the Republican Party with less difficulty than other mobsters take over the territories of rival groups of syndicated criminals.

One final point or two about the deceiving Donald: Not only is Trump the equal opportunity con artist that bullshits everybody, but also, he is excellent at it. For example, the champion of chameleons is a socially stuck up and class snob who can wine and dine or party with anyone to get the desired outcome. This especially includes his MAGA base of supporters that are quite repulsive to the germophobic ex-president. Donald also believes that his conspiracy trusting QAnon followers are a bunch of idiots, even dimmer than his trusting evangelical true believers. For the record, the Donald does not believe for one minute any of the conspiracy theories floating about nor does the Atheist-in-Chief believe in any religion. However, the realist and pragmatic Donald Trump knows that most of his sycophantic base believes in both, so he plays them as he plays everyone else with his bonafide fakery. To the best of his grifting abilities, the Donald feeds craziness, nurtures conspiracies, and exploits the absurdities for every single dollar and vote that they are worth to him.

Trumpism, the tactician, and the hatemonger

Some argue historically that narrow-mindedness or illiberalism represents the symptoms of a fascist political infection; others argue that we are witnessing an era of neo-fascist inflection. I for one do not believe either of these arguments or their envisioned political scenarios of a post-democratic authoritarian state per se. If fascism comes to America, it will come not with jackboots and disappearances but with smiley faces and reality TV series. Several decades ago, Bertram Gross referred to this cultural expression as "friendly fascism."[18] At the same time, I believe that what we are witnessing to paraphrase Stephen K. Bannon is the struggle to deconstruct the constitutional state. Or in the words of Washington Post columnist Robert Kagan:

> The United States is heading into its greatest political and constitutional crisis since the Civil War, with a reasonable chance over the next three to four years of incidents of mass violence, a breakdown of federal authority, and the division of the country into warring red and blue enclaves.[19]

The 2020 "stop the steal" crusades though a bit chaotic and amateurish were successful. For example, the campaign to overturn the election and the failed coup were very effective in organizing Republicans nationwide and have been surpassed by Republican controlled states passing restrictive election rules to ensure that Trump and Trumpism are victorious in 2024 should the Donald still be eligible to run for office.

The principal means for retuning Trump to the White House beyond voter restriction legislation is the establishment of a political infrastructure to legally nullify vote counts and overturn election results. These erroneously "rigged" and "stolen" elections and the recounts of 2020 were dress rehearsals to undermine the democratic election process. These pre- and post-election campaign efforts were very successful in delegitimizing the voting system. They also helped to spawn the Republican movement to facilitate Trump and his supporters taking control of the state and local election officials that they lacked control of in 2020. By the spring of 2021, numerous bills had already been proposed or passed in 16 Republican-controlled statehouses that allow simple majorities of state legislatures to overturn elections by voting to revoke their Secretary of State's issuance or certification of a presidential elector's certificate of election.

Now imagine in 2024 such a political-election scenario unfolding, as Trump and the Republicans have been busy organizing and planning for since early 2020. Thus, when I imagine this 2024 Trumpian scenario to repress the certification of the actual winner of the presidency, I do so as the successful alternative of what did not occur after the 2020 election and the assault on the Capitol in 2021. I also imagine "all hell breaking loose" across the streets of America between the warring red and blue enclaves. As the former president would say, "It's going to be wild." Or as Jimmy Durante the vaudevillian, film actor and pianist used to say, "You ain't seen nothin' yet!"

Some would argue that we could blame this developing electoral crisis on the Framers of the U.S. Constitution. For when they were designing the Bundle of Compromises as it had been nicknamed and working out the "checks and balances" of power, they never imagined the Trumpian phenomenon nor did they foresee political parties, let alone two nationally unified parties. In other words, while the Founders were aware of both charismatic leaders and dangerous demagogues, they had no ideas whatsoever about the national cult of a personality. In short, the Framers provided no protections to safeguard against the types of stolen elections that the Republicans have been preparing for nor did they provide any mechanisms to protect the people from one national party of senators nullifying the impeachment of a president by the other party simply because the nullifiers were members of the same party.

Several attributes have been associated with Trumpism, including political ideologies, social emotions, and styles of governance. On the one hand, Trumpism has been viewed as a national-populist movement with a unified political base. On the other hand, it has been viewed as part of a far-right U.S. variant of a neo-nationalist worldwide movement. The Canadian political scientist David Tabachnick has described Trumpism as the intertwining of contemporary and traditional political trends involving the empowerment of celebrity, anti-establishmentarianism, nativism, and populism.[20] At the most basic level, Trumpism is about white identity and resentment.[21] To drill down further, Trumpism is about grievance, victimhood, and the rise of neo-authoritarian romanticism. Trumpism is anti-democratic, anti-elitism, anti-liberal, anti-scientific, and anti-wokeness. Trumpism is also about deconstructing a structure of social relations, governmental norms, and legal rules for the purposes of suppressing human diversity, multiculturalism, and the natural amalgamation of people. Lastly, Trumpism has been a movement to acquire and expand alt-right political power both at home and abroad.

On the ground, the Trumpian reordering of things comprises diverse factions and individuals. Though similar in zeitgeist, not all Trumpians are the same. Individually, there is the non-invested Trump political supporter or the Trumper. There are also those persons that identify collectively with Trumpism and those exhibiting the characteristics of Trumpists. What holds all these folks together is not any political ideology or agenda or economic concerns but rather that the Donald is a false prophet who has come to save them from everything they fear and resent. Namely, the blending of socialists, minority groups, and sexual deviants capturing the U.S. government and society. The Trumpists not only have contempt for the Democrats, but they also have contempt for the Republican Party establishment. They view the latter

> as corrupt and weak – 'losers,' to use Trump's word, unable to challenge the reigning liberal hegemony. They view Trump as strong and defiant, willing to take on the establishment, Democrats, RINOs, liberal media, antifa, the Squad, Big Tech and the 'Mitch McConnell Republicans'.[22]

Before Trump became the 45th POTUS and there were formally no Trumpers, Trumpists, and Trumpians per se, there was Trump, the Trump Brand, the Trump family, and the Trump Organization. There had recently been the Tea Party replaced by the smaller ultra-conservative House

Freedom Caucus that formed in 2015 whose mission statement reads: "a voice for countless Americans who feel Washington does not represent them." There were also Internet companies serving an underworld of websites. Among these were those with far-right trolls and domain names such as racisminc.com, whiteencyclopedia.com, christiansagainstisrael.com, and theholocaustisfake.com.[23] Trump's campaign strategically tapped into this hard-right and angry popular movement that had been growing for decades.

With Trump as the president-elect, this reactionary movement could now come out of its racist, sexist, and xenophobic closet. As Trump became the real or imagined exponent of a dark and powerful worldview that was dominating the alt-right airwaves, he was speaking with and on behalf of voters that most other politicians did not recognize except as belonging to Hillary's basket full of deplorables. In no time, the Donald and his impassioned base of "nutcakes" took over the Republican Party. Meanwhile, Republican lawmakers across the country started trying to revamp the electoral process, take partisan control of elections, and suppress millions of votes casted principally by black, brown, and other disadvantaged urban citizens. These anti-democratic activities in the United States are not unlike or are characteristic of other historical backlash periods that not so long ago combatted "reverse racism" and tried to reinstitute "white affirmative action" after the post-Civil Rights era in the 1970s or after Reconstruction ended in 1877 when there was the passage of Jim Crow Laws or the reincarnation of the "new" black codes of the antebellum South.

After winning the White House, there were a slew of politicos that would come and go throughout the Trump presidency, including administrative officials, cabinet appointments, and West Wing advisers until Trump could secure as best as possible only those folks around him who agreed or who would always defer to him if they did not. Two of the most influential authorities behind Trumpism were Stephen K. Bannon and Stephen Miller. In tandem, they had penned much of Trump's 2017 inaugural state of the union address to Congress. Among other things, Bannon and Miller helped Trump stoke white voters' resentments toward immigrants, Muslins, Black Lives Matter protesters, political correctness, cancel culture, and the teaching of critical race theory.

Bannon the tactician and Miller the hatemonger were the twin oracles behind economic nationalism and the American First ideology with its range of combative and odious techniques. The radically pragmatic tactician certainly can take as much credit as anybody for Trump's 2016 Electoral College win as well as for the Capitol insurrection. As a business and political correspondent for Bloomberg News, Joshua Green, author of *Devil's Bargain: Steve Bannon, Donald Trump, and the Storming of the Presidency*, has argued about Trump's unlikely victory in 2016. It was a combination of Bannon's hard-edged ethnonationalism and his many years of plotting to destroy Hillary Clinton that paved the way.[24] In advance of Trumpism, there had been a barely visible subterranean political movement both at home and abroad—call it Bannonism. Bannon had been waiting for more than a decade for the politically alt-right candidate to come along to personify his vision of the deconstructed state. Bannon's imagined vessel, if not himself, more likely would have been someone like Newt Gingrich. Eventually, Trump became that vessel as the two men turned out to be kindred spirits with parallel passions.

Before the 62-year-old Bannon became Trump's third campaign manager in August 2016, the two had been having a running conversation whenever their paths crossed at various conservative political events over the preceding years. These interactions were usually at the prompting of the Donald who was always eager to know what Steve was thinking. At both the Conservative Political Action Conference in 2013 and 2014, for example, the ethnonationalist organized panels that included former House Speaker Gingrich and former Bush administration Attorney General Michael Mukasey, father of Marc Mukasey, one of Trump's trusted lawyers and legal friend of Rudy Giuliani. While these panels were busy discussing the usual Republican preoccupations like military spending and preparedness, or the attacks on the U.S. mission in Benghazi, Bannon was "speaking about sovereignty, economic nationalism, opposition to globalization, and finding common ground with Brexit supporters and other groups hostile to the transnational European Union."[25]

After winning the presidency and taking office in January 2017, Trump announced that Bannon would be his chief strategist. This newly created position was to be equal in power to Reince Priebus' appointment as the chief of staff. Long after the second appointed chief of staff John Kelly had excommunicated the radical tactician in August 2017 from the West Wing, Bannon's influence over Trump never waned. Only days before firing Bannon, Kelly, the retired four-star Marine general who had also served as Trump's first Secretary of Homeland Security for less than seven months, was brought into the West Wing. He was charged with the impossible task of establishing military-like order out of the administrative mess riddled with leaks, vipers, and palace intrigue.[26] Of course, the chaos and disorder in the Trump administration never exactly changed. In fact, it only got worse throughout the rest of Trump's term in office. In any case, some 14 months later, the general tired of dealing with all the cluserfucking gave notice that he was exiting stage left at the end of 2018.

Bannon, from a working-class Irish Catholic family, grew up in Richmond, Virginia, where he attended an all-male Roman Catholic military academy, Benedictine High School. His parents were pro-union and Jack Kennedy Democrats. After receiving his bachelor's degree in urban planning from the Virginia Tech College of Architecture and Urban Planning, Bannon joined the Navy in 1976. He was not particularly political until after he spent two tours as an officer aboard Navy destroyers in the Pacific and in the Persian Gulf. Turned off by the U.S. response to the Iranian crisis in 1979 and turned on by Ronald Reagan and neoconservativism, Bannon returned stateside. For about one year, he was a special assistant to the Chief of Naval Operations at the Pentagon writing reports about the state of the Navy fleet worldwide.

During this period, he earned a master's degree in national security studies from Georgetown University. Bannon then acquired his MBA from Harvard where one of his former classmates told The Boston Globe that when it came to "intellectual horsepower," Steve may have been the smartest student or at least in the top three out of a class of one hundred. Similarly, Benjamin Harnwell of the Institute for Human Dignity, a Catholic organization in Rome, has referred to Bannon as a "walking bibliography." Upon graduating Harvard, Bannon headed to Wall Street to make his fortune. Christopher Caldwell, a senior editor at the conservative magazine *The Weekly Standard*, penned an op ed for *The New York Times* that appeared in February 2017:

> Bannon has won a reputation for abrasive brilliance at almost every stop in his unorthodox career – as a naval officer, Goldman Sachs mergers specialist, entertainment-industry financier, documentary screenwriter and director, Breibart News cyber-agitprop impresario and as chief executive of Mr. Trump's presidential campaign.[27]

Naturally, Trump liked the abrasive style, and he admired that Steve was indeed the real deal, a self-made multimillionaire that started out with nothing unlike the false narrative that the Donald has been peddling since the 1970s. Trump loved Steve's self-confidence and his nonstop energy. He also liked that the insurgent Bannon did not appear to be intimidated by anyone, including Trump himself. However, Donald was less enamored with Bannon's star power like when he appeared on the cover of Time magazine with the caption The Great Manipulator. Whether or not

Steve was Trump's brain or the second most powerful man in the world as of February 13, 2017, the inside story suggested that Bannon was indeed Trump's go-to tactician.

Bannon's thinking had staying power with Trump because it reinforced the former president's intuition on matters both domestic and international. In particular, the two were simpatico about what the base of the GOP wanted or cared about, what the Republican elites were failing to deliver them, and how Trump could best exploit the status quo. Importantly, whenever the Republican nominee for president needed to demonstrate some political chops, Steve provided the Donald with some intellectual gravitas by mere association. Bannon had the theories and the explanations for why global capitalism had not delivered the goods for the workers. He also understood how the regulating class or the administrative state was robbing Americans of their democratic prerogatives. Steve had the ideas for how our lost sovereignty, nostalgic laments, and cultural authenticity could be reunited and how America could be made great again. To oversimplify and in no order, excessive regulation needed curtailing, the DC political swamp needed draining, and the self-serving administrative state as well as the lobbyists operating to empower corporations and enrich crony-capitalist allies needed deconstructing.

On the campaign trail in 2016, Bannon was key in helping Trump to hone his America First message. During the first seven months of the Trump administration, he exerted a powerful influence in trying to turn his political agenda into national policy. To do so, Bannon allied himself with the few other Washington insiders that shared similar views. Notably, this included the former Alabama Senator Jeff Sessions who became Trump's first attorney general pick after firing his inherited AG James Comey for failing to pledge his loyalty to the Donald at a one-on-one dinner at the White House.[28]

In August of 2020 as part of the We Build the Wall campaign, Bannon and three colleagues were arrested and charged with conspiracy to commit mail fraud and money laundering. Bannon pleaded not guilty and was released on $5 million bail secured by $1.75 million in assets.[29] Days before the election on November 6, Bannon's Twitter account was permanently suspended for suggesting that infectious disease expert Anthony Fauci and FBI Director Christopher Wray should be beheaded. Twenty-four hours before the Capitol riots began, Bannon was circumventing the ban on his Facebook "Stop the Steal" account and urging his followers on one of his other Facebook groups, "Own Your Vote" to: TAKE ACTION. THEY ARE TRYING TO STEAL THE ELECTION. Facebook then shut this group down for supporting baseless conspiracy theories about stolen elections and QAnon.[30] Days later, the lame duck president pardoned his guru buddy who clearly knows where the Trumpian insurrectionary bodies are buried.

Before Stephen Miller became a speechwriter and immigration wonk for Trump during the 2016 campaign and then one of Donald's senior policy advisors during the full four years of the administration—a rarity indeed—he was Jeff Sessions' senatorial aide. Miller was among a minority of Trump appointees to the White House, aside from daughter Ivanka and son-in-law Jared, not only to survive but also to thrive throughout the administration. In tandem initially with Bannon who had been one of Miller's later mentors, they fine-tuned the existential narrative threat to America and worked with Trump to stoke dystopian fears about migrants, their Democratic supporters, the Deep State, and American Carnage. Like Bannon, Miller often found himself in conflict with other Trump family members, especially when he encouraged or reinforced Trump's cruelest or harshest impulses. While Trump railed against illegal immigration, Miller crusaded against legal immigration:

> He targeted refugees, asylum seekers and their children, Engineering an ethical crisis for a nation that once saw itself as the conscience of the world. Miller rallied support for this agenda, even as it triggered humanitarian crises and legal battles, by courting the rage that found expression in tragedies from El Paso to Charlottesville.[31]

Miller will be remembered mostly as the architect of Trump's anti-Muslim ban, his separating children from their parents, and immigration policies more generally. He also had influence on the Department of Homeland Security narrowing its focus on protecting America from cyber threats and terrorism to sifting out the desperate and destitute people. One of his specialties was the demonization of migrants, conjuring up images of hordes of brown invaders crossing the southern borders to "rape our women, steal our jobs, and spill our blood." Leaked emails from 2019 also reveal that Miller was promoting conspiracy theories and using propaganda from white nationalist publications, which no doubt helped to secure Miller a place on the list of right-wing extremists compiled by the Southern Poverty Law Center.[32] As a spokesman for the White House for four years and as a co-conspirator of Donald's Stop the Steal campaign, Miller was also peddling unsubstantiated and false claims regarding widespread electoral fraud.

As the dynamic duo on the campaign trail, Stephen Miller and the Donald could pack a one-two punch especially when parceled for tens of thousands in attendance. Often, the opening act for one of Trump's rallies or what the Messenger-in-Chief liked to refer as their "lovefests," Miller would warm up the audience for the Donald experience. This was certainly the case when Miller addressed a sea of red MAGA caps at the San Diego Convention Center on May 27, 2016. The 31-year-old began by telling the spectators that the man who was going to save America was about to come out on stage. Waiting patiently for the erupting crowd to subside before continuing Miller would typically ask them a series of four loaded questions waiting patiently in between each question for as long as one minute: "Are you ready to secure that border?" "Are you ready to stop Islamic terrorism?" "Are you ready to make sure that American children are given their birthright in their own country?" Lastly, "Are you ready to make America great again?" As in other "call-and-response" interactions, the crowd would erupt on cue after each of the rhetorical questions.

On this evening, Miller would deviate from his script and inserted a series of demands from the audience based on his own psychodynamic history of resentment. Steve was experiencing a personally reflective and resentful get even moment many times over in classic Trumpian payback. Unlike the hisses and boos, Steve had been accustomed to growing up in politically correct Santa Monica, two hours north of San Diego, where he was well known for his teenage rages against multiculturalism; he was now soaking in the thousands of cheering people from his home state of California. When the crowd had subsided after his third query, he told them:

> I want you to shout so loud that all the people who betrayed you can hear you! Every single person who's beaten you down, and ignored you, and said that you were wrong, and mocked and demeaned and scorned you, every person who's lectured you sanctimoniously while living the high life in DC—shout so loud that their conference tables will shake![33]

Outside the convention center, more than a thousand people had gathered to protest Trump's campaign as xenophobic, racist, sexist, and so on with their signs waving "bully" and "bigot." The protesters were naturally upset about Trump describing and characterizing all Mexicans as "rapists" and "criminals" and by his calling for "a total and complete shutdown of Muslims entering the United States." Meanwhile, Trump's "troopers" were confronting his critics and eager for a brawl. "A white man spat the

N-word in a black man's face. Someone screamed 'Hitler!' A paunchy Trump supporter with a bullhorn told black men they were going to Hell."[34] Another individual responded, "God is a black man." As Trump inside was now riling up his packed arena, racial tensions were escalating, and vitriol was reaching a fever pitch outside. Punches were thrown, rags were lit on fire, and objects started flying. By the time the sun was setting on the San Diego Bay, the police had arrived with riot gear and batons on the ground and overhead helicopters were buzzing and floodlights were shining down. By the time Trump finished speaking, dozens of people had been handcuffed and hauled off to jail.

Miller grew up in the wealthy community and liberal enclave of Santa Monica, residing at the eastern edge of the Pacific Ocean and the western edge of the City of Angels. Miller was born in 1985 into a third generation of wealth accumulated mostly from real estate not unlike son-in-law Jared and with similar Eastern European heritages of pogroms and pre-Holocaust immigrants or post-Holocaust survivors in their lineages. Not exactly one of the beautiful people, Miller is prematurely bald and resembles a grownup Eddie Munster without the sideburns. Steve comes across as creepy looking even when he is dressed up in a tuxedo. Nevertheless, Miller is a showman like Trump. Miller like the Boss also has a taste for the morbid and the gruesome as when he was a 20-year-old junior at Duke University in 2005 and wrote in favor of the death penalty. In the piece for the *Duke Chronicle*, Miller informs his reader that he would take the rapist apart "piece by piece."[35]

Miller's earliest influencers on his journey away from his roots and to white nationalism, racism, and xenophobia were many. These included a subscription to *Guns & Ammo*, his daily dose of Rush Limbaugh, and Republican Governor Pete Miller's invoking the "invasion" of migrants bringing havoc to California's fiscal problems because they were subhuman welfare guzzlers. There also was the tutelage of sixties New Leftist and ex-Marxist David Horowitz who was on a national crusade to defend young conservatives in trouble for or under attack due to allegations of racism, sexism, and homophobia. Horowitz had become aware of the high school student who had been taking on the Santa Monica school board for fighting against non-existent racism and for endorsing multiculturalism and diversity. One day, the now 81-year-old Horowitz reached out to Miller when the teenager was ranting on a right-wing radio show. The two have remained friends as the adolescent boy who had first "waged an ideological war on his dark-skinned classmates and their supporters," was learning "to speak in terms of heritage and culture rather than race and skin color," and eventually went on to work from inside the White House to change the ethnic flows of migrants into the United States.[36]

At his worst, Miller "repeatedly harnessed crises to boost Trump's popularity with the base and promote delusions of a plot to ruin America."[37] When Trump faced his first impeachment trial for abuse of power and obstruction of Congress, for example, Miller used the threat of "open borders" and "turned that trouble into a doomsday pitch for reelection, helping his boss draft a long, dramatic letter to House Speaker Nancy Pelosi, accusing her of endangering democracy."[38] It read, "Your egregious conduct threatens to destroy that which our Founders pledged their very lives to build."[39]

Political style mattered more than political substance

Long before Donald and Melania descended the Trump Towner elevator in 2015, the Manipulator-in-Chief had been establishing a formidable political base and what would become millions of Americans lining up behind MAGA. Trump did so by appealing to the Obama backlash, to anti-elitism, to xenophobia and American First. At the same time, the reality TV host was forming his critical alliance with Fox News preparing for the upcoming Republican primary. It all began in the spring of 2011 when the Donald was embracing Birtherism wholesale:

> He doesn't have a birth certificate. He may have one, but there is something on that birth certificate—maybe religion, maybe it says he's a Muslim; I don't know. I have people that have been studying it and they cannot believe what they're finding.[40]

Trump knew that there was no truth whatsoever to Birtherism and that it was complete nonsense. Donald also knew that the calls to disavow birther theories were beside the point. As he understood talking Birtherism was a

> statement of values, a way to express allegiance to a particular notion of American identity, one that became the central theme of the Trump campaign itself: To Make American Great Again, to turn back the clock to an era where white political and cultural hegemony was unthreatened by black people, by immigrants, by people of a different religion.[41]

Similarly, by the 2020 campaign for reelection, Trump knew that there was no truth behind the QAnon conspiracies and the millenarian movement.

Donald had no illusions that he or anybody else was going to take the place of Jesus. Adherents of QAnon may have been dreaming of the "coming of the storm" when enemies of the MAGA movement are rounded up and executed as Trump is restored to his rightful place as the U.S. president, but the Donald knows that this is pure gobbledygook. His vision of how the scenario plays out was different as we all know by now. Back then and now, the Joker-in-Chief knows how to stoke crazy or nonsensical beliefs. As for 2024, whether he runs or not, the Donald will continue to milk conspiracy narratives of electoral fraud and stolen elections for all they are worth to him politically and economically. Astutely, Trump and his inner circle understand the relationship between the recent decline in white evangelicals and the rise of QAnon. Not too long ago, these evangelicals saw themselves as the owners of mainstream American culture, morality, and values. QAnon was at least partially a response to the feelings that white ownership of America is being suffocated by multiculturalism and ethnic diversity.[42] All of the real demographic changes and the imagined scenarios contribute to an atmosphere of fear, rage, resentment, and paranoia that Trump nurtures and exploits as part of the Donald's "cult of the personality."

The 2016 and 2020 presidential elections were first and foremost about the candidates and their styles of campaigning. In the history of U.S. elections, presidential or otherwise, Trump's style was new, unique, and deviant. It not only broke with tradition and departed from all the other political candidates Democratic or Republican, but in his authentic challenging of and defying and dancing on the normative order, the Donald was tapping into and communicating with all people regardless of their political persuasions. While breaking with modern political linguistic tradition, Donald was adopting the pre-modern linguistic tradition of court jesters, street performers, clowns, and outlaws. Love or hate the Donald, most people take subconscious delight in his anarchism and are captivated by his political shtick as entertainment. This Trumpian ability as a politician has been one of the key components of Donald's appeal across the socioeconomic spectrum. It also helps to explain one billionaire's popularity with the commoners or the working classes.

In the first part of this book, I argued that Trump does not have much of a sense of humor especially when it is at his own expense. Like in the fall of 2019 when he checked into Walter Reed Hospital to have his last colonoscopy. The Donald did not disclose the procedure to the American people because he allegedly did not want to provide late night television with any material that might make him the butt of another Stephen Colbert or Jimmy Fallon joke. However, Trump very much enjoys making fun of or putting other people down as he imagines at their expense. As part of the creation of spectacle and comedic entertainment, Trump's gestural repertoire of exaggerated facial and bodily expressions when used in coordination with verbal strategies designed to lampoon his opponents essentialize identity politics and cast members of various groups as problem citizens.[43] From Democrats to socialists, from the disabled to the mentally ill, from refuges to the lower classes, from Mexicans to Muslims, and from women to transgender persons. But never does the political Donald show disrespect for or put down any of the hatemongers from white supremacists to racists, from sexists to misogynists, and from homophobes to xenophobes.

Only secondarily were these campaigns about substance or party platforms rather than about abrasive style. This was especially the case in 2020 when for the first time in history the Republican Party did not bother to have an articulated platform that was very consistent with their anti-most things and do-nothing policies about other things. In 2016, the election became a classic political race between the "lesser of two evils." In relation to their positives with the voters, both Trump and Clinton were full of very high negatives. Deservedly or not, they both carried a lot of troubling baggage. As it turned out, Hillary's political and legal baggage was more tarnishing and damaging to her than Donald's social and legal baggage was to him. At the end of a squeaker election where less than 200,000 votes made the critical difference to Trump's winning, the loss could be boiled down to "crooked" or "corrupt" Hillary being less electable than "they let you grab them by the pussy" and "despicable" Donald.

While the Republic platform in 2016 had been presented as the most conservative one in U.S. history and the Democratic platform had been presented as the most progressive, regardless of party affiliation, most people and conventional wisdom assumed that the Donald would lose and Hillary would win. Although there was no new formal Republican platform adopted, the party did reference its 2016 platform without change or amendment in 2020. The Republicans were still very much the party of anti-science, anti-environment, and anti-regulation. For example, in deference to the Spreader-in-Chief, there was conspicuous silence and no mention of the pandemic during the Republican convention. What probably made the difference or shaped the outcome of the election in favor of Biden were the COVID-19 virus and the embarrassing daily briefings by the former president in late winter and early spring as well as his dismal overall handling of the U.S. response to the pandemic.[44]

Rhetorically, Trump and his minions' talking points shifted a bit in 2020. That is to say, the GOP's enemies' list or its emphasis on favorite scapegoats was less about the threats from anti-Muslim terrorists and more about the dangers of the popular Black Lives Matter movement, critical race theory, and Antifa. While the progressive and moderate factions of the Democratic Party had their differences and vibrant debates on policy matters during and after the 2020 primaries, their platform did not markedly change from 2016, but the political and economic conditions especially due to COVID had. When Biden had secured the necessary number of votes to win the nomination, the party despite its differences immediately united behind Joe to defeat the Autocrat-in-Chief as quite literally the sacrosanctity of democracy was at stake and is again in 2022 still threatened by the former president and Trumpian Republicans at large.

2016 Democratic and Republican differences

Before highlighting the differences between the Democratic and Republican platforms, it is worth noting that one platform moved to the left of its nominee, and one moved to the right of its nominee. The Democrat's statement of principles incorporated the viewpoints of runner-up for the nomination of Bernie Sanders and the progressive wing of the party, shifting its platform to the left of Hillary Clinton. The Republican platform shifted conversely to the right of Donald Trump as the Republican National Committee was concerned that the businessman from New York was not conservative enough. Ten of those differences included[45]:

1 Abortion

Democrats:

Every woman should have access to quality reproductive health care services, including safe and legal abortion.

Republicans:

Abortion should be illegal in all cases and the Constitution should be amended to ban the procedure.

2 Same-Sex Marriage

Democrats:

Applauded the U.S. Supreme Court decision legalizing same-sex marriage.

Republicans:

Condemned the court decision.

3 Immigration

Democrats:

Called for fixing the broken immigration system and establishing a path to citizenship for 11 million undocumented immigrants.

Republicans:

Embraced Trump's building a wall along the U.S.-Mexican border but they were silent about his wanting to deport 11 million immigrants.

4 Climate Change

Democrats:

Poses an urgent and substantial threat to the environment, to the economy, to our national security, health, and well-being as well as our children's future.

Republicans:

Casted doubt on the science by rejecting the findings of the United Nations' International Panel on Climate Change as they maintained these reflected a political mechanism without tolerance toward those who dissent from its orthodoxy and not a truly unbiased scientific institution.

5 Medicare

Democrats:

Allow Americans older than 55 to enroll and opposed any attempts by Republicans to privatize, voucherize, or phase out Medicare.

Republicans:

End the health care program for the elderly and require seniors to either enroll in a private insurance plan or face cuts in the amount covered by the government.

6 Wall Street

Democrats:

Continue to implement, enforce, and build on banking regulations to curb risky practices by financial institutions as well as oppose to any efforts to weaken regulation.

Republicans:

Blamed the Great Recession not on the actions of the mega financial institutions of Wall Street but on governmental housing policies and they referred to banking regulations as an excuse for unprecedented governmental intervention into the financial markets.

7 Iran

Democrats:

Maintain President Obama's ten-year agreement to relax economic sanctions in exchange for verifiable curbs on the development of a nuclear bomb.

Republicans:

Calling the agreement a security threat to the United States and others as well as a personal one between the president and his negotiating partners and therefore should not be binding on the next president.

8 Israel

Democrats:

Backing a secure and democratic Jewish state of Israel and for Palestinians to be able to govern themselves in their own viable state.

Republicans:

While supporting Israel security and right to exist as a Jewish state, they were silent about the two-state solution that has been a bipartisan cornerstone of the U.S. foreign policy for more than 50 years. They also called for moving the U.S. embassy to Jerusalem from Tel Aviv (that Trump executed and opened May 14, 2018).

9 Money in Politics

Democrats:

Favored the overturning of the Citizens United decision that eased restrictions on corporate (and union) campaign spending and called for an ending to secret and unaccountable money vis-à-vis more disclosure and transparency through either executive order or legislation.

Republicans:

Favored repealing or raising contribution limits and also allowing outside groups to spend millions of dollars on campaigns while hiding the donors from public disclosure.

10 Voting Rights

Democrats:

Opposed laws requiring certain forms of voter identification to preserve the fundamental right to vote.

Republicans:

Already blabbing on about non-existent voter fraud, they called for voter identification requirements while referring to the state and federal court judges as bullies for ruling that these would be discriminatory against poor and minority voters.

2020 Democratic and Republican differences

The 11 policy or ideological differences highlighted between the Democratic and Republican platforms in 2020 overlap with seven of those highlighted in 2016 if one interchanges Medicare from 2016 with Health Care from 2020. Three new issues were highlighted in 2020, Gun Rights, Mass Transit, and Corporate Taxes, while two issues were dropped, Iran and Same-Sex Marriage. Eleven of those differences included[46]:

1 Abortion

Democratic and Republican positions were essentially the same as 2016.

2 Health Care

Democrats:

While failing to adopt Sanders' call to abolish private insurance and adopt Medicare for All, they did call for a public option along with strengthening the Affordable Care Act.

Republicans:

Continued to advocate for the repeal of the Affordable Care Act of 2010 for the tenth straight year without any replacement health care plan.

3 Immigration

Democrats and Republican positions were essentially the same as 2016.

4 Climate Change

Democrats ratcheted up the existential threats to communities from coast to coast and emphasized that there was no time to waste in this global emergency. The Republicans were sticking with non-science, doubling down on reality denting, and continuing with the present levels of environmental pollution.

5 Gun Rights

Democrats:

Come fully loaded with no shortage of legislating "new" bills, including universal background checks, banning the manufacture and sale of assault weapons and high-capacity magazines, ending online sales of guns and ammunition, preventing individuals convicted of hate crimes from possessing weapons, repealing the law protecting gun companies from most lawsuits, and encouraging states to license firearm owners.

Republicans:

Opposed all weapons bans and gun licensing of any kind.

6 Wall Street

Democrats called for strengthening and enforcing the regulations passed in response to the 2018 economic downturn, while the Republicans were staying pat with blaming the government for its handling of the housing crisis rather than the fraudulent securities transactions.

7 Mass Transit

Democrats:

Committed to public transportation as a public good, providing good paying transit jobs, and investing in assessable and affordable passenger transportation for all people, including those with disabilities.

Republicans:

Called for an end to federal support for public transportation maintaining that it is a local affair and serves only a small portion of the population.

8 Voting Rights

Democrats:

Strive to restore the full powers of the Voting Rights Act referring to Section 4(b) that the U.S. Supreme Court struck down in 2013 with a 5 to 4 vote. Supported passing the John Lewis Voting Rights Act in the Senate that was essentially the same as the Voting Rights Advancement Act that was passed by the House of Representatives on December 6, 2019 and defeated in the Senate when all the Democrats voted in favor and all but one Republican voted against. They also committed to roll back recently enacted voting discriminatory voting policies recently put in place to prevent people of color from voting.

Republicans:

Continued their voter suppression course.

9 Israel

Democrats:

Stayed the two-state solution. They also opposed BDS or the anti-Israel boycott, divestiture and sanctions movement, as well as terrorism, settlement expansion, annexation, and any other unilateral steps by either the Israelis or the Palestinians.

Republicans:

Once again were silent about a two-state solution. They also called BDS "anti-Semitism" that should be denounced by advocates of "academic freedom."

10 Money in Politics

Democrats:

Maintained their position that money is not speech and corporations are not people. They proposed banning corporate political action committee contributions to candidates, requiring that all money-spending groups on campaigns identify their donors and called for a Constitutional amendment banning the private financing of elections.

Republicans:

Stayed the course of unlimited dark money contributions to campaigns.

11 Corporate Taxes

Democrats:

Favored action to reverse the Trump administration's windfall tax cuts benefitting the super-wealthy and corporations exporting American jobs overseas. Biden pledged to raise the corporate tax rate from

21 percent to 28 percent and to also raise taxes on Americans earning over $400,000 annually. The party was silent about the most important need to tax capital gains like other income where the vast majority of economic inequality comes from in the United States.

Republicans:

Were standing pat on lowering the corporate tax rate to all-time modern lows.

Policy undertakings by the Trump administration

Over the course of four years, President Trump by executive orders mostly dismantled or disrupted multilateral pacts overseas, sparked a tariff war with China, overhauled tax and immigration systems, reversed Obama-era efforts to fight climate change in conjunction with slashing environmental regulations, and tried to implement mostly repressive crime control measures with respect to powerless offenders while ignoring or assisting the crimes of the powerful. As Wonders and Danner argue in "Regulatory Rollbacks and Deepening Inequalities," most of Trump's interventions in a variety of ways were "privileging wealthy corporations and elites, while rolling over the rights and social protections historically afforded many other groups."[47] With respect to inequalities and privileges, Michalowski and Brown have argued that most of Trump's deregulation had created conditions that were likely to "increase state-facilitated corporate crimes that will result in excess deaths, avoidable illnesses and injuries, and a degradation of public health."[48]

With respect to foreign policy and trade, Trump tried to topple the NATO alliance, alienated European allies, and admired as well as indulged autocrats from the Middle East to Latin America. Specifically, the Donald engaged in a series of withdrawals from accords and bodies, including the Iran nuclear deal, the World Health Organization, the U.N. Human Rights Council (formerly the U.N. Commission on Human Rights), and The Paris (climate) Agreement. He abruptly pulled the military out from Syria. Trump also introduced new taxes and other hurdles on imported goods such as steel and Chinese-made industrial components, and challenged the operating rules of the World Trade Organization. On his third day in office, Trump quit the Trans-Pacific Partnership, a 12-country Pacific Rim trade deal that had been negotiated under Obama. His administration also renegotiated the 1994 North American Free Trade Agreement though it remained essentially unaltered except for adding digital trade rules and some stronger labor and environmental standards insisted on by the Democrats. Under Trump's watch by August 2020, the trade deficit had jumped to its highest level in 14 years.[49]

Trump's only piece of legislation of significance was the Tax Cuts and Jobs Act (TCJA) signed in December 2017. The act was the most important restructuring of the U.S. tax system since the 1981 Reagan administration had slashed the corporate tax rate from 70 percent to 50 percent. The $1.5 trillion tax cut reduced indefinitely the corporate rate from 35 percent to 21 percent. The act also cut minimum, estate, and gift taxes for the very wealthy as well as eliminated some deductions for homeowners especially in high-tax Democratic states. Consequently, the U.S. corporations brought home billions of dollars in cash from abroad. Unfortunately, rather than increase capital investment or hire more workers and support the raising of the minimum wage to $15.00, most multinational corporations simply boosted their stock buybacks further enriching the wealthy. The passage of the law added more than one trillion dollars to the U.S. deficit. Finally, TCJA lowered the federal income tax rates slightly for most individuals and raised the standard deductions a bit as well. The last two provisions were set to expire after 2025.

Making good on the central plank of his 2016 election campaign, Trump revamped the U.S. immigration system. Initially, he tightened borders, reduced refugee admissions and access to asylum, and instituted a sweeping ban that targeted mostly travelers from majority-Muslim and African nations. Trump also imposed new bureaucratic hurdles to make legal immigration more difficult than previously. Next, he pressured Mexico and Central American countries to make it more difficult for migrants to travel North through their countries to the United States. In the most widely condemned action, Trump and Stephen Miller with the Cabinet Secretaries unanimously signing off on the "zero tolerance" policy at the southwest borders that separated some 2,000 children from their families.[50] Later, another policy denied entry to almost all asylum seekers forcing them to wait in Mexico pending the outcome of their refuge case that could take several months or longer. Regarding the building of the wall on the southern border that Trump had promised Mexico would pay for during the 2016 campaign, the former president had to divert billions of dollars from military allocations because neither Mexico nor the U.S. Congress was willing to ante up any dollars.

As for climate change and policy, the Trump administration did away with environmental protections and regulations as a means of removing obstacles viewed as bad for the fossil fuel industry and aligned businesses. In withdrawing from the 2015 Paris Agreement and the international accord to fight global warming, Trump abandoned the U.S. pledge to slash emissions by 28 percent from 2005 levels by 2025. He also rescinded and weakened two Obama initiatives that would have helped to meet those Paris targets. First, there was the Clean Power Plan to cut emissions from the electricity sector, which the Republican states had been tying up in litigation, and was replaced by the much weaker Affordable Clean Energy rule that had no hard targets for reducing emissions. Second, Obama's national vehicle fuel efficiency targets that were aimed at reducing the pollution from cars and trucks were lowered.[51] Finally, the National Environmental Policy Act "governing environmental reviews of big infrastructure projects to reduce the weight climate considerations" was altered to permit these projects to go forward.[52]

Most of these regulatory rollbacks of Obama-era rules have reverted to pre-Trump 2017 under the Biden administration, such as the House Resolution and Executive Order signed by the 46th president on June 25, 2021, to curb once again leaks of methane (a most powerful greenhouse gas) from oil and gas operations. As a formality of the Congressional Review Act, the new administration of the opposite party or the Democrats were allowed to abolish rules established by Trump's previous executive orders within 60 legislative days after completing their first review.

What the Democrats will not be able to "fix" are the appointments of more than 200 judges to the federal benches, including 54 powerful appeals court judges in four years as compared to Obama's 55 appointments in eight years. Working closely with Majority Leader McConnell to reshape the federal judiciary particularly at the appellate level, Trump also appointed a smaller share of non-White federal judges than other recent presidents of both parties had. His appointment of women (24 percent) was slightly better than his Republican predecessors George W. Bush (22 percent) and George H.W. Bush (19 percent), but below the proportion appointed by Democrats Obama (42 percent) and Clinton (28 percent). By the end of 2020, more than a quarter of active federal judges were Trump appointees. Adding to Trump's legacy of conservative judiciary appointments is that in one term of office, the Donald "flipped" the balance of several appeals courts from Democratic majorities to Republican majorities. Trump in the words of Senator Bernie Sanders had a *huge* influence on the shape of U.S. Supreme Court appointing three ultra-conservative associate justices Neil Gorsuch, Brett Kavanaugh, and Coney Barrett. Each of these relatively young, appointed justices is projected to serve at least two decades.[53]

Criminal Justice Federal Policy: a timeline 2017–2020[54]

February 10, 2017

DJT signed three executive orders related to crime and public safety. First, the orders directed Attorney General Jeff Sessions to establish a task force on crime reduction and public safety. The force was directed to establish "strategies to reduce crime, including, in particular, illegal immigration, drug trafficking and violent crime" and put forth legislative proposals, as well as a report to the president within one year. Second, the orders instructed federal agencies to promote intelligence sharing between the federal government and state and local law enforcement—focusing on international drug cartels—and requested a report documenting actions to target and dismantle criminal drug organizations. Third, the orders required the U.S. Department of Justice to prosecute individuals who commit crimes against state and local law enforcement officers

May 10, 2017

Attorney General Jeff Sessions issued a memo outlining changes to federal prosecution of crimes. The memo sent to all 94 U.S. attorneys' offices stated that prosecutors should "charge and pursue the most serious, readily provable offense." The memo also stated that if a prosecutor did not want to pursue the most serious offense, the prosecutor had to receive supervisory approval such as from a U.S. attorney to the assistant attorney general. The memo reversed the Obama administrative policy issued by then-Attorney General Eric Holder in 2013, which encouraged prosecutorial discretion in pursuing mandatory minimum sentences in criminal charges, particularly in low-level nonviolent drug offenses.

July 18, 2017

Sessions announced revised federal asset forfeiture policy expanding the assets seized by state and local laws in connection to proceeds from or used to facilitate federal crimes typically illicit drug dealing and requiring annual training from all law enforcement agencies on state and federal laws conducted by the DOJ Asset Forfeiture Program.

July 25, 2017

Sessions announces criminal justice grant requirement changes for localities receiving Byrne Memorial Justice Assistance Grants adding two new "sanctuary city" criteria for JAG eligibility: (1) Funded jurisdictions had to honor requests from federal immigration officials to receive 48-hour notice prior to releasing certain detainees and (2) these jurisdictions had to allow federal immigration officials to assess local jails and prisons in order to interrogate prisoners.

In response, several lawsuits were filed by the City of Chicago on August 7, 2017, by San Francisco and the state of California on August 14, 2017, and by the city of Philadelphia on August 30, 2017. Chicago claimed that the new criteria were unconstitutional because these grants were based on a statutory formula created by the Congress. This resulted in the U.S. Court of Appeals for the 7th Circuit granting a preliminary injunction and releasing a ruling upholding a nationwide injunction on April 19, 2018. Similarly, SF and California argued that the new grant requirements were violating the U.S. Constitution and were detrimental to public safety. They also challenged federal agents, given access to correctional facilities and the 48-hour notice to Homeland Security before releasing individuals wanted by immigration authorities. On September 10, 2018, Judge Orrick granted summary judgment for California, which was appealed by the DOJ and eventually upheld by the Ninth Circuit on July 13, 2020. The DOJ appealed the case to the Supreme Court on November 17, 2020, following the presidential election. On March 4, 2021, the DOJ agreed to dismiss the appeal to the Supreme Court. Philadelphia and the city solicitor general essentially argued that the attorney general did not have statutory authority to change the Byrne justice grant requirements regarding immigration-related activities. The U.S. District Judge Michael Baylson issued a preliminary injunction on November 15, 2017. It ruled again on June 6, 2018 that the city was entitled to its grant money and that the Trump administration attempt to withhold federal funds was in violation of both statutory and constitutional laws.

September 15, 2017

DOJ announces that it was beginning to overhaul Obama's initiative on police reform effectively putting an end to the six-year-old program to reform local police departments and improve police-community relations. Reforms were put in place after Ferguson and in the wake of numerous police shootings and other controversial incidents of abuse of force. Instead of these efforts, the Trump DOJ would focus on providing more direct support to police officers fighting gangs, drugs, and violent crime as well as those officers dealing with protests over police abuse and on behalf of human rights.

These changes in policing were consistent with the lawless Trump's approach to "law and order" advocated for during the campaign and in his first several months of office when the former president was very busy lying about violent crime having soared to record highs when the opposite had been the case of record lows. Even before the murder of George Floyd occurred, Jeremy Stahl had underscored the three ways in which the DOJ and Trump were aligning rhetorically on behalf of police officers who commit brutality and undoing the modest reform efforts of Obama: First, it ended "the practice of placing police departments that violate constitutional rights under court-supervised consent decrees." Second, it ended a voluntary federal-state collaborate reform program "over the opposition of police chiefs—including Republicans—who embraced the initiative." Third, it "reversed limits on a program that has provided billions of dollars of military-grade vehicles and weapons" to local police departments as a means of demilitarizing and descaling violence.[55]

March 7, 2018

President Donald Trump issued an executive order establishing the Federal Interagency Council on Crime Prevention and Improving Reentry. The order's stated purpose was to prevent crime, improve public safety, and "provide those who have engaged in criminal activity with greater opportunities to lead productive lives." It called on the council to examine ways to reduce recidivism and improve the process for individuals re-entering society after incarceration.

No problem with establishing a council with stated purposes, however, it appears that the council may have only met once in 2020. More importantly, there is no report or evidence of activity that the council ever examined ways to reduce recidivism and improve the re-entry of federal prisoners.

March 20, 2018

A few days after Trump announced his first of two plans to fight the opioid epidemic, Sessions issued a memo to the U.S. attorneys encouraging them to seek the death penalty for drug traffickers when appropriate as when drug cases include "certain racketeering activities," "the use of a firearm resulting in a death during a drug trafficking crime," "murder in furtherance of a continuing criminal enterprise," and "dealing in extremely large quantities of drugs."

Although the timing of the announcement and the memo may not be coincidental, I am fairly confident that neither Trump nor Sessions was thinking of executing the CEOs of McKesson, Cardinal Health, AmerisourceBergen, and Johnson & Johnson who as the Big Four in the making and distribution of prescription opiates settled numerous lawsuits to the tune of $26 billion with those cities and counties across the country that had been devastated by their manufactured opiate crisis that killed millions of Americans.

April 11, 2018

Trump signs the overwhelming bipartisan Fight Online Sex Trafficking Act. The law makes it easier for victims of online sex trafficking to take legal action against websites for facilitating these crimes. The law also allows victims to seek damages and it increases fines and prison terms for individuals who promote or facilitate sex trafficking online.

December 20, 2018

Trump signs the First Step Act of 2018. By giving a judge more discretion when sentencing nonviolent repeat drug offenders, the law reformed lifetime mandatory minimum sentences and made the Fair Sentencing Act retroactive. The law also provided prisoners with drug treatment programs, vocational training and educational instruction, as well as the ability to earn credit for early release, and lastly allowed for inmates to be placed closer to their family and friends to allow for easier and more frequent visitations.

The act had bipartisan support receiving a vote of 358 to 36 in the House and 87 to 12 in the Senate. Unfortunately, the law jurisdictionally only affects federal and not state or local inmates. In other words, the First Step Act impacted less than ten percent of those persons locked up in the United States as of June 2021. Should the states adopt similar measures, then the departments of corrections would find themselves carrying out the same policies that the federal and state systems were all practicing back in the 1950s and 1960s. Welcome back to the progressive future of the past where the United States still leads the developed world in its rates of locking up people especially with respect to nonviolent offenders and people of color.

July 13, 2020

At the Federal Correctional Institution in Terre Haute, Indiana, the Trump administration carried out the first of 13 executions beginning with Daniel Lewis Lee, a convicted killer of three members of an Arkansas family in 1996.

After a 17-year hiatus, the Trump Justice Department resumed federal executions during the height of the pandemic when more than 120,000 inmates had contracted COVID-19. The 13 executions were more than the number of federal death sentences carried out in the previous 56 years combined. The first woman to be executed in 70 years was among those executed. Not since Grover Cleveland's presidency in the late 1800s had the U.S. government ever executed any federal inmates during a presidential transition period.[56]

Notes

1 Wilfred Codrington III, 2019. The Electoral College's Racist Origins. *The Atlantic*. November 17. https://www.theatlantic.com/ideas/archive/2019/11/electoral-college-racist-origins/601918/.

2 In front of an open microphone on the television set of "Days of Our Lives" where Trump was making a cameo appearance, the Donald is on tape saying among other things:

> You know, I'm automatically attracted to beautiful women – I just start kissing them. It's like a magnet. Just kiss. I don't even wait. And when you're a star, they let you do it…Grab 'em by the pussy. You can do anything.

3 Politico Staff, 2016. Full transcript: Third 2016 Presidential Debate. October 20. https://www.politico.com/story/2016/10/full-transcript-third-2016-presidential-debate-230063.

4 Joshua Green, 2017. *Devil's Bargain: Steve Bannon, Donald Trump, and the Storming of the Presidency*. New York: Penguin, pp. 8–9.

5 The *New York Times* bestselling book was authored by Peter Schweizer and published by Broadside Books, a division of HarperCollins, and was adapted into both a film and a graphic novel. Most importantly, the book was a product of a team of researchers from the Government Accountability Institute, an institution formed by Schweizer and the then Executive Chairman of Breitbart News, Steve Bannon. The Mercer Family Foundation funded the $2.6 million cost of producing the book. Meanwhile, as revealed in *Spooked: The Trump Dossier, Black Cube, and the Rise of Private Spies* (2021) by Barry Meier, there was Fusion GPS first retained by the Democratic Party to find dirt on Trump before the 2016 election, which produced the Steele Dossier that found its way into the investigations of the Russians and Trump.

6 I believed before the election and after that Bernie Sanders would have been a better adversary going head-to-head against Trump for several reasons, but primarily because he was less vulnerable than Hillary and because he would have been able to swat away the socialist charges and she could not do the same with the corruption charges. Taking off his gloves, Bernie would have taken it to the Donald by calling a spade a spade; he would have pulled no punches: "I would have loved to run against him, to tell you the truth. He's a fraud and he's a phony. That's what he is, and he has to be exposed for that." Quoted in Maureen Dowd, 2021. The Ascension of Bernie Sanders. *The New York Times*, July 11: Opinion, 7.

7 Noland D. McCaskill, 2016. Graham: We Should Have Kicked Trump Out of the Party. *Politico*. March 3. https://www.politico.com/blogs/2016-gop-primary-live-updates-and-results/2016/03/lindsey-graham-donald-trump-kicked-out-220402.
8 Daniella Diaz, 2018. Republican Sen. Lindsey Graham Says He'll Support Trump in 2020. *CNN*. April 19. https://www.cnn.com/2018/04/19/politics/lindsey-graham-donald-trump-2020-election/index.html.
9 Phillip Bump, 2021. The Government Finally Connected the Line from Trump's Campaigns to Russian Intelligence Five Months After the 2020 Election. *The Washington Post*, April 15. https://www.washingtonpost.com/politics/2021/04/15/government-finally-connects-line-trumps-campaign-russian-intelligence/.
10 Michael Cohen, 2020. *Disloyal, a Memoir: The True Story of the Former Personal Attorney to the President of the United States*. New York: Skyline Publishing, p. 208.
11 David Cay Johnston, 2016. *The Making of Donald Trump*. Brooklyn, NY: Melville House, p. xiii.
12 Ibid: xi.
13 Ibid: xi.
14 Ibid: xii.
15 Ibid: xi.
16 Ibid: xii.
17 Anna Schecter and Dareh Gregorian, 2020. D.C. Attorney Charges Trump Inaugural Committee Enriched the Family Business. NBC News, January 22. https://www.nbcnews.com/politics/trump-impeachment-inquiry/d-c-attorney-general-charges-trump-inaugural-committee-enriched-family-n1120361.
18 Bertram Gross, 1980. *Friendly Fascism: The New Face of Power in America*. New York: South End Press.
19 Robert Kagan, 2021. Opinion: Our Constitution Crisis Is Already Here. *The Washington Post*. September 23. https://www.washingtonpost.com/opinions/2021/09/23/robert-kagan-constitutional-crisis/?utm_campaign.
20 David E. Tabachnick, 2016. The Four Characteristics of Trumpism. *The Hill*. January 5. https://thehill.com/blogs/congress-blog/presidential-campaign/264746-the-four-characteristics-of-trumpism.
21 A. Graham, F. Cullen, L. Butler, A. Burton, and V. Burton, Jr., 2021. Who Wears the MAGA Hat? Racial Beliefs and Faith in Trump. *Socius* 7: 1–16. doi: 10.1177/2378023121992600.
22 Kagan, 2021.
23 Drew Harwell, Hannah Allam, Jeremy B. Merrill and Craig Timberg, 2021. Fallout Begins for Far-right Trolls Who Trusted Epik to Keep Their Identities Secret. *The Washington Post*. September 25. https://www.washingtonpost.com/technology/2021/09/25/epik-hack-fallout.
24 Green, 2017.
25 Christopher Caldwell, 2017. What Does Steve Bannon Want? *The New York Times*. February 25. https://www.nytimes.com/2017/02/25/opinion/what-does-steve-bannon-want.html.
26 Cliff Sims, 2019. *Team of Vipers: My 500 Extraordinary Days in the Trump White House*. New York: St. Martins.
27 Cardwell, 2017.

28 Sarah Childress, 2017. Stephen Bannon's Legacy at the Trump White House. PBS. August 18. https://www.pbs.org/wgbh/frontline/article/stephen-bannons-legacy-at-the-trump-white-house/.
29 Larry Neumeister, Colleen Long and Jill Colvin, 2020. Ex-Trump aide Bannon Pleads Not Guilty in Border Wall Scheme. AP. August 20. https://apnews.com/article/ct-state-wire-ap-top-news-tx-state-wire-ny-state-wire-politics-6119b50079aaf30ba54b8e40bd36033b.
30 David Gilbert, 2021. Steve Bannon Urged Facebook Followers to 'Take Action' on Eve of Capitol Riot." *Vice News*. January 15. https://www.vice.com/en/article/n7vqgb/steve-bannon-urged-facebook-followers-to-take-action-on-eve-of-capitol-riot.
31 Jean Guerrero, 2020. *Hatemonger: Stephen Miller, Donald Trump, and the White Nationalist Agenda*, quoted from the inside jacket. New York: William Morrow.
32 Michael Edison Hayden, 2019. Stephen Miller's Affinity for White Nationalism Revealed in Leaked Emails. *HATEWATCH*. November 12. https://www.splcenter.org/hatewatch/2019/11/12/stephen-millers-affinity-white-nationalism-revealed-leakcd-emails.
33 Guerrero, 2020: 1.
34 Ibid: 8.
35 Stephen Miller, 2005. "Justice." *The Chronicle*. Duke University. https://www.dukechronicle.com/article/2005/11/justice.
36 Guerrero, 2020: 7.
37 Ibid: 8.
38 Ibid.
39 Ibid.
40 Quoted in Adam Serwer, 2020. Birtherism of a Nation: The Conspiracy Theories Surrounding Obama's Birthplace and Religion Were Much More Than Mere Lies. They were ideology. *The Atlantic*, May 13. https://www.theatlantic.com/ideas/archive/2020/05/birtherism-and-trump/610978/.
41 Serwer, 2020.
42 Michelle Goldberg, 2021. The Christian Right Is in Decline, and It's Taking America with It. *The New York Times*. July 9. https://www.nytimes.com/2021/07/09/opinion/religious-right-america.html.
43 Kira Hall, Donna M. Goldstein, and Matthew Bruce Ingram, 2016. The Hands of Donald Trump: Entertainment, Gesture, Spectacle. *Journal of Ethnographic Theory* 6 (2): 71–100. http://dx.doi.org/10.14318/hau6.2.009.
44 Michael C. Bender, 2021. *"Frankly, We Did Win This Election: The Inside Story of How Trump Lost*. New York: Grand Central Publishing.
45 Jonathan D. Salant, 2016/2019. 10 Huge Differences between Democratic and Republican Platforms. NJ Advance Media for NJ.com. July 28/January 16. https://www.nj.com/politics/2016/07/dnc_2016_10_big_ways_the_democratic_platform_diffe.html.
46 Jonathan D. Salant, 2020. 11 Huge Differences between Democratic and Republican 2020 platforms. NJ Advance Media for NJ.com. August 20. https://www.nj.com/politics/2020/08/here-are-11-huge-differences-between-democratic-and-republican-platforms.html.
47 Nancy A. Wonders and Mona J. E. Danner, 2020. Regulatory Rollbacks and Deepening Social Inequalities. *Journal of White Collar and Corporate Crime* 1 (2): 103–112.

48 Raymond Michalowski and Meredith Brown, 2020. Poisoning for Profit: Regulatory Rollbacks, Public Health, and State-Facilitated Corporate Crime. *Journal of White Collar and Corporate Crime* 1 (2): 113–122.

49 Reuters Staff, 2020. Factbox: Donald Trump's Legacy – Six Policy Takeaways. *Reuters*. October 30. https://www.reuters.com/article/us-usa-trump-legacy-factbox/factbox-donald-trumps-legacy-six-policy-takeaways-idUSKBN-27F1GK.

50 Maya Pagni Barak, 2021. Family Separation as State-Corporate Crime. *Journal of White Collar and Corporate Crime* 2 (2): 109–121. See also, Julia Ainsley and Jane C. Timm, 2018. 1,995 Children Separated from Families at Border Under 'Zero Tolerance' Policy. *NBC News*. June 15. https://www.nbcnews.com/politics/donald-trump/1-995-children-separated-families-border-under-zero-tolerance-policy-n883716.

51 Ronald C. Kramer, 2020. Rolling Back Climate Regulation: Trump's Assault on the Planet. *Journal of White Collar and Corporate Crime* 1 (2): 123–130.

52 Quoted in Reuters Staff, 2020.

53 John Gramlich, 2021. How Trump Compares with Other Recent Presidents in Appointing Federal Judges. Pew Research Center. January 13. https://www.pewresearch.org/fact-tank/2021/01/13/how-trump-compares-with-other-recent-presidents-in-appointing-federal-judges/.

54 Most of the material for this section comes from BallotPedia: Federal policy on crime and justice, 2017–2020. https://ballotpedia.org/Federal_policy_on_crime_and_justice,_2017–2020.

55 Jeremy Stahl, 2020. How the Trump Administration Undid Obama's Response to Ferguson. *Slate*. June 02. https://slate.com/news-and-politics/2020/06/trump-doj-obama-policing-reform.html.

56 Michael Tarm and Michael Kunzelman, 2021. Trump Administration Carries out 13th and Final Execution. *AP News*. January 15. https://apnews.com/article/donald-trump-wildlife-coronavirus-pandemic-crime-terre-haute-28e44cc5c026dc16472751bbde0ead50.

5

A SINKHOLE OF ORGANIZATIONAL CORRUPTION

Trump has introduced the United States to "grand corruption" as Sudhir Chella Rajan has labeled it, referring to the unacknowledged "illegitimacy of elite networks exercising power over diverse social groups and ecosystems" and to the "collective incapacity" of people to see their "complicity in maintaining elite collusion of economic and political power, which is manifested in our own daily habits and routines."[1] Similarly, Michael Johnston has identified "influence market corruption" to distinguish it from Elite Cartel, Oligarch and Clan, or Official Mogul styles of corruption that typically engage in deals and connections circumventing established institutions. By contrast, IMC revolves around access to and operates from within established institutions. As Johnston explains, "Strong institutions reduce the opportunities, and some of the incentives, to pursue extra-system strategies, while increasing the risks." At the same time, "the very power of those institutions to deliver major benefits and costs raises the value of influence within them."[2] Another way of getting at grand corruption or influence market corruption is to say that like high-level white-collar and corporate crime, these are not only about obfuscating harms as a means of avoiding regulation, but also about blending their deviant conduct with what people accept as "just the way things are." By normalizing these forms of corrupt behavior, most people do not realize the actual extent of corruption or that people are daily victims collectively of politically organized crime.[3]

DOI: 10.4324/9781003221548-8

As columnist Paul Waldman has opined: Before Trump became the president, "we had a relatively simple understanding of government corruption…officials using their positions of public trust to benefit themselves and their associates."[4] Waldman continues that Trump has taught us that there is a lot more to corruption than meets the eye. In different words, the Donald "has offered us a corruption master class, presenting for our edification a kind of full-spectrum corruption" and in doing so "he has revealed that opportunities for corruption are far more numerous than we knew."[5] And from Mapping Corruption: Donald Trump's Executive Branch:

> Trump has sowed corruption of a breath and brazenness unseen in the far-from-innocent annals of our nation's history. In three years as president, he has transformed the executive branch into a giant favor factory, populated with the agents or willing partners of virtually every special interest. Add up all the routine, daily outrages—the quasi-bribery and quasi-extortion, the private raids on public funds, the handouts to the undeserving, the massive flow of cash, jobs, and freebies back in return—and Trump's attempt to squeeze a little re-election help out of the fragile government of a desperate Eastern European country does not loom particularly large in the reckoning."[6]

Trump has spent his dishonest life in search of money. His business history is filled with overseas financial deals and missed deals. Some of these have involved the Chinese state. The Donald "spent a decade unsuccessfully pursuing projects in China, operating an office there during his first run for president and forging a partnership with a major government-controlled company."[7] China along with Britain and Ireland are three nations where Trump maintains bank accounts. These foreign accounts do not show up on Mr. Trump's public financial disclosures where he must list his personal assets because these accounts are not in his name. In the case of China, the bank account is controlled by Trump International Hotels Management, LLC, whose tax records reveal that TIHM paid $188,561 in pursuing licensing deals there from 2013 to 2015 that did not pan out.[8] Until 2019, China's biggest state-controlled bank rented three floors in Trump Tower stateside, a very lucrative lease that had generated accusations of a conflict of interest for the former president. Citizens for Responsibility and Ethics in Washington (CREW) in its January 15, 2021 report on corruption identified more than 3,700 conflicts of interest while Trump was the president because of his decision not to divest from his business interests while in office.[9]

As far as offshore banking laws and accounts go specifically, I cannot imagine that Trump has not stashed away hundreds of millions of dollars in the Cayman Islands or Panama or... However, one of the key planks in Trump's tax reform plan during the 2016 campaign was supposed to end the practice of U.S. multinationals stockpiling hundreds of billions of dollars away in offshore accounts. Thereby bringing back to America trillions of dollars and millions of jobs. When asked publicly whether the U.S. citizens should be allowed to save or invest in offshore bank accounts, Trump responded: "No, too many wealthy citizens are abusing loopholes in offshore banking laws to evade taxes."[10]

For the record, the sheltered tax dollars did not come home nor have any of the outsourced jobs ever returned that Trump talked a lot about. These were merely 2016 talking points that were never going to materialize in a Trump administration. Not the least of all because of the political economy of corruption that Trump routinized as he moved into the White House. The argument is that Trump transformed governmental corruption into a for profit business enterprise whose hidden and malicious intents were often but not always criminal in nature. Over the past three decades, numerous examples from investments, securities, and control frauds (Savings and Loan, 1986 and 1995; BCCI, 1991; Waste Management, 1998; Enron, 2001; HealthSouth, 2003; Lehman Brothers, 2007; Wall Street; 2008; Bernie Madoff, 2009; Libor, 2011; Fannie Mae and Freddie Mac, 2011; FIFA, 2015; Wells Fargo, 2016; Volkswagen emissions, 2017) have repeatedly revealed that when the purposes sought after become power, profit, and/or pressure, these tend to displace or override the interests of people, principles, policy, process, and practice, thus increasing the risks of disasters, crises, and scandals.[11]

Powerful advisers whose financial backgrounds and inclinations were at odds with regulations, the public interest, and reversing trends in the social and economic growth of inequality both at home and abroad supported Trump's routinization of governmental corruption. Most importantly, Donald's corporate and state-organized corruption was also steeped in a social milieu where nations, lobbyists, legislators, the Republican Party, businesses, the nonprofits, and so on in order to play had to pay a stipend usually over and over to the Trump Organization. This established from the top-down an administrative apparatus marked by placing self-interest, profiteering, and racketeering above the public welfare. This even helped to contribute to the "deadly insurrection that was rooted in the same self-serving ethos."[12]

Stocking the swamp with free marketers

Trump's political appointments included more than its share of high rolling donors with no expertise in anything let alone with an appropriate area of specialty. Those appointments with expertise were in business, finance, and law. Their economic philosophy or orientation reinforced a laissez-faire approach to regulation and taxation. These free marketers were not about recouping billions, let alone trillions from the tax avoiding and tax evading dollars superrich or mega multinational corporations. Four of the key economic appointments had been beneficiaries of shell companies and offshore banking accounts, including Gary Cohn, Rex Tillerson, Steven Mnuchin, and Randal Quarles.

Chief economic adviser Gary Cohn was the driver behind the White House tax reform act. Leaked documents reveal that between 2002 and 2006, Cohn was either president or vice president of 22 separate offshore entities in Bermuda for Goldman Sachs. That was before Gary eventually became the president and COO of GS, one of the foremost banking, securities, and investment management firms in the world. As for the Secretary of State Rex Tillerson, leaked documents reveal that before he ascended to the chairman and CEO of ExxonMobil in 2006 and while still presiding as the president of ExxonMobil Yemen division, Rex was also a director of Marib Upstream Services Company that was incorporated in Bermuda in 1997. And Treasury Secretary Steven Mnuchin before joining the Trump administration was an offshore specialist and deputy chairman of CIT Bank. Steve provided "financing structures for personal aircraft priced at tens of millions of dollars, which customers used to legally avoid sales taxes and other charges."[13] Randal Quarles, Trump's most senior banking "watchdog," was also outed in connection with offshore banks and tax evasion as he appeared prominently in the infamous Paradise Papers.[14]

I could go on and discuss the three wealthiest cabinet members of the Trump cabinet, Secretary of Education Betsy DeVos, Secretary of Commerce Wilbur Ross, and Secretary of Transportation Elaine Cao, the spouse of Republican Senator Mitch McConnell. As we all know, the shining accomplishment or gift by the Donald was a $1.9 trillion tax cut enjoyed primarily by super wealthy individuals, mega corporations, and multinational businesses which already enjoyed the lowest rates in the corporate world at the financial expense of the general population. According to a Joint Committee on Taxation, the 2017 Tax Cut and Jobs Act will increase the deficit by $1 trillion between 2021 and 2031. The Tax Foundation analysis stated over the same period that the tax cuts would cost $1.47 trillion in decreased revenue while adding only $600 billion in growth and savings.[15] These economic projections are consistent with the same kinds of consequences to the economy by the radical Reagan and Bush II tax cuts, respectively, for the corporate wealthy in the United States. These neoliberal taxing policies produced the same failures in countries such as Argentina, Brazil, Russia, and every other nation where they have been utilized. As Bob Dylan sung in Love Minus Zero/No Limit from Bringing It All Back Home (1965) … "there's no success like failure and that failure's no success at all." In a nutshell, reducing the top income tax rates for the rich has to date had no appreciable effect on economic growth.[16]

Why does this matter? Because these kinds of fiscal policies reinforce and escalate inequality and criminal behavior. From preliterate to contemporary societies, inequality and not poverty has always been linked to rising rates of crime in the streets as well as in the suites. Thus, expanding inequality in the distribution of goods and services usually increases crime at the top and the bottom of society. Why? Because extreme inequality and relative deprivation undermine the basic sense of fairness and collective trust that humans, other primates, and even lower animals like dogs share. These are the core fabrics that hold most families, tribes, and societies together. When these basic qualities are violated, the cynicism of it is a dog-eat-dog world out there which unleashes, rationalizes, and normalizes cheating, dishonesty, theft, exploitation, and so forth. In other words, without social interaction and cooperation based on fairness and trust, group solidarity or the shared values and emotional empathies wither away as cultures degenerate.

For example, think about the consequences of extreme tax cuts that flow to the super wealthy and multinational corporations as well as the related and deliberately underfunded Internal Revenue Services budgets year after year. All those sheltered taxes in offshore accounts, loopholes, and other financial frauds that continue unabated rob the U.S. coffers and taxpayers of trillions of dollars annually. These stolen monies not only assault social solidarity and escalate class warfare, but so does the expected transfer according to Wealth-X of a combined US$ 18.2 million in net worth or more. From an instrumental or pragmatic point of view, capturing the sheltered and stolen trillions annually, for example, could pay several times over for the Build Back Better once upon a time Biden agenda of $7.5 trillion over ten years to address climate change, infrastructural and human development as well as the amelioration of a myriad of social problems caused by our growing inequality and immiseration of society.[17]

What most folks, non-criminologists and criminologists alike, fail to appreciate is the scope of the normalization of the interconnected and overlapping relationships of the trillions of dollars annually looted by the super wealthy and multinational corporations and other forms of criminal capital formation and accumulation. These include money laundering and other expressions of organized and white-collar crime. The magnitude or proportion of these thefts of capital from governmental coffers in relation to global wealth and its asymmetrical distribution is enormous and dwarfs both the human and financial costs of street crimes dozens of crimes over. For example, criminal activities from drug trafficking to extortion to illegal mining are central to the global economy. According to the United Nations, these illicit activities generate an estimated $2.1 trillion in global annual proceeds or about 3.6 percent of the world's GDP. For perspective, according to Barron's, Forbes, and Lovemoney, total global wealth rose 7.9 percent in 2020 to US$431 trillion.

Making matters worse, people do not realize, nor do they focus their attention on the economic reality that the money derived by organized and syndicated criminals flows through the same global banking institutions that oligarchs and other wealthy cheats like Donald Trump and company use as part of their criminal enterprises to accumulate capital. Politically, as Thom Hartmann wrote in *Salon* on July 22, 2021, the Republican Party "is so committed to making morbidly rich people even richer (and keeping them that way)" that Republican Senator Rob Portman announced that he "wouldn't go along with funding a bipartisan infrastructure bill by letting the IRS hire more auditors to catch rich tax cheats." Other captured Republican senators, including John Barrasso told *Axios* news that "spending $40 billion to super-size the IRS is very concerning" because law-abiding Americans "deserve better from their government than an army of bureaucrats snooping through their bank statements." And there was also Republican Senator Ted Cruz, the sleazeball from Texas that chimed in "Throwing billions more of taxpayer dollars at the IRS will only hurt Americans struggling to recover after the waves of devastating lockdowns." Ted's solution, "we should abolish the damn place."[18] This dribble comes from a Harvard law graduate, a former clerk for Chief Justice William H. Rehnquist, and a lawyer who has argued nine times before the U.S. Supreme Court.

Paying to play

Though Trump campaigned in 2016 to end the Washington insider culture of lobbying and favor seeking, he actually "reinvented it, turning his own hotels and resorts into the Beltway's new back rooms, where public and private business mix and special interests reign."[19] The line between the Trump Organization and the Trump administration was so thin that it is still unclear where the former president's public responsibilities ended, and his private financial interests began.

> Unlike any other modern president, Trump has forced the American people to ask if the decisions and policies his administration is implementing are because they're the best policies for the nation, or because they personally benefit him – either by helping his businesses directly or the special interests spending money there.[20]

Trump has never been about doing anything for the American people. More significantly, the Corrupter-in-Chief in terms of personal benefits was able to monetize or convert the office of the presidency into a cash-paying cow for both the Trump Organization and Trump family members.

Following his election to the White House, Donald pledged to recuse himself from running the operation of the Trump Organization that he never did. *The New York Times*' investigation found that over 200 companies and special interest groups and foreign governments reaped benefits from patronizing and spending monies at his properties. The Donald picked up a few fringe benefits such as the granting of 67 foreign trademarks to Trump businesses, including 46 from China. A mere 60 of those business customers with political interests at stake before Trump found them advanced by bringing into the family businesses nearly $12 million during the first two years of his presidency. The diversity of the patrons showing up spanned the political spectrum and competing special interests trumped each other at Trump's bazaar. Either way, the Donald and his immediate family made out like bandits as they doled out funding, laws, and land. Some of those winners and losers included: "foreign politicians and Florida sugar barons, a Chinese billionaire and a Serbian prince, clean-energy enthusiasts and their adversaries in the petroleum industry, avowed small-government activists and contractors seeking billions from ever-fattening federal budgets."[21]

By September 2020, the promised firewall between his businesses and the presidency had revealed 3,403 conflicts of interest or about two conflicts per day. These conflicts include foreign government officials conducting business or staying at Trump properties as well as other taxpayer and campaign spending at Trump businesses. They also involved Trump and family members or other politicos promoting an array of racketeering scams. These tabulated conflicts of interest may only be the tip of the pay to play iceberg. After 1,341 days in office: 88 political events had been held at Trump properties, including 13 foreign government events; 130 special interest groups events; 145 foreign officials and 141 members of Congress had visited a Trump business for a total of 344 times. Most of these visits (284) were to the Trump Hotel in D.C. Topping the list of pay to play was Senate Judiciary Committee Chairman Lindsey Graham with 27 visits, followed by Sen. Rand Paul (18) and Reps. Matt Gaetz (17), Kevin McCarthy (17), Jim Jordan (13), and Mark Meadows (13).

The top 10 political committees spending money at Trump properties included[22]:

1 Trump Victory, $2,282,630
2 Republican National Committee, $2,425,472
3 Donald J. Trump for President, $2,307,127
4 America First Action, $600,322
5 Republican Governors Association, $412,721
6 Great America Committee, $237,967
7 Protect the House, $232,837
8 Senate Leadership Fund, $94,626
9 Republican Attorneys General Association, $85,205
10 National Republican Congressional Committee, $81,367

During this period, Trump paid 503 visits to Trump businesses mostly to his golf courses (303), costing the American taxpayers at least one million dollars spent at the properties as well as more than $100 million to shuttle him to his properties. Besides the Donald, 334 administration officials visited Trump properties for a total of 885 times. First, family members and senior advisors Jared Kushner and Ivanka Trump visited Trump properties "more than any other executive branch officials with 39 and 36 visits, respectively."[23] Following them were runner ups Vice President Pence with 33 visits, former Counselor to the President Kellyanne Conway with 27 visits, and Secretary of Treasury Steven Mnuchin with 23. Competitive visitors worthy of dishonorable mentions were Wilbur Ross (19), Dan Scavino (19), Mick Mulvaney (18), Richard Grenell (17), and Sarah Huckabee Sanders (17).

Finally, 145 foreign officials from 75 governments have visited Trump properties with officials from Turkey leading the pack. At Trump's vaunted "Winter White House," Mar-a-Lago, the former president had hosted Chinese President Xi Jinping, the then Japanese Prime Minister Shinzo Abe, and lastly the far-right President of Brazil, Jair Bolsonaro, and a slew of his Brazilian officials.[24] The Xi visit was the most successful promotional event in the history of Mar-a-Lago and an unparalleled moneymaker.[25]

Mapping the corruption of President Trump

Grasping the enormity, the breadth, and the depth of Trump corruption is rather astonishing. Most news junkies and politicos alike are quite familiar with the in-your-face looting, skimming, and self-dealing of the president and his family members. Beyond the family corruption there is a much larger world of Trump corruption. A "sliminess perpetuated by literally thousands of presidential appointees from Cabinet officials to obscure functionaries."[26] It is certainly difficult to tabulate all the knaves, thieves, and corporate stooges as well as the nefarious schemes perpetrated. However, thanks to the work of The American Prospect and to the reporting of Jim Lardner, we have all been invited to https://prospect.org/mappingcorruption with an agency-by-agency exhibit of the Trump administration's major offenses known through March 2020. Thus, one can sort out much "more consequential crookedness" and follow "the plotlines of all the sordid stories," and "grasp the brutal consequences visited upon countless people."[27] At the interactive website there are extensive dossiers provided in relation to the self-dealing that was transpiring at the 15 federal departments, including one agency and one bureau during the Trump regime. I have selected three of these to highlight: The Consumer Financial Protection Bureau (CFPB), the Environmental Protection Agency (EPA), and the Department of Health and Human Services (HHS).

CFPB

On November 24, 2017, two acting directors of the Consumer Financial Protection Bureau were named. First, longtime director Richard Corday announced that he was retiring at the end of the day rather than at the end of the month as expected. In the process, Corday promoted his chief of staff Leandra English to become the acting director. In a letter to his staff, Corday wrote: "I have also come to recognize that appointing the current chief of staff to the deputy director position would minimize operational disruption and provide for a smooth transition given her operational expertise."[28] Corday, an Obama appointment, had assumed incorrectly that English would serve as the agency's acting director until the Senate confirmation of her replacement. The White House announced a few hours later that Mick Mulvaney the director of the Office of Management and Budget (OMB) would take over instead: "The President looks forward to seeing

Director Mulvaney take a common-sense approach to leading the CFPB's dedicated staff, an approach that will empower consumers to make their own financial decisions and facilitate investment in our communities."[29]

Although Mulvaney's appointment appeared to violate the succession provisions of the legislation that established the bureau, the White House's Office of Legal Counsel provided a supportive memo to the contrary. That resulted in Mulvaney becoming the acting director for the next two years while he continued to serve as the director of OMB. The author of the memo was Steven Engel who had also been the lead attorney for Advance America, the nation's biggest payday lending company. At the time, Advance America was in a dispute over its fees and charges to customers. After Mulvaney took charge the CFPA dropped the case against AA. Mulvaney had previously been a U.S. Congressman representing the city of Spartanburg, South Carolina where Advance America's corporate offices are still based. Thus, taking charge of the agency was a longtime defender of the payday industry as well as an ideological foe of efforts to regulate financial companies and their products in general. In fact, back in 2011, Mulvaney had opposed the creation of the CFPA when he referred to the agency as "a sick, sad joke."

During the 2016 election cycle, payday groups and companies gave $2.2 million to the Trump campaign and inaugural committees. The Community Financial Services Association of America the payday lending industry's main lobbying arm "spent roughly $1 million holding its 2018 and 2019 annual conferences at the Trump-owned Doral golf resort."[30] In May 2018, the CFPA sided with the payday industry's legal efforts to delay implementation of a rule "intended to block lenders from manipulating customers into unmanageable long-term debt."[31] A few weeks later, Mike Hodges, CEO of the mega-chain lender Advance Financial and spouse Tina Hodges, contributed $250,000 to the main super PAC working for Trump's re-election. Under Mulvaney's supervision of the bureau, there were multiple investigations stemming from consumer complaints of payday companies attempting to circumvent the law. The bureau also cut back significantly on enforcement and financial relief for defrauded customers. When Mulvaney stepped down in late 2019, Kathy Kraninger, an aide of his at OBM with no consumer protection experience, became the director of CFPB.[32]

Highlights from Mulvaney's "anti-consumer protection agency" included the suspension of hiring, rule-making, and fine collection; the dropping of a CFPB lawsuit against an "online lender that charged up to 950 percent interest while falsely claiming to be run by a Native American tribe in order to dodge state usury laws"; the calling off of efforts to regulate auto lenders accused of cheating vulnerable customers; and the proposing of a rule that would allow debt collectors to "barrage consumers with phone calls, text messages, and voice mails, immunizing them against liability for causing someone's confidential financial information to be disclosed to a third party."[33]

EPA

Trump's first Environmental Protection Agency Administrator was one of the Donald's most controversial appointments to a cabinet-level position. This appointment embodied the White House's broad support for the fossil fuel industry and disdain for climate science. Prior to his appointment, Scott Pruitt had made a career as Oklahoma's attorney general attacking the very federal agency that he would someday run. As an outspoken skeptic of climate change caused by greenhouse gas emissions Pruitt along with other Republican attorney generals led the charge and "sued the EPA to stop ozone and methane emissions rules and block regulations on coal-fired power plants." Of course, it was not Pruitt's anti-environmental policies that brought about his abrupt departure after 18 months in office because that was why he was hired in the first place.

Pruitt was fired ("resigned") because of his garden-variety corruption and lavish spending on his expenses, office and travel. He also had the habit of mixing his personal and his professional that led to more than a dozen investigations by the Office of the Inspector General.[34] For example, Scott spent more than $124,000 on unjustified first-class air travel and $43,000 on a soundproof phone booth. He used EPA staff to land a job for his wife, rented a condominium apartment on Capitol Hill at a bargain rate from a lobbyist's wife, and had his security detail drive him around on personal errands.[35] As the investigations piled up several of his close aides and EPA staffers were exiting the shop. After all the negative publicity the pressure mounted on Trump from the Congressional Republicans to oust Pruitt.

By Twitter, Trump announced on July 8, 2018 that he was accepting Scott's resignation noting: "Within the Agency Scott had done an outstanding job, and I will always be thankful to him for this."[36] Some of Pruitt's "outstanding" work included his response to an initial study requested by his aides from EPA economists to re-evaluate the effects of the Obama administration's clean-water rule. According to a 30-year veteran of the agency who left around the same time, when the study found more than a half billion dollars in economic benefits, these economists "were ordered to say the benefits could not be quantified."[37] Similarly, after

> a scientific advisory board questioned the basis for a proposed rewrite of the Obama administration rules on waterways and vehicle tailpipe emissions, more than a quarter of the panel members were dismissed or resigned, many of them being replaced by scientists with industry ties.[38]

Under Pruitt's EPA more generally the agency moved to limit the use of scientific research. They excluded numerous studies that relied on confidential personal-health data. Meanwhile, vacancies were left unfilled especially in the areas of air pollution and toxic research. The Trump EPA did not miss a beat with its anti-environmental and anti-species agenda when Andrew Wheeler became the next Administrator. For example, as a former coal lobbyist whose top client was Murray Energy and whose CEO was a major backer of Trump and a climate change denier, Secretary Wheeler ordered the EPA on June 2019 to terminate its funding to 13 health centers around the country that were studying the effects of pollution on the growth and development of children and other living things. As Trump wrote on Twitter announcing Wheeler as Pruitt's replacement: "I have no doubt that Andy will continue on with our great and lasting EPA agenda. We have made tremendous progress and the future of the EPA is very bright."[39]

While Wheeler was at the helm of the EPA, CEO Robert Murray of Murray Energy prepared a policy "wish list" and it was hand-delivered to Energy Secretary Rick Perry. Several of Murray's recommendations were acted on such as "abandoning an Obama administration rule barring coal companies from dumping waste into streams and waterways; making it easier to open new coal plants, and allowing higher levels of mercury pollution."[40] In related matters, Nancy Beck, deputy assistant administrator for Chemical Safety and Pollution Prevention, a former industry lobbyist, was leading the charge against an EPA proposal to halt the sale of three chemicals linked to birth defects, nerve damage, and deaths. Under Wheeler the EPA was completely absolved of any duty to address global warming.

Besides the EPA's capture by mega polluters, conflicts of interests, and Trump top appointments, the Mapping Corruption project has underscored the undue influence of a dozen deputy and assistant administrators dispersed throughout the environmental protection organization. Below are the first five administrators identified[41]:

- David Dunlap the deputy assistant administrator for research and development was a former policy director for Koch Industries. At the

EPA Dunlap had a role in regulating formaldehyde even though one of the country's largest producers of formaldehyde, Georgia-Pacific Chemicals, is a Koch subsidiary.

- David Fischer the deputy assistant administrator for chemical safety and pollution prevention was a former industry lawyer and senior director of the American Chemistry Council that represents chemical companies.
- Alexandra Dunn the assistant administrator for chemical safety and pollution prevention had worked for the American Chemistry Council.
- Susan Bodine the assistant administrator for enforcement and compliance assurance was a former industry lawyer that defended polluting companies against Superfund cleanup responsibilities.
- Peter Wright the assistant administrator for land and emergency management that oversees toxic waste site cleanup was a former employee of DowDuPont that had mismanaged roughly one-seventh of all toxic waste cleanup sites in the nation.

HHS

Trump's two Secretaries of Health and Human Services Tom Price and Alex Azar systematically assaulted the Affordable Care Act. They discouraged health care sign-ups by deleting enrollment links and references to the law from government web pages. They cut spending on the Affordable Care Act promotion by nearly 90 percent. HHS slashed grants to non-government groups helping people enroll, cancelled billions in payments meant to reduce deductibles and co-pays, and finally, encouraged insurance companies to market "junk health plans" as an alternative to ACA. Through spending cuts and the approval of state-level work requirements HHS pushed millions of low-income families off Medicaid. After three years of President Trump nearly three million more Americans were added to the ranks of the uninsured. Had the U.S. Supreme Court not ruled on several occasions against the Republicans and Trump to declare the ACA unconstitutional another 20 million Americans would have become former health care insured persons.

Secretary Price after spending close to a million dollars on chartered jets and government aircraft rather than using commercial flights was forced to resign from office. It might be argued that he auditioned for the part when he was a Georgia congressman. While sitting on the House Ways and Means Committee and working on legislation and regulations affecting the industry, Price bought and sold hundreds of thousands of dollars worth of shares in health care companies. During an official trip to Australia, Price also had some shading dealings with drug companies, while he held shares in an Australian pharmaceutical firm. Price's replacement Secretary Azar had previously been a pharma lobbyist before becoming a top executive and president of the multinational drug company Eli Lilly. During his tenure at Lilly, the costs of drugs shot skyward with insulin tripling. Trump's campaign promises to reduce drug prices and replace ACA with a cheaper and better alternative never materialized. While in charge of HHS, Azar refused to say that once a vaccine was available, it would be affordable for all.

Four persons with undue influence at HHS during the Trump administration included Colin Roskey, Laura Kemper, Erin Estey Herzog, and Timothy Clark. Roskey, after a 20-year lobbying career in which he represented private companies over issues that he would oversee at HHS, became the deputy secretary for mandatory health. The revolving doors swung both ways as Kemper in March 2019 left a senior-level position at the agency to become a vice president for government affairs at Fresenius. The giant lobbying firm with multiple health care clinics across the country reported more than $2.2 million in lobbying expenditures during the first six months of that year. Hertzog a top lobbyist for the Biotechnology Industry Organization, in turn, went to work as an attorney at the Centers for Medicare and Medicaid Services. Clark the president and founder of Clark Strategy group that represents pharmaceutical companies was a senior adviser to HHS secretary Price. However, he was forced to resign in July 2018 when it was revealed that Clark had sent out "pro-Trump tweets under a hashtag linked to the theory that Hillary Clinton's campaign chair John Podesta was involved in satanic practices."[42]

Anti-democracy corruption for profit

As far as the Donald's lifelong schemes of conning goes, probably none have been as financially rewarding as when Trump has run or not for the presidency of the United States. In this regard, I am more than speculating that the Donald has legitimately and illegitimately pocketed hundreds of millions of U.S. dollars, Russian rubles, Saudi riyals, Emirati dirhams, Chinese renminbi, and perhaps a few Euros tossed in for good measure. On the afternoon of July 21, 2021, I received an email invitation from the Republican National Committee HQ informing me: "Gregg, "Thanks to your loyal support of YOUR Party, you already PRE-QUALITY to become an **Official 2021 Trump Life Member**, no application necessary." The body of the email read: "Once you join, you'll be a part of the most critical group of conservatives helping to push back against the constant LIES coming from Joe Biden and his allies in the Liberal News Media." The email finished, "We plan to finalize the membership roster soon, don't miss your chance to be included." All I had to do was make a modest contribution by 11:59 PM. When I missed my chance on July 21. No problem. Even after I had unsubscribed daily for several weeks, I was still receiving my daily last chances to become an official 2021 Trump member for life.

Without equal value Trump's best grift has been the Big Steal yielding the Donald $75 million in the first six months of 2021. I am referring to his scam operation Save America a leadership PAC that Trump created in the aftermath of the 2020 stolen election not! In less than seven weeks it amassed $31.2 million. And in less than eight months the PAC raised more than $100 million. But wait folks, that's not all. There is an affiliated joint fundraising committee contributing more money to the save the America scam. I am referring to the Trump Make America Great Again Committee, which is splitting its donations with 75 percent going to Trump's leadership PAC and 25 percent going to the Republican National Coalition for Life. Accordingly, add another $50 million to the $31 million by the end of 2020.[43] In addition during the first six months of 2021, Save America paid for lodging nine times at properties owned by Trump for a scant $68,000 but still Mo' Money. Meanwhile, Make America Great Again spent about $200,000 on office and restaurant space in where else Trump Tower. A Trump-backed PAC overseen by Corey Lewandowski one of his three campaign managers during the 2016 race for the presidency paid $21,810 to rent space at Donald's summer home the Trump National Golf Club in Bedminster, N.J.[44] According to ProPublica for the first six months of 2021, Republican campaign groups have paid about $348,000 to Trump properties.[45]

Although the Donald cannot spend the PAC cash directly should he run again in 2024, he can use it to back candidates in the 2022-midterm elections, pay his political co-conspirators, travel the country, cover his daily expenses, including his legal fees that I imagine are already enormous. Most of his daily expenses of course will be spent at his own properties—cha-ching, cha-ching. As for spending "his" political money on other candidates or on the efforts in Arizona, Pennsylvania, Michigan, and Georgia to cast doubt into the integrity of the 2020 election[46] and to feed the stolen election lie, the chances of that happening would have been as likely as

Donald spending any of his own money on the 2016 or 2020 presidential campaigns zero to none. In other words, whatever Donald will not be spending on attorneys or other political candidates will simply find its way into his baggy pants—Mo' Money, Mo' Money. In any case, the Capitol assault has been a moneymaker for Trump and has helped to solidify his control of the Republican Party.

At the other end of the financial ledger, the income from Trump's sedition and other political business dealings is being offset by his accumulating deficits from his more traditional businesses that began with the loss of merchandising deals during the early days of the 2016 campaign. During the presidency, the loss of his branding and management agreements continued and culminated with a wave of partners vowing to no longer do business with him after the Capitol attack. For inquiring minds, we will all want to know how much of the stop the steal money was used to underwrite Donald's January 6th insurrection on the capitol? I suspect that the Select Committee to examine and report out on the facts and causes of the mob attack will definitively answer this real pertinent and conspiratorial question.

To paraphrase Abraham Lincoln: "You can con all the people some of the time and some of the people all the time, but you cannot con all the people all the time." Conning all the people some of the time is a stretch for me. Not conning all the people all the time is not debatable. As for conning some of the people all the time I would not have believed it could be true until Trump and his sycophantic followers proved otherwise. In a similar vein, while Donald is the virtuoso of the con he is also the connoisseur of corruption—a dynamic duo to say the least. Speaking of or exposing grand corruption on a Trumpian scale especially the sustainable and long-lasting kind becomes an exercise in identifying the small and overlapping elite networks of wealth and power.

As Rajan explains, these

> networks drive all criminal activity—from terrorist financing to manipulation of huge tax write-offs through shell companies and offshore accounts to protect ill-gotten wealth. Over time, laws may be changed to normalize these activities and to legalize the laundered financing of political campaigns, which entrenches white-collar criminal control of democracy.[47]

This political economy of grand corruption and social control is not limited importantly to those individual bureaucrats and politicians who episodically distort public goods for private gain. Rather, this is a global network of social relations in which the "inner circle" comprises "prominent and wealthy individuals, political machines, and corporations" that "may be involved in deceiving the public over a much longer time than a mere election cycle."[48] As many readers of this book are probably well aware of in *Citizen United vs. Federal Election Commission* (2010) the U.S. Supreme Court ruled to remove any limits on financial contributions from corporations to political campaigns. The terrible ruling predictably amplified the scope of parties both left and right to collude with big business.

Trump's linked elite networks of global wealth and power

What do the people listed below and the U.S. nationals have in common? First, they are all part of the overlapping elite networks of global wealth and power linked to Donald Trump. Second, with the exceptions of Rudy Giuliani and Jared Kushner who have also been under investigation by various law enforcement agencies for similarly related activities, the rest have been indicted and their cases are either pending or they have plead guilty to or been convicted for crimes investigated by Robert Mueller. Before leaving high office, Boss Trump pardoned several of his most loyal soldiers, including Manafort, Flynn, Bannon, and Stone. At this point in time, one question of significance is whether a loyal soldier for nearly 40 years and since the early 2000s CFO of Trump Organization Allen Weisselberg whose former daughter-in-law says of him, "Allen loves Donald more than his wife," will flip on Donald to save himself from going to prison?

Team USA and their foreign connections

George Papadopoulos, USA (Russia)
Paul Manafort, USA (Ukraine, Russia)
Michael Flynn, USA (Turkey)
Michael Cohen, USA (Russia)
Rick Gates, USA (Ukraine, Russia)
Steve Bannon, USA (Europe, Middle East)
Rudolph Giuliani, USA (Ukraine)
Jared Kushner, USA (Israel, Saudi Arabia)
Lev Parnas, USA (Ukraine)
Igor Fruman, USA (Ukraine)
Richard Pinedo, USA (Russia)
Roger Stone, USA (Europe)

Allen Weisselberg, USA
Tom Barrack, USA (United Arab Emirates, Qatar)

Indicted foreign nationals

13 Russian nationals, 12 GRU officers of the Russian military, and three Russian companies were all indicted, however, their lawsuits will never materialize.
Konstantin Kiiimnik, a Ukrainian national (now living in Russia) was indicted along with Manafort and Gates, but the former will never find his way to trial.

Heads of foreign states

Recep Tayyip Erdoğan, President of Turkey (Flynn)
Mohammed bin Salman, Crown Prince of Saudi Arabia (Kushner)
Vladimir Putin, President of Russia (Donald Trump)
Khalifa bin Zayed bin Sultan Al Nahyan, President of United Arab Emirates (Barrack)

One of those U.S. citizens in the overlapping networks not pardoned by Trump was Tom Barrack. Tom is a longtime associate. He was senior adviser to the 2016 presidential campaign and chair of the 2017 inaugural committee. Barrack was not indicted for a series of related crimes until six months after Trump left office.[49] He was arrested July 20, 2021, on charges that he secretly acted in the United States as an agent for the United Arab Emirates. The "sealed" federal indictment from the U.S. District Court of New York accused the 74-year-old Barrack of failing to register as a foreign agent, conspiracy, obstruction of justice, and four counts of making false statements to the FBI. He was no doubt acting secretly and not registering as an agent of a foreign government. But he was not acting without the knowledge of Trump. Quite the contrary. The two were in cahoots and have been bosom buddies for about three decades. Donald's longtime dirty trickster and collaborator Roger Stone has described Barrack as Trump's best friend. In the summer of 2016, Paul Manafort became Trump's second campaign manager on the recommendation of Tom.

What is less known about Thomas Joseph Barrack, Jr. is that he made his fortune as an American private equity real estate investor in the Middle East and elsewhere. More specifically, in June 2018, the NY Times reported that Barrack's company "raised more than $7 billion in investments since Mr. Trump won the nomination" and that "about a quarter came from the Emirates and Saudi Arabia."[50] Hence, the $250 million bond secured by $5 million in cash to get out of jail was chump change for Barrack. For what it is worth, the "judge also ordered Barrack to wear a GPS location monitoring bracelet, barred him from transferring any funds overseas and restricted his travel to parts of Southern California and New York."[51]

In 1991, Barrack founded and became the executive chairman of the publicly traded Colony Capital, Inc. and subsequently Colony NorthStar. He divested all interests in 2019 and stepped down from his executive role in March 2021.[52] In 2016, Colony managed more than $58 billion in assets making it the 5th largest real estate company globally. In 2017, Colony agreed to invest in The Weinstein Company to keep it afloat considering Harvey Weinstein's sexual misconduct. Not only do Donald and Tom go back decades, but Barrack also helped rescue Trump's real estate empire back in the 1990s. In 2010, Barrack bought $70 million of Jared Kushner's debt on 666 Fifth Avenue. Most recently at the request of Trump he agreed to reduce Jared's obligations to avoid bankruptcy.[53] Tom was also the Donald's top fundraiser for the 2016 campaign and gave personally more than $750,000. Preferring to remain an adviser from behind the scenes, Barrack allegedly turned down a cabinet position and he could also have been the White House chief of staff.[54]

To give the reader a sense of the indictment I quote from page 4, Section IV. <u>The Defendants' Actions in the United States as Agent of the United Arab Emirates</u>, paragraph 13 reads:

> Government officials in the United Arab Emirates, including Emirati Official 1, Emirati Official 2, Emirati Official 3 and Emirati Official 4 tasked the defendants RASHID SULTAN RASHID AL MALIK ALSHAHHL, THOMAS JOSEPH BARRACK and MATTHREW GRIMES with, variously and among other things, (a) influencing public opinion, the foreign policy positions of the Campaign and the foreign policy positions of the United States government; (b) obtaining information about foreign policy positions and related decision-making within the Campaign and, at times, the United States government; (c) developing a back channel line of communication with the Campaign and, at times, officials of the United States government; and (d) developing plans to increase the United Arab Emirates' political influence and to promote its foreign policy preferences.

It is worth noting that Barrack and his two co-defendants were not charged with the more customary foreign-agent statute, the Foreign Agents Registration Act, but with "a lesser-known statue typically used to charge individuals accused of working at the direction of senior officials of a foreign government."[55] Unlike FARA the foreign-agent statue used for Barrack and company does not require proof that the defendants knew that their conduct was illegal. The prosecutor Mack Jenkins handling the bail hearings in Los Angeles where the three defendants had been living stated that the infrequently used foreign-agent statute reflected the elite circles involved: "We're talking about the highest levels at the UAE and the highest levels of the United States."[56]

Going forward with Barrack's prosecution will involve questions about another meeting at Trump Tower that occurred in August 2016 with Trump campaign officials. This meeting was not with Russians as the one that occurred two months earlier in June. This meeting was between Donald Trump, Jr., George Nader at the time an advisor to Crown Prince Mohammed bin Zayed, the Emirates' de factor ruler, and Joel Zamel, owner of an Israeli private intelligence company, Psy-Group, which has been discussed in a bipartisan U.S. Senate Select Committee on Intelligence report about Russian election interference.[57] If the allegations in Barrack's indictment are true that Zamel was paid more than one million dollars for social media work done on behalf of Nader, "it means that while an adviser to the Emirates was offering Trump campaign election help, an Emirati agent was also shaping Trump's foreign policy, even inserting the country's preferred language into one of the candidate's speeches."[58] As Michelle Goldberg has written:

> Trump could scarcely have been a more accommodating ally to the Emirates and to Saudi Arabia, whose crown prince Mohammed bin Salman, was a protégé of Prince Mohammed bin Zayed. Trump's first foreign trip as president was to Saudi Arabia. He tore up the Iran deal, hated by Gulf leaders. Of Trump's 10 vetoes five dealt with concerns of the Emirates and Saudi Arabia. More significantly, he overrode Congress's attempt to end American military involvement in Yemen, where Saudi Arabia and the Emirates were fighting on one side of a brutal civil war.[59]

Aside from his overlapping networks of grand corruption, the routinization of corruption by Trump as a moneymaking enterprise is second to no other administration. Trump is in a league of his own. No other president is remotely close. Recall, for example, that Trump boasted in his recorded interviews for Bob Woodward's *Rage* that he had saved the Saudi crown prince after his agents murdered the *Washington Post* reporter and

Saudi dissident Jamal Khashoggi.[60] I cannot imagine any future president coming along, no matter how full of conflicts of interest, ever giving the king-of-corruption a run for his or anyone else's money. At the website Republic Report, a rank ordering of the 50 most disgraceful people in the Trump administration has the Donald finishing in first place with the following description

> a shameless liar and con man, ugly racist and misogynist, vile coronavirus spreader, despicable attacker of the press and whistleblowers, amoral admirer of autocrats, erratic, ignorant, incompetent, pathetic narcissist, enabler of global climate disaster, corrupt, and kleptocratic abuser of the Constitution.[61]

Similarly, in an investigation of how money corrupts democracy, David Halperin posted at Republic Report the Ten Reasons Trump is the Most Corrupt President in the U.S. History[62]:

1 Trump broke his promise to drain the swamp as he made it dirtier by giving top administration jobs to blatant grifters, such as Scott Pruitt, Ryan Zinke, Tom Price, Diane Auer Jones, and Mike Pompeo.
2 Trump while in office had personally pocked millions in taxpayer, lobbyist, donor, and foreign dollars; at least $2.5 million to rent high priced rooms at his company's hotels, for example.
3 Trump corrupted the tax system with his tax cut for the wealthiest people and corporations while bragging about it, but paid virtually no taxes of his own at the same time.
4 Trump gutted health care because of his hatred of Obama and did his best to eviscerate the Affordable Care Act, even as the COVID-19 pandemic raged, lying all the while that he had a new and better health plan, which never existed.
5 Trump sacrificed hundreds of thousands of lives to the pandemic because of his re-election strategy that necessitated the covering up and lying about the disease's contagiousness as he and his ilk became the super spreaders of virus and scientific denial.
6 Trump falsely claimed widespread voter fraud and that he won the 2020 election that has undermined the integrity of the U.S. electoral system and has resulted in voter suppression laws passing throughout the nation thanks to Republican controlled state legislatures.
7 Trump has been an ally of Russian dictator and murderer Vladimir Putin, praising him, endorsing his denials of election interference, and even

delaying for months, beyond its legal deadline, the implementation of a bipartisan veto-proof margined bill to impose new sanctions on Russia.

8 Trump repeatedly engaged in the obstruction of justice and Congress with respect to Russia, Ukraine, and other matters, including the firing of several whistleblowers that testified before Congress and he also dismissed five inspector generals who were each investigating administration misconduct.
9 Trump and his hatched man Attorney General William Barr turned the U.S. Department of Justice into an apparatus for doing the former president's corrupt bidding on behalf of his political allies and against his political enemies all the way up to the lost election and after only parting ways with the Donald in late December 2020.
10 Trump has driven racism and racist violence with far too many examples to enumerate here, including remarks to disparage Muslims, Mexicans, Black Lives Matter, members of Congress, the media, as well as defending the violent slogans and actions of white supremacists.

Notes

1 Sudhir Chella Rajan, 2020. *A Social Theory of Corruption: Notes from the Indian Subcontinent.* Cambridge, MA and London: Harvard University Press, pp. x–xi.
2 Michael Johnston. 2005. *Syndromes of Corruption: Wealth, Power, and Democracy.* Cambridge: Cambridge University Press, p. 42.
3 Gregg Barak, 2012. *Theft of a Nation: Wall Street Looting and Federal Regulatory Colluding.* Lanham, MD: Rowman & Littlefield.
4 Paul Waldman, 2020. How Trump's Epic Corruption Reveals Hidden Weaknesses in the System. *The Washington Post.* October 29. https://www.washingtonpost.com/opinions/2020/10/29/how-trumps-epic-corruption-reveals-hidden-weaknesses-system/.
5 Ibid.
6 Jim Lardner, 2020. Mapping Corruption: Donald Trump's Executive Branch: An Inquiry into How the Trump Administration Transformed Washington. *The American Prospect.* April 9. https://prospect.org/power/mapping-corruption-donald-trump-executive-branch/.
7 Mike McIntire, Russ Buettner and Susanne Craig. 2020. Trump Records Shed New Light on Chinese Business Pursuits. *The New York Times.* October 20. https://www.nytimes.com/2020/10/20/us/trump-taxes-china.html.
8 During the same period and after Donald was paying the IRS less than $1,000 annually.
9 CREW, 2021. President Trump's Legacy of Corruption, Four Years and 3,700 Conflicts of Interest Later. January 15. https://www.citizensforethics.org/reports-investigations/crew-reports/president-trump-legacy-corruption-3700-conflicts-interest/.
10 ISideWith…, ND. Donald Trump's Policy on Offshore Banking. https://www.isidewith.com/candidates/donald-trump/policies/economic/offshore-banking.

11 Thang Nguyen, 2021. On Human Decisions with Hidden and Malicious Intent in Business and Management. *American Letters*. Article 1014. https://dos.org/1020935/AL1014.

12 CREW, 2021.

13 Jon Swaine and Ed Pilkington, 2017. The Wealthy Men in Trump's Inner Circle with Links to Tax Havens. *The Guardian*. November 5. https://www.theguardian.com/news/2017/nov/05/wealthy-men-donald-trump-inner-circle-links-tax-havens.

14 NickHopkinsandHelenaBengtsson,2017.WhatAretheParadisePapersandWhat Do They Tell Us? *The Guardian*. November 5. https://www.theguardian.com/news/2017/nov/05/what-are-the-paradise-papers-and-what-do-they-tell-us.

15 Eric Estevez, 2021. A Review of *How Much Trump's Tax Cuts Cost the Government* by Kimberly Amadeo. *The Balance*. May 30. https://www.thebalance.com/cost-of-trump-tax-cuts-4586645.

16 Tyler Fisher, 2017. How Past Income Tax Rate Cuts on the Wealthy Affected the Economy. *Politico*. September 27. https://www.politico.com/interactives/2017/gop-tax-rate-cut-wealthy/.

17 Gregg Barak, 2017. *Unchecked Corporate Power: Why the Crimes of Multinational Corporations are Routinized Away and What We Can Do About It*. New York and London: Routledge.

18 Quoted in Thom Hartmann, 2021. How Republicans Unleashed a New Crime Wave in America – Through Worsening Inequality. *Salon*. July 22. https://www.salon.com/2021/07/22/how-republicans-unleashed-a-new-crime-wave-in-america--through-worsening-inequality_partner/.

19 Nicholas Confessors, et al., 2020. The Swamp That Trump Built. *The New York Times*. October 10. https://www.nytimes.com/interactive/2020/10/10/us/trump-properties-swamp.html.

20 CREW, 2021.

21 Ibid.

22 Ibid.

23 Ibid.

24 Ibid.

25 Sarah Blaskey, Nicholas Nehamas, Caitlin Ostroff, and Jay Weaver, 2020. *The Grifter's Club: Trump, Mar-A-Lago, and the Selling of the Presidency*. New York: Hachette Book Group.

26 Lardner, 2020.

27 Ibid.

28 Renae Merle, 2017. The CFPB Now Has Two Acting Directors. And Nobody Knows Which One Should Lead the Federal Agency. *The Washington Post*. November 24. https://www.washingtonpost.com/news/business/wp/2017/11/24/the-cfpb-now-has-two-acting-directors-and-nobody-knows-which-one-should-lead-the-federal-agency/.

29 Ibid.

30 Lardner, 2020.

31 Ibid.

32 Ibid.

33 Ibid.

34 NPR, 2018. Scott Pruitt Out at EPA. *NPR*. July 5. https://www.npr.org/2018/07/05/594078923/scott-pruitt-out-at-epa

35 Lardner, 2020.
36 Quoted in NPR, 2018.
37 Lardner, 2020.
38 Ibid.
39 Quoted in NPR, 2018.
40 Lardner, 2020.
41 Ibid.
42 Ibid.
43 Zach Montellaro and Elena Schneider, 2021. Trump Stocks New PAC with Tens of Millions as He Bids to Retain Control of GOP. *Politico*. January 31. https://www.politico.com/news/2021/01/31/donald-trump-pac-millions-gop-464250.
44 Isaac Stanley-Becker and David A. Fahrenthold, 2021. His Campaign Is Over. But Trump's Political Groups Are Still Spending Donor Money at His Properties. *The Washington Post*. August 1. https://www.washingtonpost.com/politics/2021/08/01/trump-pacs-hotels-spending/?utm_campaign=wp_post_most&utm_medium=email&utm_source=newsl.
45 Derek Willis, 2021. Campaign Spending at Trump Properties Down, but Not Out. *ProPublica*. July 20. https://www.propublica.org/article/campaign-spending-at-trump-properties-down-but-not-out.
46 Josh Dawsey and Rosalind S. Helderman, 2021. Trump's PAC Collected $75 Million This Year, But So Far the Group Has Not Put Money into Pushing for the 2020 Ballot Reviews He Touts. *Washington Post*. July 22. https://www.washingtonpost.com/politics/.
47 Rajan, 2020: ix.
48 Ibid.
49 On January 22, 2020, the District of Columbia Attorney General Karl Racine sued Trump's Inaugural Committee. The suit alleges that the Committee improperly used nonprofit funds to pay highly inflated prices to the Trump hotel in DC as well as to Ivanka Trump for renting the space and so on.
50 Quoted in Michelle Goldberg, 2021. A Foreign Agent in Trump's Inner Circle? *The New York Times*. July 25: SR7.
51 Eric Orden, 2021. Trump Ally Tom Barrack Strikes a $250 Million Bail Deal to Get Out of Jail. CNN. July 23. https://www.cnn.com/2021/07/23/politics/tom-barrack-bail-hearing/index.html.
52 Divorced in 2016 and the father of six, Barrack has been based in Los Angeles. He owns a 1,200-acre mountain ranch near Santa Barbara as well as Happy Canyon Vineyards in Happy Canyon and a wine tasting room in downtown Santa Barbara, California. Notably, Barrack bought a house in 2014 in Santa Monica and "flipped" it for $35 million, the highest price for a residence in the area at the time. In 2017, he purchased a home in Aspen, Colorado for a modest $15.5 million. Back in 2010, Barrack partnered with Qatar investment authority to purchase Weinstein film production company Miramax for $660 million. Six years later, he sold Miramax to the Qatari beIN Media Group at a fourfold profit.
53 David D. Kirkpatrick, 2018. Who Is Behind Trump's Links to Arab Princes? A Billionaire Friend. *The New York Times*. June 13. https://www.nytimes.com/2018/06/13/world/middleeast/trump-tom-barrack-saudi.html.
54 Michael Kranish, 2017. 'He's Better Than This,' Says Thomas Barrack, Trump's Loyal Whisperer. *The Washington Post*. October 11. https://www.

washingtonpost.com/politics/hes-better-than-this-says-thomas-barrack-trumps-loyal-whisperer/2017/10/10/067fc776-a215-11e7-8cfe-d5b-912fabc99_story.html.

55 Josh Gerstein, 2021. Trump Adviser Tom Barrack Arrested on Foreign-agent Charges. *Politico*. July 20. https://www.politico.com/news/2021/07/20/tom-barrack-arrested-foreign-agent-charges-500333?cid=apn.

56 Quoted in Ibid.

57 Mark Mazzetti, Ronen Bergman and David D. Kirkpatrick, 2018. Trump Jr. and Other Aides Met With Gulf Emissary Offering Help to Win Election. *The New York Times*. May 19. https://www.nytimes.com/2018/05/19/us/politics/trump-jr-saudi-uae-nader-prince-zamel.html.

58 Goldberg, 2021.

59 Ibid.

60 Bob Woodward, 2020. *Rage*. New York: Simon and Schuster.

61 David Halperin, 2020. Final Reckoning: The 50 Most Disgraceful People of the Trump Administration Ranked 7th through 2nd as Follows: Mike Pence, Vice President of the U.S.; Lindsey Graham, Chairman, Senate Judiciary Committee; Rudy Giuliani, Outside Counsel to President Trump; Mike Pompeo, Secretary of State; William Barr, Attorney General; and Mitch McConnell, Senate Majority Leader. Republic Report. https://www.republicreport.org/2020/final-reckoning-the-50-most-disgraceful-people-of-the-trump-administration/.

62 I have condensed the ten reasons' sections into single sentences from David Halperin's 2020 post. https://www.republicreport.org/2020/ten-reasons-trump-is-the-most-corrupt-president-in-u-s-history/.

6
STATE-ORGANIZED ABUSES OF POWER AND OBSTRUCTION OF JUSTICE

In the world of crime, criminals, and criminology, there are many types of offenses and offenders. There are also many types of routinized actions or inactions as well as organized political violations, individual and corporate. Organized corporate crime refers to dishonest or fraudulent behavior that is arranged by employees for the benefit of the incorporated business.[1] Usually, these offenses are of a corrupting nature and involve the coordinated actions knowingly (and unknowingly) between individuals working within or on behalf of a corporation.[2] Less often, these offenses also involve collaboration among personnel from both the private and public sectors.[3] Thus, the networking of organized corporate criminals does not preclude employees of the state or from not for profit organizations.[4]

State-organized crimes may include state agents acting on behalf of the state in the name of the body politic.[5] Individually a president, a premier, or a similarly titled head of state could execute these crimes. Collectively, these crimes could be executed by elected or appointed officials, by bureaucracies and institutions, as well as by other bodies and organizations comprising the apparatus of governing.[6] State crimes refer to both political acts of commission and political acts of omission. These offenses by or on behalf of the state are also among those crimes subject to "cover up" or protection by the state. Rarely are these crimes subject to the domestic or international laws that they periodically breach.[7] Rarer still are those hybrid political-state crimes directed both by and at the state such as those that involve assassinations, insurrections, and civil wars. For example, the

DOI: 10.4324/9781003221548-9

failed coup orchestrated by the former Commander-in-Chief and by his mouthpieces in Congress and elsewhere to overturn the legitimate election of President Biden as the 46th president is inclusive of criminal felonies and high crimes and misdemeanors enumerated by the U.S. Constitution.

Another hybrid form of organizational crime applies to businesses that operate their affairs both legitimately and illegitimately at the same time. Though Trump has been operating a criminal enterprise from within Trump Organization, Inc. since its beginning in 1980, the organization was only first indicted on July 1, 2021, for running one 15-year-long tax fraud compensation scheme beginning early in the 21st century. In the world of white-collar crime, the simultaneous operation of an incorporated organization in conjunction with a criminal enterprise may also involve a host of other felonies from bribery to extortion, grand larceny to tax fraud, from the obstruction of justice to wire fraud and racketeering, more commonly associated with organized crime and other non-legal enterprises. These types of organized offenses are all subject to federal and state criminal statues. These laws first emerged in the 1930s and have been modified over the years to target patterned unlawful pursuits that provide working capital for any future unlawful pursuits.[8]

For example, New York State has a money-laundering statue that corresponds with Title 18 U.S.C. § 1956, the federal money-laundering conspiracy statute that makes it a crime to knowingly conduct or attempt to conduct a "financial transaction" with proceeds from a "specified unlawful activity" (SUA) and the "specific intent" to promote SUA; or conceal or disguise the source, origin, nature, ownership, or control of the proceeds; or evade reporting requirements; or evade taxes.[9] Personally, I think that these laws should be amended further to include those proceeds from a SUA that may be used to provide capital for future lawful pursuits as well as unlawful pursuits. As Michael Cohen's Congressional testimony revealed, unlawful activities to generate personal wealth for lawful pursuits in the future was a decades-old specialization of the Trump Organization. As was the unlawful family tradition of stealing from one generation of Trumps to pay the next generation of Trumps established by Donald's father Fred, Sr. in the late 1940s and that was up and running by the early 1950s. When the Trump Organization and its CFO were finally indicted for one of its many tax-avoiding and revenue-generating schemes for its principal executives and their beneficiaries in June 2021, the Trump criminal enterprise had been engaging in this form of tax looting and control fraud for three quarters of a century without so much as a peep from the Internal Revenue Service.

A third hybrid form of criminality is state-corporate crime. These crimes occur when state-organized crime and crimes organized by corporations become accomplices whose harms or injuries result from the reciprocal relationship between the policies and practices of the state and the policies and practices of corporations for the political and/or economic benefit of both.[10] Once again for the first time in the U.S. Constitutional history, the one and same person Trump was acting in his official capacity as the head of state and as the principal owner of the Trump Organization along with its family run criminal and noncriminal enterprises. This unique state-corporate relationship was facilitated because Trump had refused to separate himself from the family business and place his financial holdings into a blind trust.[11] Instead the Donald opted to place them into a revocable trust whose trustees were his eldest son Donald, Jr. and his CFO Allen Weisselberg. On July 1, 2021, the Trump Organization and its CFO was the first Trump executive officer to be indicted for defrauding the federal, state, and city governments out of more than $900,000 in unpaid taxes.[12]

The revocable trust entitled Donald to use any of the income or profits derived from any of his businesses. These included foreign and domestic emoluments, for example, the purchasing of services at his properties while doing business, lobbying, or trying to secure one-on-one access to the Donald. The same is true of the revenue streams generated by the sitting president and his secret service staff spending time and money usually at the Trump International Hotel Washington DC or at the Mar-a-Lago Club in Palm Beach, Florida.[13] As the former president the Donald and company will continue to make money off this legally corrupt relationship established in 1965 by Public Law 89–186 as amended most recently by President Obama. Unless Trump refuses secret service protection for himself and his current spouse or is convicted of a felony he will continue to receive an annual pension of $219, 200.

Drilling further down, whether secret agents stayed or not in one of the properties where the Donald, Melania, and son Barron were calling their home in the month of May 2021, the Secret Service was billed $400 every 24 hours for more than $10,000 a month.[14] These expenditures come to $120,000 every 12 months bringing the annual stipend to $339, 200. Moreover, before leaving office in a memorandum signed by then-president Trump, he saw to it that 14 members of his extended family at no cost to them would be protected 24/7 by the Secret Service for at least six months. The protection for Ivanka Trump and Jared Kushner, along with their three children; Donald Trump Jr. and his five children; Eric Trump and wife Lara; and Tiffany Trump could be extended after July 20, 2021.[15] At two thousand dollars a day, this extended protection could cost the American taxpayers an additional $360,000 for the first six months alone. What is most interesting here is if the Trump businesses continue to lose more than ten million a year as they allegedly did in 2016 and 2017, then the self-proclaimed "king of the tax code" will continue to pay around $750.00 in federal taxes annually.[16]

For the purposes of this investigation the question became what happened when Trump's corporate and criminal net worth of not more than two billion dollars and not less than several hundred million dollars along with the power of his marketing brand were leveraged with his newly acquired political power as president of the United States? At a minimum as we have all bared witness, Trump's lifetime of lawlessness and abusing power escalated further. Ultimately, it metastasized through the body politic to the point where his inspired and orchestrated insurrection at the Capitol rotunda on January 6 was rationalized away by a mixture of bogus conspiracies theories and Big Lies adopted by the vast majority of Republican Americans and their elected officials in Washington, DC.

Unlike the 44 presidents that preceded Trump, the 45th on a regular basis flouted the limits of executive authority and the rule of law. As part of his legacy, the Donald has left behind a relic of unmatched misuses of power ranging from the mere violations of longstanding norms to the violations of civil, criminal, and constitutional laws. Moreover, on every occasion where the partisan Republican-elected officials have weighed in on Trump's clear and unambiguous violations of the law, they have politically punted the harmful behavior rather than acknowledge the wrongdoing. Not only have they failed to condemn and convict Trump, but also both the House and the Senate Republicans have collectively sought to whitewash and cover up the Donald and his associates' unlawful behavior.

By reliably excusing Trump's abuses of power while in office and by giving the former president continual free passes on his routinization of illegal misbehavior and corruption, these Republican loyalists had all become enablers, and some were even accomplices serving to reinforce and to up the ante on future depraved behavior like the failed coup on January 6. In the case of Donald's habitual "non-criminalities," we have the absences of Edwin Lemert's theory of primary and secondary deviance from the 1950s and Howard Becker's labeling theory from 1960s, respectively, playing out as deterrence theorists of criminal behavior Cesare Beccaria and Jeremy Bentham from the 18th century had predicted. In other words, by not admitting to Trump's unlawful behavior and by not negatively sanctioning his unlabeled deviant behavior, the Donald continued to engage in his "business as usual" misbehavior by not playing fair or by the rules of law as he had been doing for 40 years before becoming the president.

In the political world of gaslighting, whether we are talking about the president's abuse of power, his obstruction of justice, or his different roles in the insurrection, the Republicans were virtually all in with the fraudulent stop the steal campaigning as well as with the political machinations to decertify the winner of the 2020 election. In fact, most of these politicos like Boss Trump have continued to double down—denying, lying, whitewashing, and covering up—even as they keep learning more about the inconvenient truths that so far they have perceived as being against the collective interests of Donald's captured political party and, therefore their own naked personal power.

After having participated in what I like to think of as the Republican impeachment mistrials or exercises in jury nullification to twice acquit the former president of high crimes and misdemeanors, these same U.S. Senators on May 28, 2021 were staging their second filibuster on behalf of the Insurrectionist-in-Chief to further delay the Donald's accountability for the assault on the Capitol by voting to kill the bill to establish an independent and bipartisan commission to investigate January 6. In each of these political contests between the entrusted power of these elective representatives and the U.S. Constitution, the whitewashing Trumpian party has chosen to stand with treachery over veracity, disloyalty over authenticity, lawlessness over rules of law, and travesty over democracy.

The abuses of power

CNN in early 2021 interviewed a group of 16 politically diverse constitutional scholars, presidential historians, and experts on democratic institutions asking them to rank order Trump's ten worst abuses of power while in office. Their rankings from first to tenth were as follows:

1. Subverting the 2020 election
2. Inciting an insurrection
3. Abusing the bully pulpit
4. Politicizing the Justice Department
5. Obstructing the Mueller investigation
6. Abusing the pardon power

7 The Ukraine affair and cover-up
8 Loyalty oaths and personalizing government
9 Firing whistleblowers and truth-tellers
10 Profiting off the presidency.[17]

Should the Boss still be free to pursue a comeback in 2024 as the leader of the Trumpian party, I suspect that his anti-democratic and autocratic record will cut both ways with divided America pretty much along political party lines. Even more importantly should the Boss return to the White House in 2025 there would be virtually no proverbial guardrails to prevent him from doing whatever he wanted to since he would no longer have to face another presidential reelection. If there were not enough loyalists and yes people around during his first administration this time around it will be that much worse. As will the culture of intimidation or social and psychological abuse that the Boss maintains as a fusion of Toddler-in-Chief and Bully-in-Chief to hear what he wants to hear and to get his way.[18]

Of course, these rankings of the former president's abuses of power are subjective and represent the averaging of the 16 politically diverse scholars. Nevertheless, I have a couple of bones to pick with this collection of experts: First, although the Ukraine affair and its cover-up ranks seventh worst on the abuse of power list and even though "cover-up" might reference implicitly the Obstruction of Congress charge in Trump's First Impeachment, I would have liked to see this abuse of power spelled out by name. Second, if I had been polled, I would have rank ordered Politicizing the Justice Department as number one. Even though Trump's takeover of the U.S. Justice Department was not nearly as successful as his takeover of the Republican Party, his constant self-interested use and abuse of the allegedly independent or non-politicized organization was a very serious assault on the highest levels of U.S. law enforcement and quite damaging to the esprit de corps of the DOJ.

Specifically, these abuses of power were aided by the lack of push back or resistance and often cooperation from his two appointed U.S. attorney generals. First, there was Jefferson Beauregard Sessions of Alabama who recused himself from the Russian Inquiry, discontinued investigations into police abuse, reactivated the executions of federal prisoners, and established the unprecedented policy of taking children away from their parents as a means of deterring migration. After less than two years of the very anti-human rights and repressive Sessions, there was William P. Barr the former and not very honorable attorney general for Bush I, 1988–1992. From early 2019 to late 2020 as Trump's unabashed "hit man" and corrupt AG, the even more ethically challenged Barr should have been impeached and/or disbarred long before he resigned following Trump's loss for reelection.[19]

In Citizens For Responsibility and Ethics in Washington vs. U.S. Department of Justice, a case addressing Barr's misrepresentation of the findings from the Mueller Russian investigation into the 2016 campaign, the U.S. District Judge for the District of Columbia Amy Berman Jackson rejected the DOJ's attempt to keep secret a department opinion not to charge former President Trump with obstruction of justice during the Mueller investigation. The redacted 41 pages of Memorandum Opinion signed on May 3, 2021, begins[20]:

> On Friday, March 22, 2019, Special Counsel Robert S. Mueller, III delivered his Report of the Investigation into Russian Interference in the 2016 Presidential Election to the then-Attorney General of the United States, William P. Barr. But the Attorney General did not share it with anyone else.
>
> Instead, before the weekend was over, he sent a letter to congressional leaders purporting to "summarize the principal conclusions" set out in the Report, compressing the approximately 200 highly detailed and painstakingly foot noted pages of Volume I – which discusses the Russian government's interference in the election and any links or coordination with the Trump campaign – and the almost 200 equally detailed pages of Volume II – which concerns acts taken by then-President Trump in connection with the investigation – into less than four pages. The letter asserted that the Special Counsel "did not draw a conclusion – one way or the other – as to whether the examined conduct constituted obstruction," and it went on to announce the Attorney General's own opinion that "evidence developed during the Special Counsel's investigation is not sufficient to establish that the President committed an obstruction-of-justice offense." The President then declared himself to have been fully exonerated.
>
> The Attorney General's characterization of what he'd hardly had time to skim, much less, study closely, prompted an immediate reaction, as politicians and pundits took to their microphones and Twitter feeds to decry what they feared were an attempt to hide the ball.
>
> Even the customarily taciturn Special Counsel was moved to pen an extraordinary public rebuke on March 27: The summary letter the Department sent to Congress and released to the public in the afternoon of March 24 did not fully capture the context, nature, and

> substance of this Office's work and conclusions. We communicated that concern to the Department on the morning of March 25. There is now public confusion about critical aspects of the results of our investigation. This threatens to undermine a central purpose for which the Department appointed the Special Counsel: to assure full public confidence in the outcome of the investigations. Mueller called for the immediate release of his report, but it remained under wraps for another three weeks.
>
> On April 18, 2019, the Attorney General appeared before Congress to deliver the report. He asserted that he and the Deputy Attorney General reached the conclusion he had announced in the March 24 letter "in consultation with the Office of Legal Counsel and other Department lawyers."
>
> Citizens for Responsibility and Ethics in Washington ("CREW") immediately fired off a Freedom of Information Act ("FOIA") request for any records related to those consultations, but the Department of Justice ("DOJ") demurred on the grounds of the deliberative process and attorney-client privileges. What remains at issue today is a memorandum to the Attorney General dated March 24, 2019, that specifically addresses the subject matter of the letter transmitted to Congress.
>
> As the May 4, 2021, headlines from Law.Com and the NYTimes. Com as well as from CNN.COM on May 5th respectively read: 'Not Worthy of Credence': Ordering Release of Mueller Report Memo, Judge Blasts Trump DOJ for 'Disingenuous' Claims; Judge Says Barr Misled on How His Justice Dept. Viewed Trump's Action; and Secret William Barr memo saying not to charge Trump must be released, judge says.

An incomplete list of Bill Barr's abuses of power as attorney general the second time includes:

- Serving as the president's offense and defense lawyer.
- Bypassed Senate confirmation to install acting U.S. attorneys in New York and New Jersey—offices critical to the fate of corruption charges against the Trump administration, organization, and family.
- He has repeatedly kept evidence of Trump misdeeds from reaching agencies or officials who might have pursued them.
- He advanced a series of extreme legal arguments for noncooperation with congressional requests and inquiries.

- He overruled his own prosecutors sentencing recommendations and intervened to lessen Roger Stone's years in prisons after Trump complained.
- He was also instrumental in granting additional pardons to white-collar criminals with influence in either the White House or the Republican Party.
- Under his (and Session's) tenure at the DOJ, the number of federal prosecutions for price-fixing, tax fraud, and environmental offenses reached historical lows not seen for some 30 years.[21]
- Led the federal government targeting of Black Lives Matter protesters with harsh prosecutions to discourage the movement following the murder of George Floyd, which also exaggerated the threat of violence from protesters.[22]

The not so quick and dirty on Bill Barr and other lawless attorney generals

AG Barr played a critical role as Trump's deceitful and mostly reliable "hatchet man." While running the DOJ for a second time from February 14, 2019 to December 23, 2020, Barr probably became the most corrupt U.S. attorney general in one hundred years.[23] Other contenders for the most corrupt modern attorney general title include: A. Mitchell Palmer who served under Woodrow Wilson from March 1919 to March 1921; Harry M. Daugherty who served under Warren G. Harding and briefly under Calvin Coolidge from March 21 to April 24; John N. Mitchell who served under Richard Nixon from January 1969 to March 1972; John Ashcroft and Alberto Gonzales who served under George W. Bush from February 2001 to February 2005 and February 2005 to September 2007, respectively; and Trump's Jeff Sessions as well as his temporary replacement acting AG Matthew Whitaker before Barr returned to his old stomping ground after three decades. What all these attorney generals share is that while they each engaged in and/or facilitated lawlessness, injustice, and crime, they all presented themselves as steadfast "law and order" crusaders. They also all refused as attorney generals to cooperate with any investigations of wrongdoing by administration officials.[24] With the exception of A. Mitchell Palmer the other corrupt attorney generals were all appointed by and served at the will of Republican presidents.

In the case of Barr, he repeatedly violated the written rules of the Department of Justice and the unwritten norms and principles that constitute the "prosecutor's code." At times, he also conspired with the president for the benefit of Boss Trump and his various associates to the detriment of his opponents and the rule of law. These state-organized crimes were not rationalized in the name of national security as in Reagan's Irangate or some other tenable justification. All these actions were taken in order to protect the former president from his personal and political wrongdoing. From the instances of distorting the findings of Special Counsel Robert Mueller to trying to manipulate the law to squash the whistleblower's complaint about Trump's dealings with Ukraine to the undermining of his own DOJ prosecutors in the cases of the former president's allies, Michael Flynn and Roger Stone. Subsequently and under false pretenses, Barr fired the U.S. attorney for the Southern District of New York who was investigating both the Donald and the Trump Organization. Finally, in the months running up to the 2020 presidential election, Barr repeatedly amplified the baseless claims and conspiracy theories about massive mail-in ballot voter fraud.

None of this was particularly surprising given Barr's track record as far back as his employment at the Central Intelligence Agency from 1973 to 1977 where he learned about dirty tricks from the best and brightest, including its Director George H.W. Bush. While serving in the Agency's Office of Legislative Council William wrote the memorandums that ended the moratorium on destroying records imposed on the CIA by the Church Committee hearings to investigate the abuses of both the Central intelligence Agency and the National Security Agency during the 1960s and early 1970s.[25] In 1992, then-Attorney General Barr also supported President George H.W. Bush's Iran-Contra scandal decision that gave clemency to six officials in the Ronald Reagan administration, including the former Defense Secretary Caspar Weinberger.[26] Barr justified these blanket pardons because he viewed the investigation of Iran-Contra as a miscarriage of justice much as he would come to view the Russian investigation by Mueller.

In each of these instances where Barr dismissed or routinized away state-organized crime, he has been viewed as acting consistent with his very conservative beliefs and extremist views on the power of the executive branch. In fact, in June of 2018, Barr wrote an unsolicited 20-page memorandum to the DOJ. Barr began the memo "as a former official deeply concerned with the institutions of the Presidency and the Department of Justice."[27] The former attorney general was fundamentally questioning the scope of Mueller's investigation and arguing that Trump did not have to answer any of the questions about possible obstruction of justice. The Donald had found his Roy Cohn and on Valentine's Day eight months later, the

Senate voted 54 in favor of 45 opposed and confirmed William Barr as the Boss' third attorney general.

Attorney General Barr like tactician Steve Bannon was all in with Trump except when he was not. In the case of Steve's betrayal, it was when he got caught skimming off of Trump's proceeds for the building of a wall along the Southern border—a Trump pardon would come, nevertheless. In the case of Barr, his betrayal occurred on December 1, 2021—after president-elect Biden had defeated Trump some three weeks earlier—when Bill was not willing to say that the election was stolen or to endorse Trump's Big Lie. Recall that Barr and Bannon each had their own agendas that preceded the Donald and the age of Trump. In this sense Barr even more so than Bannon gives a whole new meaning to the term "double-agent" as he used Trump perhaps as much or more than Donald used him. In either case, it was pretty much a faceoff between Bannon and Trump and between Barr and Trump even though the former supported the coup, and the latter seems not to have been on board with insurrection. Lastly, unlike the other kneeling Republicans surrounding Boss Trump, both Barr and Bannon held their own and could go toe to toe with the Donald, especially Steve.

Historically, what is similar about Trump's state-organized crimes against the democratic state or Republic of America with other state-organized crimes from the POTAS is the probability that the Biden Administration and Attorney General Merrick Garland will not prosecute Donald Trump or try to hold him accountable. This is like when President Obama and his Attorney General Eric Holder failed to hold Bush and company accountable for their state-organized war crimes against the Iraqis, Afghans, and others. More specifically, President George W. Bush and Vice President Dick Cheney authorized those state-war crimes. Secretary of Defense Donald Rumsfeld ordered the building of clandestine prisons overseas and provided the sanctioning authority to torture prisoners in those "black sites" that was approved by the National Security Council and by the Justice Department who drafted "memos providing the brutal program with a veneer of legality."[28] On December 9, 2014, the Senate Intelligence Committee on CIA torture released a 6,700-page report. Despite its "revelations about waterboarding and week-long bouts of water-soaked sleep deprivation in the CIA's Rendition, Detention and Interrogation programme," there never was any chance that any of the top members of former president George W. Bush's national security team would ever be prosecuted for their crimes.[29]

Media attention has revolved around Barr's criminal law background especially as a former AG for the first Bush Administration. Almost no focus has been given to Barr's extensive background in corporate and financial litigation or to his selective enforcement of antitrust law. For example, from 1994 to 2008, Barr served as general counsel to GTE and later to Verizon the product of its merger with Bell Atlantic. That merger wound up making Barr a millionaire many times over. In 2008 he took early retirement from Verizon, and he received a $28 million payout cited in a watchdog group's complaint as an example of overcompensation and sloppy corporate governance.[30] Barr more recently was also a former director of the Och-Ziff Capital Management Group, a hedge fund that had been involved in the acquisition of 14 ski resort properties in the United States. Not long after he resigned from the board in 2018 as he prepared to jump on the Trump train as the attorney general, "the company paid a $412 million fine to settle charges of offering bribes in several African nations." Some of the bribe money found its way to the son of former Libyan dictator Muammar el-Qaddafi.[31]

Perhaps it is not all that surprising then as Trump's attorney general that Barr gave the green light to several mergers, including the one between T-Mobile and Sprint that had promised to be politically helpful to Trump and the Republican Party. In fact, during the time when the government was considering the deal both T-Mobile and Sprint executives were staying at the Trump International Hotel in Washington where they just happened to spend approximately $195,000. At the time 13 attorney generals from across the country as well as the District of Columbia sued to block the deal from happening. Meanwhile, the head of the antitrust division of DOJ in an unprecedented action was "involved in the negotiations to bring the deal to fruition."[32] As we previously discussed "pay to play" at some length in the previous chapter and how Trump properties became a "favorite roosting place" for many other corporate leaders as well as foreign government officials seeking policy concessions, it is worth acknowledging that a conscientious and ethical attorney general might "have asked his department to investigate this practice as a potential violation of the Constitution's emoluments clause."[33] Not only did Barr choose not to do so, but he also adopted the same practice and scheduled an annual holiday party at the Trump Hotel for a cost of $30,000.

Investigative reporting has

> unearthed smoking-gun evidence of overt attempts by former President Trump and his White House staff to use the Department of

> Justice (DOJ) to overturn the will of voters in the 2020 election and revealed the possibility that the DOJ may have targeted Democratic Members of Congress in a criminal leak investigation at Trump's behest.[34]

Most assuredly, the primary target of Trump's abuses of power was the DOJ. While Barr usually had the Donald's back the department of justice ultimately "withstood Trump's basest efforts to use its law enforcement powers for his own corrupt purposes."[35] That stated the DOJ leadership often treated "its prosecutors and civil attorneys alike – as the president's henchman."[36] This abusive treatment manifested "externally in a loss of integrity and perceived integrity; internally in the personnel lost, spirits crushed, and precedents set."[37]

It was disconcerting to learn that Biden's Attorney General Merrick Garland had indicated that he was not inclined to perform the necessary "post-mortem" on the Trump-era abuses. Again, it was not particularly surprising considering the Obama administration's failure to hold the Bush II administration and Secretary of Defense Donald Rumsfeld accountable for their crimes. Particularly the Secretary of Defense Rumsfeld who was the architect of the war crimes committed by the U.S. soldiers at Abu Ghraib prison in Iraq as well as at the Bagram Theater Internment Facility in Afghanistan. In 2005 the ACLU represented nine men who sued Rumsfeld and others for torture and the two-time Secretary of Defense was found not liable. An international group of lawyers also filed a war crimes lawsuit in 2006 against Rumsfeld in Germany to no avail. A 2008 report from the U.S. Senate Armed Forces Committee did place most of the blame for torture on Rumsfeld and other senior officials. Unlike the International Criminal Court in the Hague, the Kuala Lumpur War Crimes Commission (Tribunal), Malaysia found Rumsfeld, former vice president Dick Cheney, George W. Bush, and other senior officials guilty for crimes against the peace in 2012.

Of course, the DOJ could also indict and prosecute Trump, Barr, and other senior officials for corruption, abuse of power, and obstruction of justice. Think back to the Watergate scandal and the burglars caught in the act at the Democratic National Committee's headquarters on June 17, 1972. Those hired burglars were tried and convicted in January 1973. Subsequently, Attorney General Elliot Richardson who had replaced John N. Mitchell as AG in 1972 when the latter departed to head up Nixon's reelection campaign. Richardson then appointed Archibald Cox as special prosecutor in May 1973. On March 1, 1974, a grand jury indicted former Attorney General John N. Mitchell, H. R. Haldeman, White House chief of staff, John Ehrlichman, former assistant to Nixon in charge of domestic affairs, and Charles Colson, former White House counsel specializing in political affairs, for such crimes as conspiracy, obstruction of justice, and perjury. They were all convicted and sentenced to prison.

Back in February of 1974, the Watergate grand jury had also named Richard Nixon as an unindicted co-conspirator for his attempt to cover up the burglary. In August, Nixon resigned the presidency rather than stand trial. Former vice president Gerald R. Ford who had assumed the presidency when Nixon stepped down immediately pardoned him.[38] Certainly pending the ongoing threat that Trump has generated and the damage that the Donald has already done, caused, and continues to foment even compared to 20 years of "Tricky Dick" Nixon is far more dangerous to our democracy, especially because of the Trumpian capture of the Republican Party. For this reason alone, it warrants that the DOJ minimally prosecute the former president and his cohorts not only for inciting a rebellion or an insurrection against the authority of the United States or the laws thereof, or giving aid or comfort thereto, shall be subject to fines or up to a maximum of ten years in prison or both, and shall not be able to hold any future public office 18 U.S. Code § 2383.

Out of cautionary fear of alienating or incriminating DOJ personnel and ostensibly to avoid politicalization, Garland is shirking his duty as the attorney general should he not prosecute all persons involved in the conspiracy to overturn the lawful election of Joe Biden as the 46th President. If Merrick is truly interested in both being fair to current employees and protecting them from future presidents with autocratic impulses, then he needs to set the record straight about both the crimes and the abuses of crime control during the Trump administration. As former DOJ attorneys Kristy Parker and Rachel Homer have blogged:

> We know firsthand that fortifying the Department of justice so that it can protect the rule of law and withstand future authoritarian assaults will require *both* a comprehensive understanding of the ways in which the Trump administration abused the Department and the implementation of direct and robust measures to address the damages sustained and weaknesses identified over the past four years.[39]

The Russian investigation: Robert Mueller vs. Donald Trump

After Trump's firing of James Comey as the Director of the FBI and when his first appointed AG Jeff Sessions recused himself and stepped aside from the Russian inquiry, the Deputy Attorney General Rob Rosenstein made the decision in May of 2017 to appoint Robert Mueller, a former federal prosecutor and director of the FBI from 2001 to 2013, as the "special counsel" to lead the Russian investigation. His job was to look for evidence of alleged interference in the 2016 presidential election and to decide whether or not Trump campaign officials were complicit in that process.[40] Allegedly but not really independent of the normal chain of the DOJ command and still subject to the caprices of the attorney general conventional wisdom still had expected that Mueller "would be able to proceed without any interference, including from the White House."[41] Any person who might have assumed that expectation would apply to the Machiavellian Trump as the saying goes, that person "doesn't know jack" about the Donald.

Trump was obviously guilty of several counts of obstructing justice, especially since the Mueller Report went into detail about ten instances. There was also an abundance of evidence of collusion (not conspiracy) between Russian operatives and the Trump campaign. Nevertheless, with much assistance by AG Barr the Donald easily managed to get the best of Mueller and once again to evade culpability. This is not to suggest that Mueller came away empty handed. On the contrary, there were 25 Russians who were symbolically indicted since they will never see the inside of a U.S. courtroom. Criminal charges were also filed against nine U.S. nationals. Most notably, Trump's second campaign chairman Paul Manafort for the 2016 race pleaded guilty in September 2018 to conspiracy to defraud the United States and to witness tampering in the Russian investigation. These plea bargains were occurring as the voir dire was set to begin in a second Manafort criminal trial. These pleas had followed an earlier trial in Alexandria, VA where Manafort was convicted of eight crimes that occurred before and during the 2016 campaign. These included five counts of tax fraud, two counts of bank fraud, and one count of failure to disclose a foreign bank account. There were four other campaign workers that pleaded guilty to crimes as well, including most significantly former Army General Michael Flynn. Trump's first National Security Advisor Flynn lasted less than a month when he pleaded guilty to lying to the FBI about his contacts with the Russian ambassador during the transition to the White House.[42]

There was also lawyer Michael Cohen who had stated that he would "take a bullet" for the Donald. In November 2018, Michael pleaded guilty to lying to Congress for stating that discussions about a potential Trump Tower project in Moscow had ended in January 2016 when they had continued through June of that year. Last and not least there was Roger Stone.

The longtime friend and advisor to the former president was convicted and sentenced to prison for 44 months for seven crimes, including obstruction of justice, witness tampering, and making false statements to the FBI in relation to the Russian interference in the 2016 election.[43] Nevertheless, Trump with the help of AG Barr was able to bamboozle about half of the American people into thinking that there was nothing there as in "No Collusion, No Obstruction." Trump also played as usual his phony grievance card that he was the victim of another "witch-hunt" or some kind of conspiracy by the "deep state" to take him out of the game.

Let us return to the three specifics that Rosenstein ordered special counsel Mueller to investigate:

- The Russian government's efforts to interfere in the election.
- Any coordination between Russians and Trump campaign-linked individuals.
- Any matters that arose or may arise directly from the investigation.

To be more fully informed, the acting attorney general's specific charges to Mueller should be understood within the scope of the larger powers of a special counsel that are essentially like the powers of U.S. attorneys. Meaning that they can subpoena records or people to testify as well as bring forth criminal charges. Mueller did so 34 times. Daily, the DOJ hierarchy does not supervise special counsel the same as it does the U.S. attorneys. Special counsels are also permitted to request the widening of jurisdictions subject to the approval of the attorney general. Finally, the special counsel may prosecute anyone who engages in various crimes that interfere with their investigations. These include perjury, obstruction of justice, destruction of evidence, and the intimidation of witnesses with the debatable exception of the president of the United States.[44]

Like Trump, Robert Swan Mueller III came from an upper-middle-class family with considerable wealth. His father was an executive at DuPont and the young Bob grew up in Princeton, New Jersey. Mueller had also been born in New York City two years before the Donald in 1944. They both share German and English ancestries. Each is alleged to have underdeveloped and non-self-effacing senses of humor. It is during the Vietnam War that the life courses of the two dramatically diverge. After graduating from Princeton University in 1966, Robert tried to enlist in the Marines but because of a knee injury he had to wait. While doing so he made the most of his time and went to officer candidate school and then to Vietnam in 1968 the same year that Donald graduated from the University of Pennsylvania. No longer eligible for his student deferment a doctor practicing in a building owned by Fred, Sr. signed the paperwork so that Donald could receive a medical deferment because of bone spurs in one of his two feet. When running for office in 2016 the former two-time candidate could recall neither the foot that had suffered the bone spurs nor the doctor's name. While serving in Vietnam Mueller was awarded the Bronze Star, the Purple Heart, and the Vietnamese Cross of Gallantry. After Nam he pursued a master's degree in international studies from New York University and then Robert earned his law degree from the University of Virginia.

Over the course of their contrasting lives Mueller chose public service rather than private fortune as the narrative goes. He spent a combined 12 years as an Assistant U.S. Attorney in San Francisco and Boston. Next, he served in George H. W. Bush's Justice Department where Mueller would become an assistant attorney general in charge of the criminal division. In 1998 President Clinton appointed Mueller to be the U.S. attorney for San Francisco. After President George W. Bush nominated Mueller to become the sixth director of the FBI the U.S. Senate unanimously confirmed him in 2001. Trump as we all know chose personal wealth over anything he could do to serve his country. His demystified slogan for the race to the White House should have been: "Ask not what your country can do for you, ask yourself what I can do for the Donald?" By the time the Russian investigation began in the early summer of 2017 the personalities of these two men were very well known. One had earned a reputation for honesty and morality; the other had become famous for his selfishness and greed. Not unrelated: "Mueller has one wife and many lifelong friends; Trump had three wives, many business associates, and few friends."[45]

With respect to "goody two shoes," Mueller and his deference to the rule of law vs. the "scumbag" Trump and by any means necessary in relation to the Russian intervention into the 2016 election and the various links between the Russians and Trump that might have arisen from the investigation, Bob never laid so much as a legal punch on the Donald. I am not suggesting that Mueller took a dive for the president but rather as Tiger Woods might have stated, "Mueller didn't bring his A game." Or more accurately in his overzealousness to be fair and not to be politically biased Bob ended up getting in his own way especially in terms of what should be done. Mueller's own convoluted legal interpretation of the findings and his twisted discourse compromised an appreciation for what Trump and company had wrongfully done. Now let us review why and how this occurred. And how it could have been different had Mueller been less concerned about process, precedent, or ethics and less deferential and accommodating to the litigious 45th president. In short, Mueller should have been more transactional and assertive in nature like the adversary he was investigating. He should have played hard ball with the Donald and fought fire with fire

For example, Robert could have pursued the discretionary justice outcomes of Rosenstein's third charge without stepping on any of Donald's toes or alleged rights. If Mueller had investigated Trump's historical and ongoing business relations with Russian nationals, then he would have discovered the ongoing and patterned evidence of criminal wrongdoing involving Russians, Deutsche Bank, and the Trump Organization. I am referring to the two decades of money laundering that predated the 2016 presidential race. It is not necessarily that Donald's taxes and business affairs were off the investigative gurney because that was and is where the bodies are buried, and that Trump had insisted repeatedly that they should remain outside the investigation. As legal commentators have speculated the acquired evidence of crimes in these matters may have been passed on to other prosecutorial agencies in the State of New York.

One week after Trump had fired Mueller's successor as FBI Director James Comey and the day before Robert accepted his appointment from Deputy Attorney General Rod Rosenstein to become the special counsel in the Russian investigation, the two had met privately with Trump in the Oval Office. Comey had been removed because the Donald did not like how he was handling the investigation; specifically, James had declined the former president's request to drop the charges against General Michael Flynn, Trump's first National Security Advisor. To Trump's chagrin Attorney General Jeff Sessions had recused himself from the Russian probe because of a campaign event in the spring of 2016 where Trump, Sessions and son-in-law Kushner were in a small gathering with the Russian ambassador to the U.S. Sergey Kislyak.[46]

Mueller had finished his tenure as the Director of the FBI in 2013 after having served the legal maximum number of 12 years. Though he had never met privately with either Presidents Bush or Obama during his time as head of the FBI he had agreed to meet with Trump because when the president requests your presence it becomes your duty to appear. Mueller did not know at the time that the nefarious Trump was setting him up and creating a false narrative about the DOJ's special counsel. When the meeting began Mueller thought its purpose was that the former president was seeking his advice about the appointment of the next FBI Director. However, Trump did most of the talking about unrelated matters though Mueller found one opportunity near the end of a relatively short meeting to let the former president know that his replacement for Comey should come from outside the FBI. That did occur more of less when Christopher Wray became Trump's director. Wray was brought in from the private sector, but he had also been a former assistant attorney general in charge of the criminal division from 2003 to 2005 during the end of G.W. Bush's first and the beginning of his second term.

Afterward on several occasions, Trump lied about the meeting saying that it was about Mueller wanting his old job back as the director of the FBI and the Donald telling him "No can do." That exchange between the two men with Rosenstein present in the room was a complete fabrication that never transpired. This was simply part of Trump's game to discredit Mueller from the start of the investigation and to establish a narrative that Robert had accepted the job as special counsel not as an act of public service but as a means of pursuing a personal vendetta against the Donald. As Donald always argues, say something, anything enough times, and some people will believe it no matter how absurd it is. More importantly as Donald does with his adversaries whether in business, politics, or litigation he always personalizes the legal exchanges. As we all know by now the Projector-in-Chief has a tendency of using adolescent putdowns and nicknames to demonize and ridicule not only his legal opponents but also those who disagree with him, refuse to break the law for him, or are viewed as weak and disloyal.[47]

In a series of tweets that railed against the Russian probe in August 2018 the Donald bestowed the nicknames of "disgraced" and "discredited" Bob Mueller—from *Donald J. Trump@realDonaldTrump*, August 20, 2018. And from two other tweets on the same day:

> They are enjoying ruining people's lives and REFUSE to look at the real corruption on the Democrat side – the lies, the firings, the deleted emails and soooo much more! Mueller's Angry Dems are looking to impact the election. They are a National Disgrace!
>
> Where's the Collusion? They made up a phony crime called Collusion, and when there was no Collusion they say there was Obstruction (of a phony crime that never existed). If you FIGHT BACK or say anything bad about the Rigged Witch Hunt, they scream Obstruction!

And from a tweet on August 19, 2018:

> The Failing New York Times wrote a story that made it
> seem like the White House Council had TURNED on the President, when in fact it is just the opposite – & the two Fake reporters knew this. This is why the Fake News Media has become the Enemy of the People. So bad for America.[48]

Typically, Trump characterized the investigation as a personal contest between himself and Mueller. Their respective teams and operations reflected the two men:

> Mueller and his team were disciplined, restrained, and orderly; they avoided publicity, and their presentations to the public—especially the Mueller Report, which closed their work—hewed scrupulously to provide facts. Trump was in every way their opposite, and his public statements were medleys of invective and falsehood… his lawyers were disorganized and riven by internal rivalries, and their number was frequently in flux because of the changing moods of Trump himself.[49]

Trump played with the postmodern tools of mass media, social media, and used the power of the presidency with his usual demagoguery. As previously noted, Mueller's team did meticulous forensic examinations in a traditional sense, built compelling factual cases against numerous persons, and extracted several guilty pleas. As already implied, they were overly cautious when narrowly conceiving their mandate as obligatory under the rules and normative traditions governing the work of prosecutors. As Jeffrey Toobin has pointed out, these were Mueller's choices and costly ones. His reticence led him to fail at his two most fundamental tasks:

> Thanks to the clever actions (and strategic inaction) of Trump's legal team, Mueller failed to obtain a meaningful interview with Trump himself. Even worse, Mueller convinced himself—wrongly—that he had to write a final report that was nearly incomprehensible to ordinary citizens in its legal conclusions. By doing so, he diluted, nearly to insignificance, the extraordinary factual record he had assembled. And the opacity of Mueller's report allowed Trump's allies to define it to the president's advantage.[50]

With respect to the resolution of the Russian investigation and Trump's complicity in several crimes, Toobin is once again spot on:

> Trump's victory over Mueller was tactical, not strategic. The president and his allies outmaneuvered Mueller, but Trump's character—and his behavior—didn't change. He had muddied the public's understanding of his collusion and obstruction with regard to Russia, but his determination to collude and obstruct for political advantage never waned. Indeed, as it became clear that Trump would survive the Mueller investigation of Russia, the president took that escape as an invitation to undertake the same kind

> of effort with regard to Ukraine. But now that Trump was the president, not a private citizen running a long-shot campaign, he had vastly greater powers, which he used to collude and obstruct on a grander scale.[51]

Three years later, the five-year statute of limitations for prosecuting the former president on eleven instances of obstruction of justice have already started to expire, beginning with Trump's alleged request to then-FBI Director James Comey to drop the criminal investation of national security advisor Michael Flynn on February 14, 2022. It now appears that Attorney General Merrick Garland's vow to pursue those criminally responsible for breaking the law "at any level" does not apply to the Donald.

Trump's first impeachment: "A Perfect Call" to Ukrainian President Zelensky

The Mueller investigation into Trump's 2016 election campaign of collusion with the Russians before the Donald was president and his obstruction of justice after he became the 45th president can be distinguished from Trump's first impeachment for abuse of power and obstruction of congress. The primary distinction being that the latter offense, namely strong-arming Ukrainian President Zelensky occurred while Trump was president and ipso facto becomes a state-organized crime. The call to Zelensky was less than three months after Trump had eluded any negative results from the Russian investigation.

After Trump's request that Ukrainian President Volodymyr Zelensky investigate Democratic presidential candidate Joe Biden and his son Hunter triggered the first impeachment inquiry, the Donald made a series of false claims about the whistleblower's accurate account of the call and about what others were not saying about Trump's conversation with the Ukrainian president. First, although a White House-released memo on his July 25 phone call with Zelensky included a note of caution explaining that the text shared was "not a verbatim transcript" Trump lied and stated that it was "an exact word-for-word transcript of the conversation." Second, although the whistleblower stated in testimony that he had received "a readout of the call" and Acting Director of National Intelligence Joseph Maguire had testified that the complaint was consistent with the White House memo, Trump maintained that the whistleblower "never saw the conversation" and "wrote something that was total fiction." Donald was contradicting Maguire on both counts.

Third, although Maguire during his testimony before the House intelligence committee never characterized the phone call Trump asserted that the acting director called the phone call "very normal." Fourth and fifth, Trump misrepresented comments made by Republican Sen. Majority leader Mitch McConnell as well as Republican Sen. Rick Scott of Florida. Both men had agreed that the call was not an impeachable offense. Regarding the former Trump had claimed falsely that Moscow Mitch had "put out a statement that said that was the most innocent phone call he's read." As for the latter the Donald had claimed that Scott referred to the phone call as "a perfect conversation."[52] The whistleblower had written in his complaint that White House officials were "deeply disturbed" by the call and had acted to "lock down" all details of it.[53] Trump was impeached the first time over allegations he improperly sought help from Ukraine to improve his chances for reelection by asking his newly elected counterpart to dig up damaging information on his political rival or at least to announce publicly that an investigation into the matter would be initiated.

On December 18, 2019, the Democratic held House specifically impeached Trump on two charges–abuse of power and obstruction of Congress. Back in August 2019, an anonymous intelligence official wrote a letter expressing concern over Trump's July 25 phone conversation with Zelensky. The official spoke of an "urgent concern" that Trump had used his office to "solicit interference from a foreign country" in the 2020 election. The call had occurred shortly after Trump had blocked the release of $391 million in military aid to Ukraine. "A senior official," the acting ambassador to Ukraine, Bill Taylor who had replaced Marie Yovanovitch, "later testified the president had made it clear the release of this aid was conditional on Mr. Biden being investigated."[54]

Taylor also told the inquiry that there was "an irregular, informal channel of US policymaking" occurring in Ukraine involving AG Barr, Secretary of State Pompeo, and Donald's personal attorney Rudy Giuliani. They had been circumventing Ambassador Yovanovitch or placing her outside the loop as it were.[55] Finally, in an unprecedented move the ambassador was removed from her post and brought back to the United States in July 2019 based on complaints from allies outside the administration, including his personal lawyer Rudy Giuliani that Marie was "undermining him abroad and obstructing the efforts to persuade Kyiv to investigate former Vice President Joe Biden."[56] Trump's call had also come three months after Zelensky a famous TV personality and comedian with no political experience was elected president. Trump claimed that he had made the call merely to congratulate Volodymyr on his victory and that the impeachment trial was nothing but another witch hunt. The trial came down to whether soliciting opposition research from a foreign government constituted an impeachable offense.

The Senate trial lasted two weeks and was held in late January and early February 2020. Failing to meet the requirement of a two-thirds majority to convict a Republican-held Senate acquitted Trump by 52 to 48 on abuse of power and by 53 to 47 on obstruction of Congress. All totaled the partisan votes were as follows: The Republicans cast 105 votes to acquit and 1 to convict; the Democrats cast 94 votes to convict and 0 to acquit. Not unlike the results of the Mueller investigation and now with the help of Republican senators finding the president not guilty on February 6, 2020, Trump and his 2020 campaign were able to double down on the Donald as a victim at the hands of those "radical" Democrats.

Not content with his acquittal victory Trump ousted Army Lt. Col. Alexander Vindman, the Ukraine expert for the National Security Council from his White House role as director of European Affairs after Vindman had responded to a subpoena and testified under oath that the telephone conversation between Trump and Zelensky had been "inappropriate."[57] As part of Trump's post-acquittal purge, he also recalled one of his million dollar donors Gordon D. Sondland who was the ambassador to the European Union because he also testified against Trump during the impeachment trial.

> In the two days since his acquittal in the Senate, Mr. Trump railed about those who stood against him, calling them 'evil', 'corrupt' and 'crooked', while his press secretary declared that those who hurt the president 'should pay for' it.[58]

Notes

1 Celia Wells, 2001. *Corporations and Criminal Responsibility*. Oxford: Oxford University Press. See also, Sally Simpson, 2002. *Corporate Crime, Law, and Social Control*. Cambridge: Cambridge University Press.
2 Jonathan Pinto, Carrie R. Lena, and Frits K. Pil, 2008. Corrupt Organizations or Organizations of Corrupt Individuals? Two Types of Organizational-Level Corruption. *Academy of Management Review* 33 (3): 685–709.
3 Gregg Barak, 2012. *Theft of a Nation: Wall Street Looting and Federal Regulatory Colluding*. Lanham, MD: Rowman & Littlefield.
4 Maya Pagni Barak, 2021. Family Separation as State-Corporate Crime. *Journal of White Collar and Corporate Crime*. June 2 (2): 109–121.
5 William Chambliss, 1989. State-organized crime. *Criminology* 27: 183–208.
6 Jeffrey Ian Ross, 2000 (ed.). *Varieties of State Crime and Its Control*. Monsey, NJ: Criminal Justice Press.
7 Gregg Barak, 1991(ed.). *Crimes by the Capitalist State: An Introduction to State Criminality*. Albany: State University of New York Press. See also, Penny Green and Tony Ward, 2004. *State Crime: Governments, Violence and Corruption*. London: Pluto Press.
8 The contemporary applicable federal law is the Racketeer Influenced and Corrupt Organizations Act, enacted October 15, 1970. New York criminalized these offenses as part of its "enterprise corruption" statute that was added to

their Penal Law by the Organized Crime Control Act of 1986. Over the years, other states have enacted similar statues.

9 Martin J. Sheil, 2019. Can Trump Organization Executives Be Prosecuted for Money Laundering? *Just Security*. March 6. https://www.justsecurity.org/63084/trump-organization-executives-prosecuted-money-laundering/.

10 Raymond J. Michalowski and Ronald C. Kramer, 2006 (eds.). *State-Corporate Crime: Wrongdoing at the Intersection of Business and Government*. News Brunswick, NJ: Rutgers University Press.

11 VOA News, 2017. Report: Trump Assets in Revocable, Not Blind, Trust. February 4. https://www.voanews.com/usa/report-trump-assets-revocable-not-blind-trust.

12 Michael R. Sisak and Tom Hays, 2021. Trump Organization, CFO Indicted on Tax Fraud Charges. AP. July 1. https://apnews.com/article/trump-organization-allen-weisselberg-charges-ad7350d4f85f295eeb753658e786cd88.

13 Turns out that over the course of Trump's first three years in office, he spent 3.1 days out of 10 visiting a Trump-owned or branded property, mostly at Mar-a-Lago, Florida in the winter and at Trump National Golf Club Bedminster, New Jersey in the summer. The Donald did so primarily so he could play a round or two of golf or host a political fundraiser, setting and breaking a presidential record as one of his campaign pledges: "Because I'm going to be working for you, I'm not gong to have time to go play golf." Quoted in Philip Bump, 2019. Nearly a Third of the Days He's Been President, Trump Has Visited a Trump-branded Property. *The Washington Post*. December 30. https://www.washingtonpost.com/politics/2019/12/30/nearly-third-days-hes-been-president-trumps-visited-trump-branded-property/.

14 David Fahrenthold, 2021. Trump Charged Secret Service Nearly $10,200 in May for Agents' Rooms. *The Washington Post*. July 8. https://www.washingtonpost.com/politics/trump-secret-service-charges/2021/07/07/7f88043a-df2e-11eb-b507–697762d090dd_story.html.

15 Nexstar Media Wire, 2021. Trump Extends Secret Service Protection to 14 Family Members, Reports Say. *ABC News*. January 20. https://www.abc27.com/news/us-world/national/trump-extends-secret-service-protection-to-14-family-members-reports-say/.

16 Russ Buettner, Mike McIntire, Susanne Craig and Keith Collins, 2021. Trump Paid $750 in Federal Income Taxes in 2017. Here's the Math. *The New York Times*. Updated February 28. https://www.nytimes.com/2020/09/29/us/trump-750-taxes.html.

17 Marshall Cohen, 2021. Chronicling Trump's 10 Worst Abuses of Power. CNN. January 24. https://www.cnn.com/2021/01/24/politics/trump-worst-abuses-of-power/index.html.

18 Stephanie Grisham, 2021. *I'll Take Your Questions Now: What I Saw at the Trump White House*. New York: HarperCollins.

19 Elie Honig, 2021. *Hatchet Man: How Bill Barr Broke the Prosecutor's Code and Corrupted the Justice Department*. New York: HarperCollins Publishers.

20 United States District Court for the District of Columbia, Civil Action No. 19–1555 (ABJ)***SEALED***, filed 05/03/21. https://ecf.dcd.uscourts.gov/cgi-bin/show_public_doc?2019cv1552-27.

21 Jim Lardner, 2020. Mapping Corruption: Donald Trump's Executive Branch: An Inquiry into How the Trump Administration Transformed Washington. *The American Prospect*. April 9. https://prospect.org/power/mapping-corruption-donald-trump-executive-branch/.

22 The Associated Press, 2021. Feds Targeted BLM Protesters in Attempt to Disrupt Movement, Report Says. NBC News. August 19. https://www.nbcnews.com/news/nbcblk/feds-targeted-blm-protesters-attempt-disrupt-movement-report-says-rcna1717.
23 Honig, 2021.
24 Ronald L. Feinman, 2019. The Long History of Unjust and Lawless Attorney Generals. HNN. July 28. https://historynewsnetwork.org/article/172654.
25 JPat Brown, 2019. While at the CIA, William Barr Drafted Letters Calling for an End to the Agency's Moratorium on Destroying Records. *Muckrock*. April 16. https://www.muckrock.com/news/archives/2019/apr/16/cia-barr-crest/.
26 Carrie Johnson, 2019. William Barr Supported Pardons in an Earlier D.C. 'Witch Hunt': Iran-Contra. NPR. January 14. https://www.npr.org/2019/01/14/684553791/william-barr-supported-pardons-in-an-earlier-d-c-witch-hunt-iran-contra.
27 Quotes in Jonathan Hafetz and Brett Max Kaufman, 2019. William Barr's Unsolicited Memo to Trump about Obstruction of Justice. ACLU Speak Freely. January 11. https://www.aclu.org/blog/civil-liberties/executive-branch/william-barrs-unsolicited-memo-trump-about-obstruction-justice.
28 Anthony D. Romero, 2014. Pardon Bush and Those Who Tortured. *The New York Times*. December 8. https://www.nytimes.com/2014/12/09/opinion/pardon-bush-and-those-who-tortured.html.
29 James Reinl, 2014. Why Bush Won't Be Prosecuted over CIA Torture. *Aljazeera*. December 11. https://www.aljazeera.com/features/2014/12/11/why-bush-wont-be-prosecuted-over-cia-torture.
30 Ibid.
31 Ibid.
32 Ibid.
33 Ibid.
34 Kristy Parker and Rachel Homer, 2021. Restoring Justice to DOJ. July 15. JUST SECURITY. https://www.justsecurity.org/77454/restoring-justice-to-doj/.
35 Ibid.
36 ibid.
37 Ibid.
38 Less than one year before in October 1973, the House minority leader Ford was selected to replace Vice President Spiro Agnew for an unrelated scandal. Agnew was being investigated by the U.S. attorney for the District of Maryland on suspicion of criminal conspiracy, bribery, extortion, and tax fraud. After months of professing his innocence, Agnew pleaded no contest to a single felony charge of tax evasion, and exited stage left.
39 Quoted in Ibid.
40 Titles no longer used for these types of inquiries include "special prosecutor" or "independent counsel." The former term harks back to the Watergate scandal when Nixon's AG nominee Elliot Richardson appointed Archibald Cox as the Special Prosecutor to oversee the federal criminal investigation into the Watergate burglary and other related crimes. Since there was no law defining and regulating such an appointment, nothing prohibited Nixon from subsequently firing Cox. Accordingly, the Ethics in Government Act was passed in 1978 defining the circumstances under which an "independent counsel" could be appointed. This law was allowed to expire in 1999 after the controversy of independent counsel Kenneth Starr's wide-ranging inquiry into President Clinton and his Whitewater land deal in the Ozark Mountains near Flippin,

Arkansas morphed into having sexual relations with a White House intern Monica Lewinsky. Henceforth, 28 CFR § 600.1 Grounds for appointing a Special Counsel, passed July 9, 1999, may ensue when the investigation or prosecution of that person or matter by the U.S. Attorneys Office or litigating Division of DOJ would present a conflict of interest. Ironically perhaps, as it turned out in the case of Trump, the Special Counsel was not all that independent especially because the AG, in this case Bill Barr, had the power to fire Mueller for "misconduct," "dereliction of duty," "incapacity," "conflict of interest," or other "good cause," including the violations of department policies.

41 BBC News, 2019. Special Counsel: What Is It and What Did Robert Mueller Investigate? July 24. https://www.bbc.com/news/world-us-canada-39961732.

42 Jason Breslow, 2018. All the Criminal Charges to Emerge From Robert Mueller's Investigation. *National Public Radio*. December 9. https://www.npr.org/2018/12/09/643444815/all-the-criminal-charges-to-emerge-so-far-from-robert-muellers-investigation.

43 Sharon LaFraniere, 2020. Roger Stone Is Sentenced to Over 3 Years in Prison. *The New York Times*. February 20 (Updated July 19, 2020). https://www.nytimes.com/2020/02/20/us/roger-stone-40-months-sentencing-verdict.html.

44 Mueller maintained that a 1973 Office of Legal Counsel memorandum prevented him from pursuing criminal charges against Trump or indicting him as a sitting president. The appropriate place for dealing with a misbehaving president was impeachment. However, two other legal memorandums from the Office of Legal Counsel written surrounding Clinton's impeachment trial were split: one from Independent Counsel Kenneth Starr says that the president is immune from prosecution and other from the President's defense council Charles F.C. Ruff says that the president may be indicted. Moreover, the naming of Nixon as an unindicted co-conspirator in the Watergate was certainly a precedent that Mueller could have used to pursue criminal violations.

45 Jeffrey Toobin, 2020. *True Crimes and Misdemeanors: The Investigation of Donald Trump*. New York: Doubleday, p. 4.

46 Ken Dilanian, 2017. Did Trump, Kushner, Sessions Have an Undisclosed Meeting with Russian? *NBC News*. June 1. https://www.nbcnews.com/news/us-news/did-trump-kushner-sessions-have-undisclosed-meeting-russian-n767096.

47 See the List of nicknames used by Donald Trump at Wikipedia. It is fascinating and begs the question, does he really sit around nicknaming all these people? Though his nicknames overlap, the Donald has hundreds of nicknames for domestic political figures, foreign leaders, media figures, groups of people, organizations, television programs, and more. https://en.wikipedia.org/wiki/List_of_nicknames_used_by_Donald_Trump.

48 Saagar Enjeti, 2018. Trump Gives Mueller His Very Own Nickname. *Daily Caller*. August 20. https://dailycaller.com/2018/08/20/trump-mueller-new-nickname/.

49 Toobin, 2020: 7–8.

50 Ibid: 8

51 Ibid: 9.

52 Eugene Kiely, Lori Robertson and D'Angelo Gore, 2019. Trump's Inaccurate Claims about His 'Perfect' Call. FactCheck.org. October 3. https://www.factcheck.org/2019/10/trumps-inaccurate-claims-about-his-perfect-call/.

53 BBC, 2020. Trump Impeachment: The Short, Medium, and Long Story. *BBC News*. February 5. https://www.bbc.com/news/world-us-canada-49800181.

54 Ibid.

55 Ibid.

56 Rebecca Balhaus, Michael C. Bender and Vivian Salama, 2019. Trump Ordered Ukraine Ambassador Removed After Complaints From Giuliani, Others. *The Wall Street Journal.* October 3. https://www.wsj.com/articles/trump-ordered-ukraine-ambassador-removed-after-complaints-from-giuliani-others-11570137147.

57 Corey Dickstein, 2020. Lt. Col. Vindman, Fired by White House after Testifying in Trump Impeachment, Will Retire from Army. *Stars and Stripes.* July 8. https://www.stripes.com/branches/army/lt-col-vindman-fired-by-white-house-after-testifying-in-trump-impeachment-will-retire-from-army-1.636781.

58 Peter Baker, Maggie Haberman, Danny Hakim, and Michael S. Smith, 2020. Trump Fires Impeachment Witnesses Gordon Sondland and Alexander Vindman in Post-Acquittal Purge. *The New York Times.* July 8. https://www.nytimes.com/2020/02/07/us/politics/alexander-vindman-gordon-sondland-fired.html.

7

PARDONS, PROSECUTIONS, AND THE POLITICS OF PUNISHMENT

The Vera Institute of Justice has reported that there were 1,249,300 prisoners confined in the U.S. prisons, federal and state, combined in 2020. By late December, there also had been an additional 633,200 persons who had passed through a local lockup or jail facility.[1] However, less than eight percent of the total number were convicted of a federal offense, the rest of the incarcerated offenders were either convicted of state crimes or faced charges for the same. According to the Federal Bureau of Prisons as of July 24, 2021, there were 144,915 federal inmates broken down by type of offense as follows[2]:

Drug Offenses	66,905
Weapons, Explosives, Arson	29,825
Sex Offenses	16,211
Burglary, Larceny, Property Offenses	7,260
Extortion, Fraud, Bribery	7,241
Immigration	6,315
Robbery	4,638
Homicide, Aggravated Assault, and Kidnapping Offenses	4,576
Miscellaneous	862
Courts or Corrections Violations	515
Continuing Criminal Enterprise	286
Banking and insurance, Counterfeit, Embezzlement	243
National Security	38

DOI: 10.4324/9781003221548-10

Putting aside that 50 governors also have the authority to grant reprieves and pardons and to commute the sentences of those convicted of state crimes, the relative number of convicted persons that may be considered for presidential clemency always represents to some degree a small and insignificant form of forgiving justice. Regardless of the president or political party in power, the trifling number of lottery recipients of this particularly capricious form of criminal justice is exceedingly fortunate. These people are often connected one way or the other to economic, political, or cultural capital to help grease the wheels of forgiveness.

Sixty-seven percent of those possible cases are for drugs or weapons, explosives, and arson offenses. The other 33 percent are for sex offenses, immigration violations, robbery, homicide, aggravated assault, and kidnapping. If we combine all those individuals federally convicted of the traditional expressions of *organizational crime* inclusive of extortion, continuing a criminal enterprise, fraud, bribery, banking, insurance, counterfeit, and embezzlement, then while Trump was the president, there were some 7,770 convicted white-collar and/or corporate offenders or five percent of the total imprisoned federal population of inmates that were eligible for pardons or commuted sentences.[3]

Going back as far as President Theodore Roosevelt (1901–1909), Trump ranks as one of the stingier clemencies dispensing presidents falling more in line with his Republican rather than Democratic predecessors. With respect to the previous five presidents—Obama (D), Bush II (R), Clinton (D), Bush I (R), and Reagan (R)—each may have pardoned a handful or less of business and political criminals. These types of recipients of clemency made up the largest proportion of the Forgiver-in-Chief. There are a couple of other interesting facts that are worth thinking about when we review Donald and the power of the pardon. First, as 2022 began, Trump was still very busy dodging prosecution for allegedly a myriad of criminal offenses. These have involved most if not all categories of organizational crime, as well as sex offenses, violations of national security, and most likely some violations that fall under miscellaneous. Second, Donald has employed hundreds if not thousands of undocumented workers at his hotels and golf courses. Decades ago, most of his undocumented workers were periodically employed in the destruction and reconstruction of hotels.

White-collar crimes annually make up just over three percent of federal prosecutions. White-collar prosecutions declined steadily from 9,507 prosecutions in 2001 to a projected 4,727 prosecutions in 2021, a 50.3 percent drop.[4] Between 2010 and 2014, there were a total of 1,309 or 262 annual prosecutions of corporate offenders (215) and corporations (47).[5] For the same four years, there were 1,010,340 criminal referrals processed by federal prosecutors of which 10,879 or 1.1 percent were for alleged corporate violations. The remaining 98.9 percent were for alleged individual offenders.[6] Among these, there were 3,337 criminal corporate referrals to the FBI and 6.6 percent or 220 cases prosecuted or 54 annually.[7] Yet, the costs annually to the U.S. economy and tax payers are $300 billion from white-collar crime and $1.5 trillion from corporate crime for a total of $1.8 trillion or more than twice the $800 billion costs for all of the other crimes in society combined.[8] Unfortunately, when most folks, especially politicians, use the crime problem and underenforcement as a talking point, they are not referring to the domestic epidemic of white-collar and corporate crime committed in the wealthy skyscrapers as their eyes are always focused downward on the impoverished masses.

Like most white-collar and corporate crimes in the United States, business violations of immigration laws such as knowingly hiring people without the proper paperwork are rarely enforced. Since 1986, the number of prosecutions has averaged 15 per year and has only exceeded 20 twice. Once in 2005 under George W. Bush and again in 2009 under Barack Obama. Although almost every enforcement measure of crime in the street rose during the Trump administration, the number of business owners subject to immigration violations appears to have dropped by more than 33 percent: "From April 2018 through March 2019, 11 individuals representing employers were prosecuted" and "only three were sentenced to prison."[9] As the former Projector-in-Chief and very cynical Trump has told us many times whether it is employer fraud, tax fraud, or any other offense that Donald regularly engages in: "everybody does it and nobody gets busted for it, so why single me out?"

From Article II, Section 2, Clause 1 of the Constitution, the President "shall have the Power to grant Reprieves and Pardons for Offences against the United States, except in Cases of Impeachment." The Constitution is also silent about, and therefore, does not prohibit the president's pardoning power from extending to those convicted of federal crimes on behalf of and/or in conspiracy with the president. As we all know, the Boss pardoned several loyal members of the Trump gang, including among the most notable recipients Paul Manafort, Roger Stone, and Steve Bannon. To be specific, under the Constitution, only federal convictions, military court martial decisions, and convictions in Washington, DC are eligible for presidential clemency. These include pardons or full forgiveness of crimes, commutations or the merciful reduction of sentences, and reprieves or the temporary stay of a sentence. As we have already discussed, the power of the pardon does not extend to those convicted of state crimes.

To be considered for clemency, applicants submit a notarized petition to the Office of the Pardon Attorney in the Department of Justice. The rules "tell pardon seekers to wait at least five years after their conviction or their release from prison, whichever is later before filing a pardon application." [10] Spoiler alert: The Trump administration repeatedly violated this DOJ custom. After evaluating such factors as the seriousness of the offense and the extent to which someone has accepted responsibility for their crimes, how a person has acted since conviction, and input from the U.S. prosecutor who handled the case weighs in, the pardon office makes a recommendation and forwards it to the deputy attorney general. In turn, the deputy AG makes a recommendation of its own and forwards it along with the pardon office's up or down recommendation to the White House for a decision. In many instances, this process was totally ignored because the Trump administration viewed it as too time-consuming and cumbersome which it probably is. Trump rationalized why should he bother to conform to these rules since he could do as he pleases anyway. After all, the Donald was acting in "the spirit" of Article II...perhaps more so here than with other rules of law that he has broken.

Other informal rules or customs that Trump violated are that pardons are usually given near the end of a president's term in office and not after persons have only been charged and not even convicted of a crime. In the case of the latter, one of Trump's co-conspirators in deconstructing the state and assaulting the Capitol Steve Bannon had been arrested and indicted in August 2020 for "conspiring to swindle donors to a private fund to build a wall along the Mexican border, siphoning off more than $1million for personal and other expenses."[11] Steve was pardoned just before Christmas well before his case was scheduled for adjudication. It will be interesting to see how Steve's three co-defendants fare at trial when the time comes. In the case of the former, infamous Arizona Maricopa County Sherriff Joe Arpaio became Trump's first pardon on August 25, 2017, only seven months into his administration. Besides the violations in procedure, what makes this pardon particularly unique is that it was for only a misdemeanor rather than a felony offense. Here again, the pardoning of Arpaio was pre-emptive occurring after his conviction and before his sentencing. The former Sherriff of course had not submitted a pardon application. For the record, his conviction had been for a misdemeanor contempt of court charge for having intentionally defied a 2011 court order to stop traffic patrols that targeted immigrants.[12]

In Donald's inimical and corrupt way, he was able to turn his pardoning gig into another revenue stream for making money off the presidency. Opening bids for pardon consideration were auctioned off at $50,000. There were no guarantees. In fact, Parker Petit paid one of the largest figures—$750,000—out in mid-December to Matt Schlapp and his lobbying firm, Cove Strategies. This was done just days before Trump released his final pardons. It was denied. Petit had been a top Republican donor who served as the Georgia finance chairman for Trump's 2018 campaign. Cove Strategies had raised over $2.3 million for Trump in 2020. He was convicted of securities fraud in November 2020 and was facing up to 20 years in prison. Schlapp who is also the chairman of the American Conservative Union had also been a frequent guest on Fox News program. His wife Mercedes Schlapp worked for both the White House and the 2020 campaign. In December 2020, Trump appointed Schlapp to the trust fund board for the Library of Congress, "making him one of the many Trump-connected lobbyists to land a government appointment from Trump while continuing to lobby."[13]

The White House has credited the former U.S. Attorney Brett Tolman with having secured for a little over $75,000 clemency or pardons for four individuals as either a special group rate or a going out of business sale. A most interesting split-pardoning decision by Trump involved the granting of clemency to Nickie Davis and Elliott Broidy. In August 2020, Davis admitted that she had failed to disclose lobbying the Trump administration on behalf of a fugitive Malaysian financier. In November, Davis had paid Mark Cowan a member of Trump's transition team $100,000 to lobby the Donald to grant her clemency. While Trump did not pardon Davis, he did pardon Broidy, "a top Trump fundraiser who was the mastermind behind the covert foreign influence operation."[14]

We know about these fees because these lobbyists reported their "pay to play" to the IRS. Knowing the Donald, I suspect that these known lobbying efforts of pardon disclosures are only the tip of the "dollars for forgiveness" iceberg. We also know that Trump has all kinds of business and political relations with unknown and unregistered lobbyists domestic and international. These folks lobby the United States illegally and regularly on behalf of foreign interests such as the convicted and pardoned Paul Manafort and the indicted Tom Barrack. Neither Paul nor Tom was ever registered as lobbyists or publicly advertised their lobbying services. Not only were their transactions with Trump "off the books" but they also were clearly in violation of the Foreign Agents Registration Act (1938).

Pardoning crimes and commuting sentences

The table comparing clemency figures for Trump and the five previous presidents is from a larger Pew Research Center table for presidents 25–45, 1897–2021, that was generated the day after Trump begrudgingly left the White House.[15] Among these six presidents, only Ronald Reagan was not particularly stingy with granting clemency. The only president as unforgiving and unmerciful as Trump was G.W. Bush. Of course, when an administration has engaged in war crimes like the Reagan administration, it probably reduces one's tendencies to grant clemency as in what gives a War Criminal the right to do so? Of course, moral reluctance by our Violator-in-Chief never crossed Donald's mind. His reluctance was more a product of his lack of empathy and the fact that most of those clemency applicants had nothing of value to offer Trump.

What sets Trump's grants of clemency apart from his presidential forerunners was again the audacious inclusion of his co-conspirators whose crimes were of benefit to Trump as well as the relatively high number of "well connected donors," one of whom had been convicted of committing "crimes while holding public office." Though the elder Bush president granted the fewest number of total clemencies, he did manage to pardon five Iran-Contra conspiratorial offenders plus the Secretary of Defense Caspar Weinberg for numerous illegalities that Bush as a former CIA Director and then as Reagan's VP oversaw organizing this unlawful exercise in the first place.[16]

Please note that "other" on the comparative clemency table refers to remissions, which reduce financial penalties and respites that are temporary reprieves often granted for medical reasons, which are seldom used these days, had peaked with 489 during FDR's three terms, 1933–1945. For example, Truman, 1945–1953 used it 13 times; Hoover, 1929–1933 used it 121 times; and Wilson, 1913–1921 used it 374 times. For the record, the percentage of requests granted for clemency involving 15 presidents from McKinley, 1897–01 through Carter, 1977–1981 averaged 30. It is also noteworthy that Barack Obama received more requests for clemency, 36,544, than the other five presidents put together, 35,674. And Obama's 1,715 commutations dwarf the 182 of his five predecessors and even more than the previous 13 presidents combined. Barack's last-minute commutations and pardons were reflective of part of his larger efforts to redress the unfair, racist, and inequitable punitive system of criminal justice in America.[17] Notably, most of those pardons and commutations were for nonviolent drug offenders[18] as compared with the other presidents whose granting of clemency had been more about the political or economic grievance status of the offenders involved.[19]

President Trump

> used his final hours in office to wipe away convictions and prison sentences for a roster of corrupt politicians and business executives and bestow pardons on allies like Stephen Bannon, his former chief strategist, and Elliott Broidy, one of his top fund-raisers in 2016.[20]

Comparative Clemency Figures for Six Presidents

President	*Term*	*Pardons*	*Commutations*	*"Other"*	*Total Clemency*	*Total Requests*	*Percent Granted*
Trump	2017–21	143	94	0	237	11,611	0.02
Obama	2009–17	212	1,715	0	1,927	36,544	0.05
Bush II	2001–09	189	11	0	200	11,074	0.02
Clinton	1993–01	396	61	2	459	7,489	0.06
Bush I	1989–93	74	3	0	77	1,466	0.05
Reagan	1981–89	393	13	0	406	3,404	0.12

Source: U.S. Department of Justice Data, accessed by the Pew Research Center (1/22/21).

The Donald's 11th hour list of forgiveness recipients included 73 pardons and 70 commutations representing 60 percent of his total number of clemencies. Just before Christmas, Trump pardoned among others Charles Kushner, his son-in-law and senior adviser Jared Kushner's father and Manafort, his short-lived 2016 campaign chairman who had shared Republican campaign data with the Russians. Back in July 2020, Trump had commuted the sentence of Roger J. Stone. His longtime informal adviser and friend had been convicted of seven felony charges, including lying under oath to a congressional committee and threatening a witness. Subsequently, on December 23, 2020, Stone was also pardoned by Trump. A month earlier just before Thanksgiving, the Donald had pardoned Michael T. Flynn, the former national security adviser who had twice pleaded guilty to lying to the FBI about his conversations with a Russian diplomat. Attorney General Barr had previously tried unsuccessfully to shut the prosecution down. The rest of this section provides a large sampling of both the high-profile and low-profile crimes of mostly corrupt and wealthy allies that Trump pardoned or commuted during his administration.[21]

High-profile business, political, and media pardons or commutations issued in the final days of Trump's term included Anthony Levandowski, Kwame Kilpatrick, Duncan Hunter, Chris Collins, Steven Stockman,

Robert Hayes, Rick Renzi, Nicholas Slatten, Paul Slough, Evan Liberty, Dustin Heard, Lil Wayne, Kodak Black, Ken Nahmad, Albert J. Pirro Jr., and Sholam Weiss. Lesser known or low-profile pardons or commutations occurring at the same time included Dr. Salomon E. Melgen, William T. Walters, Paul Erickson, George Gilmore, Eliyahu Weinstein, Robert Zangrillo, and Aviem Sella. His earlier high-profile political and business pardons or commuted sentences included George Papadopoulos, Alex van der Zwaan, Rod R. Blagojevich, Edward J. DeBartolo Jr., Bernard B. Kerik, Michael R. Milken, David H. Safavian, Angela Stanton, Conrad M. Black, former Army lieutenant Clint Lorance, Maj. L. Golsteyn, Chief Petty Officer Edward Gallaher, Scooter Libby, Dinesh D'Souza, Dwight L. Hammond, Steven D. Hammond, and Trump's first pardon to Joe Arpaio, August 25, 2017.

Trump also issued three posthumous pardons to historical figures: Jack Johnson, Susan B. Anthony, and Zay Jeffries. Jackson was the first Black heavyweight boxing champion convicted in 2013 for transporting a white woman, his girlfriend, across state lines. The women's suffragist Anthony was arrested in Rochester, N.Y. for voting illegally in 1872 and was fined $100. Jeffries, a metal scientist who made contributions to the Manhattan Project and whose development of armor piercing artillery shells helped the Allies win WWII, was found guilty of antitrust violations related to his work and was fined $2,500.

Finally, there was Donald's second clemency twofer for his "poster" commutation (June 6, 2018) and pardon (August 28, 2019) of Alice Marie Johnson. She was one of only five petty clemencies issued by Trump.[22] Alice, a prison reform advocate and a friend of television personality Kim Kardashian, was extricated from her life sentence imposed after she was convicted in 1996 on eight criminal counts for her involvement in a Memphis cocaine trafficking organization. She was one of the speakers at Trump's 2020 Republican National Convention.

High & Low Profile Business, Political, and Celebrities Issued Clemencies in the Last Days.

- **Anthony Levandowski**—Pardon, January 2021—a Silicon Valley star and pioneer of self-driving car technology was sentenced in August 2020 to 18 months in prison for stealing self-driving car trade secrets from Google; he agreed to pay more than $756,000 to Waymo, a self-driving business spun out of Google.
- **Kwame Kilpatrick**—Commuted January 2021—former Detroit Mayor was sentenced to 28 years after being convicted of two dozen counts, including racketeering and extortion in 2013.

- **Robert Hayes**—Pardon, January 2021—a former chairman of the North Carolina Republican Party received a full pardon after being accused in 2019 of bribery and conspiracy to commit honest services wire fraud as well as making false statements; subsequently, he pleaded guilty to lying and was sentenced to one year of probation.
- **Rick Renzi**—Pardon, January 2021—a former Republican representative for Arizona who had been sentenced in 2013 to 36 months in prison for his involvement in a bribery scheme concerning an Arizona land swap deal.
- **Randy "Duke" Cunningham**—Conditional Pardon, January 2021—a former Republican representative had pleaded guilty and was sentenced to eight years and four months for taking $2.4 million in bribes from military contractors seeking government contracts.
- **Little Wayne**—Pardon, January 2021—born Dwayne Michael Carter, the rapper pleaded guilty in December 2020 to having illegally carried a gold-plated 45-caliber Glock handgun and ammunition while traveling on a private jet in 2019 as a felon formerly convicted of a gun crime; Lil Wayne was facing up to ten years in prison.
- **Kodak Black**—Commutation, January 2021—whose legal name is Bill Kapri though he was born Dieuson Octave had served nearly half of his four-year sentence for lying on background paperwork while attempting to buy guns.
- **Ken Kurson**—Pardon, January 2021—close friend and associate of Jared Kushner who had once appointed Jared as the editor-in-chief of *The New York Observer* was under consideration for a seat on the board of the National Endowment for the Humanities when he was arrested and charged in 2020 on cyberstalking charges that he planned to plead not guilty to.
- **Hillel Nahmad**—Pardon, January 2021—as a wealthy family member of art collectors and one of the best-known art dealers in New York, he served five months in prison in 2014 after pleading guilty to leading a sports gambling ring with ties to Russian-American organized crime figures.
- **Albert J. Pirro Jr.**—Pardon, January 2021—a Republican businessman and an ex-husband of Jeanine F. Pirro, a Fox News host, he had been convicted in 2000 and sentenced to 29 months for conspiracy and tax evasion.
- **Sholam Weiss**—Commutation, January 2021—the New York businessman in 2000 was convicted of racketeering, wire fraud as well as money laundering related to a huge insurance fraud scheme, and was

sentenced to more than 800 years believed to be the longest federal prison term ever imposed.

- **Salomon E. Melgen**—Commutation, January 2021—a major Democratic donor and West Palm Beach eye doctor who received a 17-year sentence in February 2018 for health care fraud and stealing $73 million from Medicare by persuading patients to undergo tests and treatment they did not need for diseases they did not have.
- **William T. Walters**—Commutation, January 2021—a wealthy sports gambler convicted in 2017 for his role in an insider-trading scheme and sentenced to five years in prison.
- **Paul Erickson**—Pardon, January 2021—a former boyfriend of Maria Butina, the Russian operative involved in Republican campaigning was convicted of wire fraud and money laundering in July 2020 and he was sentenced to 84 months concerning his 2017 business dealings in the Bakken oil fields of North Dakota.
- **George Gilmore**—Pardon, January 2021—a New Jersey Republican power broker was convicted in April 2019 on two counts of failing to pass over payroll taxes withheld from employees to the IRA as well as one count of making false statements on a bank loan application was sentenced to one year in prison, January 20; however, his case remained in appellate court until a three-judge panel rejected his appeal in December 2020.
- **Eliyahu Weinstein**—Commutation, January 2021—in 2014 was convicted of a real estate Ponzi scheme that prosecutors claimed caused $200 million in losses and he was sentenced to more than 20 years.
- **Robert Zangrillo**—Pardon, January 2021—a Miami real estate developer and father was one of many wealthy parents arrested in April 2019 and accused of paying $250,000 to get his daughter into the University of Southern California as a transfer student pleaded not guilty to multiple fraud and conspiracy charges and was yet to be adjudicated.
- **Aviem Sella**—a former Israeli Air Force officer indicted in 1987 by the United States on espionage charges for recruiting the convicted spy Jonathan Jay Pollard to collect military secrets for Israel that Israel never agreed to extradite.

High, Low, and Other Profile Pardons and Commuted Sentences Issued Earlier

- **George Papadopoulos**—Pardon, December 2020—a foreign policy adviser to the Trump 2016 campaign pleaded guilty in 2017 to making false statements about his contacts with Russian intermediaries during the presidential race to federal officials as part of the Mueller investigation; he served 12 days and subsequently wrote a book portraying himself as a victim of a deep state plot to "bring down President Trump."

- **Alex Rolf van der Zwaan**—Pardon, December 2020—a Belgian-born Dutch attorney that was employed by a London branch of a New York-based international law firm pleaded guilty in February 2018 to making a false statement about the Russian interference in the 2016 election in response to questioning by federal investigator; after paying a fine of $20,000 and serving a 30-day sentence, he was deported to the Netherlands.
- **Duncan Hunter**—Pardon, December 2020—former California Republican congressman pleaded guilty in 2019 to one charge of misusing campaign funds by using more than $150,000 to support a lavish lifestyle and was set to begin an 11-month sentence in January 2021.
- **Chris Collins**—Pardon, December 2020—former New York Republican congressman and early Trump endorser pleaded guilty in 2019 to making false statements to the FBI and to conspiring to commit securities fraud and was serving a 26-month sentence.
- **Steve Stockman**—Pardon, December 2020—former Texas Republican congressman was charged with stealing hundreds of thousands of dollars meant for charity and was convicted on charges of fraud and money laundering in 2018 and was serving a ten-year sentence.
- **Nicholas Slatten**—Pardon, December 2020—and three other former U.S. service members, **Paul Slough**, **Evan Liberty**, and **Dustin Heard** who were all working as security contractors for Blackwater in 2007, were convicted on charges related to the killing of Iraqi civilians.
- **Rod R. Blagojevich**—Commutation, February 2020—former governor of Illinois was sentenced in 2011 to 14 years in prison for trying to sell or trade to the highest bidder Obama's vacated Senate seat when he was elected president; while he awaited trial back in 2010, he was a contestant on Trump's reality TV series, The Celebrity Apprentice.
- **Bernard B. Kerik**—Pardon, February 2020—a former New York City police commissioner was sentenced to four years in prison after pleading guilty to eight felony charges, including tax fraud and lying to White House officials.
- **Michael R. Milken**—Pardon, February 2020—the billionaire "junk bond king" pleaded guilty in 1990 to securities fraud and conspiracy charges who had been originally sentenced to ten years and later was reduced to two years and a fine of $600 million had not applied for a

pardon or a commutation; however, Giuliani who had prosecuted him back in the day was now arguing on his behalf.

- **Edward J. DeBartolo Jr.**—Pardon, February 2020—a former owner of the San Francisco 49ers pleaded guilty in 1998 to concealing an extortion plot and was prosecuted for a $400,000 bribe to secure a riverboat gambling license in Louisiana and had avoided prison by paying a $1 million fine and a one-year suspension from the NFL.
- **David H. Safavian**—Pardon, February 2020—a top federal procurement official during the George W. Bush administration had covered up his ties with corrupt lobbyist Jack Abramoff and was convicted of obstruction of justice and making false statement in 2009 and was sentenced to a year in prison.
- **Angela Stanton**—Pardon, February 2020—television personality, motivational speaker, author of *Life of a Real Housewife* explores her difficult upbringing, her work with prisoner re-entry, and her encounters with reality TV stars after serving six months of home confinement in 2007 for her role in a stolen vehicle ring.
- **Clint Lorance, Mathew L. Golsteyn, and Edward Gallaher**—Pardons, November 2019—these members of the armed services had been accused or convicted of war crimes when the Commander-in-Chief decided that he would become the arbiter of military justice as former Army lieutenant Lorance, who was serving a 19-year sentence for the murder of two civilians, Army Special Forces Maj. Golsteyn, who was facing murder charges for killing an unarmed Afghan he believed was a Taliban bomb maker, and Chief Petty Officer Gallaher, a Navy Seal who had been acquitted of murder and convicted of a lesser offense in a war crimes case.
- **Conrad M. Black**—Pardon, May 2019—a Trump friend and former press owner of The Chicago Sun-Times, The Jerusalem Post, and The Daily Telegraph of London and other newspapers was convicted of fraud in 2007 with three other former executives of Hollinger International and was released from prison in 2012 and subsequently penned several pro-Trump opinion articles as well as a flattering book, *Donald J. Trump: A President Like No Other.*
- **Dwight L. Hammond** and **Steven D. Hammond**—Pardons, July 2018—father and son were Oregon cattle ranchers serving five-year sentences for arson on federal land that inspired the antigovernment weeks long standoff at the Malheur National Wildlife Refuge in Oregon 2016 that included the occupation led by the Bundy family and

militia members in tactical gear and long guns commandeered government buildings and vehicles.

- **Dinesh D'Souza**—Pardon, May 2018—a right-wing author, commentator, and filmmaker who has also dabbled in conspiracy theories pleaded guilty to making illegal campaign contributions in 2014.
- **Lewis "Scooter" Libby**—Pardon, April 2018—was Vice President Dick Cheney's top adviser who was convicted in 2007 of four felony counts, including perjury and obstruction of justice in connection with the public disclosure of the identity of CIA officer Valerie Plame in reaction to her former ambassador husband's Joe C. Wilson's critical op-ed piece about the absence of weapons of mass destruction in Iraq.

Bottom line: Except for a few high-profile clemencies doled out to a diversity of celebrity stars and a handful of garden variety street criminals, the bulk of the pardons and commutations were enjoyed by wealthy, white-collar, or political criminals same as the former president. Perhaps they too were being persecuted by witch-hunts and victimized by miscarriages of justice.

Civil and criminal lawsuits against the former president

As of July 27, 2021, the former president was facing a bevy of investigations and lawsuits on both the civil and criminal litigation fronts with more cases likely to materialize.[23] The Donald's lawsuits span the full range of illegalities. Some of these civil suits involved pre-presidential business dealings as well as defamation claims from women who had claimed that Trump had sexually assaulted them. Emanating from his presidency were civil actions and criminal probes examining Donald's attempts to overturn the results of the 2020 election. In the face of so many looming lawsuits, the Houdini of all types of crime and his uncanny ability to elude legal liability will certainly be challenged. Potentially, the most damaging business and political outcomes to the Donald, the Trump family, as well as the Trump Organization are about the criminal rather than the civil lawsuits. The latter are generally subject to promises not to do it again and/or fines some of which are eligible for tax deductions.

Trump has been under criminal investigation in several jurisdictions, and should he be indicted and prosecuted, he would be the first former president in American history to face criminal adjudication. In the case of Teflon Don, however, without a jury conviction, the mere stigma of criminal charges will not be enough to reshape the contemporary U.S.

political landscape as an acquittal would only add fuel to the witch-hunt fires and conspiracies of the deep state out to get the aggrieved and persecuted ex-president. Therefore, it may very well be the case that Donald, the family, and the organization might have more to lose or to be damaged by one of their many civil lawsuits, especially in terms of their looming debt obligations and overall reduction in business revenues. Think of the settled lawsuit on November 7, 2016, where the Donald was forced to pay more than $2 million in court-ordered damages for misusing charitable funds at the Trump Foundation for political purposes. The settlement among other things required the Trump Foundation to shutter its doors and dissolve under court supervision that it did in December 2016.

As we turn to the Trump lawsuits tracked by justsecurity.com for this review, please keep in mind that a slew of other litigation pending indirectly against Trump that fall into those cases against his corporate properties, water use, the Trump campaign, or to telephone spam, copyright, and discrimination lawsuits are not identified below unless there were overlapping and multiple defendants such as Trump, the family, the campaign, the organization, and so on. What follows are those civil and criminal investigations of or lawsuits filed against Trump as the lone defendant or in combination with other legal entities and sued individuals. Then, I turn to a hypothetical DOJ prosecution of Trump for the January 6th Capitol insurrection.[24] In the final section of the chapter, I review those cases where Donald Trump is either not specifically charged with a criminal offense or named as the first defendant in a civil litigation against Trump Organization, Inc., Trump family members, its businesses, and political entities aligned with the former president such as the Trump campaign or political action committees.

The breadth of the scope of the civil cases includes **defamation**—*Zervos v. Trump* and *Carroll v. Trump*; **fraud**—*Trump v. Trump*; **incitement**—DC Attorney General investigation and *Thompson v.* Trump, Swalwell *v. Trump, Blassingame v. Trump, Smith et al. v. Trump et al*; **voting rights**—*Mich. Welfare Rights Org. v. Trump*; **class action**—*Doe v. Trump Corp.*; and **criminal election influence**—Fulton County, Georgia.[25] Four groups of plaintiffs are also bringing various **constitutional and statutory claims** against defendant Donald Trump and others. These are separate yet related lawsuits concerning the law enforcement responses to protests in Lafayette Square on June 1, 2020.[26] A brief overview and status of these lawsuits are presented in the chronological order of their legal filings.

On January 17, 2017, Summer Zervos filed a suit in New York State Court against Trump for defamation. After the Billy Bush *Access Hollywood Tape* revealed Trump talking sexually and derogatorily of women,

Zervos alleged that Trump offered her employment at half the salary they were previously discussing because she would not sleep with him. Zervos claimed that during the job interview, Trump kissed her on the lips and had touched her inappropriately. Trump claimed in response to the allegations that she was lying and only making up the accusations to generate self-fame or to help the Hillary Clinton campaign. After Trump's motions during and after office to dismiss the case were rejected by the court most recently on March 30, 2021, the case is waiting to move forward.

On September 9, 2019, E. Jean Carroll, a journalist and advice columnist, publicly accused President Trump of sexually assaulting her in a New York City department store in the 1990s. Within hours, Trump had denied Carroll's allegation and accused her of making up the story to sell her upcoming book. In turn, Carroll sued Trump for defamation in New York state court. In December 2020, the parties filed opposing memoranda on Trump's early motion to stay followed by their opening briefs on January 15, 2021. Carroll's attorneys filed their final brief on April 16, urging the appeals court to uphold the decision from below. The Biden administration DOJ filed a reply brief on June 7, 2021 that backed Trump's claim that when he responded as an elected official to media inquiries about Carroll's charges, his speech was protected under the Federal Tort Claims Act. Pending an appeal, the case is still alive.

On June 4, 2020, Black Lives Matter D.C., et al., plaintiffs v. Donald J. Trump, et al., defendants, was filed in the federal District of Columbia. Subsequently, three other related lawsuits were also filed in DC: Radiya Buchanan, et al., plaintiffs v. Donald J. Trump, et al., defendants; Isabella Kavanagh, plaintiff v. Donald J. Trump, et al., defendants; and Ryan Roth, plaintiff v. Donald J. Trump, et al., defendants. On June 21, 2021, the U.S. District Court Judge Dabney L. Friedrich responded to the related lawsuits that arose out of the law enforcement responses to protests in Lafayette Square on June 1, 2020. The claims against these federal defendants were based on the alleged unprovoked violence and clearing of Lafayette Square in order that the lawless Commander-in-Chief, AG Barr, and General Mark A. Milley, the nation's highest ranking military officer, could walk across the square so that the Donald could take a photo opt in front of St. John's Church where he was inadvertently holding a bible upside down, if only until his aids pointed this out to him. Donald quickly righted the bible as he stood before the church damaged from a prior and unrelated nonviolent protest. The plaintiffs sought (1) damages under *Bivens*, (2) injunctive relief for constitutional violations under 42 U.S.C. § 1983, and alleged (3) conspiracy in violation of 42 U.S.C. §§ 1985(3) and 1986, and (4) violation of the Posse Comitatus Act 18 U.S.C. § 1385.

The defendants brought before the court 15 motions to dismiss the complaints on the grounds that the constitutional and statutory claims were not justiciable and that the individual defendants were entitled to qualified immunity. In a 51-page Memorandum Opinion, Judge Friedrich essentially granted the motions to dismiss damages under *Bivens*, the conspiracy charges, and violations of the Posse Comitatus Act. The 1983 claims for First Amendment violations by Arlington County and District of Columbia officials remain. Since the court's rulings were based solely on the allegations of the complaints and were before either of the parties had pursued discovery, the court could not draw any conclusions about why Lafayette Square was cleared on June 1 or whether the law enforcement officers' actions were justified. In sum, after discoveries have been completed, the parties will have their opportunities to litigate the facts.[27]

On September 24, 2020, Mary Trump, the former president's niece, sued her uncle Donald Trump for allegedly defrauding her out of tens of millions of dollars from her rightful inheritance after her father Fred, Jr., Donald's older brother died. The lawsuit alleges that the Donald and his siblings siphoned off revenue from her share and set up a system to automatically devalue her assets. This ongoing scheme existed for nearly two decades until Fred, Sr., her grandfather, died in 1999. When Mary took issue with the terms of his will, the Trump siblings pushed back and started maneuvering to force her out of the family holdings altogether. Mary ultimately accepted a settlement offer that undervalued her share in April 2001 although she was unaware of how she was being short changed. After learning in 2018 from *The New York Times* story that the Trump Organization had been fraudulently manipulating the values of its assets for decades, Mary decided to take legal action against her uncle and siblings. On January 4, 2021, Trump moved to dismiss the case and Mary filed her response on February 26, 2021. On January 11, 2022, New York State Judge Robert Reed asked the Donald and Mary pointed questions during a two hour video hearing over Trump's motion to dismiss the lawsuit. From the judge's comments it appears that they will proceed to discovery.

On November 20, 2020, the Michigan Welfare Rights Organization represented by the NAACP's Legal Defense & Educational Fund (LDF) sued the then-President Trump and the Trump campaign alleging that their post-election conduct violated Section 11(b) of the Voting Rights Act, 52 U.S.C. § 10307(b) that forbids intimidation of voters, those aiding voters, and various election officials. The suit claims that following the election, Trump spent weeks pressuring Republican officials not to certify the election; examining the actions of Wayne County Republican officials first not to certify and then to certify the election. A few weeks later, the complaint was amended to include the NAACP as a plaintiff and the Republican National Committee as defendant. A new claim was also alleged to include the violation of the KKK Act that prohibits conspiracies to deprive someone of equal protection under the law or the right to vote in this case.

The LDF argued that Trump's efforts to discard votes in cities with large Black populations such as Detroit, Atlanta, and Philadelphia satisfy the statutory definition. The amended complaint seeks statutory damages, a declaratory judgment, and injunctive relief to prevent defendants from intimidating voters and election officials in the future. On February 25, 2021, the defendants of this case moved to dismiss using the same arguments that they will use in several other lawsuits yet to be discussed. Namely, that defendants' conduct did not violate the statutes, the cited statutes do not allow a private party to bring litigation, and the case was filed in the wrong court.

On February 10, 2021, the Fulton County District Attorney's Office in Atlanta opened an investigation into attempted election interference by the former president. On the same day, the DA's Office sent letters to Governor Brian Kemp, Lieutenant Governor Duncan, Secretary of State Raffensperger, and Attorney General Carr informing them about the investigation and requesting that "all records relating to the election, including emails sent by employees from non-governmental accounts, be preserved."[28] On March 6, DA Willis brought on John Floyd, a national expert on state racketeering prosecution to assist in the investigation. Two grand juries were underway in the county by March 28, and they were expected to issue subpoenas for documents and recordings related to the Trump investigation.[29] While both Manhattan's District Attorney Cyrus Vance and the New York State's AG Letitia James have active criminal investigations into Trump's finances, taxes, and business practices, some believe that the case in Georgia may be the strongest criminal one.[30] On January 22, 2022 a special grand jury with subpoena power and the authority to obtain documents requested by Fulton County DA Fani Willis was approved.

The Fulton County DA's investigation is looking into whether Trump violated Georgia election laws, including the "solicitation of election fraud, the making of false statements to state and local governmental bodies, conspiracy, racketeering, violation of oath of office and any involvement in violence or threats related to the election's administration."[31] Reportedly, the Fulton County DA Fani Willis plans to investigate a phone call between Senator Lindsey Graham (R-SC) and Georgia Secretary of State Brad Raffensperger who claimed that Graham asked him if he could throw out legally casted ballots. A spokesperson for Graham claims this was not the case that the senator was only inquiring about the signature verification process. The DA was also looking into whether Rudy Giuliani violated election laws in making false statements to Georgia officials.

On February 16, 2021, Mississippi Congressman Bennie Thompson (D) sued former President Trump, Rudy Giuliani, the Proud Boys, and the Oath Keepers, for violating the Ku Klux Klan Act of 1871, 42 U.S.C. § 1985(1). In response to violence and intimidation by the KKK intended to stop Black people from voting, the law was passed with the intention of allowing members of Congress to sue individuals who conspire to violently "molest, interrupt, hinder, or impede" the discharge of official duties such as the certification of the presidential election. Thompson is seeking compensatory and punitive damages for his emotional distress suffered during the Capitol attack. Subsequently, ten other members of Congress joined the lawsuit as plaintiffs. On July 21, Thompson announced that he would withdraw from the lawsuit to avoid any conflict with his role as the Chair of the January 6 House Select Committee to investigate the Capitol riots. Those members of Congress not on the committee have remained plaintiffs in the ongoing lawsuit.

On March 5, 2021, Representative Eric Swalwell filed a similar lawsuit to Rep. Thompson accusing Trump and his co-defendants Donald Trump, Jr., Representative Mo Brooks (R-AL), and Rudy Giuliani of violating the Ku Klux Klan Act by conspiring to interfere with the Electoral College count on January 6, 2021. The Swalwell lawsuit also alleges that the defendants committed criminal incitement under the local DC code–§22–1321(a)(2) and is therefore civilly liable for negligence. Beyond the civil rights and incitement counts, Swalwell has claimed that the defendants are not only liable for aiding and abetting the rioters' violent conduct, but also for intentionally inflicting emotional distress on members of Congress.

Between late May and early July 2021, the four defendants had filed their responses to the lawsuit. Giuliani's motion to dismiss argued that he had never formed a conspiracy and that his speech did not qualify as incitement, which he maintained was also protected by the First Amendment. Rep. Brooks' motion to dismiss argued that he was acting within the scope of his employment under the Westfall Act. By late July, both the DOJ and the Chairwoman of the Committee on House Administration had submitted briefs stating that Brooks was not acting within the scope of his employment and thus should not be shielded by the Westfall Act. Both Donald Trump and Donald, Jr. filed motions to dismiss as well. Junior's motion to dismiss contended as did his father's motion that the First Amendment and the canonical *Brandenburg* test protected their speech. Additionally, the former president claimed that he had immunity because his alleged misconduct was within the scope of his official duties as the president. Both Trumps also raised arguments ranging from standing to the political question doctrine. Finally, Donald raised a unique "double jeopardy" question when he claimed that Swalwell was barred from suing him over the same conduct for which he had already been acquitted of at the culmination of his second Impeachment trial. On January 10, 2022 a five hour hearing before D.C. District Judge Amit Mehta to decide whether this most significant case can proceed.

On March 30, 2021, Capitol police officers James Blassingame and Sidney Hemby sued Trump for injuries they sustained during the January 6 riots. As with the other January 6 lawsuits, the plaintiffs claim that their injuries resulted from the former president's incendiary rhetoric before and during the violence, aiding and abetting the rioters, and negligently inciting the riot in violation of DC's public safety codes. In addition, Blassingame, a Black officer pointing to racial slurs and taunts hurled at him by the intruders, accused Trump of directing intentional infliction of emotional distress. The officers are each seeking from the Donald a minimum of $75,000 in compensatory damages and an undisclosed amount in punitive damages.

On April 28, the plaintiffs added two conspiracy claims to their lawsuit. One was based on the KKK Act and the other on common law conspiracy alleging that Trump conspired illegally with the Proud Boys and the Oath Keepers to storm the Capitol resulting in their injuries. On June 6, defendant Trump filed a 55-page Memorandum in Support of his Motion to Dismiss. Once again, Trump argues that he has absolute immunity, the Constitution foreclosures the court from exercising jurisdiction over the president's actions during his presidency, the political question doctrine bars claims against the president, and that res judicata and collateral estoppel or double jeopardy regarding his Impeachment acquittal preclude any such claims by the plaintiffs. The bench has yet to rule on these motions. In addition, three more lawsuits against Trump by officers engaged in defending the Capitol on January 6, 2021 were filed in January 2022.

On May 24, 2021, Avaaz Foundation, a nonprofit global rights organization, filed a petition in the highest civil court in Scotland to challenge a Scottish Parliament vote not to investigate the Trump Organization's golf courses through an Unexplained Wealth Order (UWO) when called to do so by the minority opposition party the Scottish Greens. UWOs were designed to prevent suspected corrupt foreign officials from laundering potentially stolen funds into the UK. These orders require individuals or organizations to reveal the source of their unexplained wealth. While they do not necessarily trigger criminal proceedings, they can result in the confiscation of assets and other fines. The issue arose in 2014 when Trump purchased the Turnberry golf course and renamed it Trump Turnberry course. The deal to purchase and refurbish the course came to about $200 million in all-cash transactions that raised eyebrows because at the time the Donald was financing large-scale purchases by selling his debt. Adding more interest to the case is the dispute over whether Eric Trump had made a statement indicating that the funds had come from Russia. On August 11, 2021, Lord Sandison of the Scottish Court of Session ruled that the petition seeking "judicial review of the Scottish ministers in determining whether to apply to the court for UWOs" should "proceed without condition or restriction."[32] At a hearing before Scotland's High Court in October, 2021, the court was told that that Scottish ministers had failed to understand their role in applying for a McMafia order as it is commonly referred to, and that they had "misdirected themselves in the law." The court had not ruled by February 2022.

In the U.S. District Court for the District of Columbia on August 26, 2021, Capitol police officers Conrad Smith, Danny McElroy, Byron Evans, Governor Latson, Melissa Marshall, Michael Fortune, and Jason Deroche, the plaintiffs, represented by the Lawyers' Committee for Civil Rights Under Law sued Donald J. Trump, Donald J. Trump for President, Inc., Stop the Steal, LLC, Ali Alexander a/k/a Ali Abdul Akbar, Brandon J. Straka, Roger J. Stone, Jr., Proud Boys, Proud Boys International, LLC, Enrique Tarrio, Ethan Nordean, Joseph R. Biggs, Zachary Rehl, Charles Donohoe, Dominic J. Pezzola, Oath Keepers, Stewart Rhodes, Thomas E. Cardwell, Jessica Watkins, Kelly Meggs, Alan Hostetter, Russell Taylor, Erik Scott Warner, Felipe Antonio "Tony" Martinez, Derek Kinnison, Ronald Mele, and John Does, 1–10, the defendants. Sharing much common ground with the lawsuits filed by Thompson, by Swalwell, and especially by Blassingame and Hemby, this case was filed several months after the others and is the most comprehensive scope of the conspiratorial lot. For example, the complaint has ten sections, perhaps the most illuminating is number nine quoted in its entirety:

> TRUMP employed, planned for, and encouraged the use of force, intimidation, and threats to try to stop the Congressional count of electoral votes on January 6. He followed the Capitol Attack on television and social media as it happened, and despite requests made to TRUMP to call off the attackers—including from House Minority Leader Kevin McCarthy—he refused to do so for hours as he watched on live television the attackers overrun the Capitol and

> threaten its lawful occupants. Instead, TRUMP encouraged and supported the attackers. While the Attack was ongoing, TRUMP and his co-conspirators contacted members of Congress, not to offer support or protection, but to pressure them to delay further and to stop the Congressional count. Even after the attackers—including white supremacists and hate groups—were finally repelled and cleared from the Capitol, TRUMP ratified their attack and praised them, "We love you. You're very special," and to "Remember this day forever!" TRUMP later confirmed that he and the attackers shared the same goal, stating, "Personally, what I wanted is what they wanted."[33]

In summation, the lawsuit claims that the defendants were responsible for the violent assaults against and injuries to the officers as well as fearing for their lives. They were accountable for Black officers becoming objects of racial slurs and epithets. And by falsely claiming that the election was rigged and stolen, Trump and his associates incited a mob of the former president's supporters to storm the Capitol to stop the Congress from confirming Biden's victory as the 46th president. Finally, by violating the federal Ku Klux Klan Act, the defendants also violated the D.C. Bias-Related Crimes Act, conspiracy, and several other laws. The lawsuit does not seek a specific monetary award but asks for compensatory and punitive damages in an amount to be determined by "the jury in trust." Trump's lawyers will contend that Trump had absolute immunity from lawsuits over official actions taken while in office and that the First Amendment shields his comments from prosecution. However, Executive privilege should only pertain to lawful actions taken by the POTUS while in office. And the First Amendment should not shield anyone, including the ex-president from inciting a U.S. insurrection on the Capitol.

In closing, the hypothetical prosecution of Donald Trump by the DOJ makes four related assumptions. First, that the current application of 18 USC 1512©(2) covering voter certification survives judicial review of at least nine legal challenges. Second, that the former president's campaign activities are excluded from the office's formal duties so as not to preclude prosecution. Third, that conspiring to attack the Capitol and inciting an insurrection were not within the scope of the president's duties. Fourth, if the DOJ prosecutes Trump, it will most likely do so for conspiring to obstruct the final certification of the vote count even though these activities overlapped with other organized efforts to obstruct the vote counts, as in the Georgia election and Trump's phone calls to Secretary of State Brad Raffensperger, or many of the other Trump-Republican efforts to overturn the elections in Arizona, Pennsylvania, and Michigan.

Other conspiracies to obstruct the vote count involved seven known groups or organizations with the number of persons involved in parentheses: Oath Keepers (17),[34] Proud Boys Media (2), Proud Boys Leadership (4), Proud Boys Kansas (6), Proud Boys North Deer (2), and 3%er SoCal (6). Besides the overlapping efforts to obstruct multiple vote counts, there are still many unanswered questions as to whether Trump can be charged with conspiracy:

- Did Trump enter a relationship with the Proud Boys after they had threatened a federal judge to serve Trump's interest when he said to the Proud Boys on September 29, "stand back and stand by?"
- When both the Proud Boys and the Oath Keepers started planning their January 6 operation days after the lost election, did they have communication with the former president and his administration then or at any time running up to the administration?
- Was Roger Stone in the room where the Proud Boys and Oath Keepers formed an alliance to lead the January 6 operation at a December event they attended in common?
- Did the Park Police receive orders that explain their failure to prepare for the assault?
- Did the Proud Boys have reason to believe that the National Guard would not protect the Capitol but instead would protect them?
- Why was the Guard delayed for four hours before responding and was the Proud Boys and Oath Keepers' decision not to pursue a second assault on the Capitol related to the 32-minute delay in relaying an order from Acting Secretary of Defense Christopher Miller to the Guard Commander to deploy the Guard who were waiting in buses?
- After the rioters had breached the Capitol building when both Rudy Giuliani and the Donald made calls to members of Congress asking them to delay the count, did they specifically talk with Arizona House of Representative Paul Gosar, and did the delay in the evacuation of the House side led to Ashli Babbitt's death who both Trump and Gosar continue to mourn as an American patriot?
- Was Rudy also in contact before or during the insurrection as he was nine days afterward when he received a texted plan from a Proud Boyd affiliate to blame the riots on Antifa?

There are still other related questions to answer or necessary dots to connect the strands of relationships before Attorney General Merrick Garland would know whether he had a prosecutorial case against Trump and others. These include:

- Agreements to or ordering subordinates to participate in an effort or plan to obstruct the vote certification.
- Proud Boys encouragements to believe they are his army.
- Personally, sowing the Big Lie that the election had been stolen.
- Asking or having working subordinates and Republican politicians lie about the election results.
- Supporting surrogates and campaign staffers to fund buses to DC.
- Applauding or celebrating violence in advance of January 6 and encouraging it on the day.
- Recruiting members of Congress to raise challenges to the vote count and to vote against certification.
- Targeting Mike Pence after he refused to act in response to Trump's unconstitutional request for him to not certify the election for Joe Biden.
- Muddling the lines of command ensuring further chaos.
- Ignoring the immediate requests for help from the leaders of Congress.

Pending lawsuits vs. Trump family members and Trump Organization, Inc.

The number of lawsuits that fall under this categorization of the diversity of claims and against whom are a smaller number compared to those suits where Trump is the primary if not the soul plaintiff or defendant. These litigated cases include *Ithaca Cap. Invs. v. Trump Pan. Hotel Mgmt.*; *Doe v. Trump Corp.*; *District of Columbia v. 58th Presidential Inauguration Comm.;* and *Supreme Court of the State of New York County of New York* and *The People of the State of New York v. Trump Corporation, d/b/a the Trump Organization, Trump Payroll Corp., d/b/a the Trump Organization, and Allen Weisselberg.* What these legal cases share is that the perpetrators of the alleged offenses had set up, coordinated, and operated fraudulent schemes (or "rackets") to repeatedly or consistently collect money or other profit.[35] As with the Racketeer Influenced and Corrupt Organizations Act (RICO) passed in 1970, anyone of these defendants could be prosecuted for racketeering and subject to both civil and criminal penalties for activities performed as part of an ongoing criminal enterprise.

After a brief round of failed arbitration proceedings, Ithaca Capital Investments on January 16, 2018 sued Trump Panama Hotel Management and Trump International (TI) Hotels Management alleging that Trump representatives, including Donald, Jr. and Eric, made exaggerated claims about the hotel's value; that TI breached their agreement by mismanaging the hotel as well as diverting hotel revenues for their own use; and finally that TI had failed to pay income taxes. This federal litigation stems over a hotel management deal gone terribly bad.

Up until 2018 TI had operated a luxury hotel in Panama. As was standard practice TI contracted with a separate owner the use of the "Trump" name and to provide management services. When that owner filed for bankruptcy in 2015 Ithaca Capital moved to purchase most of the hotel's units. Unaware of at the time of the purchase were the facts that the Trump representatives had made a series of fraudulent claims that the suit alleges underreported the costs and oversold the profitability of the hotel. In short order, the new owners ran into financial trouble and the relationship between the two parties collapsed rapidly. On March 30, 2020, the district court upheld all three of Ithaca's claims. The court also dismissed all but one of the defendants' counterclaims—for tortious interference—alleging that Ithaca interfered with TI's other hotel contracts while it was forcing TI out of their partnership. The parties were still conducting discovery over the summer of 2021, and then on September 16, 2021 the Panama owners quietly agreed to dismiss a New York federal lawsuit against the two Trump hotel management companies.

Four anonymous plaintiffs on October 30, 2018 filed a class action suit in the U.S. District Court for the Southern District of New York against the Trump Corporation, Donald Trump, Ivanka Trump, Donald Trump, Jr. and Eric Trump. The complaint alleges racketeering and that the defendants were using the Trump brand name to defraud thousands of working-class individuals by promoting numerous businesses in exchange for secret payments. Those companies included CAN Opportunity, LLC (a business based on a controversial multi-level marketing scheme), the Trump Network, LLC (another multi-level marketing scheme), and Business Strategies Group, LLC (a seminar claiming to sell the Trump secrets to success). In addition to the violations of the RICO ACT, the complaint alleges that the defendants also engaged in activity violating numerous state consumer protection laws concerning fair business practices and free completion. The lawsuit alleges that the Trump children were key to the success of this promotional scam that from 2005 to at least 2015 yielded the family millions of dollars in payments to advance CAN to people who hoped to get rich selling its products. For example, the siblings had appeared repeatedly with CAN co-founders on Trump's Celebrity Apprentice television show.

On July 24, 2019, responding to the defendants' motions to dismiss, Judge Lorna Schofield rejected the RICO claims because the plaintiffs' losses were not sufficiently the proximate cause of the defendants. She also ruled that under the Class Action Fairness Act (CAFA) that the other claims concerning the state laws could precede. The Trumps then moved to compel forced arbitration and the judge denied the motion in April 2020. Not only did the judge point out that the defendants were not party to the arbitration agreement between the CAN and the plaintiffs, but also she found that the motion to compel arbitration was in "bad faith" as the defendants were "acting in a manner that is 'substantively prejudicial towards the plaintiffs' and not within the spirit of the Federal Arbitration ACT (FAA)." The Trumps filed motions to stay or halt the legal process and were denied for failing to meet the four traditional factors for doing so. In turn, the defendants appealed these decisions and on July 28, 2021, the Second Circuit Court of Appeals issued a 3-0 decision rejecting forced arbitration and rejected ICI's efforts to turn over documents to the plaintiffs as ordered by the lower court. More than a year before on May 22, 2020, Raj Patel had filed a Motion of Permissive Intervention in order to join the Doe plaintiffs as a party to the litigation. The Second Court of Appeals had denied this motion approved by the lower court, but ultimately on April 28, 2021, the U.S. Supreme Court renamed the lawsuit, *Patel v. Trump Corp. et al.*

On January 22, 2020, the District of Columbia or the Plaintiff through its Attorney General Karl A. Racine brought a legal action against Defendants Trump Organization, the TI Hotel Washington, DC, and the 58th Presidential Inaugural Committee. Post the 2016 election and run-up to Trump's swearing-in ceremony in mid-January 2017 the inaugural committee raised a record $107 million to spend on inauguration festivities. As a nonprofit the committee was supposed to use these charitable funds for the public good and not for private gain. Hence, the DC attorney general sued the inaugural committee alleging that it spent over $1million of those funds to enrich the Trump family's private businesses.

The suit claims among other things that the committee paid exorbitant rates to rent space in the TI Hotel. For example, on the very same day that another nonprofit was paying the hotel only $5000 to rent the same main ballroom in the hotel, the presidential committee was paying $175,000. At the same time, the committee was allegedly ignoring much better deals for arranging events in other upscale locations. On January 11, 2021, the AG added another allegation that the committee had improperly used its nonprofit funds to pay a hotel bill on behalf of Trump's private business.

The case has also zeroed in on the possible misconduct by the committee's executive Rick Gates who had also played a key role in the Trump campaign. Recall that Gates had cooperated with the Mueller investigation, plead guilty to conspiracy against the United States, and to making false statements in the investigation of the Russian interference in the 2016 presidential election. For those felonies Gates received a 45-day jail sentence and a $20,000 fine. The lawsuit has requested that the court compel the Trump business to put the misspent funds into a trust where it can be used for charitable purposes. The defendants moved for dismissal of the case as well as for arbitration and both were denied. On July 28, 2021, in a 3-0 decision the 2nd Circuit Court of Appeals upheld the district court's judgment over arbitration. During discovery that was still ongoing at the end of summer 2021 the AG's office had already deposed high-level Trump executives, including Ivanka Trump and Donald Trump, Jr.

On July 1, 2021, Manhattan District Attorney Cyrus Vance charged the Trump Organization, CFO Allen Weisselberg and an "unindicted coconspirator" with tax fraud. According to the indictment this was a 15-year long tax fraud scheme where the defendants had arranged for Weisselberg to receive indirect employee compensation from the Trump Organization in the approximate amount of $1.76 million so the defendants could avoid reporting and paying taxes. The indictment states that beginning in 2005 that Weisselberg used the Trump corporation bank account to pay his rent and utility bills. The CFO was also accused of concealing "indirect compensation" by using payments from the Trump Organization to cover nearly $360,000 in upscale private school payments for his family as well as some $200,000 to lease luxury cars.

Specifically, the suit charges that the CFO intentionally caused the indirect compensation payments to be omitted from his personal tax returns knowing that those payments represented taxable income and that he knew they should have been treated as compensation for the internal records of the Trump Corporation. During the court proceedings, Carey Dunn the general counsel for the Manhattan DA's office stated that Weisselberg "directed that company records be deleted to conceal his participation in the scheme." Dunn pointed out, "there's been no attempt to impose discipline on the people involved, to report the crimes, to repay the proceeds, or even to amend any of the false tax returns."[36]

More indictments of other high-ranking Trump employees are likely to follow. Meanwhile, Weisselberg and the company pleaded not guilty to criminal charges that included grand larceny in the second degree, a nonviolent felony that carries a prison sentence from 5 to 15 years. After the indictment was unsealed Trump told ABC News that Weisselberg "is a tremendous person" and that the charges against him were a "disgrace" and "shameful." Trump also referred to the joint investigation involving the Manhattan DA Cyrus Vance and the New York AG Letitia James as another politically motivated "witch hunt" by the Democrats.

On December 20, 2021, the former president sued the New York Attorney General to stop the parallel civil investigation into his business practices two weeks after James requested that Trump sit for a January 7, 2022, deposition. Trump was seeking both a permanent injunction barring James from investigating and preventing her from pursuing civil or criminal investigations against him and his organization. He was also seeking a declaratory judgment against the attorney general for violating his free speech and due process rights. Assuming that this lawsuit is tossed out of court, then James will no doubt have to subpoena Donald for him to sit for a deposition.

Donald the racketeer

When one considers Donald's lifetime of dishonesty, deception, and defrauding as well as the breadth and diversity of his lawbreaking spread over five decades of criminality, I believe that the most appropriate label is racketeer. When people think of racketeers the first name that usually comes to mind is Al Capone. Followed by others such as Bugsy Siegel and Sam Giancana but certainly not Teflon Don the 45th president of the United States. When people think of families of racketeering, they might think about the Genovese family, the Gambino family, and the Lucchese family. Not too many people would be inclined to think of the Trump family though they should. In part this has to do with the evolution of organizational crimes. In part this has to do with the RICO statues and the historical non-appellations to state, corporate, and political criminals.

Though there are 35 types of felonies or "illegal schemes" that fall under RICO, the law has been used primarily to go after organized criminals. Specifically, crime families that have made their money by way of the protection rackets, the numbers rackets, or the drug rackets. Not all the rackets or illegal schemes necessarily involve extortion, fraud, deception, or coercive practices but most of them do. Additionally, since most of the vice crimes, for example, have been part of the black market or underground economy most of the proceeds have not been "tax free." Any related taxation derived from these criminal enterprises often comes from their legitimate front businesses such as bars, restaurants, hotels, laundromats, parking concessions, and so on.

In the case of the former president several of his illegal schemes or racketeering operations for four years circulated through and within the TI Hotel a few blocks away from the White House. These rackets included Trump's work-a-rounds of the Foreign Emoluments Clause, his foreign and domestic pay to play schemes, and his biggest money maker to date, anti-democracy for all fundraising. Talk about your legal rackets? As the Donald would tell us, "For the time being all of these scams are legal and even if they should not be until they are, cha-ching, cha-ching!" Of course, had the Donald been reelected he would still be raking in the chips at his DC Hotel that was losing on average $17.5 million per annum while Trump was in the White House. And yet Trump apparently sold the lease to this hotel in late 2021 for an alleged $300,000 million profit.

Long before Trump came to the White House his modus operandi and business model had included fraudulent and manipulated bottom lines, profits, losses, wealth, debt, taxes, loans, and so on. Depending on the financial occasion or business transaction called for, the Trump family has reported these types of data upward or downward. As part of this family tradition established by Fred, Sr. in the 1940s the Trump Organization has always engaged in a variety of nontraditional illegal schemes or criminal rackets. In other words, the Trump books are always in a state of cooking. Since the late 1980s comptroller Allen Weisselberg has been the master chef stirring the control fraud pot. Most recently, for example, while the DC hotel had lost $70 million in four years Trump had claimed to the General Services Administration that the hotel had earned $150 billion in revenue, according to the House Oversight and Reform Committee.[37] Despite the quarter of a billion-dollar discrepancy, the hotel operation was generating other revenue streams, including an estimated $3.7 million from foreign governments above board, and unknown amounts of money through the exchanging of foreign currencies above and below board.

Perhaps the blending of these different revenue streams is why the former president had "grossly exaggerated" the financial health of the property. Then again, this was a time for the Donald and company to inflate the value of the property as the hotel has been on and off the market since 2018. Here was another hotel venture where Trump was desperately trying to avoid bankruptcy and seeking to extricate himself from another failing business. To help keep the hotel afloat, for example, the Trump holding company was forced to inject $24 million into the operation as it first went on sale. Also lending a helping hand was Deutsche Bank, one of Trump's longest and oldest partners in crime even though they seem to fight and sue each other a lot. The DB "bail out" allowed the Donald to delay payment for up to six years on a personally guaranteed loan of $170 million. Meanwhile, in October 2019, the Trump Organization tried to sell the lease of the TI Hotel for the ridiculous asking price of $500 million when Trump had acquired the same for $200 million back in 2013 that had been allocated for the restoration and conversion of the 122-year-old U.S. Postal Office Building into the four-star luxury hotel. In November 2020 when bids came in at less than half the asking price the sale process was put on hold. Word on the street in December 2021 was that the Trump Organization had sold the lease for an undisclosed amount and a $300,000,000 profit.[38]

Over time and too gradually for this criminologist, the term racket has begun to expand to include white-collar and corporate criminals. For example, back in the spring of 2019, a total of 33 wealthy parents were charged with conspiracy to commit mail fraud and honest services mail fraud for their roles in an "admissions" scheme. Initially, as part of the sprawling college admissions scandal, a dozen college coaches, sports and testing administrators each pleaded not guilty to racketeering in a Boston federal court. Shortly thereafter, at least four individuals had pleaded guilty and became cooperating witnesses for the prosecution. These included Rudy Meredith, the Yale women's soccer coach, John Vandemoer, a former Stanford head sailing coach, Mark Riddell, who impersonated students and took the SATs and ACTs for them, and Rick Singer, the mastermind of the scheme.[39] The takeaway here is that a racket, a racketeer, or racketeering can refer to any illegal scheme that operates continuously or is repeated as in any organized criminal enterprise. In other words, there is no limit to the actual number of illegal schemes that could be prosecuted under RICO.

As a career criminal and the head of a criminal enterprise specializing in a myriad of rackets, the Donald could be prosecuted for many of his illegal schemes such as the way he pays his highest-level employees to avoid taxes due from the Trump Organization or from the employee, or the Trump classic of each generation of Trumps passing the wealth off to the next generation illegally as a way of avoiding once again taxes due from the giver and the receiver. Simply put, the Donald, the Trump Organization, and other members of the immediate Trump family such as children Ivanka, Eric, and Donald, Jr. under RICO all could directly or indirectly be liable for the crimes of extortion, bribery, theft, embezzlement, fraud, obstruction of justice, money laundering, bankruptcy fraud, securities fraud. wire fraud, and acts of terrorism. Most of this criminal activity reflects the Donald as the unscrupulous businessman, dishonest newsmaker, and corrupt politician that he is.

On those very rare occasions when the bosses from traditional families of organized crime have been busted and charged with a litany of crimes, whenever they were convicted and sent to prison, it is pretty much a safe bet that tax fraud helped to put them away for very long terms. Is it any wonder that the Donald has not wanted to share his cooked books and fraudulent taxes with anyone besides his CFO Weisselberg, his criminal accountants, his unethical attorneys, and the Internal Revenue Service?

Notes

1 Jacob Kang-Brown, Chase Montagnet, and Jasmine Heiss, 2021. People in Jail and Prison in 2020. Vera Institute of Justice. January. https://www.vera.org/downloads/publications/people-in-jail-and-prison-in-2020.pdf.
2 Federal Bureau of Prisons, 2021. Inmate Statistics. July 24. https://www.bop.gov/about/statistics/statistics_inmate_offenses.jsp.
3 This small number represents the lack of enforcement of white-collar and corporate crimes, not the epidemic of violations in those areas. See my two books on the subject previously cited several times by now. *Theft of a Nation: Wall Street Looting and Federal Regulatory Colluding* (2012) and *Unchecked Corporate Power: Why the Crimes of Multinational Corporations Are Routinized Away and What We Can Do About It* (2017).
4 Eva Herscowitz, 2021. White-Collar Crime Prosecutions Continue 20-Year. *The Crime Report*. June 10. https://thecrimereport.org/2021/08/10/white-collar-crime-prosecutions-continue-to-decline/.
5 TRACREPORTS, 2016. U. S. Prosecution of Corporate Crime Varies Widely by Location, Program, and Agency. January 20. https://trac.syr.edu/tracreports/crim/411/.
6 Ibid.
7 Ibid.
8 Evan Curran, 2021. New Research Examines the Cost of Crime in the U.S., Estimated To Be $2.6 Trillion in a Single Year. *Research News*. February 5. https://news.vanderbilt.edu/2021/02/05/new-research-examines-the-cost-of-crime-in-the-u-s-estimated-to-be-2–6-trillion-in-a-single-year/;
9 Roy Maurer, 2019. Do Employers Face Consequences for Hiring Unauthorized Workers? *SHRM*. September 24. https://www.shrm.org/resourcesandtools/hr-topics/talent-acquisition/pages/do-employers-face-consequences-hiring-unauthorized-workers.aspx.
10 Associated Press, 2017. A Look at the President's Pardon Power and How It Works. *PBS News Hour*. August 26. https://www.pbs.org/newshour/politics/presidents-pardon-power-works.
11 Benjamin Weiser, 2021. Trump's Pardon of Bannon Could Raise Risk for 3 Co-Defendants. *The New York Times*. January 26. https://www.nytimes.com/2021/01/26/nyregion/steve-bannon-pardon-trump.html.
12 Ibid.

13 Karl Evers-Hillstrom, 2021. Trump-Tied Lobbyists Paid Massive Sums to Push Pardons. *OpenSecrets.org*. January 22. https://www.opensecrets.org/news/2021/01/trump-tied-lobbyists-paid-massive-sums/.
14 Ibid.
15 Pew Research Center, 2021. Trump Used Clemency Power Less Often Than Nearly Every Other Modern President. January 22. https://www.pewresearch.org/fact-tank/2021/01/22/trump-used-his-clemency-power-sparingly-despite-a-raft-of-late-pardons-and-commutations/ft_21-01-20_trumpclemencyrecord_1/.
16 Andrew Glass, 2018. Bush Pardons Iran-Contra Felons. *Politico*. December 24, 1992. https://www.politico.com/story/2018/12/24/bush-pardons-iran-contra-felons-dec-24-1992-1072042.
17 Gregg Barak, Paul Leighton, and Allison Cotton, 2018. *Class, Race, Gender, and Crime: The Social Realities of Justice in America*. 5th edition. Lanham, MD: Rowman & Littlefield.
18 Eileen Rumfelt, 2017. Obama Commutes Record Number of Inmate Sentences. *ABA*. January 25. https://www.americanbar.org/groups/litigation/committees/criminal/practice/2017/obama-commutes-record-number-of-inmate-sentences/.
19 Lumumba Akinwole-Bandele and Monifa Akinwole-Bandele, 1917. Race Still Matters in Presidential Pardons. *The Hill*. January 17, 2017. https://thehill.com/blogs/pundits-blog/civil-rights/314564-race-still-matters-in-presidential-pardons.
20 Maggie Haberman Kenneth P. Vogel, Eric Lipton and Michael S. Schmidt, 2021. With Hours Left in Office, Trump Grants Clemency to Bannon and Other Allies. *The New York Times*. January 20, updated May 5. https://www.nytimes.com/2021/01/20/us/politics/trump-pardons.html.
21 The New York Times, 2021. Here Are Some of the People Trump Pardoned. *The New York Times*. January 26. https://www.nytimes.com/article/who-did-trump-pardon.html.
22 Alana Wise, 2020. Trump Grants Clemency To 5, Most Incarcerated For Drug Offenses. *NPR*. October 21. https://www.npr.org/2020/10/21/926374277/trump-grants-clemency-to-5-most-incarcerated-for-drug-offenses.
23 Karl Mihm, Jacob Apkon, and Sruthi Venkatachalam, 2021. Litigation Tracker: Pending Criminal and Civil Cases against Donald Trump. JUST SECURITY. July 27. https://www.justsecurity.org/75032/litigation-tracker-pending-criminal-and-civil-cases-against-donald-trump/.
24 Emptywheel, 2021. How a Trump Prosecution for January 6 Would Work. August 19. https://www.emptywheel.net/2021/08/19/how-a-trump-prosecution-for-january-6-would-work/.
25 Karl Mihm et al., 2021.
26 United States District Court for the District of Columbia, 2021. Case 1:20-cv-01622-DLF Document 31 Filed 06/21/21. https://www.govinfo.gov/content/pkg/USCOURTS-dcd-1_20-cv-01622/pdf/USCOURTS-dcd-1_20-cv-01622-0.pdf
27 Ibid.
28 Mihm et al., 2021.
29 Jose Paglier, 2021. The Unlikely Team of Prosecutors Hunting Trump in Georgia. *Daily Beast*. March 28. https://www.thedailybeast.com/the-unlikely-team-hunting-team-donald-trump-in-georgia.

30 Although DC Attorney General Karl Racine had stated in early 2021 that he was exploring whether to charge Trump with inciting the riots, it is not likely because he has limited or split jurisdiction and because the applicable offense in the DC statue only makes it a misdemeanor.

31 Quoted in Mihm et al., 2021.

32 Ibid.

33 Case 1:21-cv-02265 Document 1 Filed 08/26/21: pages 7–8. https://storage.courtlistener.com/recap/gov.uscourts.dcd.234873/gov.uscourts.dcd.234873.1.0_1.pdf.

34 On January 13, 2022, the leader of the Oath Keepers and 10 others were indicted by a federal grand jury in the District of Columbia for Seditious Conspiracy and other offenses related to the U.S. Capitol Breach.

35 Michelle Lou and Brandon Griggs, 2019. What Is Racketeering? The Crime, Explained. *CNN.* March 26. https://www.cnn.com/2019/03/26/us/what-is-racketeering-trnd/index.html.

36 Quoted in Aaron Katersky and John Santucci, 2021. Manhattan DA Charges Trump's Company, CFO with Tax Fraud. *ABC News.* July 1. https://abcnews.go.com/US/manhattan-da-charges-trumps-company-cfo-tax-fraud/story?id=78535462.

37 Ted Johnson, 2021. Donald Trump Concealed D.C. Hotel's $70 Million in Losses with "Misleading" Disclosures, House Committee Says. *Deadline.* October 8. https://deadline.com/2021/10/donald-trump-hotel-washington-70-million-losses-1234852771/.

38 TRD, 2021. "Trump Org in "Advanced Talks" to Sell DC Hotel Lease. *The Real Deal.* September 7. https://therealdeal.com/2021/09/07/trump-org-in-advanced-talks-to-sell-dc-hotel-lease/.

39 Eric Levenson and Mark Morales, 2019. Racketeering Suspects All Plead Not Guilty in College Admission Scheme. *CNN.* March 25. https://www.cnn.com/2019/03/25/us/college-admission-court/index.html.

PART THREE

Following the presidency

8

INSURRECTION, DIVIDED SELVES, AND THE AFTERMATH OF A FAILED COUP

By electing a failed business mogul and a reality television celebrity as the President of the United States on November 9, 2016, the stage was set for the dissolution of reality politics and for the emergence of a post-reality politics in America. These two politics faced off on January 6, 2021, courtesy of a Trump's orchestrated assault on Capitol Hill. Were we all tuned in to what we thought we were watching live in real time—an attempt to stop the certification of the 46th President Joe Biden—or were we all unknowingly plugged into the episode "Tourist Day at the Capitol" from the reality TV spectacle the Fake Presidency? In the era of mediated social realities, my sociological imagination has room for both political set-ups.[1]

Trump's multiple attempts to steal back the White House from the president-elect in the late 2020 as well as his failed coup or insurrection at the beginning of 2021 are the most shameful and politically corrupt behavior of a president in the history of the United States. Yet, the Trumpian Republican Party and at least 50 million Republican voters have been into absolving, downplaying, and excusing the horrendous behavior of the former Anarchist-in-Chief. Once again, these members of the Trump gang are quite willing if not eager to give the Boss another "do over" on his criminal behavior even when it includes political treason and sedition. The ignoble Republicans in Congress that have given the Donald another "get out of jail" free card have made a political travesty of both the federal government and the U.S. Constitution.

DOI: 10.4324/9781003221548-12

In this final chapter, it would be a dereliction of duty if I did not address the criminological elephant in the room. I am referring to the extensive amount of *political crime* inclusive of wrongdoing, corruption, and criminality supported by certain sectors of the Trumpian base, by key power brokers in the Trump orbit, by political groups, corporate bodies, and learned societies behind the scenes, and by other faceless collaborators in this assault on democracy. Historically, what holds the lawlessness of Boss Trump, and these folks are that they all share and believe in a common white minority and anti-democratic agenda. There is also the nihilistic pleasure that Trump loyalists derive from watching the Houdini of White-collar, State, and Corporate Crime get away with his smorgasbord of criminal activities like the Donald was a 19th-century mythical rebel-outlaw from the Wild West.

More importantly, the former Republican Party turned Trumpian Party and its elected officials post the Trump administration have aligned themselves criminally with the former president like a mafioso Boss that they are afraid to cross. They are not only the party of Trump's base, but they are also the party of his violent mob. They are dedicated to denying Biden his legitimacy as the president, to whitewashing the existence of the Capitol riots, and to covering up the roles played by the insurrectionists, the treasonous Trump, his Chief of Staff Mark Meadows, many others as well as themselves. They are also political criminals because they are violating their oaths of office as they use the government apparatus not for the public interest but for what they perceive to be their own personal interests. Moreover, their political crimes specifically the omitted Trump sanctions and the abuses of power in these and other matters are directed against our national interests, our political system, and our democracy.

Since the emergence of modern capitalism with the establishment of mercantilism between the 16th and 18th centuries, mass rebellions have been organized from the bottom-up. They are usually choreographed collectively in resistance to selfishness, gluttony, the denial of human rights, the crimes of capital, the crimes of state, and the crimes of the powerful.[2] Violent coups, however, are usually organized from the top-down and they are often accompanied by military support. Historically, these coups happen when Commanders-in-Chief lose their legitimate authority and are trying to hold on to power by any means necessary. For five months prior to Trump losing in November 2020, the Donald had been busy working his MAGA crowds and priming the base as well as the rest of the Republican Party for what he understood was likely to be the losing election outcome as his inside pollsters were telling him.

Trump knew that he would once again lose the popular vote only he did not know by how much he would lose. Hence, the Donald was preparing the political ground for his post-election defeatist strategies of denying certification of the president-elect that would ultimately play out at the Capitol on January 6. The Big Lie was a rather rudimentary narrative that succeeded in "overturning" the election in the minds of Republican America. Simply put, the lie that caught on and stuck was that there was no way Trump could possibly lose his bid for reelection to Sleepy Joe. And if he did lose, it was only because of voter fraud or that the Democrats had rigged the election. Here the narrative gets a bit more satirical if not conspiratorial. It turns out that the Democrats stole the election from Trump with the assistance of aliens from outer space, pedophiles from inner space, and agents from the Deep State. Rhetorically, what other reasons could explain Trump's losing the popular vote to Biden by seven million votes when he only lost the popular vote to Crooked Hillary by three million votes, and she was a woman?

Trump's insurrection was different from your typical top-down insurrections especially in terms of the overlying hordes of his political followers that had gathered in DC from across the nation. Many of them had flown in from thousands of miles away for what would be the capstone rally of Donald's administration. Their several hundred attendees at Trump's rally-turned-riot were prepared for violence and stormed the Capitol at the behest of the president. Many of these rioters were kitted up in tactical gear, adorned in flak jackets, and moved in formation. There were many more demonstrators, however, who were surprised and unprepared for the mass violence.

The core of "militants" was mostly white men between the ages of 18 and 50. In the name of a stolen election, they busted windows, kicked in doors, and beat up Capitol police. The befuddled "patriots" were an eclectic group of white folks. They had prepared for a MAGA Trump rally or to what has also been referred to as a jamboree atmosphere of revolutionary tourism.[3] They were taking selfies with other rally attendees as well as with Capitol police officers. Many of these protestors who were caught up in Trump's universe that day clearly did not understand the gravity of the choices that they may not have even realized they were making. Most all these persons, militant or patriotic, were also the victims of several absurd and overlapping conspiratorial stories about a fraudulent election that blended well with their mythical understandings of 1776. Their unreal or false states of consciousness or their state of fantasy politics allowed many of these "freedom-fighters" to see themselves as god-fearing Christian patriots rather than as bamboozled revolutionaries.

Situated within 150 years of "apocalyptic" agitation, the lame duck president and his sycophantic kowtowing anti-democratic loyalists with the help of Russian hackers, social media, shameful attorneys, and right-wing pundits were simply using and abusing their Trumpian audiences by mollycoddling them with their very own nonsensical conspiracies and homespun fantasies of fiction and misinformation. At the same time, those Trumpian supporters at the Capitol on January 6 were of the correct belief that they were righteously participating in the "cultural wars" of our times to preserve the American Republic from the evils of democracy, socialism, science, people of color, aliens from inner and outer space, Satan, or whatever other poppycock they can create out of make believe.

Amid this eclectic collectivity of divided selves and dangerous patriots were QAnon adherents, neo-Nazis, anti-Semites, neo-Confederates, white supremacists, political morons, revolutionary cosplayers, and finally the evangelical faithful and most Republicans. The anti-women Christians in particular view themselves as the vanguard of god's end-times army and are so trusting in their belief that they saw themselves as having no other choice but to try to overthrow the Congress. These religious insurgents carried signs that read "Jesus Saves," "In God We Trust," and "Jesus 2020." They carried flags adorned with "Jesus Is My Savior, Trump Is My President." Two of these evangelicals were videoed marching nonviolently through the Capitol building, one holding a Christian flag and the other a Bible. Together, the men were chanting over and over, "The blood of Jesus covering this place."[4]

Sociologists, economists, political scientists, and others have argued for more than 150 years that in the wake of modernity came the decline of community. From Emile Durkheim and Karl Marx in the 19th century to Robert Bellah, Robert Putnam, and Sherry Turkle in the present. The same concepts of anomie, alienation, disenchantment, ennui, false consciousness, illusion of companionship, and individualism have each been used to describe the deterioration of the modern community.[5] As for post-modernity and the online world of interpersonal communication, Andrew Marantz has written about the shocking speed in which social media has

> decimated professional media, abraded our civic life, coaxed us into unhealthy relationships with our phones and with one another, harvested and monetized our personal data, warped our brains and our politics, and made us brittle and twitchy and frail, all while a few entrepreneurs and investors continue to profit from our addiction and confusion.[6]

Meanwhile, social media as the medium of contemporary choice provides us subconsciously with a false sense that these online platforms are somehow meeting our emotional needs for communal connection. However, these virtual realities or online communities are without warm bodies and should not be misconstrued with the brick-and-mortar communities that are made up of real people. As substitutes for the authentic thing, these are at best ephemeral or shadow communities. At the same time, social psychologists have informed us that with the decline or loss of community comes the decline or loss of selves.

More revealing perhaps and not surprising are the damaging algorithms and monetized social media that are intentionally conflating information and misinformation for profit. Media analysts, data scientists, and computer engineers, for example, like Facebook whistleblower Frances Haugen with thousands of pages of Facebook's own data reveal how the social network's algorithms are tweaked or set to amplify misinformation over information resulting in more lies, more harm, more threats, and more violence.[7] Others have suggested that social media has even been ushering in a new dark age of autocracy, repression, and myopia.[8] Research has also exposed many of the other downsides associated with social media. Some arguing that its gravest harm so far has been the correlation between social media use and suicide, especially among teenage girls. The negative fallout of this online misogyny extends throughout American society.

In similar ways, social media contributes to chronic depression, loneliness, and anger. It also tends to narrow rather than expand individual worldviews. Recently, this type of social media has been associated with the rising rates of racially and sexually motivated hate crimes, the most reactionary U.S. Supreme Court since the pre-New Deal 1930s, the banning of access to abortion and its enforcement by citizen bounty hunters, the developing voter suppression laws across the United States, and the movement among the alt-right of an alleged First Amendment right to infect others with a deadly virus.[9]

With respect to Trump's deluded supporters, R.D. Lang argued some 60 years ago that human psychosis or obsession at its core was an existential condition driven by a fragmentation of the self and a sense of being disconnected from the world. In order to resist this existential condition of psychosis, one must suppress the tension of the "divided self" between the two personas within us all—the private, the real, and the insane "me" vs. the public, the false, and the sane "me." Concurrently, all people need to defend their "integrated selves" from human disconnection and the possibility of slipping away into a state of meaninglessness. Individuals struggling even lightly with these psychic issues of alienation often find themselves in markets—social and cultural—to reconnect with other human beings experiencing similar emotions of disconnections. In other words, many of those individuals find themselves connecting with others who are also struggling with the same types of psychic malaises. As the saying goes "misery loves company" and these folks can assuage their heretofore experienced feelings of alienation and not belonging by coming together with likeminded MAGA and Save America Trumpists.

Lang further argued that psychosis was not necessarily a medical condition or a mental problem. Rather, psychosis was an ontological condition of feeling disconnected from the emotions of existing for others and of others existing for us. Without this type of human connection, Lang argues that people usually experience ontological insecurity. In different words, their lives find it difficult to take for granted the authenticity, autonomy, and identity of others or of themselves for that matter. Thus, hooking up with QAnon adherents, the Oath Keepers, MAGA cultists, white supremacists, conspiracy theorists, and other likeminded people can be emotionally satisfying. Unfortunately, for these mesmerized Trumpian cultists, the chaotic cosmos of Donald's world holds the seeds of cathartic destruction or the power to unleash the worst instincts of human disregard and cruelty.[10] Similarly, these conspiratorial dark horses or alienated pessimists of human destructiveness as Eric Fromm has referred to them provide another explanation or viable alternative vision to Freud's "death wish."[11]

There are many other Freudian-oriented Marxists, historians, or sociologists besides Fromm that have directly and indirectly linked the social development of the human species and the repression of individual selves to the ontological conditions of insecurity generated fundamentally from the exploitation of labor and capital. These Freudo-Marxists and likeminded social philosophers are many and have most famously included Wilhelm Reich, author of *Character Analysis* and *The Mass Psychology of Fascism* published in 1933 as well as *The Sexual Revolution* in 1936; Herbert Marcuse, author of *Eros and Civilization* in 1955 and *One-Dimensional Man* in 1964; and French West Indian psychiatrist Frantz Fanon, author of *Black Skin, White Masks* in 1952 and *The Wretched of the Earth* in 1961. I would be remiss not to mention a book that I also referenced in the introduction to this book, the 1953 *Character and Social Structure: The Psychology of Social Institutions*, by Hans H. Gerth and C. Wright Mills. These books all published between 50 and 90 years ago are still very relevant in explaining the strange and destabilizing phenomenon of Trumpism and the American people's intense "love-hate" relationship with the Donald. The contemporary cognitive dissonance between Democrats and Republicans helps to explain the extreme reactions to Donald Trump.

For example, since the Pew Research Center started measuring Republican and Democratic attitudes on policy issues and political values in 1994, the two parties have never been further apart on the issues. In the summer of 2017, Pew sampled more than 5,000 respondents on government regulation and aid, same-sex marriage, environmental regulations, race, education, and religion. They found that the gap between the two parties had increased 21 points in 23 years from 15 to 36 across the board; the widest two gaps pertained to views on race and poverty.[12] Pew also found that 20 years after 9/11, anti-Muslim sentiment and Islamophobia were ascribed to by 33 percent of Republicans.[13] Contemporary political psychologists tell us stories about groupthink as a developing behavioral phenomenon. While Trump's victory in 2016 may have been a political anomaly of sorts or socially deviant in several ways, "it resulted from a long period of evolution in terms of how and why people in the U.S. identify with different political parties."[14]

The recent historical origins of Trump's rise to presidential power can be traced back to when the prevailing liberal U.S. political economy was challenged and overcome subsequently by a concerted confederacy of big businesses, CEOs, religious extremists, and right-wing economists and lawyers. Working together, they were bent on changing the prevailing rules and policies that had been established after the Wall Street crash of 1929. Those New Deal policies, programs, and laws as they came to be labeled were credited for enabling a growing middle class for most Americans, if not those racially discriminated against. Though Trump has no real ideological stance politically and has changed his party affiliation five times since he first registered as a Republican in 1987, the chameleon, the con, and the egocentric Trump has much more in common with 21st-century Republicans than he does with 21st-century Democrats.

With the election of President Ronald W. Reagan who first coined the Make America Great Again slogan, there were the same kinds of demands for "law and order," "local and state rights," and unregulated "free enterprise." There were also the anti-"civil rights" tropes and backlash appeals to racism, white nationalism, and the nostalgia for androcentric privileges harking back to the days before the 1960 Lunch Counter Sit-in at Woolworth's in Greensboro, NC and the 1955–1956 Montgomery Bus Boycott. As part of a backlash to the civil rights advances of the 1960s, the political movement of the 1980s and 1990s also ushered in the rise of neoliberal ideology and reactionary social and economic policies. Once again, the political and economic arrangements were striving for the "good old days" of worker exploitation and of social and ethnic inequalities. During the first era of U.S. "trickle down economics," "reverse discrimination," and "market deregulation" capitalist greed, conspicuous wealth, and selfishness were anointed as good or the new normal. In opposition, "big government" or the federal state became bad. The insidious problem to be reduced and deconstructed, if not eradicated. Shrink the commons and the public services, privatize this and privatize that. In these political and cultural environments, workers lost much of their former power, multinational corporations took over the political economy, finance capitalists become the supreme rulers of the global order, and the quality of life began to decline for most Americans.

Over the arc of four decades, economic inequality expands, and identity politics and multicultural diversity intensifies. At the same time, the subterranean movements of aggrieved white nationalists and anti-governmental militia build. These white nationalist movements reappear once again as they have several times since the rise and fall of the Ku Klux Klan in the 1920s and the neo-Nazi American groups in the1930s. By the 2016 race for the presidency, the electoral constituents of the Republican mainstream along with extreme right-wing social movements, coupled with an assault on the rarefied policies of free trade and neoliberalism, and the spreading conspiratorial theories set the political table and readied the landscape for the weaponized Donald J. Trump. Four short years later, the wave of antidemocratic authoritarianism emanating from the White House had become the order of the day for most elected Republicans from coast to coast.

As we prepare ourselves for the 2022-midterm elections, we are culturally experiencing déjà vu à la the Lincoln vs. Douglas Debates, the Dred Scott Case, and a post-Civil War Reconstruction all over again. As Michael Bellesiles contended after the Capitol riots, the Confederacy surrendered to Union forces in April 1865. In January 2021, Confederate forces had seized the Capitol again proving the accuracy of William Falkner's observation: "The past is never dead. It's not even past."[15] The well-known American historian further explains:

> With the election of Barack Obama as President, white supremacists rose up against this hated system of multicultural democracy, seeking to end birthright citizenship for leading to too many non-white Americans, charging without evidence that Obama had not been born in the United States, and working to suppress the votes of non-white citizens. In 2016 this faction seized control of the federal

> government, banning some people based on religion, putting some children in cages based on ethnicity, and rejecting the will of the majority. For the next four years, they attempted to claw back white man's rule by wielding citizenship as a weapon, only to be stymied by the election in November 2020.
>
> They could not accept the election and dismissed the legitimacy of Democratic voters. In doing so they realized the worst fears of the Framers that a corrupt electorate would elevate a tyrant to the presidency, while also working to restore the original white male republic.[16]

Trump's 2016 winning election was not so much a political fluke, a dislike of Hillary Clinton, or unexpected disruption of radicalization. Rather, Trump's election was the culmination of a right-wing movement within and without the Republican Party. Divided selves as well as the prevailing political economy of capitalism helps to explain the cultural means of propaganda that Trump used to exploit the social order of privilege and inequality in the United States so that he could further divide "red" and "blue" Americans from each other. At this moment, the antipathy between Republicans and Democrats has grown to the point that political partisanship can now be thought of as the new mega-identity inclusive of and even transcending gender, sexual orientation, and race at the same time.[17]

The contemporary politics of the hatred of the other is not limited to Trumpists but also includes many anti-Trumpists as well. The fact that persons of left or right persuasions are both humanly susceptible to ego-defense mechanisms and to the social-psychological processes of hating the other anonymous tribal members should not be considered as equivalencies as the objects of their contradictory hatreds are the antithesis of the other.[18] Despite the Donald's claims to the contrary when he publicly, for example, reacted to the violent protests in Charlottesville on August 15, 2017: "You also had people that were very fine people, on both sides." Or during the summer of 2021 when the former president started trying to make Capitol rioter Ashli Babbitt, a QAnon believer and fervent supporter of Trump who had been shot and killed by a Capitol police officer into a political martyr for Trump World. The Donald even recorded and released a birthday video on October 10th of 2021 when she would have turned 36 years old. The video was played at a weekend rally in Freeport, Texas held by her family and other Babbitt supporters. Despite the homicide being ruled a justifiable murder, the Donald was calling for the DOJ to reopen the investigation.[19]

As for others that conduct research on the social psychology of human interaction, several studies of cognitive orientation, motivation, and endorsers of either left-wing or right-wing ideologies have found that the former tend to be analytical and the latter intuitive. There are several competing explanations for this difference. None of these have anything to do with intelligence per se. The popular "blunting theory" of cognition hypothesizes that there is a psychological defensive advantage to intuitive or myopic thinking if one's subconscious objective "is to avoid information and thinking that threatens one's worldview." Regardless of why, the research is suggestive and has led some researchers to conclude "individuals holding right-wing beliefs are less likely to think about political issues in complex ways" when compared to those holding left-wing beliefs. Similarly, believers in right-wing ideology compared to believers of left-wing ideologies are "typically associated with a tendency to engage in selective attention and reasoning to sustain beliefs" compared to believers of left-wing ideologies, which allows for a critical willingness "to reflect on the intuitively appealing answer."[20]

Stolen election vs. election tampering

On October 6, 2021, 11 months after Trump had lost the 2020 election, the former president released a public statement. Trump declared that the select committee to investigate the events of January 6 should conclude that the "real insurrection happened on November 3rd, the presidential election." January 6, the Donald said, was a "day of protesting the fake election results."[21] One year earlier in the aftermath of his lost bid for a second term and up through the deadly assault on the U.S. Capitol, Trump and his co-conspirators like Steve Bannon, Mark Meadows, Roger Stone, and others were doing whatever they could within their fields of power to discredit and overturn the election results. This was at a time when many of Trump's aides and staff were becoming scarce. Some had tested positive for COVID and were quarantining. Others were exiting stage left or resigning like Attorney General Barr, Ivanka Trump and husband Jared Kushner, close advisor Hope Hicks, and the cabinet billionaire and multimillionaire secretaries Betsy DeVos and Elaine Chao, respectively. Donald's attorneys of any caliber especially those interested in future legal careers had all headed for the hills as well.

Besides General Milley, there were others who were concerned with Trump's state of mind and what trouble the Donald could get into while he and his colleagues were trying to steal the election from the legitimate winner Joe Biden. They were preparing for the potential damage that Donald could cause in the waning days of his administration. There were also a host of persons pushing back and resisting Trump especially inside of the DOJ where lawyers were doing battle with Trump over the certification of the 2020 election and his attempt to overturn the election results. People should read the Executive Summary of the U.S. Senate Judiciary Committee's interim 395-page Majority staff report released on October 6, 2021—*Subverting* Justice: How the Former President and His Allies Pressured DOJ to Overturn the 2020 Election.[22]

The matter all came to a head on January 3, 2021, when then-acting AG Jeffrey Rosen, his deputy Richard Donahue, and a handful of other administration officials met in the Oval Office with the Donald. The meeting became a three hour confrontation over "Trump's plan to replace Rosen with Jeffrey Clark, a little-known Justice Department official who had indicated he would publicly pursue Trump's false claims about mass voter fraud."[23] According to Rosen's testimony to the Senate Judiciary Committee, Trump opened the meeting by saying, "One thing we know is you, Rosen, aren't going to do anything to overturn the election."[24] During the discussion, Rosen and the others in the room threatened that they would resign rather than go along with Trump's plan. Even Pat Cipollone the top White House lawyer at the time and his deputy said that they would resign as well. The Senate report also made it clear that not only would Donohue resign if Trump replaced Rosen with Clark, but he also informed the president that it was not likely that mass resignations would end there. Donoghue suggested that the U.S. Attorneys and other DOJ officials across the nation "might also resign en masse."[25]

While the curtain was coming down on the Trump dystopia show the Donald was not left alone to simmer and rage with his "nutcase" attorneys Rudy Giuliani and Sidney Powell. They may have been leading the fraudulent election charge outside of courtrooms but inside the halls of justice judges were hammering their baseless claims of fraud. Facts aside, the Big Lie narrative of a stolen election had immediate and overtime growing traction with the Trumpian Republicans. Even after the failed coup and insurrection, Trump still had the support of 75 percent of Republican voters. One third believed that political violence is an acceptable course of action because the election had been stolen. The Boss also had nearly all the elected Republicans in DC and across the nation in his hip pockets. Their obedience to Trump was not only out of the fear of his wrath but also of their own survivability and the perceived inability of the Republican Party to win future presidential races without changing the rules of the election game and legally cheating. Ergo, between January 1 and May 14, 2021, at least 14 states had enacted 22 new laws that restrict access to the vote.[26] In battleground states like Pennsylvania, Michigan, Wisconsin, and elsewhere, Republicans were also busy trying to pass bills that would allow them to overturn election results certificated by their Secretaries of State.

Without any evidence of election fraud, Trump and these attorneys as well as more than a dozen other attorneys filed some 65 cases that had zero chance of seeing the light of day. But that was never the point of these bogus or fraudulent claims. These lawsuits were straight out of the Cohn and Trump playbook. Since they had no evidence of voter fraud, they knew they were going to lose each one of the cases. The goals were to cast aspersions on the process and doubt on the legitimacy of the election. Their success was in the court of Republican opinion as more than 75 percent of their voters came to believe that Biden was not the bonafide president of the United States. Better yet as Trump would say the spurious lawsuits were a trifecta of shorts. In the immediate and long terms, they fueled the bogus Stop the Steal movement. In turn, they fueled the storming of the Capitol on January 6. And in the long term, the Big Lies provided the cover for the discriminatory voter suppression laws passed by Republican majorities across the country.

Like Michael Cohn, some of these disreputable attorneys working unethically on behalf of Donald Trump have suffered legal consequences for their misdeeds. On August 2021, Sidney Powell of Texas and a team of eight other lawyers, one from Georgia, three from Michigan, one from Virginia, one who practices in Washington DC, New York, and New Jersey, one who practices in Washington DC, New York, and Nevada, and one who practices in New York and New Jersey that all sought to overturn Michigan's 2020 election were each slapped with sanctions by the U.S. District Judge Linda Parker.[27] As part of these sanctions, they were to pay the state and city of Detroit for the cost of defending the suit and to complete a continuing legal education course.

Parker's decision was sent to the Michigan state disciplinary boards for possible suspension or disbarment of the nine attorneys. In her 110-page opinion announcing the sanctions, she wrote:

> It is one thing to take on the charge of vindicating rights associated with an allegedly fraudulent election. It is another to take on the

> charge of deceiving a federal court and the American people into believing that rights were infringed, without regard to whether any laws or rights were in fact violated.[28]

This was the same case not only in Michigan but also in the other 65 frivolous lawsuits filed throughout the country on behalf of Trump's bogus claims of election fraud. Finally, as Michigan Attorney General Dana Nessel commented in response to Parker's opinion: "It has remained abundantly clear from the outset that this lawsuit aimed to do nothing more than undermine our democratic process." Nessel was also "pleased to see that the Court has ensured there is accountability for attorneys who perpetrated meritless arguments in court."[29]

Not unlike Trump's loyal attorneys who were spooling a bunch of crap for mass consumption if not before actual judicial officials when legal push came to shove, high profile Republican officials with no legal accountability to the bench were doing more of the same. For example, Senator Ron Johnson of Wisconsin (R) was one of the biggest pushers of the Big Lie that Trump had somehow been cheated out of a second term as president. As the chair of the Senate Homeland Security and Governmental Affairs Committee, Johnson used the December 16, 2020, committee session to raise doubts about the legitimacy of the election results. During his committee meeting, the "king of false claims" as he is known around the Capitol Hill without any evidence categorized the alleged irregularities into three groups: (1) Lax enforcement or violations of election laws and controls, (2) fraudulent votes and ballot stuffing, and (3) corruption of voting machines and software that could be programed to add or switch votes. While Senator Johnson was peddling these falsehoods, he was also lending his support to a bogus audit of the electoral results that was being pursued by Trump-aligned Wisconsin legislators.[30]

Similarly, Trump's always dependable projections of accusing others of having done to him what he has been busy doing to them were also adopted by the Republicans that were also participating in the "pot calling the kettle black." After Trump lost the election, Republicans were mimicking and acting on behalf of the Donald's Big Lies. They too were engaging in the same kind of gaslighting and bullying behavior as Boss Trump. Keep in mind that they have been doing so ever since they learned in early December that Trump had received 7,052,770 fewer votes than Biden and that he had also lost the electoral college by a margin of 306-232, the largest defeat by an incumbent president since FDR defeated Herbert Hoover in 1932.

Nevertheless, a sizeable majority of House Republicans and more than a handful of Senate Republicans were mimicking Trump and his lies about the election. Namely, they were falsely accusing the Democrats of doing exactly what the former president and they were actively doing—trying to steal the election. Needlessly, they were over and over counting the vote tallies through the months of November and December in order to manufacture doubt about an election that they all knew had been both legitimate and secure. Without democratic principles of any kind and only a concern for raw Republican power they were doing whatever they could to undermine, interfere, and disrupt the presidential contest before and after the votes were counted. Mostly, these Republican crooks were trying to steal the election from Joe Biden by tossing out enough lawfully casted Democratic votes so that they could declare victory and install Trump. These joint tampering efforts by the former president and his minority-controlled party had the intended effects of undermining the integrity of the election in the Republican mind-set and providing them with an alleged justification for the storming of the Capitol Building on January 6, 2021. From more than 6,000 documents turned over by the Chief of Staff Meadows to the House's bipartisan investigation of January 6, including texts from the U.S. Republican congressional representatives and senators as well as from Don, Jr., Fox TV personalities Laura Ingraham and Sean Hannity demonstrate the extent to which these persons were all a part of Trump's criminal conspiracy to commit treason against the United States.

It is important to distinguish between bogus conspiracies in theory and bonafide conspiracies in practice. In the case of the former, these included, for example, rigged elections, the Deep State, and QAnon. In the case of the latter, these included the pre- and post-election efforts organized by the Republican Party officials to interfere in the electoral process. They also include the introduction of dozens of bills to disenfranchise American voters and to allow for the overturning of future presidential election results. More widely or structurally, the attacks on our democracy by Trump and others have had the financial and organizational backing of politically dark money not to mention very rich and powerful conservative groups such as the Heritage Foundation, the American Legislative Council, the Federalist Society, the Election Integrity Project California, and Freedom Works. Since the Citizens United Supreme Court decision in 2010, Senator Sheldon Whitehouse (D) from Rhode Island has talked extensively about the "flotilla of front groups" that have been acting for years to capture the courts for the purposes of resisting global warming and climate control. Now that they have successfully taken over the courts, they have turned their attention and support to voter suppression.[31]

Whitewashing the failed insurrection vs. investigating the capitol riots

As early as 2017 Trump's lifelong advisor, confidant, and co-conspirator Roger Stone had warned: "Try to impeach him. Just try it. You will have a spasm of violence in this country—an insurrection like you have never seen."[32] As it turned out, this was no idle threat but an insider's understanding of the lengths to which Trump would go to retain his power. At the time, Stone was referring to his, Donald's, and the 2016 Trump Campaign Committee's collusion with the Russians. He was not referring to either the December 18, 2019, articles of impeachment against Trump for "abuse of power" and "obstruction of justice" with respect to Ukraine or to the Capitol riots and the January 13, 2021, article of impeachment for the "incitement of insurrection." Back in 2017, neither Stone nor anyone else for that matter would have imagined that the Republicans in one year's time through a process of "jury nullification" would have twice acquitted the lawless president of high crimes and misdemeanors. Once on February 5, 2020, and again on February 13, 2021, without the former president's attorneys presenting any substantive defense to counter the overwhelming evidence against the president the unprincipled and shameful Republicans voted to acquit on all three articles of impeachment.

As for establishing the narrative lie about the election and setting in motion what occurred at the Capitol on January 6, Trump had been planning for the possibility of a violent showdown since at least June 2020 should the Donald both lose and fail to overturn the election before certification day. Back then, Trump, AG Barr who was still all in on how easy it was to rig an election with mail-in ballots, and others like Donald Trump, Jr. were already propagating doubt about the 2020 election and planting the seeds of a fraudulent election with Trump's prophetic, "The only way we're going to lose this election is if the election is rigged."[33] Flash forward to 2:00 AM eastern time on the morning of November 4 and it is not surprising that with Hail to the Chief playing at the party in the White House East Room, out walked Trump followed by the First Lady, Vice President Mike and Karen Pence. Turning away from the teleprompter and ignoring the prepared remarks by Stephen Miller and his speech writing team, Trump delivered one of his streams of consciousness riffs claiming victories in both states that he had won and in those states that had not yet been decided, including Arizona, North Carolina, and Pennsylvania:

> We were winning everything and all of sudden it was just called off…This is a fraud on the American public. This is an embarrassment to our country. We were getting ready to win this election. Frankly, we did win this election. We did win this election. So our goal now is to ensure the integrity for the good of this nation. This is a very big moment. This is a major fraud in our nation. We want the law to be used in a proper manner. So we'll be going to the U.S. Supreme Court. We want all voting to stop. We don't want them to find any ballots at four o'clock in the morning and add them to the list, okay? It's a very sad moment. To me, this is a very sad moment, and we will win this. And as far as I'm concerned, we already have won it.[34]

Almost five months later, March 25, 2021, Trump is peddling the same narrative crock of lies on Fox News's *The Ingraham Angle*: "If you look at the last election, it was disgraceful. It was a third-world election. It was a disgrace. Legislatures didn't approve much of what happened… And if you look at the numbers, they were vastly in favor of us in the presidential election. It was disgraceful that they were able to get away with it. The Supreme Court didn't have the courage to do what they had to do."[35] During the same interview with Laura Ingraham one month after Trump's second impeachment acquittal for instigating an insurrection, the Donald had pretty much solidified his narrative on the Capitol riots. Despite the hundreds of injured police and at least five related deaths, including two post-riot police suicides, the former president was claiming that his protesters had posed "zero threat" to those lawmakers who had assembled to certify the Electoral College vote confirming Biden as the 46th president.

As the former president Trump was using his limited airtime not only to complain about how law enforcement had been "persecuting" the Capitol rioters, but also to point out how unfair it was that "nothing happens" to the protesters from the left. Even with the extensive news and security footage of the failed insurrection shown live and repeatedly to people in the United States and across the world, Trump was still busy trying to portray the actions of the rioters as peaceful: "Some of them went in and they're, they're hugging and kissing the police and the guards. You know, they had great relationships. A lot of the people were waved in and then they walked in, and they walked out."[36] Trump's narrative lies about the election and the insurrection have remained essentially unchanged since this broadcast. And there is no doubt that this narrative will continue as long as he lives even though the Donald knows perfectly well that it is total bullshit. This is simply how Donald the conman and non-pathological liar rolls.

Less than two weeks earlier, GOP Senator Ron Johnson and Trump sycophant had attempted to give the former president some racist cover for why there was no real threat at the Capitol on January 6. Like a fool he told a local radio audience that he "never really felt threatened" by the white protesters because they were largely "people that love this country, that truly respect law enforcement, would never do anything to break a law." Johnson continued this lie about the day in question by telling host Joe Pagliarulo: "Had the tables been turned and President Donald Trump won the election and those were thousands of Black Lives Matter and antifa protesters I would have been concerned."[37] Spoken like a true racist. Moreover, your average anti-racist could have informed the Cheesehead Senator from Wisconsin that had Trump won the election there would have been zero Black Lives Matter or antifa protesters anywhere near the Capitol on certification day. As a matter of fact, they would all have been at home crying.

More generally, Republican lawmakers trying to whitewash the January 6th insurrection and to change the narrative went further than Boss Trump and sycophant Johnson. After initially agreeing that the rioters were no different than ordinary tourists visiting the Capitol did not find any traction outside of Trump World, they attempted to place the blame for the insurrection on their political opposition. First, they stated that Antifa and Black Lives Matter protestors had dressed up, putting on "whiteface" no doubt, as Trump supporters and were the actual perpetrators of the violence. When those absurd racist claims were ridiculed and dismissed by all but the lunatic fringe, the Republican legislators then attempted to blame Trump's failed insurrection on FBI agents to no avail. No matter though. These dumber than dumb talking pointed-lies about the insurrection were simply piled onto to the other bogus lies about how Joe Biden and the democrats had stolen the election with the assistance of Hugo Chavez who had been dead for years,[38] Jews from outer space,[39] and Italian satellites.[40] Unfortunately, most Republicans have adopted these or other conspiratorial lies about the election. At the same time, the only actual colluding, trickery, and conspiracy to defraud and harm American democracy has been between Trump, his allies, and others in the Republican Party. Welcome to *Brave New World* and *Nineteen Eighty-Four* rolled into a very real, nonfictional, and dystopia Trump World featuring DJT as the evil of darkness and his cast of ten million minions.

Flash forward and on June 30, 2021, with all but two Republicans voting no the House established a committee to examine the security failures and root-causes that contributed to the Capitol riot. The organizing resolution of the House Select Committee on the Investigation of January 6 calls for an inquiry into "the facts, circumstances and causes related" to the "domestic terrorist attack." Originally, the 13-member panel with subpoena power was to consist of eight members named by the majority party and five recommendations to come from the Republicans. After the committee members had been agreed to and announced publicly the Republicans backed out and declined to participate in the investigation. Many of these Republican officeholders were also privy to the PowerPoint presentation developed in part by Retired Army colonel Phil Waldron, titled "Election Fraud, Foreign Interference & Options for 6 Jan" distributed before the failed insurrection, recommending among other things that Donald Trump declare a national security emergency in order to return himself to the presidency.

Shortly thereafter two independent or non-Trumpian Republicans Liz Cheney from Wyoming who also became the Vice Chair and Adam Kinzinger from Illinois joined the committee. The select committee had only been formed after Senate Republicans had blocked the formation of a bipartisan independent commission to scrutinize the assault on the Capitol. As Speaker Pelosi stated at the time, "We have a duty to the Constitution and to the American people to find the truth of Jan. 6 and to ensure that such an assault on our democracy can never happen again."[41] On the other side of the isle, the Republicans could not have disagreed more. Their only agenda was to pretend that the assault on the Capitol never happened preferring to erase, whitewash, and cover up the events of this infamous day in American history.

One of the more over the top attempts to whitewash the Capitol riots occurred on July 27, 2021, during the opening day of the House Select Committee Investigation into the January 6 attack on the Capitol. While the committee members and all the world were watching live and listening to the testimony of four police officers telling their stories of what it was like during the violent attacks, at least six Republicans members of the House were not in attendance. Instead, they were marching in front of the U.S. Department of Justice to speak up for those they were calling "political prisoners," escorted by a man in a giant Trump costume with the message "TRUMP WON."

As Rep. Paul Gosar (AZ) stated during the news conference adjacent to the DOJ headquarters: "These are not unruly or dangerous, violent criminals. These are political prisoners who are now being persecuted and bearing the pain of unjust suffering."[42] These lawmakers were also distributing copies of a letter alleging falsely that the January 6 defendants had been denied "potentially exculpatory evidence" and were being subjected to "cruel and unusual punishment." The lawmakers had signs as well that read: "Free the Jan. 6 Political Prisoners" and "Jan. 6 Was an Inside Job."

Among these six "runaway" lawmakers were Rep. Matt Gaetz (FL) and Rep. Marjorie Taylor Green (GA). They were underscoring what the Republican lawmakers, including Kevin McCarthy (CA), the minority leader of the House, Mitch McConnell (KY), the minority leader of the Senate, and Lindsay Graham (SC), were all saying about January 6 since the three performed flip flops once again as each had done during the 2016 primary election. This time, they were changing their tune on their initial reactions condemning Trump and his insurrectionists. For example, in the immediate aftermath of the insurrection, Graham took to the Senate floor to inform everyone that he was cutting ties with the president. "I hate it to end this way. Oh my God. I hate it...All I can say, is count me out, enough is enough."[43] Until a few days later when it no longer mattered because "the party could not grow without Trump." So once again Graham was all in and back golfing with the former president.

It is also common knowledge that McCarthy was not pleased with Trump's inaction while the Capitol was being ran shanked by Donald's storm troopers. In fact, McCarthy pleaded with the former president to call off the dogs in the middle of the riot to which he was sharply rebuffed. At the time, Trump was both fixated and giddy as he watched TV in the White House private dining room boasting about the size of the crowd and arguing with aides who wanted him to call off his rioters.[44] By the end of the summer, August 31, 2021, House Minority Leader Kevin McCarthy was warning telecom firms that the GOP would not forget if they handed over the phone records of alleged January 6 collaborators. A group of 11 House Republicans echoing McCarthy also sent letters to various technology company CEOs warning them against complying with subpoenas from the House January 6 select committee. Those sycophant Trump backers included such far right GOP extremists as Louie Gohmert (Tex.), Paul A. Gosar (Ariz.), and Mo Brooks (Ala.).[45]

In fact, within a few weeks, everyone had returned to the Trumpian fold. They were all siding with and defending the Seditionist-in-Chief and those rioters that had attempted a violent coup. While sucking up to Trump once again the party of lawlessness and disorder was busy blaming the violence on the Capitol Police as well as on the House Speaker Nancy Pelosi (D-CA). As one of the defenders of the insurrectionists Rep. Elise Stefanik (R-NY) shouted as Pelosi stood before the Capitol Dome. "The American people deserve the truth that Nancy Pelosi bears responsibility, as the Speaker of the House, for the tragedy that occurred on Jan. 6."[46] However, Meadow's documents reveal another story. The reason the National Guard did not show up to protect the Capitol from the insurrectionists was because their charge at the time was to protect Trump's protestors.

Recall that McCarthy in addition to Meadows was one of several prominent Republicans who has key knowledge about what Trump was saying and doing during the time of the Capitol riots. Thus, as part of trying to cover up what the minority leader knew about Trump in the moment, he went so far as to call out democratic Reps. Adam Schiff from California, Jan 6th Co-Chair Bennie Thompson from Mississippi, and House Speaker Pelosi for what McCarthy himself was doing, attempting "to strong-arm private companies to prevent them from turning over individuals' private data." Finally, the deceitful Kevin asserted that such a forfeiture of information would "put every American with a phone or computer in the crosshairs of a surveillance state run by Democrat politicians."[47] In response to McCarthy and the other Trump soldiers' threats, Cheney responded: "We owe it to the American people to investigate everything that led up to and transpired on Jan. 6. We will not be deterred by threats or attempted obstruction and we will not rest until our task is complete."[48]

Trump and his cohorts need to be prosecuted for rebellion and insurrection

When the House Select Committee releases its final report on the insurrection, hopefully before the 2022-midterm elections and well ahead of the 2024 presidential election, though not a court of law, and most likely without the testimony of the key players, including the former vice-president and president as well as their subordinate political and legal associates, will prove beyond a reasonable shadow of a doubt that the Donald was "guilty" of both inciting (e.g. a "crime of commission") and not curtailing (e.g. a "crime of omission") the violent assault and coup attempt on the Capitol.

As investigative journalism had reported by mid-summer 2021, the Chairman of the Joint Chiefs General Mark Milley post-election had been anticipating a showdown of some kind with the Commander-in-Chief because he feared that Trump and company were going to attempt a coup d'état.[49] There were other military personnel besides Milley preparing to get in the way of an attempted coup by Trump.[50] These non-partisan, independent, and apolitical state workers were more or less in agreement with Milley who had labeled Trump's claims about the fraudulent election as "the gospel of the Führer" and who had told his aides "this is a Reichstag moment."[51] Fortunately, in less than four years the Donald had not been able to co-op the military, the CIA, or the FBI as he had done with the Republican Party though he tried his best to do so. Trump fired more high-ranking officials during his four-year administration than his two predecessors did in their eight-year terms of office in order to get the type of toadies that the Donald always wants by his side.

Think about the telephonic conversation between General Milley and Liz Cheney as she was reporting her exchange with Republican Congressman Jim Jordan as the riots were unfolding in real time. JJ: "We need to get the ladies away from the aisle. Let me help you." LC: "I smacked his hand away and told him, Get away from me. You fucking did this."[52] As revealed in *I Alone Can Fix It*, Cheney was holding Jim Jordan responsible for the Capitol riot on that day. Jordan hardly acted alone. There were many folks inside and outside of Congress assisting Trump in the hastening of that violent insurrectionary day. Several of the very same Republican power brokers, such as Kevin McCarthy and Jim Jordan had his back as they were doing their best to suppress their verbal exchanges with Trump during the riots and to sabotage the initially formed bipartisan commission to investigate January 6. Next, they were doing whatever they could to obstruct the House Select Committee's investigation into that infamous day in American history.

Less than 24 hours after the revelations of Milley and his concerns were aired publicly to the American people on the evening of July 14, 2021, the former president in his Trumpian facile way had this didactic retort and hidden admission:

> I never threatened, or spoke to, anyone about a coup of our government. So ridiculous! Sorry to inform you, but the election is my form of 'coup', and if I was going to do a coup, one of the last people I would want to do it with is Mark General Milley…the world's most overrated general.[53]

This is par for Trumpian doublespeak or akin to whenever the Donald for instance is denying having sexually assaulted another woman because "She's not my type."[54] In case you might be wondering, Milley is the same general that prevented Trump as he was about to leave office from starting a war with Iran.[55] Milley was also the general who at commencement told the graduating officers at the National Defense University that his accompanying Trump to the church on June 1, 2020 for a photo-op was a big mistake on his part.[56] As the saying goes: "fool me once, shame on you; fool me twice, shame on me."

Similarly, before the events unfolded at the Capitol on January 6 the FBI in an internal memo had warned of a violent "war" that was not acted on by the Capitol police who had the same intelligence by December 23, 2020 for reasons that are still unclear.[57] FBI investigators have also found plenty of evidence that various cells of protesters, including followers of the Oath Keepers and Proud Boys were planning to break into the Capitol though they apparently had no detailed plans with respect to what they would do after gaining entrance. And, while Trump allies Roger Stone the self-described "dirty trickster" and Alex Jones, a founder of a conspiracy-driven radio show and webcast, were participating in pro-Trump events in DC on January 5, the FBI had found no evidence of a grand scheme between Stone, Alex, and these self-proclaimed militia groups to storm the Capitol and take hostages.[58]

As for proving Trump's intent to the contrary with respect to his phone call to Georgia Secretary of State Brad Raffensperger demanding he "find" enough votes to deliver the state or with respect to indicting the former president for his inciting the insurrection, there are also the records that Trump pressed his acting attorney general at the time Jeffrey A. Rosen and his deputy Richard P. Donoghue to acknowledge the false voter fraud claims by Trump and others. They pushed back and told the president that they had no power to change the election outcome. Trump had replied that he understood, and he told them, "Just say that the election was corrupt and leave the rest to me" and the Republican Party.[59]

Trump was wrong about himself and the majority of Senate Republicans but not about the House Republicans. On the day of certification and after the riots were over, all the Democratic House majority members voted to certify president-elect Biden. However, only 27 Republican members did the same while the rest voted not to confirm the election. In the case of Arizona's electoral outcome, 121 House and six Senate Republicans backed the objections to certifying the election. Similarly, in Pennsylvania 138 House and seven Senate Republicans supported the objections to certification.[60] The objections by the Republicans were totally without any evidence, foundation, or proof. Their naked and self-serving votes to challenge the election results were based on scuttlebutt, irrelevant excuses, and illogical circularity. In short, these elected members of Congress were allegedly representing the bogus concerns of their constituencies about the election's illegality emanating from the very lies they had been fabricating for the public.

Former House Intelligence Committee counsel Dan Goldman who prosecuted Trump in the first impeachment trial has stated publicly that Trump's statements on December 27 to former Acting AG Rosen and then-acting AG Donoghue demonstrate that Trump "knew he did not have true concerns about the legitimacy of the election but he simply wanted to corruptly overturn it without any factual basis." Likewise, by

> asking the DOJ to lie so that he and the Republican congressmen could use the lie to reverse the outcome of the election, Trump plainly intended to corruptly overturn the election. Any state or federal prosecutor can use these statements against him.[61]

After Impeachment 2.0, Goldman also pointed out with respect to the open question, "to what extent was Trump aware of the plans to violently storm the Capitol that existed online before January 6th?" By way of his conversation with the DOJ attorneys the Donald had admitted that he was "very familiar with what is on the Internet," thus demonstrating to prosecutors that "he knew of those plans when he incited the crowd to 'fight' and go to the Capitol." All of which "is powerful proof that he conspired with the rioters to interfere in the lawful functioning of Congress."[62] Similarly, given everything that Trump said and did after losing the election, including strong-arming Raffensperger as well as pressuring Vice President Mike Pence not to certify the election, legal and Constitutional scholar Laurence H. Tribe has opined "established Trump's intention to hold onto power regardless of the actual election results."[63]

With respect to finding out much more about what Trump was doing in the days leading up to and on the day of the Capitol assault, the January 6th Select Committee on September 23, 2021, issued its first subpoenas for both documents and direct testimony from fours aides to the former president. These included former White House chief of staff Mark Meadows, former communications official Dan Scavino, former Defense Department official Kash Patel, and Trump advisor Steve Bannon. Other subpoenas followed, including one for acting assistant AG Jeffrey Clark who allegedly was willing to do the former president's bidding.[64]

Immediately, the talking heads presumed that these Trump loyalists like the Donald should he be subpoenaed, and that they would choose not to comply and seek out some sort of presidential privilege against testifying that does not exist. At the same time, a former Assistant U.S. Attorney and committee member Rep. Adam Schiff (D-CA) could be heard warning those that refuse to comply with subpoenas that they would be guilty of criminal contempt. Unlike the House committees that struggled to force members of the Trump administration to comply with subpoenas such as the former White House counsel Don McGahn. Schiff who was also one of the key investigators in the first impeachment of Trump and the lead manager in the second impeachment stated that now that he has the cooperation of the Biden administration that he did not have with Barr's Department of Justice, so he would likely use Garland's DOJ to enforce the subpoenas for testimony,[65] resulting in criminal contempt of Congress charges or taking the 5th against self-incrimination for the key conspirators involved in the failed coup.

Even more important than the House investigation of the insurrection and the time spent trying to get testimony from these key players about their conspiratorial actions to violate 18 U.S. Code § 2,383 Rebellion or Insurrection is the fact that it makes a lot more sense for the DOJ to get down to business and prosecute Trump and his close co-conspirators, such as attorney John Eastman who outlined the stupidest six-step plan in a two-page legal memo ever conceived of. It was allegedly designed for the purposes of getting Vice President Mike Pence to subvert the Constitution and throw out the 2020 election results.[66] Charging and trying these individuals would certainly be the most efficient and effective way to proceed and to find legal closure on Donald J. Trump and company. With the indictments on January 11, 2022, of a baker's dozen of Oath Keepers for seditious conspiracy and other crimes against the U.S., it now appears that the DOJ may indeed, on behalf of the people, be building its prosecutorial case against the former president and his allies from the ground up. Time will tell.

Teflon Don the Racketeer-in-Chief

Michael Wolff in his third Trump book, *Landslide: The Final Days of the Trump Presidency*, argues non-persuasively that the Donald was too crazy, experiencing mood "swings of irrationality and mania," that he "was someone who has completely departed reality," and that Trump was incapable of forming specific intent based "on the calculated and 'coordinated' misuse of power."[67] Wolff is not alone, a slew of books documenting Trump's final days in office tend to agree, or the conventional wisdom is, including that of television's talking heads with the exception of those appearing on

FOX News and friends, is that Donald's loss to Sleepy Joe on election night broke him. That his fantasies about "*Frankly, We Did Win This Election*" were proof that Trump was deluded and not acting:

> Losing the election untethered him from whatever scraps of reality his advisers had still managed to tie him to, and up he went like a lost balloon with anger management issues. By the end he was (is) wallowing in delusion, ordering staff to do impossible and/or illegal things, absolutely convinced that everything was a conspiracy and that anyone who didn't tell him what he wanted to hear was in on it.[68]

Let me argue otherwise. Trump has never been tethered to reality but that does not necessarily have anything to do with believing one's delusions. Similarly, while his many advisers may have resisted to varying degrees or pushed back against the Donald's desired actions, they never tied him up or put him away in a strait jacket. Even though cabinet members had been talking about the crazy or unstable Trump and using the 25th Amendment since the first day of his administration, nothing ever materialized. Moreover, Donald has enough control of the Donald and Donald appreciates or understands that something the Donald might do could be going "too far" and that those ramifications might not be in his best interests. In these instances, the Donald usually moves sideways with the rules that Donald will not violate. In the case of losing the election, Donald could not move on or sideways for several reasons.

First, there is Donald's intense aversion to being seen as a weak loser. To have not fought back would have been to acknowledge the legal, political, and social reality of his fair and square electoral defeat to Biden. Second, always the "child" throughout his pre-pubescence and adult life as well as in his role as the Toddler-in-Chief the Donald has always had anger issues. However, these are less about his going off or up like a lost balloon, and more a byproduct of his manic-depressive personality. Third, Donald certainly wallows in self-pity and grievance. But these are less about believing his delusions and more about his defensive deflections and projections. Even his "paranoia" that everyone, including the Deep State, is conspiring against him is all part of a narrative performance. Of course, part of the narrative has also had to do with Donald defending himself from all the things that Donald knows that he is guilty of. Most importantly, Trump knows, as Bannon says, that he is a scumbag and in his heart of hearts that everybody should be coming for him.

As I have argued all along, Trump is neither self-deceived nor has he departed social reality for some alternative Trump World that he has spun and trapped millions of other people in. Trump is simply an exemplary performer and with a lot of help from his associates has had the ability to get some 40 million people to believe or at least to act like they believe all his bullshit even though to the Donald he is merely sticking to the scripted reality of the grift. It is interesting to me that Wolff has explained that he knew that in order to not have his post-insurrection interview with the former president at Mar-a-Lago ended abruptly by Trump, he had to go along with the lies, especially the stolen election. So rather than challenge Trump he simply asked him to explain how the fraudulent election was pulled off. Of course, Trump's only explanation was a bunch of nonsense, which was neither satisfying for Wolff or for the former president. Irrational or not, Trump simply zigzags along as he sloshes around in a deepening pile of manure.

In sum, it is my view that Trump is not at all deluded. He does not believe that he won the election or that the rioters at the Capitol were very nice people. He certainly feels no empathy or love for any of these people—not for one moment. Rather, the Racketeer-in-Chief is the penultimate con man, performance artist, and demagogue who never publicly abandons his narratives no matter how absurd or false they are. Because sooner or later, the Donald knows the opposition will get tired of fighting or will have exhausted the legal, financial, and political means for doing so. That's been the story for 50 years. Eventually, most if not all, his lies prevail at the end of the day.

At the same time, I must add that Trump has sucked in Wolff and a whole lot of other people. These folks believe that Donald is not only deluded and crazy, but also that he could not possibly be stable or sane enough to form intent, let alone organize a coup. Really? From the man who quite literally "takes care of business" every day while watching the tube or tweeting 24/7 except of course when he is playing 27 holes of golf three times a week. No, this is precisely what Donald the fox would like everybody to believe. In the immortal words attributed to everyone from P.T. Barnum to W. C. Fields, "There's a sucker born every minute." Or in the inimical words of the Donald, "Got you again, sucker."

Meanwhile, Donald has always been bipolar, irrational, paranoid, narcissistic, and sociopathic. This does not mean that he is legally insane, has no mens rea, or is even crazy in the popular sense. In fact, I am more than confident and would bet the farm if I had one that even though it is extremely rare not to convict somebody arguing that they are not guilty by reason of legal insanity, the Donald could pull it off brilliantly (lol). Possibly becoming as Trump would claim the "greatest insanity defense" of all time. In different words, I acknowledge that Trump is a mentally ill person and a "sick fuck" to boot. However, the Donald knows the differences between right and wrong as anyone else does. The impulsive Donald also has a great deal of self-control and does not cross lines when he thinks the consequences would be bad for him. Thus, Trump is fully liable for his behavior and his sickness does not preclude his abilities to calculate, strategize, or to form intent, even if he was unable to bring about the conditions wherein he hoped that if push came to shove the Commander-in-Chief could have used the Insurrection Act for declaring Marshall Law and remaining in office who knows for how long.

Again, Donald Trump has spent a lifetime of deception conning other people, including those who have worked for him or with him. As a connoisseur of racketeering with numerous illicit schemes or rackets under his financial belt, Trump's litanies of fraud and wrongdoing have crisscrossed the private and public spheres. This especially occurred when he became president as the Donald, the Trump Organization and his political and economic allies continued fleecing consumers everywhere and stealing from the U.S. taxpayer as they had for the past half-century. Most recently, the 2020 reelection, the Capitol riots, and Trump's economic bottom lines are indicative of numerous overlapping political rackets designed to circumscribe campaign finance laws and to benefit the former president's criminal enterprise as well as Trump Organization, Inc., which includes Boss Trump and other members of his nuclear family.

According to data analyzed by the Center for Responsive Politics, a research and government transparency group that tracks money in politics and its effects, "Trump's 2020 campaign and joint fundraising committee, the Trump Make America Great Again Committee, spent more than $771 million through American Made Media Consultants LLC," including more than $3.5 million in direct payments to people and firms involved in organizing and arranging for the Stop the Steal rally at the White House.[69] Back in June 2019, the Center had also revealed that "layers of shell companies" were used to pay for 2020 Trump campaign adds.[70] One month later, the Campaign Legal Center (CLC) filed a complaint with the Federal Election Committee. The CLC filings claim that the Trump reelection campaign and its joint fundraising committee had laundered nearly $170 million in spending through firms headed by Trump's former campaign manager, Brad Parscale, and other firms created by Trump campaign lawyers. All for the purpose of hiding millions of dollars provided to companies engaged in significant work for the campaign, including "payments to Trump family members or associates."[71]

With respect to some $100 million received from associates of Russian syndicated crime, whether in the forms of direct leasing or purchasing of Trump properties in the Borough of Manhattan, or indirectly from loans passed through Deutsche Bank to the Trump Organization amounting to $300 million, these traditional forms of money laundering practiced by the Donald have been ongoing for some three decades.[72] The patterns of using layers of shell companies should also be recognized as one of the more common modus operandi employed by Trump's criminal enterprise and political cartel. With respect to the Trumps and their associates looting monies from the coffers of the 2016 and 2020 political campaigns, these criminal thefts represent simply another classic application of the family's business model that excels at borrowing and stealing money at the same time. This fraudulent financial behavior conducted from Trump Tower, the Oval Office, Trump International Hotel DC, or Mar-a-Lago is simply the latest "art of the steal" that the Donald has fully exploited as a unique entrepreneurial opportunity and new political-economic market.

Notes

1 Laurie Ouellette, 2019. Fake President: Telemorphosis and the Performance of Grotesque Power. In Rosemary Overell and Brett Nichols (eds), *Post-Truth and the Mediation of Reality: New Conjunctures.* London: Palgrave Macmillan, pp. 15–37.

2 Matt Clement, 2016. *A People's History of Riots, Protests, and the Law: The Sound of the Crowd.* London: Palgrave MacMillan.

3 Ian Kivelin Davis, 2021. Capitol Riots and the Mythic Meaning of 1776. *Academic Letters.* March. https://doi.org/10.20935/AL292.

4 Matthew Avery Sutton, 2021. The Capitol Riot Revealed the Darkest Nightmares of White Evangelical America. *The New Republic.* January 14. https://newrepublic.com/article/160922/capitol-riot-revealed-darkest-nightmares-white-evangelical-america.

5 For more recent treatises, see Robert Bellah et al. 1985 (2007). *Habits of the Heart: Individualism and Community in American Life.* Berkeley: University of California Press; Robert Putnam, 2000. *Bowling Alone: The Collapse and Revival of American Community.* New York: Simon and Schuster; and Sherry Turkle, 2011 (2017). *Alone Together: Why We Expect More from Technology and Less from Each Other.* New York: Basic Books.

6 Andrew Marantz, 2021. The Importance, and Incoherence, of Twitter's Trump Ban. *The New Yorker.* January. https://www.newyorker.com/news/daily-comment/the-importance-and-incoherence-of-twitters-trump-ban.

7 Bobby Allyn, 2021. Here Are 4 Key Points from the Facebook Whistleblower's Testimony on Capitol Hill. *National Public Radio.* October 5. https://

www.npr.org/2021/10/05/1043377310/facebook-whistleblower-frances-haugen-congress.

8 Michael McCallion and Kevin McCallion, 2021. *Reflections on Social Media. Academic Letters.* April. http://doi.org/10.20935/AL329.

9 See, for example, Nicholas Christakis, 2019. *Blueprint: The Evolutionary Origins of a Good Society.* New York: Little, Brown Spark; and Greg Lukianoff and Jonathan Haidt, 2018. *The Coddling of the American Mind: How Good Intentions and Bad Ideas Are Setting Up a Generation for Failure.* New York: Penguin Press.

10 R.D. Lang, 1965. *The Divided Self: An Existential Study in Sanity and Madness.* New York: Penguin Books.

11 Erich Fromm, 1973. *The Anatomy of Human Destructiveness.* New York: Henry Holt and Company.

12 Jessica Taylor, 2017. Republicans and Democrats Don't Agree, or Like Each Other – And It's Worse Than Ever. *NPR.* October 5. https://www.npr.org/2017/10/05/555685136/republicans-and-democrats-dont-agree-dont-like-each-other-and-its-worst-than-eve.

13 CNN Newsroom, 2021. 3pm ET. September 8.

14 Christopher Federico quoted in Kirsten Weir, 2019. Politics is Person. *Monitor on Psychology* 50 (10). November 1. https://www.apa.org/monitor/2019/11/cover-politics.

15 Michael Bellesiles, 2021. Weaponizing Citizenship. *Academia Citizenship*, Article 591, p. 7. https://do1.org/10.20935/AL591.

16 Ibid.

17 Lilliana Mason, 2018. *Uncivil Agreement: How Politics Became Our Identity.* Chicago, IL: University of Chicago Press.

18 Yves Smith, 2021. The Bizarre Civil War-Stoking Impulses of the Professional-Managerial Class in the US. *Nakedcapitalism.* September 7. https://www.nakedcapitalism.com/2021/09/the-bizarre-civil-war-stoking-impulses-of-the-professional-managerial-class-in-the-us.html.

19 Jemima McEvoy, 2021. Trump Records Birthday Video for Ashli Babbitt, Calls for DOJ to Reopen Investigation. *Forbes.* October 11. https://www.forbes.com/sites/jemimamcevoy/2021/10/11/trump-records-birthday-video-for-ashli-babbitt-calls-for-doj-to-reopen-investigation.

20 Christian Rigg, 2016. New Study Sheds Light on the Link between Right-Wing Ideology, Cognitive Performance, and Motivation. *Cognitive Science, Political Psychology.* June 16. https://www.psypost.org/2021/06/new-study-sheds-light-on-the-link-between-right-wing-ideology-cognitive-performance-and-motivation-61174.

21 Jenni Fink, 2021. Trump Says 'Real Insurrection' Happened on Election Day, Praises Pence's Jan. 6 Comments. *Newsweek.* October 6. https://www.newsweek.com/trump-says-real-insurrection-happened-election-day-praises-pences-jan-6-comments-1636196.

22 U.S. Senate Judiciary Committee, 2021. *Subverting* Justice: How the Former President and His Allies Pressured DOJ to Overturn the 2020 Election. October 6. https://www.judiciary.senate.gov/imo/media/doc/Interim%20Staff%20Report%20FINAL.pdf.

23 Devlin Barrett, 2021. Senate Report Gives New Details of Trump Efforts to Use Justice Dept. to Overturn Election. October 7. https://www.washingtonpost.com/national-security/durbin-report-trump-pressure-justice/2021/10/07.

24 Quoted in Ibid.

25 Ibid.

26 Brennan Center for Justice, 2021. Voting Laws Roundup: May 2021. *BCJ*. May 28. https://www.brennancenter.org/our-work/research-reports/voting-laws-roundup-may-2021.

27 Craig Mauger and Beth LeBlanc, 2021. Pro-Trump Lawyers Slapped with Sanctions over Michigan Election Lawsuit. *The Detroit News*. August 25. https://www.detroitnews.com/story/news/politics/2021/08/25/election-lawyers-ordered-pay-state-city-costs-may-face-disbarment/8162355002/.

28 Gus Burns, 2021. Pro-Trump Lawyers Sanctioned. *The Ann Arbor News*. August 26. https://enewsaa.mlive.com/data/7383/reader/reader.html?t=1630098841704#!preferred/0/package/7383/pub/13034/page/1.

29 Ibid.

30 John Nichols, 2021. Ron Johnson Gets Caught Debunking the Big Lie. *The Nation*. August 2. https://www.thenation.com/article/politics/ron-johnson-donald-trump/.

31 Jane Mayer, 2021. The Big Money behind the Big Lie. *The New Yorker*. August 2. https://www.newyorker.com/magazine/2021/08/09/the-big-money-behind-the-big-lie.

32 Quoted in Jean Guerrero, 2020. *Hatemongers: Stephen Miller, Donald Trump, and the White Nationalist Agenda*. New York: William Morrow, p. 8.

33 Morgan Chalfant, 2020. Trump: The Only Way We're Going to Lose This Election Is If the Election Is Rigged. *The Hill*. August 17. https://thehill.com/homenews/administration/512424-trump-the-only-way-we-are-going-to-lose-this-election-is-if-the-election-is-rigged.

34 Carol D. Leonnig and Philip Rucker, 2021. 'I Alone Can Fix It' Book Excerpt: Inside Trump's Election Day and the Birth of the Big Lie'. *The Washington Post*. July 13. https://www.washingtonpost.com/politics/2021/07/13/book-excerpt-i-alone-can-fix-it/.

35 Tom Porter, 2021. Laura Ingraham Cut Trump Off When He Tried to Repeat False Claims the Election Was Stolen, as Fox News Faces Defamation Lawsuits. *Insider*. March 26. https://www.businessinsider.com/laura-ingraham-stops-trump-repeating-election-fraud-claims-2021–3.

36 AP, 2021. Trump Defends Capitol Rioters, Says There Was 'Zero Threat.' March 26. https://apnews.com/article/joe-biden-capitol-siege-donald-trump-electoral-college-laura-ingraham-fab1b4858ad854b7544d3169bf4a93e5.

37 Allison Pecorin, 2021. GOP Sen. Ron Johnson Says He Didn't Feel 'Threatened' by Capitol Marchers But May Have If BLM or Antifa Were Involved. *ABCNews*. March 13. https://abcnews.go.com/Politics/gop-sen-ron-johnson-feel-threatened-capitol-marchers/story?id=76437425.

38 Will Sommer, 2020. Here's How Hugo Chavez, Dead Since 2013, Became Responsible for Trump's Election Loss. *Daily Beast*. November 19. https://www.thedailybeast.com/heres-how-hugo-chavez-dead-since-2013-became-responsible-for-trumps-election-loss.

39 Josh K. Elliott, 2021. 'Jewish Space Laser' Among Wild Hoaxes Backed by GOP's Marjorie Taylor Greene. *Global News*. January 28. https://www.thedailybeast.com/heres-how-hugo-chavez-dead-since-2013-became-responsible-for-trumps-election-loss.

40 Aaron Blake, 2021. 'Pure Insanity': Here's Perhaps the Craziest Election Fraud Conspiracy the Trump Team Pushed. *The Fix*. June 15. https://www.washingtonpost.com/politics/2021/06/15/pure-insanity-heres-perhaps-craziest-election-fraud-conspiracy-trump-team-pushed/.

41 Luke Broadwater, 2021. House Opens Jan. 6 Investigation Over Republican Opposition. *Washington Post*. July 27. https://www.nytimes.com/2021/06/30/us/house-jan-6-capitol-riot.html. https://www.washingtonpost.com/politics/2021/09/07/gop-effort-hamstring-jan-6-investigation-enters-new-phase/.

42 Quoted in Dana Milbank, 2021. As Jan. 6 Hearings Begin, Republicans Side with Terrorists. *The Washington Post*. July 28. https://www.washingtonpost.com/opinions/2021/07/27/jan-6-hearings-begin-republicans-side-with-terrorists/.

43 Chris Cillizza, 2021. How Lindsey Graham Is the Perfect Vessel to Understand Donald Trump's Death Grip on the GOP. *CNN Politics*. August 24. https://www.cnn.com/2021/08/24/politics/lindsey-graham-donald-trump-mark-sanford-2022/index.html.

44 Jonathan Karl, 2021. *Betrayal: The Final Act of the Trump Show*. New York: Penguin.

45 Aaron Blake, 2021. GOP Effort to Hamstring the Jan. 6 Investigation Enters a New Phase. *The Washington Post*. September 7. https://www.washingtonpost.com/politics/2021/09/07/gop-effort-hamstring-jan-6-investigation-enters-new-phase/.

46 Ibid.

47 Myah Ward, 2021. McCarthy Threatens Companies That Comply with Jan 6 Probe's Phone Record Requests. *Politico*. August 31. https://www.politico.com/news/2021/08/31/mccarthy-january-6-thre.

48 Luke Broadwater, 2021. House Panel Requests McCarthy's Phone Records Be Preserved in Jan. 6 Inquiry. *The New York Times*. September 2. https://www.nytimes.com/2021/09/02/us/politics/liz-cheney-jan-6-committee.html.

49 Jamie Gangel, Jeremy Herb, Marshall Cohen and Elizabeth Stuart, 2021. 'They're not going to f**king succeed': Top Generals Feared Trump Would Attempt a Coup after Election, According to New Book. *CNN Politics*. July 14. https://www.cnn.com/2021/07/14/politics/donald-trump-election-coup-new-book-excerpt/index.html.

50 Carol Leonnig and Philip Rucker, 2021. *I Alone Can Fix It: Donald J. Trump's Catastrophic Final Year*. New York: Penguin Press.

51 Dana Milbank, 2021, Opinion: American Democracy Survived Its Reichstag Fire on Jan. 6. But the Threat Has Not Subsided. *Washington Post*. July 15. https://www.washingtonpost.com/opinions/2021/07/15/american-democracy-survived-its-reichstag-fire-jan-6-threat-has-not-subsided/.

52 Quoted in Lexi Lonas, 2021. Cheney Reportedly Told Jim Jordan 'you f------ did this' During Jan. 6 Riot. *The Hill*. July 15. https://thehill.com/homenews/house/563127-cheney-told-jim-jordan-you-f-ing-did-this-during-jan-6-riot.

53 Grace Panetta, 2021. Trump Claims He's 'Not into Coups' and Wouldn't Want to Do One with Gen. Mark Milley Anyway. *Insider*. July 15. https://www.businessinsider.com/trump-says-hes-not-into-coups-gen-mark-milley-response-2021–7.

54 Associated Press, 2019. 'She's Not My Type,' Trump Says of E. Jean Carroll, Who Accused Him of Sexual Assault. *NBC News*. June 25. https://www.nbcnews.com/politics/donald-trump/she-s-not-my-type-trump-says-e-jean-carroll-n1021331.

55 Ibid.

56 David Welna, 2020. Gen. Mark Milley Says Accompanying Trump to Church Photo-Op Was A Mistake. *National Public Radio*. June 11. https://www.npr.org/sections/live-updates-protests-for-racial-justice/2020/06/11/875019346/gen-mark-milley-says-accompanying-trump-to-church-photo-op-was-a-mistake.

57 Devan Cole, 2021. Washington Post: FBI Warned of Violent 'War' at Capitol in Internal Report Issued Day Before Deadly Riot. *CNN Politics*. January 12. https://www.cnn.com/2021/01/12/politics/fbi-report-warning-capitol-riot/index.html.

58 Mark Hosenball and Sara N. Lynch, 2021. Exclusive: FBI Finds Scant Evidence U.S. Capitol Attack Was Coordinated. *Reuters*. August 20. https://www.reuters.com/world/us/exclusive-fbi-finds-scant-evidence-us-capitol-attack-was-coordinated-sources-2021–08–20/.

59 Jennifer Rubin, 2021. The Most Damaging Evidence against Trump. *The Washington Post*. August 2. https://www.washingtonpost.com/opinions/2021/08/02/most-damning-evidence-against-trump/.

60 Li Zhou, 2021. 147 Republican Lawmakers Still Objected to the Election Results after the Capitol Attack. *Vox*. January 7. https://www.vox.com/2021/1/6/22218058/republicans-objections-election-results.

61 Ibid.

62 Quoted in Ibid.

63 Ibid.

64 Ivana Saric, 2021. Jan. 6 Select Committee Subpoenas Four Trump Aides. *AXIOS*. September 23. https://www.axios.com/jan-6-select-committee-subpoenas-trump-aides-ae66211f-e159-48ca-9657-8526ec878f32.html.

65 Adam Schiff, 2021. *Midnight in Washington: How We Almost Lost Our Democracy and Still Could*. New York: Penguin Random House.

66 Jamie Gangel and Jeremy Herb, 2021. Memo Shows Trump's Lawyer's Six-Step Plan for Pence to Overturn the Election. *CNN Politics*. September 21. https://www.cnn.com/2021/09/20/politics/trump-pence-election-memo/index.html.

67 Michael Wolff, 2021. *Landslide: The Final Days of the Trump Presidency*. New York: Henry Holt and Co.

68 Hunter, 2021. New Trump Books Show Trump's Election Delusions Weren't an Act. Election Night Broke Him. *Daily Kos*. July 13. https://www.dailykos.com/stories/2021/7/13/2039681/-A-spate-of-new-books-show-how-the-presidency-broke-Donald-Trump?detail=emaildkre.

69 Anna Massoglia, 2021. Trump's Political Operation Paid More Than $3.5 Million to Jan. 6 Organizers. *OpenSecrets*. February 10. https://www.opensecrets.org/news/2021/02/jan-6-protests-trump-operation-paid-3p5mil/?utm_source=twitter&utm_medium=social&utm_campaign=twitt_jan-6-tp35q-02/09/20.

70 Anna Massoglia, 2019. Trump 2020 Campaign AD Payments Hidden by Layers of Shell Companies. *OpenSecrets*. June 13. https://www.opensecrets.org/news/2019/06/trump-2020-campaign-ad-payments-hidden-by-layers-of-shell-companies/.

71 CLC, 2020. CLC Files Complaint against Trump Campaign for Hiding $170 Million in Spending from Donors and Voters. July 28. https://campaignlegal.org/update/clc-files-complaint-against-trump-campaign-hiding-170-million-spending-donors-and-voters.

72 Craig Unger, 2019. Trump's Businesses Are Full ofDirty Russian Money. The Scandal Is That It's Legal. *The Washington Post*. March 29. https://www.washingtonpost.com/outlook/trumps-businesses-are-full-of-dirty-russian-money-the-scandal-is-thats-legal/2019/03/29/11b812da-5171-11e9-88a1-ed346f0ec94f_story.

html. See also, Michael Hirsh, 2018. How Russian Money Helped Save Trump's Business. Foreign Policy. December 21. https://foreignpolicy.com/2018/12/21/how-russian-money-helped-save-trumps-business/; and Luke Harding, 2019. Deutsche Bank Faces Action over $20bn Russian Money-Laundering Scheme. *The Guardian*. April 17. https://www.theguardian.com/business/2019/apr/17/deutsche-bank-faces-action-over-20bn-russian-money-laundering-scheme.

EPILOGUE

Entrepreneurship is the creation or extraction of something of value in the market or in society at large.[1] Entrepreneurship is a verb and is associated with change. It is about timeliness, the exploiting of opportunities, and the ability to deal with uncertainty typically associated with a variety of markets.[2] In economics, it is generally viewed as entailing financial risks beyond the normal risks encountered when starting up a business and therefore greater profitability margins. There are other kinds of entrepreneurship such as political, institutional, and extreme entrepreneurships. Political entrepreneurships can be divided between those that have more in common with economics and those that have more in common with politics. In free and allegedly unregulated markets, the former refer to those persons or agencies that oversee "the direction of coercively obtained resources by the state toward processes of production which would not otherwise have taken place."[3] The latter refer to street-savvy politicians that may, for example, establish a new political party through the use of "commercial means to communicate a political message by means" typically used in other marketplaces.[4]

In fact, ABC News Chief Washington Correspondent Jonathan Karl has written in his third book on the Donald, *Betrayal: The Final Act of the Trump Show*, about a phone conversation that took place between the outgoing president and the Republican National Chairwoman Ronna McDaniel shortly after Trump boarded Air Force One allegedly for the last time. Trump was finished with the Republican Party for not fighting hard enough to keep him as the president. Hence, he was taking what he thought was his political money and would form a new party altogether. This idea lasted for about one week before McDaniel and other top Republican Party members were able to convince the Donald that he would lose millions of dollars to defend him from numerous lawsuits and "his" list of 40 million emails belonging to Trump supporters worth an "estimated $100 million because the Trump campaign could lease it to other Republicans for a price."[5] This economic reality forced the financially hemorrhaging and cheapskate Donald to stay with his Trumpian-controlled Republican Party.

Donald Trump may be a con artist and he may be an elite racketeer but when it comes to being an entrepreneur, the Houdini of White Collar Crime is the real deal. His spirit of and commitment to entrepreneurship has served to animate both Donald's rise to and fall from the pinnacle of political power. Being a con, a racketeer, and having an abundance of charisma coupled with narcissistic personality disorder have all contributed to his destructive accomplishments as a political entrepreneur, including his seditious conspiracy to overturn the 2020 election. As a multiservice entrepreneur, Trump has to say the least incorporated the full range of entrepreneurial risk-taking.

What makes Trump so unique among "top dog" entrepreneurs is that Donald combines the identities of businessman and politician in ways that benefit him and his family to the neglect of almost everyone else. What makes Trump so chaotic as a risk taker in business and politics alike is that Donald is forever getting in the way of the Donald or is the Donald forever getting in the way of Donald? I think that both of these psychic social realities play out at the same time as exemplified by Trump's lifelong ability to always think of Donald in the first and third persons. However, when Donald and the Donald are in conflict, Donald generally but not always wins. As an actor in the real world of make believe who is caught between his own dualistic persona of Donald and the Donald, Trump, the reality TV celebrity, for example, would never win one for the Gipper or for the legendary Notre Dame football coach as in *Knute Rockne, All American* played by the former Republican icon Ronald Reagan in the 1940 B movie. Not because the Donald is incapable of doing so, but because real Donald and not fake Donald is incapable of doing so.

As almost everyone knows that voted against him in 2020, Trump does not care a wit about other human beings or any social, political, and economic concerns except in relation to whether he thinks they are beneficial to his power, needs, desires, and interests. As for the favorable voters that constitute Trump World, these political mannequins and the other "frankly my dear, I don't give a damn" what outlandish things he does, the Donald has stated, "I could stand in the middle of Fifth Avenue and shoot somebody, and I wouldn't lose any voters." Despite all the harm and damage that Donald Trump had racked up during his four years of anarchistic governance, including his thunderous parting shots as the Commander-in-Chief of a failed coup and insurrection, Trump's political appeal does not appear to have faded since the 2020 election. Polling from October 2021 suggested that one-third of Republicans would like to see another Republican running against the Democratic candidate in 2024.

In other words, the remaining majority of Trumpists all seem to be still smoking the same poppycock the Donald has always been peddling. However, we do not really know and neither does Donald what his or the Trumpian party's political fate or value will be in the future, especially should Trump be on trial defending himself for a myriad of criminal offenses before or after the 2022 elections. Otherwise, we will have to wait at least until the upcoming midterm elections to see how his backed candidates and the Republicans perform. With respect to political power and the Trumpian Republican officials currently hanging out in the Capitol as well as those residing in state and local governmental bodies across the United States, it certainly appears that the exiled Boss in Club de Mar-a-Lago seems to have these politicos all in check if not checkmate. By December 2021 Trump had already endorsed 46 candidates in Republican primaries for the U.S. Senate, U.S. House and state governorships as well as endorsing down-ballot candidates, especially in election-administrative roles. On the other hand, should Trump and his storm trooping Republicans underperform in 2022, then the power of the Donald would probably start to wane if not turn precipitously south with all but his sycophantic cult of the personality base.

Conventional wisdom views entrepreneurial activity—economic or political—and institutional arrangements, especially legal ones as countervailing forces. However, it is not really that simple. As history teaches us, institutions direct entrepreneurial talent into productive, unproductive, and even destructive uses as we have been experiencing of late.[6] There are two other forms of "institutional" and "extreme" entrepreneurships that need to be incorporated into the entrepreneurial equation. The former refers to those institutional entrepreneurs that change the rules and the order.[7] The latter refers to those extreme entrepreneurs that operate in the cultural and social spheres of society.

Some extreme entrepreneurs may serve to hold a mirror up to society to alert us about certain concerns without necessarily taking or proposing constructive action. Other extreme or destructive entrepreneurs may work to resist and undermine those institutions. Now enter the Donald with his politically destructive entrepreneurship propelled by his fabrication and distribution of alternative facts and by his frontal attack on verifiable data and science vis-à-vis the bully pulpit, alt-right news, and other social media platforms. As a hyper extremist entrepreneur, there have been few if any legal rules that the Donald has not challenged or abided by while at the same time using and abusing the very same set of rules to protect himself.

I should also point out that the economic and political worlds of entrepreneurship are not necessarily separate. For example, they do indeed overlap in the political economy of the criminal enterprises operated by the former president. In similar ways, both economic and political entrepreneurships are subject to the vagaries of the rules of law, normative orders, and institutional stabilities. As for the Donald, he is habitually finding himself in conflict with this, that, and the other thing, so Donald is tirelessly rallying his political base and weaponizing the U.S. politics against all who are not loyalists, for the purposes of undermining the democratic state. To accomplish his overriding entrepreneurial mission of the acquisition of autocratic power, the Donald's modus operandi has always been about propagating lies, peddling propaganda, defending the indefensible, accusing or blaming others for exactly what he was doing, and finally, never acknowledging let alone accepting responsibility for any of the harm, damage, and destruction that he has caused.

In any case, I think that we can agree that Trump deserves to be tagged with the labels of economic and political entrepreneur. We should also be able to agree that the Donald has been a much better political entrepreneur than an economic entrepreneur. This is certainly the case as measured by the comparative values of his influence, revenue streams, and branding both as a businessman and as a politician. With respect to the former, Trump has had very little impact on the world of economics. What is more, as an economic entrepreneur, the Donald and the Trump businesses have been losing millions of dollars for decades.[8] As for Trump's marketing brand, it has been falling precipitously since he became the president in 2017. By contrast, as a political entrepreneur, Trump's brand and the value of the Trumpian party so far have been fanatismo. Moreover, with a little help from a lot of people, Trump has launched a 21st-century anti-democratic revolution in America. The question of course is how long will this entrepreneurially destructive revolution in America last? In the meantime, the former president and the Trump Organization will be politically monetizing all things Donald for mass consumption from candy bars to MAGA hats to autographed photos to shots of vodka.

With respect to Robert Merton's criminological theory of anomie or strain, Trump is a classic Mertonian "innovator" who ignores the legitimate means to success. At the same time, the Donald is a Mertonian "rebel" without a cause and with a dark and sinister vision. He is also part Mertonian "retreatist" as the Donald rejects the legitimate means to success, while paradoxically he is ostentatious and conspicuous with his wealth; winning and being perceived as wealthy are more important than the money itself.[9] In other words, when it comes to profits or rewards—economic, legal, or political—what gets Donald off has much more to do with winning and not losing contests, with "killing it" rather than being "killed by it," and with spawning cruelty and attaining revenge. Let me put it another way; for the Donald, it really is not about the money as much as it is about the leveraging of money, people, power, or whatever in order to defeat his opponents whomever they may be. Also, for the Donald, the "icing on the cake" or "the brass ring" has always been about the satisfaction that Trump derives from getting over on his marks. Of course, the Donald would never publicly say to the American people what he truly thinks of them: "What a bunch of fools, real idiots, it's amazing, it's absolutely amazing what suckers they all are, I'm telling you." And, as the political dolts that we all are, we "deserve to be taken for whatever we are worth" according to Trumpian logic.

Lastly, losing the 2020 election was so devastating to Trump that the bipolar lame duck withdrew into a depressive funk and yet he could rally his other manic state of mind into fulltime overdrive. Meaning Trump could push back against all those legal obstacles that were preventing his fragile ego from accepting defeat and allowing him to become the fabricated winner that he always must be regardless of the actual outcomes. Even though the disturbed Trump knew fully well that he was the real loser and was very depressed about it, the repressed Donald was getting madder and angrier, and the projective Trump was preparing for raging against democracy at the peril of the great red, white, and blue. Not even 74 million Republican voters could soothe the Toddler-in-Chief or calm the "return of the revenge." Nor could they make him feel any better about his real political defeat because in his own eyes, Donald and not the Donald was the humiliated schmuck who had lost the election to sleepy Joe by more than seven million votes.

Notes

1 Charles Spinosa, Fernando Flores and Hubert Dreyfus, 1997. *Disclosing New Worlds: Entrepreneurship, Democratic Action and Cultivation of Solidarity.* Cambridge, MA: MIT Press.

2 Israel M. Kirzner, 1978. *Competition and Entrepreneurship.* Chicago, IL and London: The University of Chicago Press.

3 Matthew McCaffrey and Joseph T. Salerno, 2011. A Theory of Political Entrepreneurship. *Modern Economy* 2 (4): 552–560.

4 Bengt Johannisson, 2021. Donald Trump's Return Ticket to Presidency – A Spectacular Entrepreneurial Journey. *Academic Letters,* Article 2441: 1–6.

5 Aaron Parsley, 2021. Trump Was 'Done' with Republican Party Until Officials Said They'd Ruin a $100M Political Tool: Book. People.com. November 8. https://people.com/politics/donald-trump-was-done-with-republican-party-inside-the-blowup/.

6 William J. Baumol, 1990. Entrepreneurship: Productive, Unproductive, and Destructive. *Journal of Political Economy* 98 (5): 893–921.

7 Cynthia Hardy and Steve Maguire, 2008. Institutional Entrepreneurship. In Greenwood, R. et al. (eds). *The Sage Handbook of Organizational Institutionalism.* Thousand Oaks, CA: Sage, pp. 198–217.

8 Had Trump simply taken his father's estate valued at $2 billion and invested it all in mutual funds and spent his entire life doing nothing else but playing golf, Donald would be worth about $10 billion rather than maybe $1 billion today.

9 Robert K. Merton, 1938. Social Structure and Anomie. *American Sociological Review* 3: 672–682.

A TRUMP BIBLIOGRAPHY

Wayne Barrett, 1992. *Trump: The Deals and the Downfall*. New York: HarperCollins.

Michael C. Bender, 2021. *"Frankly, We Did Win This Election: The Inside Story of How Trump Lost*. New York: Grand Central Publishing.

Andrea Bernstein, 2020. *American Oligarchs: The Kushners, the Trumps, and the Marriage of Money and Power*. New York: W.W. Norton & Company.

Sarah Blaskey, Nicholas Nehamas, Caitlin Ostroff, and Jay Weaver, 2020. *The Grifter's Club: Trump, Mar-A-Lago, and the Selling of the Presidency*. New York: Hachette Book Group.

Michael Cohen, 2020. *Disloyal, a Memoir: The True Story of the Former Personal Attorney to the President of the United States*. New York: Skyline Publishing.

David Enrich, 2021. *Dark Towers: Deutsche Bank, Donald Trump, and an Epic Trail of Destruction*. New York: HarperCollins Publishers.

Justin A. Frank, 2018. *Trump on the Couch: Inside the Mind of the President*. New York: Avery.

David Frum, 2020. *Trumpocalypse: Restoring American Democracy*. New York: HarperCollins Publishers.

Joshua Green, 2017. *Devil's Bargain: Steve Bannon, Donald Trump, and the Storming of the Presidency*. New York: Penguin.

Stephanie Grisham, 2021. *I'll Take Your Questions Now: What I Saw at the Trump White House*. New York: HarperCollins.

Jean Guerrero, 2020. *Hatemonger: Stephen Miller, Donald Trump, and the White National Agenda*. New York: William Morrow.

David Cay Johnston, 2016. *The Making of Donald Trump*. New York: Melville House.

Jonathan Karl, 2021. *Betrayal: The Final Act of the Trump Show*. New York: Dutton.

Bandy X. Lee, 2017 (ed.). *The Dangerous Case of Donald Trump: 27 Psychiatrists and Mental Health Experts Assess a President*. New York: Thomas Dunne Books.

Carol Leonnig and Philip Rucker, 2021 *I Alone Can Fix It: Donald J. Trump's Catastrophic Final Year.* New York: Penguin Press.

Dan P. McAdams, 2020. *The Strange Case of Donald J. Trump: A Psychological Reckoning.* New York: Oxford University Press.

Paul McGuire and Tony Anderson, 2018. *Trumpocalypse: The End-Times President, a Battle against the Globalist Elite, and the Countdown to Armageddon.* New York: Little, Brown.

Barry Meier, 2021. *Spooked: The Trump Dossier, Black Cube, and the Rise of Private Spies.* New York: HarperCollins Publisher.

Malcolm Nance, 2019. *The Plot to Betray America: How Team Trump Embraced Our Enemies, Compromised Our Security, and How We Can Fix It.* New York: Hachette Books.

Barbara A. Res, 2020. *Tower of Lies: What My 18 Years of Working with Donald Trump Reveals About Him.* Los Angeles, CA: Graymalkin Media.

Adam Schiff. 2021. *Midnight in Washington: How We Almost Lost Our Democracy and Still Could.* New York: Penguin Random House.

Adam Serwer, 2021. *The Cruelty Is the Point: The Past, Present, and Future of Trump's America.* New York: Penguin Random House.

Cliff Sims, 2019. *Team of Vipers: My 500 Extraordinary Days in the Trump White House.* New York: St. Martins.

Jeffrey Toobin, 2020. *True Crimes and Misdemeanors: The Investigation of Donald Trump.* New York: Doubleday.

Mary R. Trump, 2020. *Too Much and Never Enough: How My Family Created the World's Most Dangerous Man.* New York: Simon & Schuster.

Vicky Ward, 2019. *Kushner, Inc.: Greed. Ambition. Corruption: The Extraordinary Story of Jared Kushner and Ivanka Trump.* New York: St. Martin's Press.

Michael Wolff, 2021. *Landslide: The Final Days of the Trump Presidency.* New York: Henry Holt and Co.

Bob Woodward, 2020. *Rage.* New York: Simon and Schuster.

Bob Woodward and Robert Costa, 2021. *Peril.* New York: Simon & Schuster.

James D. Zirin, 2019. *Plaintiff in Chief: A Portrait of Donald Trump in 3,500 Lawsuits.* New York: St. Martin's Publishing Group.

NAME INDEX

Note: **Bold** page numbers refer to tables and page numbers followed by "n" refer to end notes.

SUBJECT INDEX

Note: Page numbers followed by "n" denote endnotes.